Psychotherapy
in Christian
Perspective

Psychotherapy
in Christian
Perspective

Baker Encyclopedia of Psychology. Selections
''

Edited by
David G. Benner

BAKER BOOK HOUSE
Grand Rapids, Michigan 49516

Contents

Part 2: Individual Therapies

Part 3: Couple, Family, and Group Therapies

Preface

Contemporary Christians are unsure about how they should view psychotherapy. Is it an ally or an enemy? Some view it as an invaluable resource in support of the goals of Christian ministry. Others regard it as an interloper, an illegitimate profession encroaching on territory belonging to religion in general and Christianity in particular. Yet few Christians have been able to completely ignore it.

Believers are not exempt from the personal need for professional psychological help. Perhaps they have friends or family members receiving such help. It is not uncommon for them to come for help like Nicodemus at night, concerned about how others will regard their problems. They come at the end of their resources and in desperation, often with shame and guilt, but ready to ask for help.

While it is unfortunate that Christians are often reluctant to avail themselves of psychotherapy, their apprehension is understandable. Horror stories of people losing or having their faith subjected to attack in psychotherapy are readily circulated in Christian circles. Such tragedies do, in fact, occur. However, because of the stigma of admitting psychological needs, stories of many who

have received help through psychotherapy do not tend to be circulated in the same manner.

How should Christians view psychotherapy? Are some therapies
more or less Christian than others? How can a Christian understand
the goals and techniques associated with any of the major approaches to psychotherapy and attempt to evaluate their correspon-
dence to the Christian view of persons? These are a few of the questions which are addressed in this volume.

The articles in this book are drawn from the larger collection
presented in the *Baker Encyclopedia of Psychology* (Benner 1985).
The intent of reproducing some of the best of these articles is to
make them more readily available. After a discussion of some general issues in counseling and psychotherapy, fifty-one of the most
common individual, group, marital, and family psychotherapies are
presented and evaluated. The authors of these articles are psychologists, psychiatrists, and family counselors drawn from the ranks of
practicing therapists and academic researchers and theoreticians.
Although they represent a broad range of theological traditions,
they share an interest in relating Christian faith to psychotherapy.

Choosing among the bewildering array of therapies requires some
basic knowledge about each of them. It is hoped that this collection
of articles will be of assistance to those who wish to be more informed about psychotherapy. More importantly, it is hoped that
these articles will help Christians think responsibly about psychotherapy.

Reference

Benner D. G., ed. *Baker Encyclopedia of Psychology*. Grand Rapids: Baker
  Book House, 1985.

Contributors

Elizabeth M. Altmaier, Ph.D.
Associate Professor
Division of Counselor Education
University of Iowa

Dean E. Barley, B.S.
Graduate Student
Brigham Young University

Clark E. Barshinger, Ph.D.
Codirector
Barrington Counseling Associates
Lake Zurich, Illinois

David G. Benner, Ph.D.
Professor of Psychology
Wheaton College

Allen E. Bergin, Ph.D.
Professor of Psychology
Brigham Young University

William G. Bixler, Ph.D.
Oklahoma Christian Counseling
  Center
Oklahoma City, Oklahoma

Jeffrey M. Brandsma, Ph.D.
Professor and Director of Clinical
  Psychology Internship
Department of Psychiatry
Medical College of Georgia

David W. Brokaw, Ph.D.
Assistant Professor of Psychology
Azusa Pacific University

Christine V. Bruun, Ph.D.
DuPage County Mental Health
  Center
Westmont, Illinois

Rodger K. Bufford, Ph.D.
Chairman and Associate Professor
  of Psychology
Western Conservative Baptist Seminary

Brian L. Carlton, Ph.D.
DuPage County Mental Health
  Center
Wheaton, Illinois

John D. Carter, Ph.D.
Professor of Psychology
Rosemead School of Psychology
Biola University

Paul W. Clement, Ph.D.
Professor of Psychology
Director, The Psychological Center
Graduate School of Psychology
Fuller Theological Seminary

Arlo D. Compaan, Ph.D.
Executive Director
Center for Life Skills
Chicago, Illinois

Creath Davis, M. Div.
Executive Director
Christian Concern Foundation
Dallas, Texas

William L. Edkins, M. Div., Psy. D.
Assistant Clinical Professor
Rosemead School of Psychology
Biola University

J. Harold Ellens, Ph.D.
Executive Director
Christian Association for Psycho-
   logical Studies
Farmington Hills, Michigan

Robert R. Farra, Ph.D.
Professor of Family Sociology
Adrian College

John G. Finch, Ph.D.
Consulting Psychologist
Gig Harbor, Washington

Dennis L. Gibson, Ph.D.
Wheaton Counseling Associates
Wheaton, Illinois

Cedric B. Johnson, Ph.D.
Director
Bethesda Counseling Clinic
Santa Monica, California

Stanton L. Jones, Ph.D.
Associate Professor of Psychology
Wheaton College

Richard K. Kahoe, Ph.D.
Christian Haven Homes
Wheatfield, Indiana

Michael J. Lambert, Ph.D.
Professor of Psychology
Institute for Studies in Values and
   Human Behavior
Brigham Young University

Lojan E. LaRowe, Ph.D.
Barrington Counseling Associates
Deerfield, Illinois
Assistant Professor of Psychology
Trinity College

H. Newton Malony, Ph.D.
Professor of Psychology and Direc-
   tor of Programs in the Integration
   of Psychology and Theology
Graduate School of Psychology
Fuller Theological Seminary

Clinton W. McLemore, Ph.D.
Associate Professor of Psychology
Graduate School of Psychology
Fuller Theological Seminary

S. Bruce Narramore, Ph.D.
Professor and Dean
Rosemead School of Psychology
Biola University

E. Mansell Pattison, M.D.
Professor and Chairman of the De-
   partment of Psychiatry and
   Health Behavior
Medical College of Georgia

L. Rebecca Propst, Ph.D.
Assistant Professor of Psychology
Lewis and Clark College

Robert J. Salinger, M.D.
Madison Psychiatric Associates
Madison, Wisconsin

John A. Sanford, M. Div.
Certified Jungian Analyst
Private Practice
San Diego, California

Bethyl J. Shepperson, Psy. D.
Claremont Psychological Services
Claremont, California

Vance L. Shepperson, Ph.D.
Associate Adjunct Professor
California Graduate Institute
California State University at Los
  Angeles

Darrell Smith, Ph.D.
Professor and Director of Training
Counseling Psychology Program
Department of Educational Psychol-
  ogy
Texas A & M University

Siang-Yang Tan, Ph.D.
Assistant Professor
Graduate School of Psychology
Fuller Seminary

Glenn C. Taylor, M.Th., M.Ed.
General Director
Yonge Street Mission
Adjunct Faculty
Ontario Theological Seminary

Harry A. Van Belle, Ph.D.
Professor of Psychology
Redeemer College

Hendrika Vande Kemp, Ph.D.
Associate Professor
Graduate School of Psychology
Fuller Theological Seminary

James H. Vander May, M.A.,
  F.T.E.P.
Chairperson
Activity Therapy Department
Pine Rest Christian Hospital
Grand Rapids, Michigan

Bryan Van Dragt, Ph.D.
Private Practice
Gig Harbor, Washington

Henry A. Virkler, Ph.D.
Adjunct Faculty Member
Psychological Studies Institute
Georgia State University
Director of Counseling Services
Ministry Counseling Center
Atlanta, Georgia

Frances J. White, Ph.D.
Professor of Psychology
Wheaton College

Rod Wilson, Ph.D.
Dean of Students and Director of
  Counseling Program
Ontario Theological Seminary

Ellie L. Wright, B.S.
Graduate Student
Brigham Young University

H. Norman Wright, M.A.
Director
Family Counseling and Enrichment
Santa Ana, California

Part **1**

General Issues

1

Counseling and Psychotherapy: An Overview
Clinton W. McLemore

Few professional services are as difficult to define as counseling and psychotherapy. Both terms have been used to mean a wide variety of things, from the giving of legal advice to the administration of antipsychotic medications. Except for the vague sense that psychotherapy is somehow a more serious and perhaps professionally respectable service than counseling, few people—including mental health professionals—could summon up clear and nonoverlapping definitions of the two. Even these professionals, if pressed, might fall back on some kind of distinction grounded in credentials: therapy is what doctors do and counseling is what every other psychological helper does. Alternately, a distinction might be drawn on the basis of frequency and duration of sessions: therapy is a long-drawn-out endeavor, sometimes involving several sessions per week, while counseling is a brief and less intense process. Yet another distinction that might be made is that therapy is what sick people get, whereas counseling is for normal people.

Definitions and Clarifications

There is an important difference between counseling and psycho-therapy, but it relates only tangentially to the above distinctions. Counseling and therapy are actually opposite points on a continuum. Any particular helping relationship may move all over this continuum as the needs of the client change from moment to moment and session to session.

Psychotherapy is, at root, the process of increasing a person's emotional capacity and self-sufficiency. This implies a more or less permanent change in the personality. Such change often takes considerable time, but it can occur within a matter of minutes—for example, in response to a life challenge or a catastrophe. Thus, sheer duration of treatment or frequency of visits does not ensure that any real therapy has taken place.

Similarly, the mere possession of professional credentials, however impressive, is no guarantee of the ability to render competent psychotherapeutic service. There are some people with prestigious permaplaques on the wall who probably could not facilitate the psychological growth of anyone. On the other hand, certain persons without very much in the way of formal qualifications are superbly capable of being therapeutic. For the term *psychotherapy* to be specific enough to be useful it should probably be restricted to services that are rendered in a professional setting, under conditions in which there is at least an informal understanding that therapy is to be attempted.

Finally, it makes little sense to try to define psychotherapy as a medical treatment given to the sick, since such a definitional effort only adds one set of ambiguities to another. Who exactly are the sick? As many writers have pointed out, describing persons with nonorganic psychological difficulties as "ill" is a regressive metaphor that stigmatizes recipients of psychological services. This metaphor once served an important social function in that it markedly decreased the outrageous persecution to which psychologically disordered persons were often subjected. At this juncture in history, when there is little persecution to compare to that of previous centuries, whatever benefits the medical model may afford are heavily outweighed by its inherent stigmatization. Part of this stigmatization is the idea that there is a clear qualitative difference between the mentally ill and the rest of us. Persons with profound psychoses tend to blind us to the fact that all people fall somewhere on a continuous scale of psychological functioning. Since psychotherapy is the process of facilitating emotional growth and self-sufficiency, just about anyone could probably profit from it.

At the opposite end of our psychological service continuum counseling is explicitly concerned with exactly what the good therapist tries to avoid: concrete advice giving. The counselor wants to help the client with immediate practical problems. These can range from choosing a career to coping with a tragedy. No permanent change in personality is necessarily expected. If such change occurs, it is a by-product of the counselor's central objective, which is to better enable the person to face a specific situation.

During the process of providing psychotherapy to a person, troubling practical problems may arise in the client's life. At such times the therapist may, without even thinking much about it, offer advice about how to respond to these problems. Some therapists fluidly move in and out of giving the client advice about decisions with respect to money matters, in-law troubles, job difficulties, and the like. Others of a more psychoanalytic persuasion believe that the giving of any advice about how to deal with concrete problems only fosters neurotic dependence and thus undermines the long-term goals of therapy. These therapists tend not to give such advice, even in the face of potential disaster for the client. All therapists probably engage in some advice giving, and it may well be that the best therapists are those who know when to "do therapy" and when to "give counsel."

Basic Dimensions of Psychological Change

Setting aside for the moment the distinctions we have drawn between counseling and therapy, it may be useful to highlight some of the ways in which different people benefit from psychological services.

Actions

As a result of professional services people may learn to behave in new ways, or learn not to behave in old, dysfunctional ways. For example, a shy person who perhaps tends to feel worse and worse during the course of a party may learn to speak up early and thereby interrupt a self-defeating pattern of mounting withdrawal. Or a child may learn to inhibit aggressive behaviors such as hitting other children.

Feelings

As a result of psychological assistance people can develop new emotional reactions or learn better ways of handling already existing feelings. For example, a person may begin to feel tenderness toward others that he or she has never felt before. Or a person may learn to express anger that previously had expressed itself only in unconscious anguish.

Perceptions

Some individuals, as a direct result of help, gradually see things in a new light. For example, a client may decide that the world is, after all, not a hostile place, "out to get you." Or a person may decide that her mother or father is not such a bad person after all.

Physiology

Many persons respond to psychological help with an improvement in physiological functioning. A business executive may be less troubled by ulcerative stomach pain after consulting a psychologist, or a client's blood pressure may go down.

Thoughts

In response to psychological services persons often undergo changes in how they think. Instead of telling themselves all sorts of terrible things—for example, "I'm no good"—they may come to think of themselves as worthwhile. Or a person may change from thinking in a confused, anxiety-ridden manner to thinking in a clear, relaxed way.

Values

Some people, as a result of psychological interventions, undergo a change in values. They may come to care more deeply about other people and less intensely about occupational success. Or they may esteem certain of their feelings in a way they never did before.

Historical Roots

The roots of psychotherapy and counseling are intricate and lengthy. No doubt from earliest times people have tried to comfort, advise, and nurture each other in countless ways. Nevertheless, within Western society there have been several major turning points on the way to psychological services as they exist near the end of the twentieth century.

While Augustine's *Confessions* and a few lesser volumes will always stand as early examples of brilliant psychological analysis, it was probably the French philosopher and mathematician René Descartes who most encouraged Western civilization in the direction of psychology. Once people turned their attention to the exploration of subjective realities and processes, it was only a matter of time before society attempted to ameliorate psychological difficulties through subjectively oriented helping methods.

The first person to construct an eminent career upon this foundation was, of course, Sigmund Freud. During the latter part of the nineteenth century neurology and psychiatry were essentially one discipline. While Freud wanted to pursue an academic career within medicine and physiology, his marriage forced him to enter clinical practice as a way to support his family. Beginning as a neurologist-psychiatrist, Freud was immensely influenced by one of his teachers to explore the benefits of "talking cures." Always the scientist-researcher-theoretician and only secondarily the practitioner, Freud was intrigued with the workings of the human psyche. His lifetime of clinical investigation has come down to us in what we know as psychoanalysis.

A second major turning point was John Watson's inauguration of behaviorism. Whereas psychoanalysis grew out of medicine, which has continued to dominate its development to this day, behaviorism developed out of academic psychology. Watson came along at the right time to persuade university psychologists of the wisdom of his approach. For many years prior to the publication of Watson's initial and ultimately most influential writings (between 1910 and 1920), introspection had been the main method of psychological research. In this period introspection involved training observers to monitor and report some aspect of their experience. Unfortunately, because of introspection's inherently subjective nature, the "trained observers" of different researchers disagreed on a regular basis. Psychology, which had begun with great promise, threatened to end up in unresolvable arguments. Watson encouraged psychologists to throw out all consideration of mental events in favor of the study of observable behavior. While Watson's excursions into clinical phenomena were few, a great many subsequent psychologists have applied his methods to the remediation of psychological disorders, in the form of what is now known as behavior therapy.

The so-called third force or, as we are calling it, the third turning point was the emergence of what is usually known as humanistic psychology. Carl Rogers, who was raised in a conservative Christian home and who began as a divinity student, left Union Seminary to study psychology across the street at Columbia University. He later held a job for many years at another college, where he provided a great deal of clinical service to students. Out of these experiences Rogers developed what has traditionally been known as client-centered (or person-centered) therapy. While the psychoanalysts focused on unconscious processes and the behaviorists focused on observable actions, Rogers and his followers focused on conscious subjectivity, in particular on feelings.

Many other forms of therapy and counseling have been advanced, so many in fact that it would be ludicrous even to attempt to review them all here. We will, however, mention those which have received the most attention, omitting such specialized forms of counseling as vocational and rehabilitational.

Major Forms of Counseling and Therapy

Because psychoanalysis has been such a strong influence on psychiatry and psychology for so many decades, it has spawned numerous offshoots and innovations. Thus, in addition to classical psychoanalysis we find direct psychoanalysis, object relations therapy, ego psychology, and a number of other variations. Still, common to virtually all analytic therapies is an emphasis on the therapeutic benefits of *insight*. Psychoanalysts have traditionally defined insight as the coming into consciousness of that which previously had been unconscious. Good analysts understand that for insight to be helpful it has to be more than intellectualization (i.e., it has to have emotional impact). And into what is the analysand seeking insight? His or her psychodynamics—those subtle mental processes, typically characterized by conflict, which create symptoms. An example of a psychodynamically based symptom is the soldier who, fearing to be called (and, perhaps more importantly, to call himself) a coward, but fearing even more that he might be killed, develops hysterical blindness (a true inability to see without any organic reason for this inability). The classic analytic position is that by allowing the nature of his conflicts into conscious awareness, the soldier will be cured of his visual impairment.

The therapies that have evolved out of Watson's behaviorism have been influenced to a great extent by Harvard psychologist B. F. Skinner and, to a lesser extent, by psychiatrist Joseph Wolpe. Wolpe is the originator of systematic desensitization, in which the patient's fears are, in the ideal, replaced by relaxation responses. The methods that have come from Skinner's work are based on the idea that people do what they do as a result of previous rewards and punishments. While Skinner has never been a clinician, a great variety of techniques have come from his research into operant conditioning. Some of these techniques have yielded excellent results (e.g., with heretofore regressed schizophrenics who, perhaps for the first time in years, learn to attend to personal grooming and to answer when someone else greets them). Operant methods have also been put to use in the classroom. Collectively, these methods are usually known as *behavior therapy*, although the more generic term *behavior modification* is also widely used. A new twist has been given to the behaviorally oriented therapies by the advent of *cognitive-behavior therapy*, which is the name for a group of clinical techniques that are designed to alter behavior by altering thought processes. Moreover, in cognitive-behavior therapy the techniques themselves are more or less patterned along the lines of traditional behavior therapy. For example, a client might be taught to say "I can do it, I am capable" in the face of previously debilitating challenges.

Client-centered (person-centered) therapy, as we have noted, developed out of work with college students. The Rogerian helper tries above all to provide the client with three essential things: unconditional positive regard (the client is accepted by the therapist no matter what the former says or feels); genuineness (the therapist accurately portrays his or her own feelings to the client); and accurate empathy (the therapist places a premium on coming to understand exactly how the client feels and, further, communicating this understanding). A central thesis of Rogerian counseling/therapy has always been that there is an innate growth tendency in people which will be released when these three conditions are met during any human encounter.

These three therapeutic traditions have been most influential. Some other schools of therapy will be described more briefly.

Adlerian psychotherapy, which seems to have decreased in prominence, is concerned with helping the individual clarify constructive life goals and plans, develop proper social interest (concern for others), and better understand his or her life style and how this relates to psychological development.

Jungian analysis, which has often been geared toward persons in their 40s, focuses on the deep unconscious (including one's ancestral unconscious, or what Jungians ordinarily call the collective unconscious) and in particular on the latent unexpressed parts of the person. Almost mystical at times, Jungian therapy is very philosophical in tone compared with most others. Jung was one of Freud's close associates who ultimately broke with him. Adler was another.

Interpersonal psychotherapy derives from the work of Harry

Stack Sullivan, an American psychiatrist who was intensely interested in the clinical significance of how people act toward others. Therapists who are interpersonally oriented attend carefully to what causes the client anxiety and to the defensive behaviors this anxiety triggers. These behaviors hinder intimacy and augment idiosyncratic (autistic) thinking.

Transactional analysis (TA) is concerned with helping the client understand, and put an end to, the games he or she plays. Games, according to TA, are anything but light and breezy fun. Indeed, they can be lethal, such as those games that revolve around alcohol or suicide. Transactional analysts use humor, blackboard diagrams, and group feedback in their work with people.

Family therapy is the general name for just about any clinical method in which the family rather than the individual is the focus of treatment. Specific methods range from psychoanalytically to behaviorally oriented ones. Closely related to family therapy is marital therapy and counseling, but the latter term, like the former, refers more to a "target population" than to a specific school of therapy.

Gestalt therapy is primarily concerned with the client's awareness. Gestalt therapists try to facilitate clients' knowledge of disowned feelings and to encourage them to take responsibility for these feelings and, indeed, for their whole lives. Like interpersonal psychologists, therapists of the Gestalt orientation attend carefully to what is going on in the present between therapist and patient.

Biofeedback typically involves using technological devices, such as EEG (electrical brain activity) monitors, to teach people how to bring under voluntary control physiological processes that were previously automatic. Thus, a business executive with high blood pressure might be taught to lower his blood pressure at will.

Hypnotherapists employ hypnosis—a treatment method with a noble heritage as well as a sideshow reputation—to help people stop smoking, learn to study better, and so forth. There is still much debate among scholars over what hypnosis is, whether an altered state of consciousness, a form of role playing, or something else entirely.

Existential psychotherapy is a philosophically oriented therapy that deals with such issues as what gives the client's life meaning. Emphasis is placed on the thesis that each person creates his or her own life as a project, and that choices are therefore of paramount importance.

Sensitivity and encounter groups are methods for helping people become more aware of their feelings and of their impact on others.

Most such groups involve a good deal of confrontation among participants. Sometimes this confrontation is gentle and sometimes not.

There are, of course, many other therapies, but these are the ones most often practiced and, therefore, those the reader is most likely to encounter.

A Three-Dimensional Model for Classifying Therapies

Therapies can be classified according to how much they emphasize thought, feeling, or action. Some therapies—for example, Gestalt—lay heavy stress on feeling and pay relatively little explicit attention to thought or action. Others, such as behavior therapy, stress action to the relative exclusion of thought and feeling, although the rise of cognitive-behavior therapy has shifted this stress for some practitioners. Still others, such as rational-emotive therapy, place primary emphasis on the client's thoughts.

It is often useful to find out exactly what is stressed by a particular therapist, since there should be at least a reasonably good match between what the therapist offers and what the client needs. Given that there is a finite amount of time and energy to distribute during the course of any therapy session, it is best to make sure that these resources will be wisely spent.

Licensing and Regulation

Most states now have licensing laws governing who can and who cannot hold himself or herself out to the public as a psychologist. *Psychiatrist* has always clearly implied the possession of a medical license, so there has traditionally been fairly tight regulation over who could use this title. The title *counselor* is almost totally unregulated. Thus, just about anybody can advertise as a counselor, as long as terms like *psychological* and *psychiatric* are not used.

What makes matters even more confusing is that psychotherapy is not a profession per se, and psychotherapist is not a formal professional title. A psychotherapist is simply one who conducts psychotherapy. Some states, recognizing the danger of leaving these two terms unregulated, stipulate by law that they cannot be used except by persons who fall into certain professional groups. In certain states, however, there is excessively wide latitude in defining which groups of professionals are included. Thus, a nurse without any training in verbal psychotherapy can be a psychotherapist. This is not to say that some nurses are not excellently therapeutic but merely to point out how loosely regulated the psychotherapy field really is.

State licensing boards are primarily responsible for policing the actions of their licensees, although in certain instances of gross misconduct criminal prosecution may occur. The most the licensing board can ordinarily do is to suspend or revoke the license, but the state attorney general can seek more serious action, if appropriate, by formal prosecution.

Most reputable professionals belong to one or more professional societies, such as the American Psychological Association. Such societies can expel members who fail to conform to their standards of conduct.

Psychological Help as Persuasion

We cannot deal thoroughly here with the subject of counseling and therapy as persuasion. But we should at least note that clients who come for help usually invest in their helpers a great deal of trust, especially if the relationship endures for any length of time. As a result, psychological helpers have more than an ordinary amount of persuasive power. The proper use of this power is the express purpose of nearly all licensing laws and codes of ethics.

Some theorists regard therapy/counseling primarily as a means of giving people new philosophies of life, new ways to make sense of old experiences. If so, therapy may be more of a religious activity than any of us heretofore have been willing to admit.

Additional Reading

McLemore, C. W. *The scandal of psychotherapy: A guide to resolving the tensions between faith and counseling.* Wheaton, Ill.: Tyndale House, 1982.

2

Christian Counseling and Psychotherapy
David G. Benner

One of the more visible products of attempts to integrate psychology and Christian theology has been the development of a number of systems of counseling and psychotherapy qualifying themselves with the adjective *Christian*. While many have viewed these developments with enthusiasm, some have argued that it is ridiculous to describe psychotherapy as Christian. To do so, they feel, suggests that there is a unique procedure that a Christian should employ for every action. If it is appropriate to talk about Christian psychotherapy, then why not Christian plumbing or Christian penmanship? However, the focus of psychotherapy is obviously much closer to that of Christianity than is the case in activities such as plumbing or penmanship. Also, the value-laden nature of the therapy process necessarily makes it either more or less Christian.

A more serious criticism is raised by Bobgan and Bobgan (1979), who view psychotherapy and Christianity as fundamentally incompatible. Contrasting the psychological way to health to the spiritual way, these authors assert that psychotherapy is not a neutral set of scientific techniques but rather a religious system, and a false one at that. The attempt to "Christianize" psychotherapy is therefore seen as a further erosion of the spiritual ministry of the church.

While agreeing that psychotherapy cannot be seen as a value-free set of techniques, a good many Christian mental health professionals and lay persons have seen that this is precisely why it is imperative that Christians subject their theories and practice of therapy to rigorous biblical evaluation. Others have gone further than this, arguing that since existing secular theories of therapy are built upon non-Christian presuppositions, a truly Christian approach must begin (and in some cases end) with the biblical view of persons. Concepts and techniques are then drawn from secular systems if they are found to be compatible with the new foundation.

Current Approaches

One factor that makes it difficult to overview and classify current Christian approaches to therapy is the often unclear line of differentiation between pastoral counseling and other forms of Christian therapy. Hiltner and Coltson (1961) demonstrated that the context of pastoral counseling (usually a church) and the symbols and expectations attached to the role of the clergy all serve to make it somewhat different from therapy offered outside an explicitly pastoral context. However, as pastoral counselors have sometimes moved physically out of the church to secular centers of pastoral psychotherapy, and as some psychotherapists have made a more explicit and visible identification with Christianity and its values, the differences are often less apparent.

In a recent summary of the major current approaches to Christian therapy Collins (1980) identifies seventeen systems, including four that are explicitly pastoral, which he suggests to be distinctively Christian. While these vary tremendously in their sophistication, for the most part they are quite simplistic and fall far short of being a comprehensive system or model of therapy.

Ford and Urban (1963) suggest that a system of therapy needs to include a theory of personality development, a theory of psychopathology, a statement of the goals of therapy, and the conditions and techniques for producing behavior change. These ideals of a comprehensive system are met imperfectly by most, if not all, models of psychotherapy. For example, Gestalt therapy and reality therapy are usually seen to be deficient in terms of their assumptions about both normal and abnormal personality development. Existential therapy has most commonly been judged to be weak in terms of its therapeutic techniques.

The current approaches to Christian counseling are no more adequate in terms of these criteria. In fact, in the majority of cases they are much less comprehensive. For example, relationship counseling (Carlson, 1980) includes assumptions only about the conditions for change, ignoring personality development, psychotherapy, and goals of therapy. Similarly growth counseling (Clinebell, 1979), love therapy (Morris, 1974), and integrity therapy (Drakeford, 1967) all give only very minimal treatment to the processes of normal or abnormal personality development, focusing on goals and techniques of therapy. Only biblical counseling as developed by Crabb (1977) explicitly sets forth a model of personality development and psychopathology and then relates goals and techniques of therapy to this foundation. In this regard it stands as probably the most comprehensive of the existing Christian approaches. However, in comparison to psychoanalysis, client-centered (person-centered) therapy, or behavior therapy, it still must be seen as simplistic and far from a comprehensive model.

To be fair, however, it is important to realize that it was probably not the intention of these authors to present their ideas as a comprehensive system of counseling but rather as an *approach* to counseling. For example, Carlson (1980) states that his intent is to present a style of counseling that is based on Jesus' style of relating. He goes on to assert that "there is no recognized set of techniques that are exclusively Christian" (p. 32) and that there is "no agreed-upon focus of change" (p. 33). His focus, therefore, is on a style of relating, which he feels is the point where a counselor or therapist is most able to be explicitly Christian.

There is one additional point that should be noted in evaluating existing Christian approaches to counseling. With the exception of biblical counseling and nouthetic counseling none of the other approaches have been explicitly developed from Christian theology. Rather, they are adapted forms of existing secular theories which the authors argue are consistent with Christian truth. Thus, we find transactional analysis (Malony, 1980), reality therapy (Morris, 1974), and family systems therapy (Larsen, 1980) at the basis of approaches to therapy which are argued by respective advocates as being basically compatible with biblical theology.

This leads to the question of how these approaches differ from others that are not called Christian. Is Christian psychotherapy anything more than a Christian doing psychotherapy? Vanderploeg (1981) argues that "there is no difference between Christian and non-Christian therapy. The goals are the same, . . . the means are the same. . . . The difference lies not within therapy but within the therapists themselves. One group is Christian and the other is not" (p. 303). Those who have disagreed with this position and have argued for an approach to psychotherapy that is uniquely Christian have usually done so on the basis of either uniqueness in theory or uniqueness in role and/or task. These two major arguments will be considered separately.

The Bible and Personality Theory

For a number of authors the answer to the question of what makes a particular approach to counseling Christian has been quite simple and direct. They assert that Christian counseling is based on the biblical model of personality. In other words, they assume that Scripture contains a unique anthropology and theory of psychotherapy. Adams (1977) argues that the Bible is the only textbook needed for the Christian to learn all that is needed for counseling. He asserts that "if a principle is new to or different from those that are advocated in Scriptures, it is wrong; if it is not, it is unnecessary" (p. 183).

Others (Carter, 1980; Crabb, 1977) have avoided the assumption that nothing useful can be learned about counseling apart from the Scriptures, but have retained the expectation that Scripture does contain a unique personality theory and implicit model of counseling. The striking thing, however, is that seldom do these people agree as to just what Scripture suggests to be this unique model. This is reminiscent of Berkouwer's (1962) assertion that the failures to find a system of personality or psychology in Scripture "have only made clear that because of the great variety of concepts used in the Bible, it is not possible to synthesize them into a systematic Biblical anthropology in which the structure and composition of man would be made clear. . . . It is obviously not the intention of the divine revelation to give us exact information about man in himself and thus to anticipate what later scientific research on man offers" (p. 199).

Although the Scriptures should not, therefore, be expected to provide a comprehensive theory of personality or psychotherapy, they obviously do contain a view of persons that is most essential to the individual wishing to provide Christian therapy. In fact, whatever else Christian counseling is, surely it must be based on and informed by these biblical perspectives on human nature. Three biblical themes seem particularly relevant: the unity of personality, creation in the image of God, and the reality of sin.

Psychospiritual unity

Historically, attempts to understand what Scripture teaches about human personality have often begun with a discussion of the so-called parts of persons (heart, soul, mind, etc.). In fact, one long-standing debate in biblical anthropology has been over whether man is best seen as a dichotomy (body-soul) or trichotomy (body-soul-spirit). Significantly, this debate is now receding into history, as the consensus of many theologians has increasingly been that the primary biblical emphasis is on the unity of personality. The suggestion is that while Scripture does present a number of characteristics of persons, these were never intended to be interpreted as components or parts. Always they are to be seen as perspectives on the whole.

The implication of this is that man does not *have* a spirit, man *is* spirit. Similarly, man does not have a soul or a body, but *is* soul and *is* body. Further, this means that since we do not have spiritual or psychological parts to our personality, neither do we have problems that are purely spiritual or purely psychological. All problems occur within the common substrate of psychospiritual processes and affect the totality of a person's functioning. The Christian therapist must therefore resist the temptation to artificially separate problems and people into psychological and spiritual parts. Similarly, the Christian therapist cannot ignore a problem just because it has a superficial religious or spiritual appearance.

Created in God's image

The second aspect of the biblical view of persons that needs to be considered is the concept of the *imago Dei*. Although Scripture directly discusses the fact of our creation in God's image in only a few passages, theologians have usually given it a central place in their doctrine of man. Vanderploeg (1981) has similarly argued that it must be seen to be foundational to any understanding of psychotherapy. The fact that we were created in God's image establishes human beings as essentially relational, called to relationship with God and with each other. Viewing the major goal of psychotherapy as helping individuals deal with and enhance their relationships, Vanderploeg then argues that this represents helping people expand and explore the *imago Dei* within them.

The doctrine of the *imago Dei* also helps us understand man's religious nature. Hart (1977) has argued that because we were created in the image of God, our whole life is intended to mirror God. We were created to serve God and to lose ourselves in joyous fellowship with him. By his gift of free will he allows us to choose whether we will, in fact, serve him or not. However, we will serve someone or something, and that is the heart of our religiosity. Religion therefore defines mankind. It is not something added on to an otherwise complete being. It describes our essential meaning, our need to be self-transcendent and to lose ourselves in service to God and others.

The reality of sin

While the fact of our creation in God's image validates the good and noble aspects of human functioning, the Christian view of persons must be balanced by the reality of sin. More than just a tendency to fail to meet our personal expectations or those held of us by others, sin has traditionally been viewed by Christian theology as active rebellion against God and his holy law. This rebellion results in alienation from God, self, and others. These consequences of sin are therefore ultimately, although not necessarily personally or directly, at the root of all our problems.

This reality informs a Christian approach to counseling. If sin is real, then guilt may not always be neurotic. Sometimes it will be real, and forgiveness and repentance will then be necessary. Pattison (1969) states that "the task of the psychotherapist, then, is not to assuage guilt feelings, although that is often a necessary preamble to successful therapy. Rather, the therapist seeks to help the patient see himself and his relationships with others in the light of how the patient violates the relationships to which he is committed. . . . Patients would quite willingly settle for pacification of their superego, but they are reluctant to undergo the pain of changing their pattern of relationships so that they no longer need to feel guilty" (pp. 106–107).

When combined with other equally important biblical themes such as grace, the incarnation, and life after death, the concepts discussed above should be at the foundation of any theory of personality that calls itself Christian. However, they are far from adequate as a complete personality theory. While we therefore may conclude that the Scriptures should not be expected to yield a comprehensive system of therapy, it is clear that they contain perspectives on persons that ought to be foundational for Christian therapy.

Roles and Tasks

The second possible basis for the uniqueness of Christian therapy is the role and tasks of the Christian therapist. In his sociological analysis of psychiatry and religion, Klausner (1964) suggests four different ideological positions based on the differentiation of the task and role in counseling or psychotherapy: reductionist, dualist, alternativist, and specialist. Reductionists maintain that there is only one role and one task. This is because there is only one type of personal problem and only one type of person equipped to address it. Material reductionists view this problem in scientific psychological terms and see the person trained in this system as the only one equipped to handle such problems. Spiritual reductionists view the problem in spiritual or religious terms and see the minister as the only one equipped to handle such problems.

Dualists believe that there are both psychological and spiritual problems. However, they also believe that one qualified person can address both these types of problems. Alternativists are opposite to the dualists, claiming only one basic type of problem but allowing for the two separate roles in the treatment of this problem. Mental health professionals and clergy are viewed as equally valid, functionally equivalent alternative roles, both groups being appropriately involved in the treatment of the one basic problem experienced by people. Finally, specialists argue that there are two discrete tasks and therefore there must be two roles. Ministers and therapists are, respectively, spiritual specialists and psychological specialists, each dealing with one of the two basic types of problems.

All four of these positions are represented in the contemporary Christian counseling literature. The spiritual reductionist position is probably best represented by Adams (1977) and Bobgan and Bobgan (1979). These authors argue that nonorganic psychological problems are really mislabeled spiritual problems. The one person equipped to provide help for such problems is the Christian who draws his mandate, goals, and techniques from the Bible and from this source alone. While this position has been well received by many conservative Protestant pastors, most Christian mental health professionals have viewed it as providing an inadequate account of psychological functioning and a limited understanding of the role of the therapist.

This assumption of one basic type of problem is shared by the alternativists. Benner (1979) represents this position, arguing that all emotional or psychological problems are at core both spiritual and psychological. Because of the fundamental unity of personality, depression is as much an issue of spiritual significance as guilt is a matter of psychological significance. The challenge is for the Christian therapist to view people as spiritual beings regardless of their religiosity and to be sensitive to spiritual dimensions of their functioning. The challenge to the minister is to similarly view a person as a psychospiritual unity and to resist the tendency to either reduce psychological problems to spiritual problems or to ignore psychological problems since these are beyond his competence. This is not to suggest that all ministers or psychotherapists will be adequately equipped to handle the broad range of problems encountered in pastoral counseling and in psychotherapy, but rather to encourage both groups to view problems within the matrix of psychospiritual unity and to respond accordingly.

The alternativist position is attractive to many because it seems to combine something of the simplicity of the reductionist model with a more adequate understanding of psychological processes. Its major weakness lies in its difficulty in explaining what often appear to be differing levels of psychological and spiritual health within a person. If psychospiritual processes are as unified as argued, the parallels in psychological and spiritual functioning should be even more pronounced than those often seen.

The dualist position is perhaps the most popular in contemporary Christian therapy. Tournier (1963) has been a very influential representative of this position. Minirth (1977) is perhaps an even better representative, arguing that Christian therapy must be responsive to the unique problems of body, soul, and spirit. The first step is therefore the differential diagnosis of the problems of each sphere. Each type of problem is then treated by appropriate and unique methods. Advocates of this position view it as a psychology of the whole person in that the therapist is prepared to respond to both spiritual and psychological problems. Critics view it as more a total treatment approach than a whole-person approach in that the person is not viewed as a whole but rather as the sum of a number of different parts.

A related criticism questions the possibility of differential diagnosis and treatment of spiritual and psychological problems. When is depression a psychological problem and when is it a spiritual problem? Perhaps more difficult to resolve are the technical questions associated with the different tasks required for work with explicitly religious issues versus nonreligious issues. For example, Pattison (1966) asks when the therapist should treat religious questions as grist for the therapeutic mill and when he or she should enter into either a Socratic dialogue or perhaps an explicit instructional role. Also, what are the effects of such movement between roles on transference and countertransference? These questions do not as yet seem adequately answered.

The specialist model has been argued by Pattison (1966), who suggests that different roles are appropriate for the unique tasks of

the therapist and minister. The role of the minister, who wor
definer of social and moral values and behavior, is best serve(
close social-emotional relationship with the parishioner. In con\
the task of changing personality argues for the therapist to ren..ove
himself from a direct involvement in the patient's social value system and maintain more personal and emotional distance.

The problem with this position is that the distinction which it
makes between the goals of therapists and ministers may be exaggerated. Perhaps personality change and changes in social values
and behavior are not as discrete as presented. However, if the goals
are as represented, Pattison's conclusion as to the role that best
supports each set of goals appears helpful.

Goals

What goals should then guide Christian therapy? Ward (1977)
suggests that the ultimate goal of Christian therapy must always be
to assist the client in becoming more like Jesus Christ. Arbuckle
(1975) claims that the desire of the Christian to convert and to
change others to his own personal faith appears to be contradictory
to general counseling philosophy, which values client self-determination. But are these incompatible? First we must realize that therapy is never value free and that all therapists either implicitly or
explicitly communicate their values and personal religion. Therefore, the question is not whether the therapist has certain personal
values or goals but how these influence the therapy process. A therapist who uses the therapy relationship to force his or her beliefs on
another person is obviously behaving in an unprofessional manner.
Christ clearly had the goal of bringing people into relationship with
the Father, but his relating to individuals was never characterized
by coercion. He clearly was willing to allow people their right of
self-determination.

This suggests that while the Christian therapist will have the
ultimate spiritual welfare and growth of the client as a part of his
concern and goals, he will be willing to work with less ultimate
concerns if this is most therapeutically appropriate. Again, Christ's
own behavior illustrates this. His frequent healings of individuals
apart from an explicit verbal proclamation of the gospel show his
concern to meet people at their point of need. His ministry was not
always in ultimate dimensions, even though he never lost sight of
those ultimate concerns.

Ellens (1980) points out how easy it is for Christian therapists to
substitute private philosophy for demandingly sound psychothera-

peutic practice. He states that "the practice of the helping professions which is preoccupied with the final step of wholeness, spiritual maturity, will usually short circuit the therapeutic process and
play the religious dynamic of the patient or therapist straight into
the typical religious patient's psychopathology" (p. 4).

The goals of the Christian therapist will also be guided by the
picture of the whole mature person that is presented as the goal of
Christian growth in Scripture. Thus, for example, the Christian therapist would seek to encourage the development of interdependence,
this in contrast to the autonomy and independence valued in many
therapeutic approaches. Other aspects of Christian maturity are also
readily translatable into therapeutic goals for the Christian counselor. The Christian therapist will be likely, therefore, to share many
of the goals of his secular counterpart. However, the goals that direct Christian therapy should grow out of the overall Christian view
of persons discussed earlier.

Techniques

Is Christian therapy unique by virtue of its employment of certain
techniques? Are there uniquely Christian or non-Christian techniques? Adams (1977) answers these questions affirmatively and,
assuming techniques to be dependent on their presuppositional
base, has judged the techniques of secular therapies to be inappropriate for the Christian therapist. The relationship between most
techniques and the theory with which they are primarily associated
seems, however, to be very loose indeed. One has only to note the
very diverse theoretical orientations laying claim to the same techniques to see this point.

Most techniques seem to be neither Christian nor non-Christian.
Therefore, they should be judged not on the basis of who first described them but rather their function. Do they support the therapeutic goals? Also, they should be evaluated for their consistency
with the overall theoretical framework guiding the therapy. The
Christian therapist will thus be cautious of pragmatic eclecticism as
the sole guide to which techniques to employ.

Some Christian therapists do employ explicitly religious resources such as prayer, Scripture reading, or even laying on of
hands. While any of these interventions may well be appropriate
under some circumstances, the responsible therapist would want to
understand clearly the significance of using them for the client and
the therapy process.

Summary

Christian therapy is clearly not a monolithic development. Little consensus exists on such basic questions as the role and task of the therapist and even the question of whether Scripture should be expected to yield a definitive model for Christian counseling. A recent survey of the membership of the Christian Association for Psychological Studies (Cole & DeVries, 1981) indicated that 48 percent of the Christian mental health professionals responding do not expect Scripture to yield a unified biblical model of counseling. The same percentage do expect such a development. Also, 87 percent see an eclectic approach as most faithful to Scripture, which they see as consistent with a great diversity of styles of counseling.

If Christian therapy is not simply the application of some biblical theory of personality and therapy, what then is it? This chapter has suggested that it is an approach to therapy offered by a Christian who bases his or her understanding of persons on the Bible and allows this understanding to shape all aspects of theory and practice. This suggests an ongoing process rather than a finished product. Seen thus, the Christian therapist is not one who practices a certain type of therapy but one who views himself in God's service in and through his profession and who sees his primary allegiance and accountability to his God, and only secondarily to his profession or discipline.

References

Adams, J. E. *Lectures in counseling.* Nutley, N.J.: Presbyterian and Reformed Publishing, 1977.

Arbuckle, D. S. *Counseling and psychotherapy.* Boston: Allyn & Bacon, 1975.

Benner, D. G. What God hath joined: The psychospiritual unity of personality. *The Bulletin of the Christian Association for Psychological Studies,* 1979, *5*(2), 7–11.

Berkouwer, G. C. *Man: The image of God.* Grand Rapids: Eerdmans, 1962.

Bobgan, M., & Bobgan, D. *The psychological way/the spiritual way.* Minneapolis: Bethany Fellowship, 1979.

Carlson, D. Relationship counseling. In G. R. Collins (Ed.), *Helping people grow.* Santa Ana, Calif.: Vision House, 1980.

Carter, J. D. Towards a biblical model of counseling. *Journal of Psychology and Theology,* 1980, *8*, 45–52.

Clinebell, H. *Growth counseling: Hope-centered methods of actualizing human wholeness.* Nashville: Abingdon, 1979.

Cole, D. T., & DeVries, M. The search for identity. *The Bulletin of the Christian Association for Psychological Studies*, 1981, 7(3), 21–27.

Collins, G. R. (Ed.). *Helping people grow*. Santa Ana, Calif.: Vision House, 1980.

Crabb, L. J., Jr. *Effective biblical counseling*. Grand Rapids: Zondervan, 1977.

Drakeford, J. W. *Integrity therapy*. Nashville: Broadman, 1967.

Ellens, J. H. Biblical themes in psychological theory and practice. *The Bulletin of the Christian Association for Psychological Studies*, 1980, 6(2), 2–6.

Ford, D. H., & Urban, H. B. *Systems of psychotherapy*. New York: Wiley, 1963.

Hart, H. Anthropology. In A. DeGraaff (Ed.). *Views of man and psychology in Christian perspective*. Toronto: Institute for Christian Studies, 1977.

Hiltner, S., & Coltson, L. G. *The context of pastoral counseling*. New York: Abingdon, 1961.

Klausner, S. Z. *Psychiatry and religion*. New York: Free Press, 1964.

Larsen, J. A. Family counseling. In G. R. Collins (Ed.), *Helping people grow*. Santa Ana, Calif.: Vision House, 1980.

Malony, H. N. Transactional analysis. In G. R. Collins (Ed.), *Helping people grow*. Santa Ana, Calif.: Vision House, 1980.

Minirth, F. B. *Christian psychiatry*. Old Tappan, N.J.: Revell, 1977.

Morris, P. D. *Love therapy*. Wheaton, Ill.: Tyndale House, 1974.

Pattison, E. M. Social and psychological aspects of religion in psychotherapy. *Insight: Quarterly Review of Religion and Mental Health*, 1966, 5(2), 27–35.

Pattison, E. M. Morality, guilt, and forgiveness in psychotherapy. In E. M. Pattison (Ed.), *Clinical psychiatry and religion*. Boston: Little, Brown, 1969.

Tournier, P. *The strong and the weak*. Philadelphia: Westminster, 1963.

Vanderploeg, R. D. Imago dei as foundational to psychotherapy: Integration versus segregation. *Journal of Psychology and Theology*, 1981, 9, 299–304.

Ward, W. O. *The Bible in counseling*. Chicago: Moody Press, 1977.

3

Theology and Psychotherapy
J. Harold Ellens

Responsible Christian professionals acknowledge a necessary relationship between the art of Christian living and that of psychotherapy and counseling. They recognize that behind those applied arts is an essential interaction between the science of theology and the science of psychology, each science forming and informing the other.

There are four levels at which the two sciences interact: theory formulation, research methodology, data base, and clinical application. At each level the two sciences interact specifically within the anthropology that is functioning in each science. More specifically, it is the personality theory in that anthropology which is the locus of the interaction of the two sciences.

Since Christians acknowledge that all truth is God's truth, no matter who finds it or where it is found, the information derived from both psychology and theology is taken with equal seriousness. God's message in the special revelation of Scripture and God's general revelation in the created world are both sought diligently to ensure the maximum constructive interaction between theology and

25

psychology. The concern in this is not to integrate the two sciences but to acknowledge that each, as science, has its own domain and data base and must be done in the light of or from the perspective of the other.

In this perspectival model (Ellens, 1982) which acknowledges that the science of biblical theology examines special revelation and the science of psychology examines general revelation, the development of sound personality and psychotherapy theory requires careful attention to the cardinal themes of both psychology and theology. In the art of counseling and psychotherapy those theological themes have clear-cut and palpable import.

Principles and Themes

The first theological principle for counseling and psychotherapy is that godliness or Christian authenticity requires thorough responsibility. To be a Christian counselor or therapist means first to be the best therapist it is possible to be. The second principle is that Christian and professional authenticity requires incarnation in the person of the therapist of that grace-shaped redemptive quality which reflects how God is disposed toward humans and how God designs humans to be disposed toward each other. To be a Christian counselor or therapist means to be God's incarnation for the patient or client, as Jesus Christ is for all of us in everything necessary to our redemption.

Eight theological themes crucially shape a Christian personality theory and counseling or psychotherapy. The first is grace: radical, unconditional, and universal. In the creation story humans are never referred to as children or servants of God but are depicted as compatriots, colaborers, and coequals of God in the kingdom enterprise. That royal status is not abrogated by the fall. The *protoevangelium* (Gen. 3:15) affirms that, whereas God recognized that the human predicament had changed and therefore that the divine redemptive strategy had to change, the objective remained the same. Humans exist to grow into the divinely ordered destiny of full-orbed personhood, in the image of God. To ensure that, God's disposition is not one of judgment but of unconditional acceptance of humans as we are, for the sake of what we can become. It is a disposition of grace, freedom, and affirmation. That covenant is "for the healing of the nations." It renders irrelevant all strategies of religious legalism, psychological defensiveness, and self-justification. Grace is God's ambition for all humanity; it cuts through to the center of our alienation and disorder, and outflanks all our techniques for creating a conditional relationship with God and each other.

The second theme is alienation. The fallenness of humanity is obvious. Its psychological consequences are evident everywhere. Humans are as children thrust out of the maternal womb and unable to catch hold of their father's hand. The biblical story of the fall depicts the spiritual and psychological disorders caused by this experience. The confusion of identity, role, focus, and relationship pervades life like that confusion attendant upon all birth trauma and adolescent disengagement. That is undoubtedly why the biblical account of the fall spontaneously seems so authentic. In the face of generic human fallenness and alienation life becomes an endeavor at anxiety reduction. Most human strategies for that, and for increasing control and security, are pathogenic compensatory strategies. All religion is such an anxiety-reduction strategy. Apart from the Judeo-Christian grace theology, all other religions increase the human sense of alienation and disorder because they provide only strategies for self-justification. Unconditional grace cuts through that pathogenesis and affirms humans as God-compatriots, in spite of ourselves. Even in Judeo-Christian history there have been frequent reversions to pagan conditionalism, but the essence of grace theology transcends that.

The third theme is therefore the biblical theology of personhood. From the biblical tradition of the Jahwist, through the theology of the prophets, to the gospel incarnated in Jesus' way of handling people, it is clear that humans are unconditionally cherished by God. Human personhood is rooted in the fact that we are created as imagers of God and arbitrarily assigned the status of coequals with God in keeping the garden kingdom. So human persons have only two potential conditions: to be in a posture which rings true to that God-given status and, therefore, to self; or to be inauthentic, alienated from God and our own true destiny, and suffering the dissonance and disease inherent to our inauthenticity. In all that, since God is God and grace is grace, God remains preoccupied with human need, not naughtiness; human failure of destiny more than duty; and with our redeemed potential, not our wretched past. Health then means not merely absence of disease but freedom and affirmation for growth to our destiny. We are free in spite of ourselves, to be what we are, for the sake of what we can become before the face of God.

The fourth theme is sin, the failure to achieve authenticity to self and the full-orbed personhood in Christ. Sin is a distortion and distraction to lesser achievements. Nothing can compensate for it. One can only be converted from it. Repentance is the only solution:

turning from our pathogenic compensatory behavior to acceptance of God's unconditional acceptance of us. God's law, then, is not a threat but a constitution for the life of the kingdom, wholeness in the whole person. Having freed us by his grace, God simply waits for us to achieve the self-actualization which expresses the regal status of God-compatriot. Sin is "falling short of his glory," his glorious destiny for us—true selfhood as imagers and compatriots of God.

The fifth theme is discipline and discipleship. It is the endeavor of beginning down the way of grace: forgiveness and acceptance of self and others and unconditional caring for self and others. It is not structuring life in a controlled legalism of personal purity and piety designed to gain credit with God. Discipleship is a troth with self and God to incarnate that divine grace dynamic that infuses the universe. It is a troth to forsake all other *foci* and keep only to the kingdom destiny of God's imager, compatriot, and incarnator of grace.

The sixth theme is that of the suffering servant or wounded healer. Nouwen (1972) suggests that there are four doors through which God and the Christian can touch humans: the woundedness of the world, of a given generation, of the individual, and of the healer. Grace, growth, and healing are communicated through the brokenness of the healer to the person to be healed. The humanness and brokenness of both must be affirmed. The healer's role is not to remove the pain of life but to interpret it. The evidence in the healer of woundedness and pain and of the constructive uses and endurance of it helps to heal the patient. The wounded healer can become the model and the sign of hope, of the risk taking inherent in growth and healing.

The seventh theme is celebration. People who can be grateful can be healthy. People who cannot be grateful cannot be healthy. They do not have access to the psychological and spiritual machinery of health. The Christian life is celebration. The Bible makes it clear that Christianity is not a command to be obeyed, a burden to be labored under, nor an obligation to be met. It is an opportunity to be seized, a relief to be celebrated, and a salvation to be savored. The celebration of gratitude may take the form of the childlike posture of prayer or the exhilarated enjoyment of God's providence.

The eighth theme is mortality. The Bible gives little impetus to the perfectionist notions that building the kingdom will eliminate mortality. It affirms the world's brokenness and pathology and that we are dying persons in a world of malignancy as well as of magnificence. It is acceptable to age, wrinkle, weaken, become more dependent, and even die. Maturation, not youthfulness, is the focus of meaning. People needing healing need to feel in their counselors the Christian realization that it is a supportable and perhaps even a celebratable condition to be a human mortal before the face of God.

Implications for Therapy

The consequences of these themes for counseling and psychotherapy are direct and practical. First, they imply that the patient possesses a pre-established identity, arbitrarily imputed by God in his grace. The patient is, in spite of himself or herself, an image bearer of God. That identity needs to be recovered. Therapy is the process of recovering it and propelling the patient into the certified and secure destiny of purposeful self-realization as imager and compatriot of God. That may not be overtly explained in therapy but will be implicit in the perspective, goals, expectations, and values inherent in the therapist's incarnational role.

Second, the themes of grace-shaped identity, growth, healing, and destiny introduce into the therapeutic milieu dynamics which can erode neurotic guilt, remorse, grief, hopelessness, self-pity, compulsivity, and rigidity of personality. The Christian perspective potentially decreases the need for the self-defeating processes of denial and self-justification as well as the various compensatory reactions so often produced by them. The biblical perspective frees the patient and the therapist for self-acceptance and a life style of dignity. It is a perspective shaped by God's unconditional positive regard for humans.

Third, the Christian perspective removes the anxiety of the therapy responsibility for the therapist and so decreases the degree of iatrogenic psychopathology (therapist-induced psychopathology). It also affords a base for wholesome transference and countertransference and frees the therapist to be human and healthily humorful.

Fourth, the Christian perspective can reduce the anxiety and distraction of the patient. This may come by means of the sense of relief and affirmed self-esteem implied in the fact that his or her worthiness is imputed and inherent rather than a worthiness earned and dependent upon his or her health or behavior.

Fifth, this Christian perspective of freedom and affirmation expands the potential for risk taking toward growth by its constructive anxiety-reduction value. It affords relief from constraints that distract the patient from Christian self-actualization. It releases persons to accept humanness and mortality, and thereby it mollifies that ultimate threat which stands behind all pathology: the fear of death and meaninglessness.

Theology and faith are cognitive-emotive processes. Their functions for good or ill are relevant to all cognitive and emotive disorders, even those of an organic or body chemistry source. Therefore, concerns about theological perspective, faith commitment, religious experience, and spiritual maturity are vital therapeutic issues. The concern to be a *Christian* professional is a crucial one.

References

Ellens, J. H. *God's grace and human health.* Nashville: Abingdon, 1982.

Nouwen, H. J. *The wounded healer.* Garden City, N.Y.: Doubleday, 1972.

4

Religious Resources in Psychotherapy
Cedric B. Johnson

The process of psychotherapy involves the relationship between a mental health professional and a client who is seeking a solution to his or her problem. The therapist applies the findings of the behavioral sciences in a relationship characterized by genuineness, unconditional positive regard, and empathy. The goal is the solution of the person's problem in living. The extent to which religious resources (such as prayer, Scripture reading, laying on of hands, or use of devotional literature) are included in the therapeutic process is a matter of concern for Christian therapists who wish to be clinically responsible and yet make full use of all resources at their disposal.

A variety of theoretical perspectives inform Christians who practice psychotherapy. Like their non-Christian colleagues a majority seem to be identified with eclecticism, where the therapist selects techniques from different systems of psychotherapy and applies these to the client's problem. Very few Christian therapists articulate their reasons for the incorporation of religious resources in therapy. Furthermore, no theory of personality has been developed that incorporates a theology and psychology of prayer, the most commonly utilized resource. In most cases the prayer of the therapist or client is an extension of his or her way of life. Practice has outstripped theory building and testing.

Prayer and the use of the Bible seem to be the most commonly employed religious resources in psychotherapy. The principles involved in their utilization would seem to provide general guidance for the use of other resources.

Prayer

A broad definition of prayer includes the variety of human endeavors wherein people focus their attention on God. The process goes beyond simply talking with God to include other ways of experiencing the divine. In Christianity the experience is mediated through a personal relationship with Jesus Christ. To what extent, then, can this component of religious practice be included in psychotherapy?

Prayer is one dimension that can make the psychotherapeutic process uniquely Christian. The client has an opportunity to connect with the source of meaning in his life and recognize alternative sources of wisdom. A transcendent and supernatural element can be introduced in the therapy. However, there are certain theological and psychological dangers inherent in the use of prayer in therapy.

A theological danger is for the therapist or client to give prayer a value and place less than its biblical importance. This may be done by employing prayer as a psychological technique until a better strategy is found. Such a transitory view of the usefulness of prayer diminishes the biblical statement of its place in the life of the believer. Biblically prayer is not a technique but the way of life of the believer in relationship to God. At all times prayer is to be addressed to God and not to serve the function of two humans speaking to each other. The therapist must remain sensitive to the whole spectrum of the prayer experience, including confession, petition, intercession, and thanksgiving. The therapist models for the client his own ultimate dependence on God, even if he only says to the client, "I will be praying for you."

One of the psychological dangers that emerges when a client asks the therapist for prayer comes under the general category of avoidance. The client may be avoiding painful issues and may suggest prayer rather than further exploration and talk. If the therapist resists this avoidance, as would be correct, his theological orthodoxy may be called into question. This also must be seen as resistance. People seek to evade personal responsibility through an infantile desire that God make everything better. Such expectations require the therapeutic skill of confrontation in a context of acceptance.

Sometimes the therapist may resort to prayer with the client as an avoidance strategy. He may be experiencing the client's sexuality, feel threatened, and avoid the intimacy issue through prayer. Questions such as "How does the client want to *use* prayer?" "Am I as a therapist seeking to please the client with my prayers?" and "Is this prayer consistent with the client's need and theological tradition?" help the therapist avoid improper use of prayer and yet remain open to its appropriate use.

Notwithstanding the dangers, the use of prayer in therapy can mobilize the client's inner spiritual resources and provide help in dealing with problems. For example, prayer of thanksgiving and praise can change the focus of a person's life away from habitual complaints. Hope, essential to change in psychotherapy, can be generated through referring the client's life to God in prayer. The spoken prayer of the client can also be the reaffirmation of a covenantal relationship with God and others. The presence of the therapist stimulates accountability on the part of the client. With a prayer of confession the therapist can act in a priestly fashion and affirm the promise of divine forgiveness. Prayer can also open a person up to his potential and assist in the discovery of fulfillment once again. Such processes are central to psychotherapy.

The Scriptures

The use of the Bible also has dangers, challenges, and great potential. One problem with reading Bible passages to Christian clients is that they may be overfamiliar with the verses to the point of being unresponsive to their impact. The truth of the Bible may have minimal penetration in the day-to-day reality of their lives. To clients having problems with authority the Bible, a symbol of authority, evokes an unquestioning compliance or reflexive rebellion. The naïve therapist may seek either to browbeat the rebel or to shape the compliant person's behavior through proof texting. Such responses on the part of the therapist could well be a case of counter-transference where his problems get in the way of effective therapy.

The Bible can also be misused through its simplistic application to human problems. One illustration of simplistic use of Scripture is when a therapist obtains behavioral change with the prescription of a particular verse. Such a change may be a transference cure—that is, symptom removal through which the client seeks, consciously or unconsciously, to please the therapist. Such cures are superficial and not in the best interests of the client.

Another problem encountered by therapists who use the Bible in therapy is that they may have different interpretations of Scripture from those held by the client. For example, the therapist holds to an equalitarian view of the marriage relationship while his client has a hierarchical perspective. At this point the therapist needs to decide whether he will explicitly or implicitly subvert the client's values, terminate the therapeutic contract, or drastically sublimate personal values and work within the personal values of the client. In no instance, however, can there be a value-free therapy. Biblical interpretation will certainly influence the therapist's and client's therapeutic relationship.

The assets of the use of the Bible in therapy must not be minimized by its dangers. Like prayer it can refer the therapeutic endeavor to the divine dimension and help people realize their God-given potential. The Bible also gives direction and content to personal growth, and can lead a person to a deeper relationship with the divine Author. Such a journey can be facilitated through bibliotherapy. Here the client is encouraged to read portions of Scripture and apply them to life problems or challenges. For example, the unforgiving person may be referred to the parables of Jesus dealing with forgiveness. The feelings and thoughts generated by such an exercise may be fruitfully explored in subsequent sessions. In instances where the client is patently ignorant of the tenets of his faith, a referral may be made to a clergyman. Such concurrent treatment requires intelligent consultation, mutual trust, and the clarification of confidentiality issues.

The Question of Evangelism

One area of special concern in the use of prayer and Scripture in psychotherapy is evangelism. Should the therapist attempt to lead the client to Christ? One problem with such a question is that coming to Christ is viewed as a boundary that needs to be crossed. Evangelism is more than telling a person, "You are a sinner who needs to be saved." If conversion is also a process, evangelism may take place through the breaking down of the client's stereotypes of Christianity in the context of therapy. Here the client through the process of being respected, heard, and accepted by the therapist comes to see Christianity as something more than a list of don'ts.

Psychotherapy can also be evangelistic when negative views of a punitive God are rectified. Such images of God may be a legacy of childhood development where the client related to an earthly father in a context of much hurt. Ideas of earthly father are here closely tied to heavenly Father. In therapy the client may learn to develop new bonds of trust with the therapist. Such bonds, together with appropriate interpretation of the earthly/heavenly father connection, may lead to the possibility of new faith. Such a process is also evangelism.

Broader Questions

The debate over whether prayer and Scripture have a place in psychotherapy will continue unresolved until some central issues are dealt with by those involved in the integration of theology and psychology. Two of the most pressing of these are the need for a Christian theory of personality and the need for better understanding of the ingredients and process of change in therapy. The need for a personality theory consistent with the biblical record is crucial, not just to these questions but to the whole understanding of Christian psychotherapy. To date no such theory exists. In its absence Christians tend to approach prayer with eclecticism and pragmatism ("If it works, then pray"). This makes it an addendum rather than an integral part of therapy. Little thought may be given to the effects of an activity such as prayer on the total personality development of the client. Furthermore, without an overarching personality theory the therapist is hard pressed to explain why prayer sometimes does not work in the life of the client. Even when prayer seems efficacious, an eclectic approach can trade off short-term gains in psychotherapy for long-term benefits. Christian psychology is in search of a theory that will consistently integrate practices such as prayer and Scripture reading.

The process that produces change in psychotherapy also needs to be better understood. Research indicates both nonspecific and specific factors to be involved in the psychotherapeutic process. The nonspecific factors transcend theoretical approaches and emerge from a study of the relationship between the therapist and client. The ideal relationship is where the therapist and client relate well, the therapist sticks closely to the client's problems, and in an atmosphere of mutual trust and confidence the client feels free to say what he or she likes. In the context of such a relationship the therapist mobilizes powerful influencing forces that assist the patient toward the reversal of self-defeating patterns and toward growth. The nonspecific factors are not always curative in and of themselves. They are a necessary but not sufficient condition for a therapeutic reversal.

Specific factors can be viewed as the science of psychotherapy. They also transcend the theoretical perspective of the therapist and include the prescription of new responses to old and habitual maladaptive ways of responding; feedback to the client regarding his thinking, emotions, and behavior; and the generation of hope through a new perspective on the problem coupled with some possible solutions. The art of therapy is seen in the selection of these specific factors at the right moment. Means such as prayer and Scripture reading must be coupled with these specific and nonspecific factors so as not to violate both theological and psychological factors. For example, change for the growing Christian includes the development of a biblical mindset (Rom. 12:2). Such renewal requires a scriptural content, understanding of the psychology of cognition, appreciation for the developmental issues involved in an unbiblical mindset, and a therapeutic context that works with the Holy Spirit to reverse unhealthy cognitions and their outworking in behavior. Scripture and prayer in the hands of a sensitive therapist can be the agents of change and growth.

5

Spiritual and Religious Issues in Therapy
Frances J. White

Increasingly the problems for which people seek help from psychotherapists involve spiritual and religious issues. These problems, caused or exacerbated by the increasing complexities of modern life, include life-span adjustment, conflicts, trauma, situational crises, problem-solving deficits, and interpersonal struggles, as well as existential issues in which counselees are searching for meaning to life and death, a sense of inner integration, a release from anxiety or despair, and greater fulfillment. As a result psychotherapists are being confronted with cries for help in areas that were formerly the domain of the clergy. The dilemma they face is how to handle the spiritual issues inherent in these problems in a way that assures their own as well as their clients' integrity.

Therapists can resolve this dilemma by attempting to maintain a neutral stance vis-à-vis the spiritual dimension of persons; ignoring the dimension; exhibiting a negativistic or, conversely, a patronizingly benevolent attitude; or recognizing the dimension as a crucial aspect of human life and seeking to find responsible ways to address it in therapy. For the Christian therapist who accepts God's revelation through the Holy Scriptures, only the last option is viable. Although the Bible does not present a systematic anthropology, it is clear in its teaching that human beings are created in the image of God and that it is impossible to understand them accurately apart from their intended relationship to the Godhead. In fact, nowhere in Scripture is that relationship presented as an appendage to one's identity; it is the very essence of humanness (Berkouwer, 1962). The individual is portrayed as a whole being who cannot be divided into component parts. Although parts (e.g., body, soul, spirit) are referred to in Scripture, they overlap in meanings; they describe rather than compartmentalize persons. Therefore, ferreting out a person's spiritual dimension and treating it as a separate, more highly relevant (or irrelevant) category prevents a true understanding of personhood. Since "any view which abstracts man from this relation cannot penetrate the mystery of man" and "can make no more than a partial contribution to our understanding of man" (Berkouwer, 1962, p. 29), the Christian psychotherapist must take very seriously any issues that involve the client's relationship to the Creator.

Incorporating spiritual issues into the therapeutic process in a maximally beneficial way makes certain demands on the therapist. First, it is essential that the therapist possess a good level of clinical competence in order to deal sensitively with these therapeutic issues. Second, it is important that therapists identify and understand the beliefs and values inherent in their own world view and how these affect them personally. For Christians this includes a concerted effort to grapple in depth with the Word of God to arrive at an ever-growing, integrated, cognitive, and experiential understanding of the Scriptures. Christian therapists who develop the habit of contemplating the attributes of the Godhead and their meaning to themselves arrive at a third basic qualification, an understanding of self. Calvin observed most aptly that a person never attains true self-knowledge until he has first contemplated the face of God and then looked into himself. Therapists who meet these prerequisites are in a unique position to relate to clients and guide their growth in ways that are congruent with a scriptural understanding of God and his relationship to human beings created in his image. Moreover, when therapists develop an awareness of how every aspect of their world view governs their conduct, they should have a better understanding of their clinical functioning.

The compelling need for therapists to be aware of the ways their total being influences clients is highlighted by studies indicating that clients' changes in therapy are attributable more to personal characteristics of the therapist than to techniques (Bergin & Lambert, 1978). These studies are even more significant in light of a review of research done by Beutler (1979), which supports the hypothesis that clients tend to appropriate the attitudes, values, and beliefs of their therapists. Psychotherapists who are reputed to be Christians carry a particular responsibility in view of Halleck's (1976) observation that clients tend to seek help from therapists who share their belief and value system. If that is true, clients who seek out Christian therapists will expect the therapist's Christianity to affect the counseling process.

Principles for Dealing with Religious Issues

In dealing with religious issues the therapist who sees the importance of the above conditions would perceive the spiritual dimension of clients as part of their inherent nature and therefore accept the necessity of dealing with issues that arise from it. This implies the responsibility to examine thoroughly what a religiously expressed belief, affect, or behavior means to a client and how it translates itself in his total functioning. Glock (1962) suggests five dimensions—ideological (beliefs), experiential (feelings), intellectual (knowledge), ritualistic (practice), and consequential (effects)—that need examining in order to determine the significance of a religious issue for a person.

Pruyser (1978) stresses the necessity of making a religious assessment an integral part of the diagnostic evaluation. He proposes that clergy be trained to work with therapists, thereby mitigating the danger that therapists extend their interventions beyond their theological competency. An adequate assessment enables a therapist to be in continual touch with the spiritual disposition of his clients and to develop the acumen to recognize the nature and depth of healthy, neurotic, or even psychotic elements in religious stances. He would also learn to sense the times when addressing religious issues will be optimally effective. If religious issues are confronted too soon, some aspects of the client's faith might be undermined. Even when therapists sense the appropriate moment to deal with a religious issue, they must go gently, at the client's pace, uncovering the issue when it works naturally into the session but never imposing their own convictions.

In situations where supportive therapy is indicated in order to prevent or retard disintegration, a person may need to have his religious persuasion reinforced, regardless of how neurotic it may seem to the therapist. This judgment would be made in a similar manner to that involving a decision to reinforce existing defenses in order best to cope with life. In other cases the therapist may choose to be relatively inattentive to religious issues because they are not specifically a part of the problem being dealt with (although if a religious issue emanates from or contributes to the problem, it will be necessary to address it at the relevant time and in a beneficial manner).

In some cases spiritual issues may be appropriately and effectively dealt with in an explicit way in the process of therapy; at other times circumstances may dictate that they be more implicit in the therapeutic process. But whether these issues are dealt with explicitly or implicitly, therapists must always work within the parameter of respecting the client's freedom and responsibility to make personal decisions.

Unconditional acceptance—expressed by a person's responding comfortably and remaining fully present to an individual whose beliefs, values, or behavior are at variance with one's own—could be the significant factor that contributes to freeing the client in a way that will someday allow him to respond positively to the heavenly Father. In the meantime the therapist, as servant, is at the disposal of the client, thus fulfilling the biblical mandate to be willing to be an agent of caring even if not always of curing (see the parable of the good Samaritan, Luke 10:33–37), letting the ultimate outcome rest with the Creator. It appears that the proper view of the source of change includes the seeming paradox of accepting both God's sovereignty and the client's free choice.

Concerns in Handling Religious Issues

Christian therapists have both valid and invalid concerns about dealing with religious issues in therapy. One troubling area is the role of religious constructs. On the one hand, some therapists ascribe to the shibboleth that religious beliefs are inherently value laden and therefore subjective and not amenable to scientific investigation. Thus, dealing explicitly with them in the therapeutic process would jeopardize the therapist's neutrality by violating a frequently propagated supposition that counselors' values have no ethical place in the therapeutic process.

That objection has been refuted by philosophers (Kuhn, 1970) who have demonstrated that the objectivity of even a research hypothesis supposedly based purely on observed facts is tainted by the controlling beliefs behind its creator's world view. In the field of psychotherapy Bergin (1980) has argued for the impossibility of the therapist maintaining a neutral stance. Therapists have a responsibility, therefore, to recognize the subjective presuppositions of their own world views lest they fall prey to the influence of those presuppositions and thereby unwittingly be more subjective than those who have defined their position.

Paradoxically some therapists who themselves accept the tenets of Scripture as objective truth tend to resist their use in therapy for fear that they be employed as resistance to facing painful feelings. Strunk (1979) points out that "in the extreme form, the notion even denies the motivational power of a person's *Weltanschauung*, since a view of the universe requires an intellectual component" (p. 194). To perceive spiritual constructs merely as defensive strategies could actually increase resistance and eliminate their potency as a growth-inducing factor in an individual's life, since for many clients significant religious constructs are as indispensable to their self-concept as is an understanding of their feelings. Often a rational cognitive structure helps them identify values and understand affect and behavior (see Rokeach, 1973). Their beliefs could also be their most powerful coping mechanisms, enabling them to function in a relatively constructive manner in spite of nefarious influences in their lives.

A second source of concern lies in the concept of transference. Therapists are vulnerable to being perceived by the client as parent figures. When God enters the picture, they become additionally subjected to possible distortions displaced from the client's relationship to God and projected onto the therapist. At these points the parent-God-therapist triad can develop into an undifferentiated system (Pattison, 1965). When this involves a true transference neurosis, it takes a skilled, dynamically trained therapist to enable the client to work it through and arrive at a correctly differentiated concept of self, God, and therapist.

Pattison (1965) points out how transference can also lead to distortions in relation to God. Feelings generated consciously or unconsciously by a critical father are easily translated into doubt of God's unqualified acceptance. However, reactions can be used advantageously to facilitate development of a correct belief and a corresponding corrective experience vis-à-vis the Godhead as well as toward any present human relationships. To ignore these distortions would be to fail to lead the person to a healthier view of what is potentially the most vital, health-producing relationship possible—relationship with God himself.

Another potential danger is the therapist's countertransferential response to his or her own relationship to the Godhead. Any spiritual issue that is not resolved in a way that reduces reactivity increases the possibility of countertransference that is potentially detrimental to the therapeutic process. A related source of countertransference is the therapist's lack of appreciation of, or even disdain for, the beliefs and practices of particular religious groups. For example, a therapist may feel negative toward fundamentalism; specific denominational or nondenominational churches; or specific practices such as speaking in tongues, certain abstinences, set rituals, or stereotyped vocabulary. Unless the therapist can neutralize such potentially strong reactions, the client will sense the negative attitudes and these will interfere with therapeutic progress.

A further distortion that makes therapists hesitant to encourage the use of religious concepts is their frequent employment in the service of resistance. For example, Scripture passages may be taken out of context and proferred as a personal directive from God, as in the case of a person who resists looking at the obviously disastrous consequences of a decision because she is not to lean on her own understanding (Prov. 3:5) or the one who interprets "Honor your father and your mother" as legitimate reason not to individuate healthily from them.

Lovinger (1979) discusses several strategies similar to cognitive reframing to nondestructively counteract such resistances. First, he suggests what he calls joining the resistance. For example, in cases where patients are plagued by a lack of security he helps them appreciate the role of doubt in fortifying correct beliefs. Second, he advocates correcting false interpretations of Scripture by introducing alternate, more accurate, translations. This might include giving some instruction in a correct use of hermeneutics. For example, for the counselee who refuses to recognize anger, "let not the sun go down upon your wrath" (Eph. 4:26) can be shown to indicate the necessity to work through hostile feelings rather than suppress or even repress them. Third, understanding the role of culture in applying certain texts can help an individual distinguish between unchanging biblical truth and cultural relatives that allow for various applications of a text according to culture and historical setting. For instance, standards of dress differ among Christians of different nations and epochs, but acceptance of the doctrine of the bodily resurrection of Jesus Christ does not.

Appropriation of Spiritual Resources

An understanding of valid principles as well as an awareness of the potential hazards in dealing with religious issues can encourage the therapist and, in turn, the client to appropriate the resources available to Christians. Nicholi's (1974) research among college students showed highly significant positive changes in self-esteem and meaning to life among new converts to Christianity. This suggests that therapists should take seriously the potential healing in a client's relationship brought about by appropriating spiritual resources. Similar research has been done with different problems and age groups (Horton, 1973).

In guiding a Christian client to appropriate the resources available to him or her the therapist must be aware of the particular attributes of the Godhead that can be the healing factor in the client's case. For example, clients who have had a weak, punitive, abusing, or absent parent may be more prone with the therapist's help to recognize and attempt to claim the deeper healing possible through gradually internalizing God as their own Abba, Father (Gal. 4:6)—that is, experience him as their intimate "Daddy" yet perfect, omnipotent Father. Allison's (1968) research offers evidence that a late adolescent's relationship to the Lord as God, the Father, can mitigate an undue struggle to differentiate from parents.

Another member of the Godhead, the Holy Spirit, offers incalculable resources for healing. In his role as convictor he leads individuals to the recognition of and repentance for sins (John 16:8–9). As the encourager (John 14:26) he reminds them of the forgiveness offered through the redemptive work of Jesus Christ (1 John 1:9). This forgiveness can bring a client to a conscious realization of the healing effects of God's unconditional love. In the process the grace and mercy of Jesus Christ may become significant healing factors.

The therapist may find that he or she must depend upon Spirit-given discernment to guide clients to distinguish between actual scriptural truths and unhealthy internalized beliefs inculcated by their environment. This is particularly the case when it is necessary to separate true guilt from unwarranted guilt-producing injunctions from authority figures.

In his role as convictor, comforter, and guide, the Holy Spirit can be called upon to bring to the surface repressed memories that block healing. Although therapists differ in the strategies they follow in being open to the Holy Spirit working through them to facilitate the process, the aim is the same—that is, to encourage the affective reliving of the actual events in order to arrive at a resolution of the emotional pain embedded in the memory. In the healing process the therapist needs to be comfortable with the possible expression of negative feelings that have been transferred to the Godhead. Alerting clients to instances where biblical characters were able to express such feelings can be helpful.

A further resource ordained by Scripture to promote healing is fellowship in the body of Christ (James 5:16). The group provides a source for authentic mutual caring, expressed through interaction and support. By encouraging the client to become a part of a local group—one as congruent as possible with the client's preferred style of fellowship—the therapist could also assist in the separation process in the terminal stage of therapy.

In utilizing any of these spiritual resources it is important that the therapist avoid becoming enmeshed in denominational differences—for example, views of the manner in which the Holy Spirit works, what prayer format should be followed, or styles of worship that have no relevance to the issue at stake. Used appropriately, spiritual provisions can be an invaluable source of strength and a starting point for exploration of neurotic relationships. Then as insight into the neurotic aspects of human relationships develops, increased healing in those relationships can be a stabilizing factor, permitting an examination of the unhealthy elements that might have been transferred to the person's religion. Likewise, as the neurotic components in the individual's spiritual perspectives are resolved, the person has an even stronger base from which to explore more deeply rooted conflicts stemming from past relationships. In effect, it is a balancing process that fosters health in all relationships.

During the last stage of therapy an evaluation of the changes that have taken place in the client's spiritual perceptions is in order. This is particularly important in long-term therapy, where profound changes may have taken place in all relationships. It is possible that in spite of release from psychological pain, clients are confused about how their Christian faith fits into the healthier patterns of functioning. Their recognition of the part religious concepts played in their problems or of how much of their unhealthy functioning had been transferred to their relationship to the Godhead could create a confusion about the very relevance of faith. This problem is more apt to arise when the relationship with the Lord was not included as a vital part of the therapeutic process. Nonetheless there has probably been a metamorphosis in the client's beliefs, feelings, attitudes, and even religious behavior toward the Godhead in proportion to the degree of growth that has transpired.

For example, the client who enters therapy with a clinging, undifferentiated relationship with a parent figure probably relates to God in a parallel way, with magical expectations and behaviors following a symbiotic pattern. As she individuates from her parent, she may no longer be comfortable with former ways of relating to the Lord. Comfort with a new style of relating comes gradually. Christian therapists should be alert to such issues, which actually emanate from salutary changes, and draw them out in the session. The client may need help to learn a new repertoire of ways to affiliate with the Godhead. Intercession for others, thanksgiving, and worship may become gradually a more natural part of the relationship.

It is enriching to the client and glorifying to the Godhead when individuals terminate therapy as more fully integrated persons because healing has transpired and has begun to translate itself into every area of their lives as they relate to God, the world, and themselves.

References

Allison, M. Adaptive regression and intense religious experience. *Journal of Nervous and Mental Disorders*, 1968, *145*, 452–463.

Bergin, A. E. Psychotherapy and religious values. *Journal of Consulting and Clinical Psychology*, 1980, *48*, 95–105.

Bergin, A. E., & Lambert, M. J. The evaluation of therapeutic outcomes. In S. L. Garfield & A. E. Bergin (Eds.), *Handbook of psychotherapy and behavioral change* (2nd ed.). New York: Wiley, 1978.

Berkouwer, G. C. *Man: The image of God*. Grand Rapids: Eerdmans, 1962.

Beutler, L. Values, beliefs, religion, and the persuasive influence of psychotherapy. *Psychotherapy: Theory, Research, and Practice*, 1979, *16*, 432–448.

Glock, C. Y. On the study of religious commitment. *Religious Education*, 1962, *42*, 98–110.

Halleck, S. L. Discussion of socially reinforced obsessing. *Journal of Consulting and Clincal Psychology*, 1976, *45*, 146–147.

Horton, P. C. The mystical experience as a suicide preventive. *American Journal of Psychiatry*, 1973, *130*, 294–296.

Kuhn, T. S. *The structure of scientific revolutions* (2nd ed.). Chicago: University of Chicago Press, 1970.

Lovinger, R. J. Therapeutic strategies with religious resistances. *Psychotherapy: Theory, Research, and Practice*, 1979, *16*, 419–427.

Nicholi, A. M. A new dimension of the youth culture. *American Journal of Psychiatry*, 1974, *131*, 396–401.

Pattison, E. M. Transference and countertransference in pastoral care. *The Journal of Pastoral Care*, 1965, *6*, 193–202.

Pruyser, P. W. The seamy side of current religious beliefs. *Pastoral Psychology*. 1978, *26*, 150–167.

Rokeach, M. *The nature of human values.* New York: Free Press, 1973.

Strunk, O. J. The world view factor in psychotherapy. *Journal of Religion and Health*, 1979, *18*, 192–196.

6

Moral and Ethical Issues in Treatment
Clinton W. McLemore

Psychological treatments are inextricably connected with moral and ethical issues. Virtually all forms of verbal psychotherapy, for example, embody some conception of the good life or of how one ought ideally to think, feel, and act. Moreover, Frank (1961) has argued with considerable force that psychotherapy is, at root, persuasion. The patient comes in demoralized, and the therapist assists the patient to a new way of viewing his or her life and of assessing what is and is not desirable. Szasz (1961) argues that even defining mental health is a subjective if not arbitrary enterprise.

London (1964) also emphasizes the great extent to which therapy is a metascientific undertaking, at best an art grounded in bits and pieces of science. The bulk of what therapists do might be best viewed as "clinical philosophy." While attorneys specialize in the use of logic to enhance clients' concrete advantages, most therapists seem to use some combination of metaphysics and ethics to enhance clients' psychological sense of well-being.

The Nature of Ethics

It is important to understand that moral-ethical questions cannot, in principle, be answered by science. Such questions are by nature speculative, meaning that there are no universally accepted standards, no laboratory observations that will certify which answers are correct. Science cannot address such questions as, "Should I put my mother in a nursing home?" or, "Should I leave my husband?" However, such questions are frequently encountered in psychotherapy, and the therapist must realize that at these points he or she leaves the realm of science and enters what is here being called the realm of clinical philosophy.

One might argue that the Bible tells us what is right and wrong, and therefore that its prescriptions and proscriptions are scientific. Such an argument amounts to little more than an expression of one's confidence in the Bible itself, since the word *scientific* is being used here in an unconventional way. Whatever else it may mean in this context, *scientific* cannot mean demonstrable or provable, as is required by the canons of twentieth-century physical science.

Questions of ethics and personal morality are by nature philosophical. If one is a Christian, much of one's philosophy is conditioned by one's understanding of, and level of commitment to, Christ. Thus, for the Christian most if not all of the philosophical questions that touch on ethical issues are also in some way theological questions; they concern the nature of God and the cosmos, including his ways with us and his desires regarding our ways with each other.

The Nature of Psychological Treatment

Almost everything that positively affects human thoughts, feelings, or actions can be held to be a psychological treatment. Drugs, biofeedback, hypnosis, hospitalization, conditioning, talking, reading, and even ordinary education may be included. Note that within this framework of understanding, the defining characteristic of a treatment is its psychological effects.

It is possible, however, to turn this conceptualization around and to define as psychological treatment only those things which, via alterations of thought, feeling, or action, alter something else, whether physical (e.g., level of adrenalin) or psychological (other thoughts, feelings, or actions). Within this framework the defining characteristic of a treatment is the psychological nature of its mode of action.

One important ethical issue in any psychological treatment relates to the presence of coercion. Seldom is coercion as overt as a threat of harm for noncompliance. However, in a great many subtle but powerful ways therapists can act coercively. When, if ever, is such coercive action ethical? Who decides that coercion is appropriate? When should the client be required to provide informed consent? How much comprehension of risks and benefits must the consenter have in order for the consent to be valid? When, if ever, ought society override the will of the individual to obtain or refuse a treatment? These are only a few of the complex ethical questions involved.

To the degree that a treatment is not coercive, a partially overlapping set of issues emerge. There are still the complexities of informed consent. A more important issue, however, involves the kinds of potentially persuasive "advices" that a therapist ought and ought not to give, as well as the manner in which such advice should be given. Therapists seem to have more than an ordinary amount of influence over their clients. How is this power to be used?

Finally, it should be noted that the issue of coercion in treatment is not synonymous with that of the voluntary or involuntary status of the client. Voluntary clients may be persuaded to undergo a certain treatment without full awareness of the alternatives or the advantages and disadvantages of this particular treatment. Many of these ethical issues are examined and standards provided in *Ethical Principles of Psychologists* (APA, 1981). Similar standards exist for other mental health professionals. Ethical standards in involuntary treatment are usually established by legislation (see Schwitzgebel & Schwitzgebel, 1980).

The Interpenetration of the Moral and the Psychological

God, we believe, desires that we do the right. God, if he is who we believe he is, also desires that we be psychologically healthy. If the cosmos is both orderly and benevolent, it seems reasonable to conclude that all of the Creator's intentions are interlocking—that there is, therefore, an intimate connection between goodness and health. God's laws cannot be arbitrary unless we are the victims of a cruel joke. Whatever he commands must on the whole be in our best interests. Striving to live morally must have positive psychological consequences. And striving for true psychological well-being has to lead us in the direction of a higher morality.

However, sometimes what seems to promote our health flies in the face of Christian teaching. Similarly, obeying God's will as we understand it sometimes appears to hurt us psychologically. Just as there is "pleasure in sin for a season," there seems at times to be health in sin for at least a while.

Few human experiences bring these issues and ambiguities into such sharp relief as the psychotherapeutic encounter. When persons come for psychological help, they are typically in turmoil and pain. "Should I get a divorce?" "Should I have an affair?" "Why am I so discouraged?" "What does life mean?" "Why did my fourteen-year-old son die in that awful car accident?" These are the sorts of questions that bring people to therapists, and not one of them is devoid of theological and therefore moral implication.

On the other side of the health-morality connection there is also a complex and often subtle interpenetration of sin and sickness. While it is possible to be seriously disturbed without being particularly bad morally, and while it seems possible to be immoral without being psychologically disordered in any conventional sense, psychopathology and baseness are sometimes closely related. Thus, a therapist who attempts to ameliorate psychological disorder sometimes seems to end up affecting the moral character of the person as well.

Law and Ethics

As noted earlier, standards of practice relating to many of these ethical areas exist both within each of the mental health professions and within state legislation. Within the professions serious ethical violations result, at worst, in peer censure, expulsion from an association, and loss of one's license or state registration. However, violation of state criminal or civil law can result in prosecution by government attorneys and conviction by the courts, which may impose fines or imprisonment. Harm to clients may result in their lodging a civil suit against the practitioner, who may be ordered to compensate the aggrieved party.

Many things are unethical that are not illegal, but illegal acts that relate to a practitioner's performance of professional duties are routinely unethical. The range of unethical behavior, therefore, is wider than that of illegal behavior.

Conflicts of interest frequently underlie ethical infractions, and in civil proceedings such conflicts as are relevant to the "cause of action" typically cast the practitioner in an unfavorable light. Courts tend to assume that practitioners cannot properly perform their duties when they have an interest in potential conflict with these duties. Accepting stock market tips from clients, engaging in sexual activities with patients, and serving as a therapist to one's students are examples of unacceptable practices. In each case the practitioner's singleness of purpose and, by implication, clarity of judgment fall under suspicion.

Malpractice suits are civil proceedings. Some malpractice actions are brought on the basis of alleged breach of contract. The plaintiff may argue, for example, that the practitioner did not perform what, for a fee, he or she promised. Most malpractice suits are filed on the basis of an alleged wrong—some for malice (deliberate injury) but the vast majority for negligence. Typically the plaintiff will hold that the practitioner did not adhere to the standard of care prevalent in the community in the way that a reasonable person (practitioner) of ordinary prudence would have, thus failing to fulfill a duty that he or she owed the client and thereby causing injury. Taking negligent action (e.g., administering a harmful treatment) or negligently failing to take appropriate action (e.g., not responding to clear signs of suicidal intent immediately prior to a self-destructive act) are grounds for legal action.

Some professional behavior can be grounds for both a civil suit and a criminal prosecution. For example, a psychotherapist who injures a client with a physically damaging treatment may be brought to trial for assault and battery by the district attorney as well as named in a civil suit by the client.

Religion and Cultural Values

The issues surrounding religion in therapy are complex and are dealt with separately (see chapter 5). When religion (in general, or of a particular sort) is in disfavor in a society, practitioners who offend their clients with religious material are likely to be viewed as negligent or even fraudulent. Since one's professional peers are routinely called on to render opinions in malpractice actions, a negative disposition toward religion by society at large or by particular professional segments could adversely affect the fate of a religiously oriented practitioner facing a malpractice suit. On the other hand, during times of religious fervor there may be a negative bias toward any practitioner who dares even to question the possible neurotic nature of a religious behavior.

We seem to be at a point in history when esoteric religions (e.g., cults or Eastern religions) or quasi-religions (e.g., astrology) may enjoy more favor than traditional ones. Although there have been a number of important church-state clashes recently, the place of Christianity in psychological services has yet to receive major legal attention; neither has the place, if any, of religious dissuasion in psychotherapy. (See McLemore & Court, 1977, for further discussion of this latter issue.)

Strongly held ethical principles tend to get reflected in laws, which are society's rules for conduct. These rules and the principles from which they derive have more than a casual connection with cultural values—in particular, with what society views as desirable and healthy behavior. Since the specification of desirable and healthy behavior is fundamentally a philosophical—and, in the opinion of Christians, a theological—activity, laws and ethics are heavily informed by speculative ideas. Christian ideas ought therefore to be injected into the shaping of societal standards (codes of ethics and systems of legislation). Because of the intimate relationship between psychological procedures and ideals of health, which in turn relate directly to morals and thus to theology, ethical and legal issues bearing on psychological treatments are of more than trivial significance to Christians.

References

American Psychological Association. *Ethical principles of psychologists.* Washington, D.C.: Author, 1981.

Frank, J. D. *Persuasion and healing.* Baltimore: Johns Hopkins Press, 1961.

London, P. *The modes and morals of psychotherapy.* New York: Holt, Rinehart, Winston, 1964.

McLemore, C. W., & Court, J. H. Religion and psychotherapy: Ethics, civil liberties, and clinical savvy: A critique. *Journal of Consulting and Clinical Psychology,* 1977, *45,* 1172–1175.

Schwitzgebel, R. L., & Schwitzgebel, R. K. *Law and psychological practice.* New York: Wiley, 1980.

Szasz, T. S. *The myth of mental illness.* New York: Hoebel-Harper, 1961.

Additional Readings

McLemore, C. W. *The scandal of psychotherapy: A guide to resolving the tensions between faith and counseling.* Wheaton, Ill.: Tyndale House, 1982.

Sharkey, P. W. (Ed.). *Philosophy, religion and psychotherapy: Essays in the philosophical foundations of psychotherapy.* Washington, D.C.: University Press of America, 1982.

7

Values and Psychotherapy
Allen E. Bergin

Freud defined psychotherapy as a technical procedure applied to mental disorders. Like surgery it was intended to be an objective procedure that did not involve the personality or beliefs of the practitioner in a direct way. Since the time of Freud it has been standard procedure for therapists to avoid disclosing their own values and to avoid shaping the values of the client. Such an objective, professional attitude is admirable, and it has been a standard for training and practice for many years.

Unfortunately it has been impossible to maintain such an objective approach to therapeutic counseling. As it turns out, the nature of client psychological difficulties and the interaction between therapist and client required to overcome these difficulties necessarily involve values. This insight has been slow in coming. It has been stimulated in part by developments in the humanistic therapies, such as those espoused by Rogers, Fromm, May and others. These therapists have recognized that many of the difficulties that we call psychological are in fact difficulties of moral choice and lifestyle. Because of this, such therapists gradually became more open about

53

their values and the ways in which values might operate in the psychotherapy process. Certainly their definitions of good mental health or of the personalities that were expected to result from good therapy have been highly value laden.

In contrast to the humanistic therapists who employ the relationship between therapist and client as one of the means of mediating therapeutic change, behavior therapists have resisted this trend. Although they object to the theories and techniques of Freud, they agree with the Freudian perspective in the sense that they consider therapy to be the application of technical procedures involving values to a minimal extent. The revival of the concept of psychotherapy as a kind of technology by behavior therapists is somewhat ironic in that it places them on the same side of the fence as their arch rival, psychoanalysis.

However, modern scholarship and research indicate that behavior therapy is no less value laden than psychoanalysis or humanistic psychotherapies. There is a growing consensus in the mental health disciplines that psychotherapy is a value-oriented procedure and that one cannot avoid making value choices in the process of attempting to help a troubled client.

The notion that values are an inevitable and pervasive part of psychotherapy is supported by a number of scholarly papers and research articles that examine both the process and the outcome of treatment. Strupp, Hadley, and Gomes-Schwartz (1977) have argued that there are at least three different value systems at play in every therapeutic enterprise: the values of the client, the values of the practitioner, and values in the community at large. They point out that our ways of defining mental health are all based on cultural choices as to what is good functioning and what is a good life style. While the standards by which these choices are made are often implicit, a careful examination of the mental health literature shows the value themes threaded throughout. For example: "If following psychotherapy, a patient manifests increased self-assertion coupled with abrasiveness, is this a good or a poor therapy outcome? . . . If . . . a patient obtains a divorce, is this to be regarded as a desirable or an undesirable change? A patient may turn from homosexuality to heterosexuality, or he may become more accepting of either; an ambitious, striving person may abandon previously valued goals and become more placid. . . . How are such changes to be evaluated?" (Strupp et al., 1977, pp. 92–93). In addition: "In increasing number, patients enter psychotherapy not for the cure of traditional 'symptoms' but (at least ostensibly) for the purpose of finding meaning in their lives, for actualizing themselves, or for maximizing their potential" (Strupp et al., 1977, p. 93).

The amazing thing about this type of literature is that it shows that psychological procedures are intricately interwoven with secularized moral systems (London, 1964; Lowe, 1976). As this literature has developed, it has become more and more evident not only that values are involved in psychotherapy, but that the values of the community of professional therapists have a certain slant or bias. Standards for good living are thus being established by the mental health disciplines as they increasingly influence the attitudes, beliefs, and values of both clients and public. Therapists therefore are becoming secular moralists who are promoting changes in life styles and in the values of the culture or community while at the same time appearing to apply a technical method to psychological disturbances as though these applications were objective and value free (Bergin, 1980a).

The impossibility of a value-free therapy can be illustrated by the work of Rogers, who personally values the freedom of the individual and attempts to help his clients choose their own values in a free and permissive atmosphere. Despite Rogers's admirable devotion to the client's freedom from coercion by the therapist or others, two separate studies done a decade apart (Murray, 1956; Truax, 1966) showed that Rogers systematically rewarded and punished verbal behavior that he did and did not approve of in his clients. His values influenced the format of the therapy sessions as well as their outcomes. If a person who intends to be nondirective cannot be, then it is unlikely that others can be objective and value free in their very human interactions with their clients (Bergin, 1971).

Another way of documenting the influence of values on the mental health enterprise is to consider the way in which change in mental health is judged by practitioners and researchers. These judgments are based on rating scales or measures of personality, behavior, and attitudes. It has been shown that even in the modern technical behavior therapies, as well as other therapies, value choices are being made in the selection of these criteria of measurement (Bergin, 1963, 1980b; Kitchener, 1980).

Types of Values in Psychotherapy

Almost every conceivable type of value is endorsed by one psychotherapist or another. However, there are certain trends that reflect the humanistic and mechanistic backgrounds of most psychotherapists. This is seen most vividly in the tendency of therapists to endorse a relativistic approach to values, or what is frequently referred to as situation ethics. From the viewpoint of

Christian psychologists or religious clients, many of the values commonly endorsed by therapists may be considered counterproductive or even immoral. There is also an antireligious and antitraditional morality trend among a fairly large minority of therapists. One of the common complaints among more conservative, religious people is the lack of harmony they often experience between their values and those of their counselor or therapist.

It is a fact that the values of mental health professionals differ on the average from those of the public at large, and especially the more religious public. These contrasts have been documented at general levels, such as in the great differences between professionals and the public who endorse traditional beliefs in God, the reality of the spiritual, the efficacy of prayer, and belief in the divinity of Christ. The contrasts also exist with respect to specific values such as those pertaining to sex, authority, family life, etc. (Bergin, 1980b).

The existence of this contrast has opened the way for a rather full debate and consideration of how values may be dealt with in psychotherapy in the most fruitful way. Some professionals argue that their values are superior to those of the public at large and that their values are mentally healthy (Ellis, 1980). However, there is no evidence that this position is valid. The tendency for professional therapists to assume that their values are superior and that they are healthy and enlightening for the average person has been challenged. It has also been pointed out that the assumption by mental health professionals that their values have some inherent psychological validity puts therapists in the role of secular priests, who act as though they have the right to promote their personal and subjective views through what is supposed to be an objective and professional practice (Bergin, 1980c). The debate over these matters has led to the question of whether specific value orientations should be used to develop specific therapies.

Development of Value-Oriented Therapies

One of the controversial developments in psychotherapy is the attempt to organize therapy goals and processes in terms of specific values. While this is an attempt to do overtly what is often done covertly under the guise of professional clinical work, it is still an unpopular approach. It has been promoted, however, by people from opposite ends of the value spectrum. For example, Ellis (1980) argues that positive therapeutic change is inevitably a value modification process, and he attempts to implement what he considers to be mentally healthy values by means of his cognitive and behavioral

interventions. Some of his valued outcomes, such as greater rationality and self-control, are endorsed by many therapists of various
persuasions; but many of his objectives, such as "sex without guilt,"
are the exact opposite of what orthodox religious people value, as
these values are derived from interpretations of Scripture. A number of attempts have been made to frame therapeutic procedures
within the context of a traditional, spiritual perspective. Some of
these are overtly and explicitly Christian in orientation. Others endorse moral values similar to those of orthodox Christians, but omit
references to theology or Scripture. Still others concern themselves
with a more eclectic approach to values in the therapeutic setting
(cf. Collins, 1981).

As different groups emerge who espouse value orientations consistent with their particular religion or subculture, the problem arises
that a kind of therapeutic denominationalism may result. To the
extent that values are an essential part of the therapeutic enterprise,
perhaps this is inevitable; but it can go too far and cause schisms
that prevent cooperative use of new discoveries regarding effective
treatment.

The enlightened approach seems to be to take one's values and
place them in the midst of the therapeutic marketplace for competitive evaluation and testing. Some Christian psychologists are carefully examining in a research context the effectiveness of merging
spiritual imagery and values with some of the traditional therapeutic techniques (Propst, 1980). This approach holds promise in that it
merges the spiritual or philosophical approach that is basic to values with the empirical approach that is basic to the psychological
and psychiatric sciences.

Values Common to the Therapies

One of the consequences of encouraging openness about values
has been that more agreement may be emerging from the different
vantage points than would have been expected. An informal survey
(Bergin, 1983a) has revealed a possible consensus regarding a number of values that affect the life style and morality of clients in
psychotherapy. While this consensus is nowhere near 100%, the
amount of agreement on some subjects pertinent to psychological
functioning has been surprising. For instance, there seems to be a
great deal of agreement regarding the advantages of marital fidelity,
even though some highly visible writers and therapists do not seem
to value this particular behavior. It may be that the majority favoring fidelity is not a large majority; but its existence is surprising in

light of what we often read in professional textbooks and in the media accounts of professional opinions. But it remains to be shown by careful empirical study just what the consequences of infidelity are. Although there is a massive amount of evidence in the clinical and research literature, it has never been systematized. The sources and consequences of many other values are now being addressed in light of the growing interest in the effects of value dimensions upon life styles and mental health. The question is, "Are there mentally healthy values or life styles?" Scripture implies that this is likely to be so; but such a belief does not yet have a persuasive position within the the professional milieu (Bergin, 1983b).

Another consequence of the growing openness regarding values is that clients increasingly have the option of selecting a therapist according to his or her orientation. One no longer simply chooses between a psychoanalyst or behavior therapist, but between an analyst or behaviorist who does or does not have spiritual convictions and biblically based moral values. Therapies especially relevant to specific groups or subcultures thus seem to be emerging gradually.

Some Dangers

While religious therapists have a strong interest in explicit value discussions and emphases, their enthusiasm for this aspect of life and of therapeutic change can lead to problems if it is emphasized too strongly. Obviously it would be unethical to trample on the values of patients or clients with whom we disagree. It would also be unwise practice to focus largely on value issues when other issues may be at the nucleus of the disorder. Thus, an emphasis on technical expertise, the ability to diagnose accurately the causes of a problem, and the capacity to sympathetically guide a person through a difficult change process should be the primary concerns. It is vital for the therapist interested in the role of values in psychotherapy to be open but not coercive, to be a competent professional and not a missionary for his particular system of belief while at the same time being honest enough to recognize his own value commitments and the ways in which they may be health promoting. Mature professionals will recognize that their own beliefs and values can introduce biases in their thinking and perceptions, and that immersion in value discussions can sometimes be an escape into cognitive intellectualizing and an avoidance of the hard work of effecting personality reconstruction. As value-oriented discussion becomes more common, it is likely that good practice will require referral also to become more common, since value clashes will be antitherapeutic.

While the dilemmas involved are very real, exciting new developments in the psychotherapeutic arena are promised. Many difficulties in past approaches were caused by a failure to discern some of the real value issues that may underlie what look like simply psychological matters. It is instructive to realize that psychotherapy is but one example of the dilemma common to all applied psychologies; namely, that any attempt to apply a technique requires a decision as to the goals or outcomes the technique is attempting to obtain. Any time we select goals we are implementing values; therefore, all applied psychologies are inevitably value laden.

References

Bergin, A. E. The effects of psychotherapy: Negative results revisited. *Journal of Counseling Psychology*, 1963, *10*, 244–250.

Bergin, A. E. Carl Rogers' contribution to a fully functioning psychology. In A. Maher & L. Pearson (Eds.), *Creative developments in psychotherapy* (Vol. 1). Cleveland: Western Reserve University Press, 1971.

Bergin, A. E. Psychotherapy and religious values. *Journal of Consulting and Clinical Psychology*, 1980, *48*, 95–105. (a)

Bergin, A. E. Behavior therapy and ethical relativism: Time for clarity. *Journal of Consulting and Clinical Psychology*, 1980, *48*, 11–13. (b)

Bergin, A. E. Religious and humanistic values: A reply to Ellis and Walls. *Journal of Consulting and Clinical Psychology*, 1980, *48*, 642–645. (c)

Bergin, A. E. Proposed values for guiding and evaluating psychotherapy. In A. P. Gomez & F. B. Currea (Eds.), *Psicoterapias 1983*. Bogota: Universidad de los Andes 1983. (a)

Bergin, A. E. Religiosity and mental health: A critical reevaluation and meta-analysis. *Professional Psychology*, 1983, *14*, 170–184. (b)

Collins, G. R. *Psychology and theology: Prospects for integration*. Nashville: Abingdon, 1981.

Ellis, A. Psychotherapy and atheistic values: A response to A. E. Bergin's "Psychotherapy and religious values." *Journal of Consulting and Clinical Psychology*, 1980, *48*, 635–639.

Kitchener, R. F. Ethical relativism and behavior therapy. *Journal of Consulting and Clinical Psychology*, 1980, *48*, 1–7.

London, P. *The modes and morals of psychotherapy*. New York: Holt, Rinehart, & Winston, 1964.

Lowe, C. M. *Value orientations in counseling and psychotherapy: The meanings of mental health* (2nd ed.). Cranston, R. I.: Carroll Press, 1976.

Murray, E. J. A content-analysis method for studying psychotherapy. *Psychological Monographs*, 1956, *70* (13, Whole No. 420).

Propst, L. R. The comparative efficacy of religious and nonreligious imagery for the treatment of mild depression in religious individuals. *Cognitive Therapy and Research*, 1980, *4*, 167–178.

Strupp, H. H., Hadley, S. W., & Gomes-Schwartz, B. *Psychotherapy for better or worse: An analysis of the problem of negative effects*. New York: Aronson, 1977.

Truax, C. B. Reinforcement and non-reinforcement in Rogerian psychotherapy. *Journal of Abnormal Psychology*, 1966, *71*, 1–9.

8

Research in Psychotherapy Effectiveness
Michael J. Lambert, Dean E. Barley, & Ellie L. Wright

Psychotherapy by trained professionals can be viewed as an industry with a therapeutic product. In an effort to monitor the industry and to provide the best services possible, the profession must continually upgrade its practices through sound research. Practitioners have the moral responsibility to protect consumers from potentially harmful therapy techniques and to ensure the most effective treatment will be appropriately used in the most cost-efficient manner. Possible researchers are faced with the monumental task of establishing an empirical base for this kind of psychotherapy practice.

In 1952 H. J. Eysenck revealed his controversial findings from a review of insurance company files that 72% of those diagnosed as psychoneurotic are improved in two years with or without professional psychological intervention. At the time a 60–70% success rate was being reported by most well-known psychology clinics (Eysenck, 1952). As a result the academic world responded with several decades of aggressive research to discover the causative components of psychotherapy and to ascertain its efficacy. The resulting research on psychotherapy outcome has thrown much doubt on Eysenck's original findings, resulting in the conclusion that psychotherapy has modestly positive effects (Bergin & Lambert, 1978). For example, Meltzoff and Kornreich (1970) conducted a review of fifty-seven methodologically adequate and fourty-four methodologically questionable studies concerning the general effectiveness of psychotherapy and found that 84% of the adequate and 75% of the questionable studies reported overall positive results from psychotherapy. In a more recent review of 475 similar studies Smith, Glass, and Miller (1980) reported that the average client receiving therapy was better off than 80% of the people who do not. Although such generalized proclamations about the general effectiveness of psychotherapy are comforting to practitioners and academicians in the field, they do not reveal a great deal about specific processes of change in therapy, nor do their results indicate what can be done to improve psychotherapy.

A generic definition of psychotherapy implies an interpersonal process between two people, one needing help to improve personal functioning and the other offering assistance. From such a broad definition spring multiple questions. What kinds of problems are best handled by "trained" professionals? What is so special about trained professionals that qualifies them to help another person? Can't a friend, parent, minister, paraprofessional, stranger on the bus, or fortune teller perform the same function? Is the therapist's role that of a tutor, coaching a person through an intense period of psychological suffering, or is he a doctor, treating symptoms without much collaborative effort from the patient? What are the exact psychotherapeutic processes that are most likely to ensure improvement? Research may have shed light on such broad issues as the general effectiveness of psychotherapy, but before any assessment can be made of psychotherapy, one must arrive at some general consensus as to what constitutes "improvement" in personal functioning.

Improvement in Personal Functioning

This issue is of particular concern to the Christian counselor as well as to the believer seeking professional psychological help who may be faced with conflicting value systems within the therapeutic setting. For example, most would agree that murder is not the best way to resolve a death wish toward one's spouse, yet many would equivocate about whether it is improvement in personal functioning to help a homosexual learn to more effectively solicit dates from others of the same sex. There are many areas of potential conflict between traditional psychological values and those values espoused by revealed religion. For example, ministers often help sufferers overcome guilt feeling through the process of repentance and through encouraging closer adherence to gospel-based principles. On the other hand, a psychologist might prescribe that guilt is best overcome through relaxing repressive tendencies and abandoning a condemning value structure. Does real improvement in personal functioning mean giving up one's part in a "collective delusion" of a Supreme Morality or rather in putting one's life more in order by adhering more closely to religious codes of conduct? To the nonbeliever such questions may seem irrelevant, but to the believer they are all-important. At such points of discrepancy between counselor and client a decision concerning an appropriate referral needs to be made. Ultimately the responsibility for the decisions made on what constitutes improvement in each individual case lies with those participating in psychotherapy. Obviously there is a need for moral clarity. Though some may try to provide psychotherapy in a moral vacuum, many practitioners acknowledge that their values are inherent in their personal definitions of improvement. Such definitions are expressed in such language as "increased social adjustment," better "reality testing," or a decrease in the "presenting symptoms." The Christian counselor needs to be keenly aware of his or her own system of values and those of the client while striving to meet appropriate goals within a mutual definition of improved personal functioning.

In order to assess the effectiveness of psychotherapy it becomes necessary to devise means of measuring psychological functioning so that comparisons can be made between personal adjustment before and after treatment. The field of psychometrics—that is, measuring and describing behavioral, mental, and emotional functioning—offers the researcher many psychodiagnostic tools: structured interviews, projective tests, behavioral tally sheets, self-report personality tests, objective rater systems, symptom checklists, etc. By the careful selection of psychometric measures dealing with the specific goals of psychotherapy, the researcher is able to draw at least tentative conclusions about the general effectiveness of the therapy provided. Criticism of research on psychotherapy outcome centers on the inadequacy of psychodiagnostic measures accurately to assess human functioning and on the misapplication of psychometrics in the course of such study (Lambert, 1983).

Most psychotherapy outcome studies have used traditional measures of change that focus to a great extent on either symptomatic relief or on subjective discomfort, without attending to the broader philosophical questions and implied values. The consumer of psychotherapy research should be aware that most researchers have attended to three major value sources: (1) the values of society at large in assessing the extent to which people perform social roles (e.g., work and school performance); (2) the values of the client, largely in the form of relief of subjective discomfort; (3) the values of professionals, or the extent to which people approach notions of ideal mental health (Strupp & Hadley, 1977). Religious values that differ from these perspectives are rarely represented in outcome studies.

Spontaneous Remission and Negative Effects

Having established a general definition of improvement in personal functioning and ways to measure it, the researcher must be aware of several variables that can cloud conclusions on the effectiveness of therapy. Early researchers coined the term *spontaneous remission* to describe the phenomenon of patient improvement without professional psychological treatment. Close scrutiny shows that most people with emotional problems do not seek out mental health professionals for help, but instead turn to ministers, doctors, lawyers, friends, and family members (Bergin & Lambert, 1978). It is conceivable that these lay therapists may be more adept than trained professionals at forming therapeutic relationships, inducing insights, and giving needed counsel. Professionals could benefit from studying these natural therapeutic agents in the environment. Thus, what some researchers have thought to be individual characteristics of the client that lead to improvement are now believed to include certain elements of lay therapy that may be available to everyone: self-help materials; religious, legal, and medical personnel; family members and friends. The concept of spontaneous remission may also be used to describe the fact that in many studies using wait-list clients as treatment controls, these control-group clients often feel somewhat helped by the initial interview and assessment. Researchers using control groups to establish baseline differences between subjects who received therapy and those who did not receive therapy must therefore be extremely careful in defining no-therapy groups since "therapy" may be readily available in the natural environment or subtly within the confines of the study itself.

Another issue that blurs the validity of global ratings of the general effectiveness of psychotherapy is that although therapy is undertaken with the aim of improvement, research has shown that a percentage of patients are worse after treatment. This "deterioration effect" could be due to many different variables in psychotherapy: the therapist and the techniques he or she employs; the ill effects of diagnosing and labeling; the appearance of new symptoms; the unrealistic expectations on the part of the client; and the resulting guilt, failure, and disillusionment (Lambert, Bergin, & Collins, 1977). When it appears that certain techniques or therapist styles show consistently poor results, methods should be seriously scrutinized and perhaps abandoned entirely. Global studies of the effectiveness of psychotherapy often lump various techniques, methods, psychological orientations, and therapist styles together. Thus final conclusions about causal attribution are blurred by the various success rates of the different techniques, some of which may even have negative effects on clients. Those variables that seem to contribute the most to negative effects, aside from the traits clients bring with them to the relationship, include the level of therapist interpersonal skills such as warmth, empathy, and unconditional positive regard; the manner in which therapists terminate their relationship with clients (therapist rejection); and confrontive techniques, especially those that emphasize client weaknesses rather than strengths. A recent study (Sandell, 1981) indicated that poor results, if not negative effects, were the result of passive involvement by the therapist who did not help the client find and deal with a focal issue in therapy. In general, however, research on this topic suggests that most of the negative effects of therapy are related to the therapist as a person. This points up the need for careful selection and training of therapists as well as sound methods for restricting the practice of credentialed therapists.

Effects of Psychotherapeutical Methods

While there is empirical evidence that many therapies have beneficial effects, support for the superiority of one school of therapy over another is weak. Early reviews of this question (Bergin, 1971; Meltzoff & Kornreich, 1970; Luborsky, Singer, & Luborsky, 1975) concluded that no difference existed between the major schools. Most recent analysis (Bergin & Lambert, 1978; Smith, Glass, & Miller, 1980; Shapiro & Shapiro, 1982) using more reliable review techniques has drawn the same conclusion.

Shapiro and Shapiro (1982), for example, reviewed 143 outcome studies that compared two or more treatments and were listed in psychological abstracts between 1975 and 1979. In all there were 414 treated groups that were exposed to a variety of traditional methods such as dynamic, humanistic, behavioral, and cognitive methods. In general, mixed methods appeared to be most effective, with behavioral and cognitive methods following, and dynamic and humanistic methods showing the least effectiveness. Behavioral and cognitive methods had a definite superiority over verbal methods, yet differences between the outcomes of treatment methods were minimal. While individual therapy seemed to have better outcomes than group therapy, the difference in outcomes was not great. Surprisingly, length of therapy did not necessarily predict a positive outcome. Favorable results were reported when self-ratings and behavioral counts were analyzed, with unfavorable outcomes reported from hard nonpsychological data. The review suggests that therapy does have a moderate, relatively uniform, positive effect.

Client Variables

A great deal of psychotherapy research has centered on the client's contribution to the outcome of treatment. In fact some believe client variables are the most powerful determining force in positive and negative change (Bergin & Lambert, 1978). Those who seek treatment from professionals often feel demoralized, socially isolated, helpless, and overwhelmingly anxious and depressed. In addition to degree of pathology, which is clearly related to outcome, there are numerous other client variables that distinguish those who profit from therapy from those who do not.

Research focusing on patient demographic variables reveals that patients from lower socioeconomic backgrounds often want symptomatic relief and attribute their difficulties to physical problems rather than emotional ones. They also show a lack of desire for psychotherapy and its processes (Heitler, 1976). As a result, patients of lower socioeconomic status typically measured in income, level of education, and occupation, tend to be referred for inpatient and drug treatments, while those of higher socioeconomic status are more often accepted for individual outpatient, insight-oriented therapies. Education level also appears to correlate positively with length of stay in therapy. Lower socioeconomic status patients more often fail to keep initial appointments and drop out of treatment sooner than patients of higher educational levels and socioeconomic status (Garfield, 1978). Despite this trend there is no clear indication of a positive relationship between socioeconomic status and success or failure of psychotherapy for those lower-class patients who do remain in therapy until mutual agreement for termination is reached. Research on other demographic variables (such as race and sex) as predictors of continuation in and outcome of psychotherapy have been generally inconclusive or even contradictory (Lambert & Asay, 1984).

Many practitioners have suggested using a pretherapy role induction interview that prepares the patient by stating appropriate goals and expectations for therapy. The interview deals with the tendency toward premature termination among lower socioeconomic status patients. These brief interventions are intended to model ideal therapy behavior that facilitates productive psychotherapeutic processes among less psychologically sophisticated clients. The use of this procedure has resulted in substantial improvement in attendance rates among the socially disadvantaged (Lambert & Lambert, 1984). Other strategies include the use of alternative treatments and methods of changing the expectations of therapists for lower socioeconomic status patients.

Researchers have also studied the relationship of client personality variables (as measured by scores on traditional personality tests) to continuation in and outcome of psychotherapy. Certain personality variables such as associative ability, rigidity, wide interests, sensitivity to the environment, "feeling deeply," high energy level, and freedom from bodily concerns correlate with positive outcomes in psychotherapy. These variables when considered together may be labeled *ego strength*. Research has shown that client ego strength has a good prognostic value (Kernberg, 1973).

The nature of most psychotherapies requires active involvement of the patient; there is considerable agreement among therapists that a well-motivated client will have a greater chance of success. However, research on motivation is inconclusive, because the term is vague and various studies have used different definitions. In addition, the liquidity of this trait has made it difficult to study. Some patients may be highly motivated at the outset of therapy and then quickly lose their motivation. Despite these difficulties current research points out that patient involvement, defined as a positive manner of participating in therapy, is consistently a strong predictor of outcome and is relatively independent of therapist techniques and the level of relationship variables offered by the therapist (Gomes-Schwartz, 1978; Lothstein, 1978; Perry, Gelfand, & Marchovitch, 1979; Pomerleau, Adkins, & Pertschuk, 1978; Marziali, Marmar, & Krupnick, 1981).

Therapist Variables

Research exploring the relationship of therapist characteristics to therapeutic outcome is based on the assumption that such characteristics are fairly stable, constant for all clients, and manifested independently of the client. Much research has been undertaken to identify those therapist styles, behaviors, attributes, and attitudes (apart from specific intervention techniques) that enhance the client's chances for improvement. These variables are of great interest because it is possible to alter therapist attitude, behavior, and style through training or use them to select therapists for training.

Therapist demographic variables such as gender, age, race, and socioeconomic status, have shown no clear pattern in relationship to outcomes. Nor has extensive research on therapist personality variables yielded a clear relationship to therapeutic outcome. It does appear that a better adjusted, more integrated, less anxious, and less defensive therapist will have better results in treatment. Therapists with emotional problems or neurotic needs may be hindered in offering effective treatment to clients (Lambert, Bergin, & Collins, 1977).

The role of training and experience in therapy outcome remains controversial. There is no evidence that trained and experienced therapists from one discipline (e.g., social work, psychiatry) are superior to another in obtaining positive results from treatment (Meltzoff & Kornreich, 1970). Durlack's (1979) review of empirical literature suggests that paraprofessionals can be as effective as professionals, especially when they are offering time-limited, highly structured treatments such as assertiveness training. On the other hand, they are not as likely to offer effective unstructured treatments (dynamic therapies, marital therapies, etc.) that require moment-to-moment decision making. There is evidence that carefully selected and rigorously trained noncredentialed therapists have an impact on clients that is every bit as potent as that of experienced credentialed therapists. However, the relative impact of professionals and paraprofessionals is hard to judge because they are not using the same procedures, since their role in mental health delivery is not the same.

In an effort to pinpoint the particular things that a therapist does during the therapy hour which lead to client improvement, many researchers have closely monitored the interpersonal processes of actual therapy sessions. It seems plausible that the most successful therapists are not successful because of their theoretical orientation or therapeutic techniques, but because of other variables. There are obviously successful therapists from all orientations, and their success may very well be due to common factors such as interpersonal styles, warmth, voice tone, gestures, etc.

The study of therapist-initiated process variables has necessitated the development of rating scales to code therapeutic interaction between therapists and clients. Such scales usually employ trained objective observers who rate speech content and the manner in which it was given. This coding is often done from audiotaped or videotaped segments chosen from a therapy session. Raters code interactions on specified scales such as genuineness, warmth, and empathy according to speech content, tone of voice, gestures, facial expression, and other nonverbal behavior. The relationship of process variables to outcome is correlational in nature and therefore cannot establish causality. Nevertheless, process studies have shed some light on the therapeutic exchange.

Process studies have yielded fairly consistent conclusions about what constitutes desirable therapist behavior. Active and positive participation by the therapist coincides with an improvement in outcome, while critical and judgmental therapist statements correlate with little improvement. Again the question of causality arises; it is plausible that good progress could lead to more positive and active therapist participation, while little improvement could lead to criticism by the therapist. Other process variables that correlate with positive outcome include fresh, vivid language; warm, empathic expressions; encouragements toward independence; and statements high in personal relevance to the client (e.g., statements about the client's defense mechanisms or anxiety source). Conversely, an artificial voice quality and stereotypic language correlate with a less favorable outcome (Rice, 1982).

Process studies have generally supported the Rogerian hypothesis that therapist behavior which communicates high levels of empathy, congruence, and unconditional positive regard leads to client improvement. Research regarding these conditions traditionally uses complex observer rating systems that focus on various components of therapist style such as communication patterns, speech content, and connotative meanings. It is assumed that a concerned, empathic, and genuine therapist will impart these feelings during therapy by the manner in which he or she participates. Research in this area has been plagued by differing definitions of what constitutes the minimal level of these facilitative conditions and by the obvious difficulties incurred in measuring therapeutic interactions. Impartial judges, using rating scales to score segments of the therapy while in process, have been able to achieve fairly consistent reliability, but their ratings do not always correlate adequately with the client's and therapist's ratings of the same segment. Although many studies have supported the original Rogerian hypothesis, other studies have been equivocal. Overall, therapist attitudes of the Rogerian variety have been shown to have a modest positive relationship to psychotherapy outcome (Lambert, DeJulio, & Stein, 1978). The importance of these factors is suggested even with behavioral and cognitive approaches (Lambert, 1983). However, because of the correlational nature of most process studies, causality is at best inferred and conclusions are viewed as tentative.

Client-Therapist Matching

Utilizing the concepts of client and therapist variables that influence outcome, researchers and practitioners have attempted to match clients and therapists on pertinent variables to form therapeutic dyads with the highest probability of positive outcome. The hypothesis is a simple one supported by common sense. People who tend to get along better because of complementary personality styles, similar interests, backgrounds, race, sex, social class, values, and expectations would naturally have an easier time forming a therapeutic or helping relationship. Although the idea seems basic enough, establishing empirical support has not been so simple.

Whitehorn and Botz (1954, 1960) pioneered a major thrust in matching client and therapist according to personality variables by categorizing therapists into two groups: A and B. Type A therapists are active during therapy, show high personal participation, and form trusting relationships with their clients. Type B therapists are passive, permissive, and demonstrate a marked use of interpretation and an instructional style during therapy. Through experimentation with the Strong Vocational Interest Blank, a 23-item scale was devised to categorize therapists according to these two types. It was found that Type A therapists typically reject manual and mechanical activities and show interest in leadership, while Type B therapists show interest in manual and mechanical professions. Traditionally Type A therapists are seen as being more effective in working with schizophrenics and Type B therapists in working with neurotics; however, the most recent review of empirical research shows that there is little support for the use of A-B scales to form client-therapist dyads for optimal outcome (Razin, 1977).

Of particular interest to the Christian counselor is the issue of congruence of client and therapist value systems and their influence on therapy outcome. This area of study is distinguished by its marked paucity of research. Of all the factors that could possibly influence therapy, values seem to be one of the most important; yet even though it is the backdrop against which all human interaction is displayed it has somehow been overlooked in research on variables influencing the outcome of psychotherapy. Amid bold declarations concerning client ego strength, the therapeutic relationship, necessary and sufficient conditions for improvement, and client and therapist variables, very little that is definite and useful has been said concerning the relative effects of value systems, or client-therapist congruence of values, on therapy outcome.

Although the commonsense notion of improving the results of psychotherapy through client-therapist matching is alluring, it has proven extremely difficult to support empirically. Research matching therapists and clients on demographic variables such as age, sex, socioeconomic status, and race, as well as therapists' personality variables and client diagnosis through the use of the A-B scales, has shown no clear relationship to outcome. It does appear that clients continue in therapy and report higher satisfaction when the client and therapist have similar expectations for therapy; as previously discussed, outcome can be improved by pretherapy training sessions with both therapists and clients to increase congruency of expectations. More research is needed to establish the relationship between the client and therapist and how this affects outcomes.

Conclusion

To date there are a few broad generalizations that can be made concerning research in psychotherapy and its outcomes. It appears that on the whole, participation in psychotherapy is better than having no therapy at all, and that above-average therapy can lead to excellent results. Research provides an empirical base for the traditional therapies: psychoanalysis, humanistic or person-centered, many of the behavioral procedures, and some of the cognitive therapies. All of these therapies have a broad range of usefulness in treating a variety of psychopathologies; however, research also indicates that certain disorders such as phobias, sexual dysfunctions, and compulsions are more successfully treated by more specially designed behavioral techniques. It seems obvious that the crisis-oriented and brief therapies are as successful as the more traditional long-term therapies, and may be more valued because they are more cost efficient.

Studies have shown that verbal therapies are worthwhile in improving personal functioning with a broad spectrum of disorders. The interpersonal factors that facilitate communication in therapy, such as warmth, interpersonal style, and personal influence, are important to therapy process and outcome. The techniques that a therapist uses give a rationale and practical approach to problem solving for the client who perhaps previously had been unable to grasp his particular source of difficulty or to conceive of an avenue for resolution. It appears that among the multiple variables affecting therapy outcome, client variables are most important (severity, onset, and duration of the presenting symptoms, support systems in the environment, personal ego strength, motivation for change, etc.). These are followed by the therapist variables (personal styles, attitudes, genuineness, etc.) and finally by the technique used during therapy.

One of the main problems concerning research in psychotherapy is the choice of measures used before and after therapy to determine change. There are many types of measures available to researchers—self-report measures, therapist evaluations, and trained detached observers to give ratings of behavioral scales. It is recommended that all these be used when evaluating therapy outcome. Comparison between these measures during the process of change may help reveal what exactly is happening as a result of therapy.

Most recent research avoids lumping therapies together by school or orientation since this does little to define what the therapist actually does during therapy. Instead, more recent studies name very detailed intervention procedures and their effects on very specific types of clients suffering from well-defined pathologies. This is a wise shift in emphasis, since most of the past global studies have left a heritage of vague generalizations that have no definite conclusions about change as a result of psychotherapy.

Researchers and practitioners involved in so human an endeavor as helping others through the practice of psychotherapy must continue to utilize all possible means to upgrade therapeutic services. Future studies will continue to add much to our growing knowledge of how best to help our fellow men and women through psychological intervention.

References

Bergin, A. E. The evaluation of therapeutic outcomes. In A. E. Bergin & S. L. Garfield (Eds.), *Handbook of psychotherapy and behavior change.* New York: Wiley, 1971.

Bergin, A. E., & Lambert, M. J. The evaluation of outcomes in psychotherapy. In S. L. Garfield & A. E. Bergin (Eds.), *Handbook of psychotherapy and behavior change: An empirical analysis* (2nd ed.). New York: Wiley, 1978.

Durlak, J. A. Comparative effectiveness of para-professional and professional helpers. *Psychological Bulletin*, 1979, *86*, 80–92.

Eysenck, H. J. The effects of psychotherapy: An evaluation. *Journal of Consulting Psychology*, 1952, *16*, 319–324.

Garfield, S. L. Research on client variables in psychotherapy. In S. L. Garfield & A. E. Bergin (Eds.), *Handbook of psychotherapy and behavior change: An empirical analysis*, (2nd ed.). New York: Wiley, 1978.

Gomes-Schwartz, B. Effective ingredients in psychotherapy: Prediction of outcome from process variables. *Journal of Consulting Clinical Psychology*, 1978, *46*, 1023–1035.

Heitler, J. B. Preparatory techniques in initiating expressive psychotherapy with lower-class, unsophisticated patients. *Psychological Bulletin*, 1976, *83*, 339–352.

Kernberg, D. F. Summary and conclusion of "Psychotherapy and psychoanalysis: Final report of the Menninger Foundation's psychotherapy research project." *International Journal of Psychiatry*, 1973, *11*, 62–77.

Lambert, M. J. Introduction to assessment of psychotherapy outcome: Historical perspective and current issues. In M. J. Lambert, E. R. Christensen, & S. S. DeJulio (Eds.), *The assessment of psychotherapy outcome*. New York: Wiley, 1983.

Lambert, M. J., & Asay, T. P. Patient characteristics and their relationship to psychotherapy outcome. In M. Hersen, L. Michelson, & A. S. Bellack (Eds.), *Issues in psychotherapy research*. New York: Plenum, 1984.

Lambert, M. J., Bergin, A. E., & Collins, J. L. Therapist-induced deterioration in psychotherapy. In A. S. Gurman & A. M. Razin (Eds.), *Effective psychotherapy: A handbook of research*. New York: Pergamon, 1977.

Lambert, M. J., DeJulio, S. S., & Stein, D. M. Therapist interpersonal skills: Process, outcome, methodological considerations and recommendations for further research. *Psychological Bulletin*, 1978, *85*, 467–489.

Lambert, R. G., & Lambert, M. J. The effects of role preparation for psychotherapy on immigrant clients seeking mental health services in Hawaii. *The Journal of Community Psychology*, 1984, *12*, 263–275.

Lothstein, L. M. The group psychotherapy drop-out phenomenon revisited. *American Journal of Psychiatry*, 1978, *135*(12), 1492–1495.

Luborsky, L., Singer, B., & Luborsky, L. Comparative studies of psychotherapies. Is it true that "Everyone has won and all must have prizes?" *Archives of General Psychiatry*, 1975, *32*, 995–1001.

Marziali, E., Marmar, C., & Krupnick, J. Therapeutic alliance scales: Development and relationship to psychotherapy outcome. *American Journal of Psychiatry*, 1981, *138*, 361–364.

Meltzoff, J., & Kornreich, M. *Research in psychotherapy*. New York: Atherton, 1970.

Perry, C., Gelfand, R., & Marcovitch, P. The relevance of hypnotic suscept-ibility in the clinical context. *Journal of Abnormal Psychology*, 1979, *88*, 592–603.

Pomerleau, O., Adkins, D., & Pertschuk, M. Predictors of outcome and reci-divism in smoking cessation treatment. *Addict Behavior*, 1978, *3*, 65–70.

Razin, A. M. S. A-B variable: Still promising after twenty years. In A. S. Gurman & A. M. Razin (Eds.), *Effective Psychotherapy. A handbook of research*. New York: Pergamon, 1977.

Rice, L. N. The relationship in client-centered therapy. In M. J. Lambert (Ed.), *Psychotherapy and patient relationships*. Homewood, Ill.: Dow Jones-Irwin, 1982.

Sandell, J. A. *An empirical study of negative factors in brief psychotherapy*. Nash-ville: Vanderbilt University Press, 1981.

Shapiro, D. A., & Shapiro, D. Meta-analysis of comparative therapy out-come studies: A replication and refinement. *Psychological Bulletin*, 1982, *92*, 581–604.

Smith, M. L., Glass, G. V., & Miller, T. I. *The benefits of psychotherapy*. Baltimore: Johns Hopkins University Press, 1980.

Strupp, H. H., & Hadley, S. W. A tripartite model of mental health and therapeutic outcomes: With special reference to negative effects in psy-chotherapy. *American Psychologist*, 1977, *32*, 187–196.

Whitehorn, J. C., & Botz, B. A. A study of psychotherapeutic relationships between physicians and schizophrenic patients. *American Journal of Psy-chiatry*, 1954, *111*, 321–331.

Whitehorn, J. C., & Botz, B. A. Further studies of the doctor as a crucial variable in the outcome of treatment of schizophrenic patients. *American Journal of Psychiatry*, 1960, *117*, 215–223.

9

Eclecticism in Psychotherapy
Darrell Smith

Professional psychotherapy had its beginning with the work of Freud at the turn of the twentieth century. A number of eager disciples were attracted to the founder of psychoanalysis, but Freud was unable to hold the loyalty of most of these equally ambitious men. Surprisingly soon, individuals such as Adler, Jung, Rank, and Reich proceeded to launch their own schools of psychotherapy. Since the founding of Freudian psychoanalysis and the various neo-Freudian spin-offs there has been a proliferation of theoretical approaches to psychotherapy. Each new system of therapy has faulted, to some degree, all of its predecessors and claimed a status superior to them on one ground or another. Although adherence to a particular school of psychotherapy often appears to be more prestigious, many psychotherapists have shown a consistent disenchantment with exclusive systems of psychotherapy and a preference for an eclectic orientation that integrates the essential features of the various theories about human behavior into a more comprehensive theory.

The word *eclectic* has its origin in the Greek verbal root *eklego*, a composite of *ek* (from or out of) and *lego* (to pick, choose, or select).

75

Eclectic literally means then to pick out or to select from. A typical definition of eclecticism emphasizes the practice of choosing what appears to be best from the doctrines, works, or styles of others. English and English (1958) define it as "the selection and orderly combination of compatible features from diverse sources, sometimes from otherwise incompatible theories and systems; the effort to find valid elements in all . . . theories and to combine them into a harmonious whole. The resulting system is open to constant revision even in its major outlines" (p. 168).

Brief History

Theoretical eclecticism is not a new phenomenon either in psychology or the practice of psychotherapy. James (1907) sought to bring together the thoughts of tender-minded rationalists and tough-minded empiricists via the pragmatic method. He considered pragmatism as being a mediator and reconciler that eschewed fixed principles, rigid dogma, pretense of finality in truth, and closed systems. He viewed it as marked by openness and a flexible empiricist attitude that invites the application of any and all principles, concepts, and methods that can be assimilated, validated, corroborated, and verified in reality.

Woodworth (1931) referred to himself as a "middle-of-the-roader" who saw some good in every school of psychology and believed that none of them was ideal. He maintained that each school or system makes its special contribution to the whole of psychological knowledge but no single one possesses the final answer. For a half-century Woodworth encouraged rapprochement of overtly competitive factions.

Allport (1964, 1968) was a self-described "polemic-eclectic" who was theoretically open, yet prepared to challenge any psychological idol. His concept of a theoretical system was "one that allows for truth wherever found, one that encompasses the totality of human experience and does full justice to the nature of man" (1968, p. 406).

Numerous eclectic approaches to psychotherapy have been developed in the last half century. The psychobiology of Meyer (1948) is generally accepted as the first serious attempt at an eclectic psychotherapy. Meyer wanted an integration of the psychological, sociological, and biological dimensions of human behavior. He insisted on a comprehensiveness that included the life history of the individual, a thorough diagnosis of the clinical situation, and the application of a variety of techniques that fit the person and the problem presented.

Dollard and Miller (1950) endeavored to integrate the psychoanalytic concepts of Freud, learning theory, and cultural influences aim was "to combine the vitality of psychoanalysis, the vigor of the natural science laboratory, and the facts of culture" (p. 3).

Wolberg (1954) made an initial effort to extract methods from the field of psychoanalysis, psychobiology, psychiatric interviewing, casework, and therapeutic counseling and to blend these into an eclectic system of methodology. He has broadened the scope of the inclusions in two subsequent editions of *The Technique of Psychotherapy.*

For better than thirty years the late Fredrick Thorne was the prince of the eclectics. He wrote prolifically on eclecticism, and each of his several major works is encyclopedic in content. A quote from his *Psychological Case Handling* well illustrates his position: "to collect and integrate all known methods of personality counseling and psychotherapy into an eclectic system which might form the basis of standardized practice; . . . to be rigidly scientific . . . [with] no priority given to any theoretical viewpoint or school . . . [but] to analyze the contributions of all existing schools and fit them together into an integrated system . . . [that] combines the best features of all methods" (Thorne, 1968, Vol. 1, p. vi).

The *Therapeutic Psychology* of Brammer and Shostrom, published in 1960 and now available in the third edition, is a landmark in the evolution of eclectic psychotherapy. They use the term *emerging eclecticism* to define their efforts to develop a comprehensive and dynamic perspective on personality structure and change as a basis for clinical practice. They assimilate extractions from psychoanalytic, humanistic, existential-phenomenological, and behavioral approaches to form a multidimensional system of therapy.

Another substantial work on eclectic theory, *Beyond Counseling and Psychotherapy* by Carkhuff and Berenson, appeared in 1967. These authors sought to build around a central core of facilitative conditions an armamentarium of clinical methods judged to be compatible with the facilitative core. The methods were derived from client-centered, existential, behavioral, trait-factor, and psychoanalytic orientations.

The work of Lazarus (1976, 1981) represents some of the latest, and perhaps best, efforts to craft an eclectic psychotherapy. His multimodal therapy approach espouses a technical rather than a theoretical emphasis. Starting with social learning theory and behavioral principles Lazarus develops a broad-spectrum system that deals with the clients' "salient behaviors, affective processes, each of his/her five senses, basic images, cognitions, and intrapersonal relationships" (1976, p. 4).

Several other psychotherapists have presented excellent eclectic themes, though these have been less substantial in nature than those cited above. A sample of these titles and their authors include *Psychological Counseling* (Bordin, 1968), *Psychobehavioral Counseling and Therapy* (Woody, 1971), *A Primer of Eclectic Psychotherapy* (Palmer, 1980), and *Psychotherapy: An Eclectic Approach* (Garfield, 1980).

Criticism

A mixed audience exists regarding eclecticism in psychotherapy. Some of the attitudes toward the eclectic approach from both the pro and con perspectives are given below.

Positive views

1. Since there is no single "best" kind of psychotherapy, an eclectic alternative is essential if maximum assistance is to be offered to each and every client (Wolberg, 1954).

2. As desirable and necessary as particular systems might be, the only way to comprehend the nature of human beings and their situation in life is by a reasoned and systematic eclecticism marked by a conceptual and theoretical openness. A comprehensive metatheory is preferred to a plurality of dogmatized and separatistic particularisms (Allport, 1964).

3. Individuals, as free beings, cannot be confined to monolithic systems. In order to enable clients to live effectively, the therapist must select from many systems those elements that promise to be most useful in given situations. Empirical data suggest that the most effective approach is an open-ended, systematic, eclectic model fashioned around a central core of caring relationship conditions and complemented with a variety of techniques derived from several theoretical orientations (Carkhuff & Berenson, 1967).

4. A psychotherapist can hardly afford to ignore any technique proven to be effective, regardless of its theoretical origin. The therapist who maintains a strict adherence to a particular school of thought arbitrarily excludes from his or her repertoire many effective procedures. Technical eclecticism has decided potential to enrich the practitioner's therapeutic effectiveness without jeopardizing his or her position (Lazarus, 1967).

5. Eclecticism is the prerequisite for complete or total psychotherapy that serves best the needs of clients at various stages or phases in the therapy process. Therapy must match the personality

needs of the particular client, and sectarianism unavoidably limits therapeutic efficacy (Slavson, 1970).

Negative views

1. Eclecticism is a namby-pamby process in which directionless eclectics are comparable to jackdaws who aimlessly carry anything and everything to their nests (Goethe, as cited by Allport, 1964).

2. Essentially eclecticism is a bag-of-tricks and trial-and-error approach that has no adequate information regarding the criteria to govern what techniques to use when and with what clients. It has no general principles of counseling and lacks a logical rationale; it is simply a random collection of techniques held together in a manipulative manner (Patterson, 1959).

3. Eclecticism makes it easy for lazy or inept individuals to choose bits and pieces indiscriminately from a wide spectrum of counseling theories and methods and to concoct a hodgepodge of contradictory assumptions and incompatible techniques (Brammer, 1969).

Current Status

Surveys of counseling and clinical psychologists indicate that the majority of therapists identify with some form of eclecticism (Garfield & Kurtz, 1976; Smith, 1982). At the same time there seems to be a growing dissatisfaction with the traditional label, since *eclecticism* suggests laziness, undisciplined subjectivity, mediocrity, and poor systemization (Smith, 1982). The current trend in labeling such approaches appears to be in the direction of such terms as masterful integration (Smith, 1975), creative synthesis (Shostrom, 1976), general systems theory (Ivey & Simek-Downing, 1980), and systematic multimodal therapy (Lazarus, 1981).

References

Allport, G. W. The fruits of eclecticism: Bitter or sweet? *Acta Psychologica,* 1964, *23,* 27–44.

Allport, G. W. *The person in psychology.* Boston: Beacon Press, 1968.

Bordin, E. S. *Psychological counseling* (2nd ed.). New York: Appleton-Century-Crofts, 1968.

Brammer, L. M. Eclecticism revisited. *Personnel and Guidance Journal,* 1969, *48,* 192–197.

Brammer, L. M., & Shostrom, E. L. *Therapeutic psychology.* Englewood Cliffs, N.J.: Prentice-Hall, 1960.

Carkhuff, R. R., & Berenson, B. G. *Beyond counseling and psychotherapy.* New York: Holt, Rinehart & Winston, 1967.

Dollard, J., & Miller, N. E. *Personality and psychotherapy.* New York: McGraw-Hill, 1950.

English, H. B., & English, A. C. *A comprehensive dictionary of psychological and psychoanalytic terms.* New York: Longmans, Green, 1958.

Garfield, S. L. *Psychotherapy: An eclectic approach.* New York: Wiley, 1980.

Garfield, S. L., & Kurtz, R. Clinical psychologists in the 1970s. *American Psychologist,* 1976, *31,* 1–9.

Ivey, A. E., & Simek-Downing, L. *Counseling and psychotherapy.* Englewood Cliffs, N.J.: Prentice-Hall, 1980.

James, W. *Pragmatism.* Cambridge: Harvard University Press, 1975. (Originally published, 1907.)

Lazarus, A. A. In support of technical eclecticism. *Psychological Reports,* 1967, *21,* 415–416.

Lazarus, A. A. *Multimodal behavior therapy.* New York: Springer Publishing, 1976.

Lazarus, A. A. *The practice of multimodal therapy.* New York: McGraw-Hill, 1981.

Meyer, A. *The common sense psychiatry of Dr. Adolf Meyer.* New York: McGraw-Hill, 1948.

Palmer, J. O. *A primer of eclectic psychotherapy.* Monterey, Calif.: Brooks/Cole, 1980.

Patterson, C. H. *Counseling and psychotherapy.* New York: Harper & Row, 1959.

Shostrom, E. L. *Actualizing therapy.* San Diego, Calif.: EDITS Publishers, 1976.

Slavson, S. R. Eclecticism versus sectarianism in group psychotherapy. *International Journal of Group Psychotherapy,* 1970, *20,* 3–13.

Smith, D. *Integrative counseling and psychotherapy.* Boston: Houghton Mifflin, 1975.

Smith, D. Trends in counseling and psychotherapy. *American Psychologist,* 1982, *37,* 802–809.

Thorne, F. C. *Psychological case handling* (2 vols.). Brandon, Vt.: Clinical Psychology Publishing, 1968.

Wolberg, L. R. *The technique of psychotherapy.* New York: Grune & Stratton, 1954.

Woodworth, R. S. *Contemporary schools of psychology.* New York: Ronald Press, 1931.

Woody, R. H. *Psychobehavioral counseling and therapy.* New York: Appleton-Century-Crofts, 1971.

10

Prevention of Psychological Disorders
Siang-Yang Tan

This subject has received significant attention in recent years. A large body of literature is now available, including review articles (e.g., Kornberg & Caplan, 1980), a series of annual volumes based on the Vermont Conference on Primary Prevention of Psychopathology (e.g., Joffe & Albee, 1977), a textbook on primary prevention (Bloom, 1981), and even a journal, the *Journal of Prevention*. This increased interest in prevention is understandable in light of the shortage of mental health professionals to meet the needs of the emotionally disturbed and the great cost of mental illness, estimated recently to be more than $40 billion annually (see Hatch, 1982). Albee (1982) has pointed out that the mental health community actually sees fewer than one in five of the estimated 15% (32 to 34 million) of the American population who are seriously disturbed emotionally. Christian authors have also begun to focus on the need for Christian counselors and churches to be more involved in preventive interventions.

Prevention of psychological disorders has usually been divided into three types: primary, secondary, and tertiary (see Zax & Cowen, 1976). Primary prevention involves preventing the development of psychological dysfunction and hence reducing the rate of occurrence of new cases of disorder (its incidence) in the general population. Secondary prevention refers to the reduction of the prevalence of disorder by shortening its duration and negative consequences. It therefore seeks to stop mild disorders from becoming prolonged or acute, and focuses on early identification and prompt, effective treatment of psychological dysfunction. Tertiary prevention aims at reducing the severity, discomfort, or disability associated with psychological disorder that is already well established. A number of authors have suggested that the terms *secondary* and *tertiary* prevention be replaced by *treatment* and *rehabilitation*, respectively, in order to reduce confusion over terminology. The term *prevention* will therefore be used in this article to refer mainly to primary prevention aimed at reducing the incidence of new cases of psychological disorder. Attempts at primary prevention, by definition, occur in a population that is free of the disorder being prevented.

Examples of Primary Prevention

There are many excellent examples of preventive intervention with a wide variety of populations (see Bloom, 1981). Heber's (1978) study of prevention of sociocultural mental retardation is one frequently cited example of successful primary prevention. Children of mothers with IQs less than seventy-five were given day care in an intense program from infancy until they entered public school. The mothers simultaneously received remedial education as well as training in home management, home economics, interpersonal relations, and child care techniques. At the final assessment (age six) children's IQs in the group that received the preventive intervention averaged 120.7, while children in the control group had an average IQ of only 87.2. The results of this study therefore seem to indicate that it is possible to modify or prevent sociocultural mental retardation. The preventive intervention appears to have improved the intelligence and reduced behavior problems of children reared by parents of limited intellectual capacity living in disadvantaged economic circumstances. However, the trustworthiness of these findings has recently been questioned (see Sommer & Sommer, 1983).

Another well-known and significant prevention program is the Primary Mental Health Project conducted by Cowen and his colleagues in Rochester (see Cowen, Trost, Dorr, Lorion, Izzo, &

Isaacson, 1975). This is a program for early detection and prevention of school adjustment problems in children. Cowen found that many of the children identified as high risk but who received no intervention continued to have problems or had worse difficulties during the later school years. His intervention involved the use of housewives as nonprofessional child aides who worked directly with high-risk children in the schools. The children were typically seen about twice a week, usually for the entire school year. The housewives provided an empathic and accepting relationship with the children on an individual basis. Research has shown that this preventive intervention has provided both immediate and long-term benefit to the children who received it, and has significantly reduced later school adjustment problems.

More recently Durlak (1977) used teachers and college students to implement a more specific behavioral preventive intervention. Verbal and token reinforcement were used to modify maladaptive social behaviors in school children. Evaluation of the eight-week intervention program using ratings by teachers and aides showed that children who received the intervention improved significantly in classroom adjustment at both completion of the program and at a seven-month follow-up. However, longer term follow-up is needed to determine whether these short-term effects last.

Shure and Spivack (1980) reported that significantly fewer young children who were trained in interpersonal cognitive problem-solving skills showed signs of impulsivity or inhibition when compared to a control group of children a year after the intervention. They concluded that problem-solving training prevented the emergence of these behaviors as well as helped children who were already having difficulties. Their study was therefore only partly preventive in nature. Attempts by other investigators to duplicate these results with other age groups and settings have not been as successful (see Cowen, 1980).

Another example of a successful and systematic preventive program is the behavioral work done by Poser and his colleagues (see Poser & Hartman, 1979). In a series of studies they have shown the effectiveness of preexposure and symbolic-modeling strategies for the prevention of maladaptive fear responses in children in situations involving dental treatment and handling of snakes (Poser & King, 1975). More recently measures of psychological vulnerability and environmental adversity or "press" have been validated and used to identify asymptomatic school students who may be at risk for psychological disorder (Poser & Hartman, 1979). Hartman (1979) found that students who received an eight-week group intervention of coping and social skills training improved significantly more than those who did not. There was a strong trend for these gains to be maintained at a three-month follow-up. Once again, longer term follow-up is needed before more definitive conclusions can be made. However, the results do suggest that coping and social skills training may be a very effective preventive intervention.

Another recent successful prevention program involved reducing child abuse and neglect with families identified to be at risk by using parent support groups, parent education, school system coordination, and the utilization of other agencies during prenatal, childbirth, and postpartum care (Turkington, 1983a, b). However, it should also be pointed out that not all efforts at prevention of psychological disorders have been successful. Examples of failure include attempts at preventing juvenile delinquency and crime (e.g., McCord, 1978) and "immunizing" children for speech anxiety (Cradock, Cotler, & Jason, 1978).

The Church and Prevention

Several authors have recently proposed that the prevention of mental disorders should be a concern of the church (Collins, 1980; Uomoto, 1982). Uomoto argues that the church is a potent mental health resource because of its proximity in the community, its independent financial set-up, its consistency in providing a stable social environment, and its mission to enhance the physical, emotional, and spiritual well-being of its members. He suggests three levels of preventive interventions as options for the church: individual interventions, social system interventions, and the provision of a healing community.

Individual interventions could include mental health education (i.e., educating church leaders on psychological principles, mental health resources, mental disorders, referral methods, skill training); skills and competence training (i.e., conducting problem-solving workshops, language skills training, and lay counselor training); and the facilitation of stress reduction and coping (i.e., teaching preventive stress inoculation techniques, relaxation training, and cognitive restructuring procedures). Social system interventions might include the development of social support groups for high risk individuals such as divorcees, single parents, business executives, jobless people, families with disabled members, and former mental patients; regular visitations to peripheral members of a church; connecting people with specific needs to appropriate agencies or resources; establishing a telephone network; and working more closely with other community agencies. Finally, the over-all goal would be the establishment of a healing climate in which all of the preceding interventions can be optimally undertaken. Uomoto suggests that such a climate can best be developed within a caring community of believers who are experiencing newness of life in Christ, living according to the law of love, and reaching out to the world.

Barriers to Prevention

Albee (1982) has argued that one-to-one psychotherapy is inde-fensible because of the unbridgeable gap between the large num-bers in need and the small numbers of helpers. Furthermore, he argues that support for primary prevention as an alternative de-rives from the demonstrated role of poverty, meaningless work, unemployment, racism, and sexism in producing psychopathology, and from the demonstrated effectiveness of programs promoting social competence, self-esteem, and social support networks in re-ducing psychopathology. He therefore asks why most mental health professionals continue to practice an individually oriented approach to treatment, ignoring the arguments for movement from treatment to prevention.

Bloom (1981) suggests several barriers to prevention: the personal tendency to avoid making immediate sacrifices in order to obtain remote goals in the future, which runs counter to what prevention often requires; the professional reluctance to shift one's focus of practice from traditional psychotherapy after having invested years in it; conceptual inadequacies and the lack of more sophisticated and systematic theory in prevention; the lack of data, especially long-term follow-up data, to support the efficacy of preventive inter-ventions; the great costs of some preventive programs; and ethical objections to the invasion of privacy or the tampering with self-choice, especially among minority or disadvantaged groups. Albee (1982) adds to this list the challenge that prevention represents to the traditional defect model (or medical model) of psychopathology. Focusing on social and environmental factors, prevention efforts are grounded in more of a social learning model. Thus they are resisted by those trained in the more traditional model, who are predisposed to see preventive efforts as modifying human unhappiness and mis-ery but not affecting mental illness.

Albee (1982) has also proposed a religious source of resistance to prevention, arguing that opposition to prevention comes as a result of Calvinistic theology. Believing that neither the individual nor society is perfectable because of the stigma of original sin, Calvinists oppose efforts to better society and the lot of the individual sinner, according to Albee. However, while it is true that Christians do not believe that individuals or society can be made perfect by purely humanistic efforts, it is not true that they therefore have to oppose prevention.

The biblical view of prevention is centered in the redemptive work of Christ, since ultimately only Jesus Christ can meet the deepest psychospiritual needs of human beings. However, this does not mean that psychological, social, and environmental changes are not helpful for healthy mental functioning. While they are inadequate without the new birth in Christ, which alone can deal with the fundamental problem of sin, they are important and legitimate spheres of Christian service.

Bloom (1981) is of the opinion that barriers to prevention can be overcome by rigorous and systematic research. Albee (1982), however, argues that what is needed is something more like ideological reeducation for mental health professionals. He suggests that significant forward movement toward the prevention of psychopathology will come as more and more people line up with those who believe in "social change, in the effectiveness of consultation, in education, in the primary prevention of human physical and emotional misery, and in the maximization of individual competence" (p. 1050).

References

Albee, G. W. Preventing psychopathology and promoting human potential. *American Psychologist*, 1982, *37*, 1043–1050.

Bloom, M. *Primary prevention: The possible science.* Englewood Cliffs, N.J.: Prentice-Hall, 1981.

Collins, G. R. The future of Christian counseling. In G. R. Collins (Ed.), *Helping people grow.* Santa Ana, Calif.: Vision House, 1980.

Cowen, E. L. The wooing of primary prevention. *American Journal of Community Psychology*, 1980, *8*, 258–285.

Cowen, E. L., Trost, M. A., Dorr, D. A., Lorion, R. P., Izzo, L. D., & Isaacson, R. V. *New ways in school mental health: Early detection and prevention of school maladaptation.* New York: Human Sciences Press, 1975.

Cradock, C., Cotler, S., & Jason, L. A. Primary prevention: Immunization of children for speech anxiety. *Cognitive Therapy and Research*, 1978, *2*, 389–396.

Durlak, J. A. Description and evaluation of a behaviorally oriented school-based preventive mental health program. *Journal of Consulting and Clinical Psychology*, 1977, *45*, 27–35.

Hartman, L. M. The preventive reduction of psychological risk in asymptomatic adolescents. *American Journal of Orthopsychiatry*, 1979, *49*, 121–135.

Hatch, O. G. Psychology, society, and politics. *American Psychologist*, 1982, *37*, 1031–1037.

Heber, F. R. Sociocultural mental retardation: A longitudinal study. In D. G. Forgays (Ed.). *Primary prevention of psychopathology* (Vol. 2). Hanover, N.H.: University Press of New England, 1978.

Joffe, J. M., & Albee, G. W. (Eds.), *Primary prevention of psychopathology* (Vol. 5). Hanover, N.H.: University Press of New England, 1977.

Kornberg, M., & Caplan, G. Risk factors and prevention intervention in child psychopathology: A review. *Journal of Prevention*, 1980, *1*, 71–133.

McCord, J. A 30-year follow-up of treatment effects. *American Psychologist*, 1978, *33*, 284–289.

Poser, E. G., & Hartman, L. M. Issues in behavioral prevention: Empirical findings. *Advances in Behavior Research and Therapy*, 1979, *2*, 1–25.

Poser, E. G., & King, M. C. Strategies for the prevention of maladaptive fear responses. *Canadian Journal of Behavioral Science*, 1975, *7*, 279–294.

Shure, M. B., & Spivack, G. A preventive mental health program for young "inner city" children: The second (kindergarten) year. In M. Bloom (Ed.), *Life span development*. New York: Macmillan, 1980.

Sommer, R., & Sommer, B. A. Mystery in Milwaukee: Early intervention, IQ, and psychology textbooks. *American Psychologist*, 1983, *38*, 982–985.

Turkington, C. At risk: Project helps hard-to-reach parents, kids. *A.P.A. Monitor*, 1983, *14*, 6. (a)

Turkington, C. National center supports prevention efforts. *A.P.A. Monitor*, 1983, *14*, 7. (b)

Uomoto, J. M. Preventive intervention: A convergence of the church and community psychology. *Journal of Psychology and Christianity*, 1982, *1*, 12–22.

Zax, M., & Cowen, E. L. *Abnormal psychology: Changing conceptions* (2nd ed.). New York: Holt, Rinehart, & Winston, 1976.

11

Paraprofessional Therapy
L. Rebecca Propst

Anthony and Carkhuff (1977) define the paraprofessional, or "functional professional" (the term they prefer), as that individual who, lacking formal credentials, performs those functions usually reserved for credentialed mental health professionals. They include in this group such people as psychiatric aides, community workers, parents, college students, and mental health technicians. Pastors and various church workers would also fall in the category.

While functional professionals have been around a long time, they have been legitimatized only since the mid-1960s. A number of reasons have been advanced for the increase in the number of functional professionals in mental health:

1. the demise of the disease model of mental health (newer approaches do not demand as much advanced schooling);
2. the development of the community mental health concept, along with the recognition of the need for change agents who come from the same background as the clients;

3. the availability of federal money to prepare unemployed and low-income persons for positions as functional paraprofessionals.

Even though paraprofessionals have become common in mental health, the question that has repeatedly been raised is whether or not paraprofessional therapists are effective. A review of the research in 1968 found that paraprofessionals could be trained to effect significant constructive changes in the clients they worked with. There has, however, been little recent research on the effectiveness of paraprofessionals. So many people have become involved in paraprofessional training that the idea of its effectiveness seems to have been forgotten.

Anthony and Carkhuff (1977) argue that paraprofessionals should be taught skills that have been found to be effective. It does no good to teach paraprofessionals skills that in themselves are not effective even when used by trained professionals. However, this often seems to have been done, and consequently most paraprofessional training is not very effective. For example, training for lay counselors usually consists of didactic lectures and discussion groups—an approach that has not been shown to make any difference in terms of observable client change. The most effective paraprofessional, therefore, is one who has had specific training in interpersonal skills and program development skills, as well as training in additional therapeutic skills that have been found to be effective.

Two skills that appear to be easily taught to paraprofessional counselors are empathy and basic skill in cognitive behavioral therapy. Training in these skills would consist of a small amount of lecturing on their nature, modeling by the instructor, and an opportunity for the trainees to practice the skills and receive feedback on their development. Practice could occur within the context of the training program by role playing with other participants.

Summarizing the literature, the following principles of paraprofessional counseling seem to be important. First, goals for any program in the church or elsewhere focusing on paraprofessional training should be specifically defined in observable, measurable terms. That is, the individual should be taught some specific skills so that an observer is able to ascertain that he or she indeed has those skills. Second, the training process should be designed to teach trainees skills that previous research has found to be effective. Finally, the selection of trainees for any program should be based on how well they perform in a situation that is similar to that for which they are going to be trained. Not everyone will benefit equally from a paraprofessional training program.

The substantial amount of literature on community mental health suggests that pastors and other church leaders can play an important role in mental health concerns. Haugk (1976) suggests that clergy can play a uniquely important role in primary prevention because they are closer to the members of their congregation. They can disseminate basic mental health information and make sure everyone is integrated into the community. They could also play a role in secondary prevention because they are in a unique position for the early detection of problems. Finally, they could play a unique role in tertiary prevention, not only by being involved in actual counseling but also by encouraging members of their congregations who are in professional counseling to stay in counseling.

References

Anthony, W. A., & Carkhuff, R. P. The functional professional therapeutic agent. In A. Gurman & A. M. Razin (Eds.), *Effective psychotherapy: A handbook of research.* New York: Pergamon, 1977.

Haugk, K. C. Unique contributions of churches and clergy to community mental health. *Community Mental Health Journal,* 1976, *12*(1), 20–28.

Part 2

Individual Therapies

12

Adlerian Psychotherapy
Dennis L. Gibson

It would not be easy to find another author from which so much has been borrowed from all sides without acknowledgment than Adler (Ellenberger, 1970, p. 645). Fifty years after Alfred Adler's death present-day thinkers are coming up with ideas similar to Adler's without apparent awareness of his work. Cognitive behavior therapy and rational-emotive therapy view personality and approach psychotherapy much as did Adler, yet have not derived their theories from his body of work. Adlerians regard this as proof that Adler drew his concepts from a well of truth self-evident to any alert student who takes an uncomplicated, commonsense approach to understanding human nature.

Psychology textbooks routinely list Adler as a dissident disciple of Freud. Adler's disciples view his years with Freud (ca. 1902–1911) as a collegial relationship of two genius physicians in search of psychological truth. They attribute the subsequent dominance of Freud's ideas to his more voluminous writing, his greater elegance of expression, and his choice to orient to the intelligentsia of the medical profession. Adler opted instead to popularize his views. He wrote

93

rather loosely organized materials for the lay public and eschewed arcane jargon in favor of commonsense terms.

Theoretical Roots

The primary precursor who shaped Adler's views was the philosopher Vaihinger (1924). Vaihinger taught that none of us can know truth exactly; we all formulate our own approximations of reality, then live by these fictions as if they validly represent the truth. Adler expanded this basic idea into his concept of life style, by which he meant the particular arrangement of convictions each person establishes early in life concerning self, others, and reality. Adler emphasized life style as something a person uses rather than something the person possesses. He called it the person's unique law of movement. His view of the uniqueness and holistic cohesiveness of each individual's personality resulted in the term *Individual Psychology* for his school of thought.

Theory of Psychotherapy

To the Adlerian therapist the primary problem with any person seeking therapy is low social interest. The neurotic preoccupied with striving for glory thus evades the normal tasks of life: love and sexual adjustment, work, and friendship. The primary goal of therapy is to arouse the patient's social interest, or sense of commonality with all fellow humans, who, by the very nature of human limitations, need each other's cooperation in order to live.

Adlerian therapists function as educators. In supportive therapy they identify and build on strengths the client already shows. They encourage the person to use those talents for the benefit of other persons. In more intensive therapy they seek to identify and revise crippling perceptions of self, others, and the world in the client's life style. Since there is no perfect cognitive map for people to follow, the goal of lifestyle revision is to replace big mistakes with smaller ones.

Process of Psychotherapy

From the first contact Adlerians work to establish a friendly relationship with their clients. They make themselves models to follow in being humorous rather than anxious, unimpressed by their own mistakes rather than perfectionistic, and curious rather than defensive about flaws in thinking or acting. They realize as educators that much of what clients take away with them will be caught rather than taught. Adlerian therapists are seldom sphinx-like and passive; they are usually active and talkative.

Many Adlerians do a formal life-style assessment early in therapy. Part of this assessment focuses on the family constellation in which the person grew up. Adlerians ask more about birth order and sibling relationships than do therapists of most other persuasions, who tend to emphasize parental influences in the person's childhood.

A second aspect of lifestyle assessment is early recollections, which Adlerians use as a projective technique. Analyzing these much as they do dreams, therapists distill themes that indicate what directions of movement a client considers important vis-à-vis the tasks of life.

Therapists make this assessment an actively therapeutic process. They involve clients thoroughly in refining the final, written lifestyle formulation. They offer an interpretation and ask, "Does that seem to fit you?" Clients who say, "Yeah, that's me all right," take responsibility for the guidelines they follow in living. In reviewing the lifestyle assessment findings over the course of one- to three-hour-long therapy sessions, therapists teach that people form their fundamental beliefs about life, themselves, and other persons early in life as they strive to find a place of significance in their families of origin. Thereby therapists set the stage for future repeated references to cognitions and the purpose they serve for the client's felt sense of security and significance.

Adlerian therapists rely largely on interpretations to promote insight. Insight implies that a person grasps some bit of self-knowledge with the zest of an "aha" experience. This energizes behavioral change in the direction of social interest. Ideally an interpretation of a thought or action should illuminate its purpose and dynamic effects as well as the use the client makes of it. Purpose, movement, and use, three central Adlerian constructs, are thus the three criteria for a good interpretation. For example, an interpretation may sound something like this: "You use your tears as water power to arouse sympathy in others, to get them to excuse you from tasks you agreed to take on but at which you don't want to look inadequate. A skill you began using with your mother long ago you still use today even with your own grown children."

The Adlerian typically embeds such an interpretation in good-natured humor and in back-and-forth talk with the client. An interpretation like the above might arise in a group setting in which the therapist comments on a client's here-and-now behavior. One such group setting which Adlerians like involves multiple therapists with one client.

Long before the cognitive behavior therapies flourished in the late 1970s Adlerians directed their clients to do tasks outside of therapy that would change their beliefs, feelings, and habits. They often assigned roles for clients to play: *as if* they were successful, *as if* they were beautiful, or courageous, or happy, or whatever clients said they lacked.

Adler loved paradoxical tactics. He often prescribed that clients do more of some resistant action they were already doing, so that they could continue resisting him only by doing less of the prescribed action. For example, a depressed client who was hardly doing anything more than getting out of bed each day might ask desperately at the end of the first interview, "But Doctor, what can I do till next time?" Adler characteristically might answer, "Don't do anything you don't want to do."

Adler is reported to have said that neurosis, in a word, is vanity. Both he and Karen Horney repeatedly cited the godlike strivings behind the neurotic's vain search for glory. In this they echo biblical views of pride as the central human sin (Gen. 3:5; Isa. 14:14).

Adler saw no basic clash between his views and those of Christian theology. He wrote that individual psychology and religion have things in common, often in thinking, in feeling, in willing, but always with regard to the perfection of mankind (Adler, 1979, p. 281). This quotation comes out of thirty-seven pages of exchange between Adler and a Lutheran clergyman, Ernst Jahn. Adler agreed heartily with Christian teachings that we must love our neighbors as ourselves. His concept of social interest was the bedrock of his own humanistic rather than theistic faith.

References

Adler, A. *Superiority and social interest: A collection of later writings* (3rd ed.) (H. L. Ansbacher & R. W. Ansbacher, Eds.). New York: Norton, 1979.

Ellenberger, H. F. *The discovery of the unconscious.* New York: Basic Books, 1970.

Vaihinger, H. *The philosophy of "as if."* New York: Harcourt, Brace, 1924.

Additional Readings

Adler, A. *The practice and theory of individual psychology.* New York: Harcourt, Brace, 1924.

Mosak, H. H. Adlerian psychotherapy. In R. J. Corsini (Ed.), *Current psychotherapies* (2nd ed.). Itasca, Ill. Peacock Publishers, 1979.

13

Applied Behavior Analysis
Paul W. Clement

Applied behavior analysis has its historical origins in operant conditioning and the experimental analysis of behavior. Skinner introduced the basic concepts of operant conditioning in 1938 in *The Behavior of Organisms.* He insisted that observable behavior is the proper concern of psychology and that individual variability in behavior can be accounted for in terms of environmental variables without making reference to unobservables such as thoughts or feelings. He did not deny the presence of covert processes. He simply denied that they are necessary in giving an account of what controls behavior.

Fifteen years after publishing his first book on operant conditioning Skinner wrote *Science and Human Behavior.* In this work he tried to illustrate how to account for complex human processes in terms of environmental factors. Among the topics covered were self-control, thinking, the self, social behavior, government, religion, psychotherapy, education, and cultures. The book was a catalyst for many investigators and theorists. Skinner's approach to psychology was distinctive in at least two ways. First, he insisted on the possibility and importance of analyzing even the most complex behaviors in terms of their publicly observable controlling variables. Second, he insisted on studying individuals rather than data averaged across groups of subjects. This focus on the individual led to research designs and methodologies not used by most other psychological investigators. At least partially because the Skinnerian approach to research was different from that used by most other psychologists, journal editors were often not receptive to publishing articles by operant investigators. In 1957 this publishing problem was alleviated by the introduction of the *Journal of the Experimental Analysis of Behavior*. The title of this new journal communicated the essence of operant conditioning. Skinner's followers were committed to analyzing behaviors of individual animals or persons by systematically manipulating those variables which may have a controlling influence. Rather than first developing a comprehensive theory and then experimentally testing the validity of the theory, the operant investigators were committed to gather experimental data, determine trends in those data, and repeatedly replicate those trends before articulating laws or principles.

Another landmark in the development of the experimental analysis of behavior was the publication of Sidman's *Tactics of Scientific Research* in 1960. Prior to this there had been no comprehensive text explaining how to do intensive experimental studies on individual subjects. Sidman's book made the concepts and procedures of the experimental analysis of behavior available to a broader audience.

At the same time these methodological advances were occurring, other researchers were beginning to explore means of applying the procedures that had been developed with rats and pigeons to people and their problems in living. These early explorations were part of the beginning of a major movement within education, medicine, and psychology.

Behavior Modification and Behavior Therapy

Beginning in the 1950s an increasing number of researchers became interested in applying the experimental analysis of behavior to problems that occur in the "real world." For example, Bijou and Baer of the University of Washington analyzed the behavior of developmentally disabled persons as well as that of normal children. In the process of experimentally analyzing what variables controlled the individual's behavior, they discovered ways of helping the person behave more effectively or appropriately. Obviously persons responsible for the care of individuals with problems did not want simply to know what environmental variables control what behaviors. They wanted a psychological technology that could be used to strengthen appropriate behaviors and to weaken inappropriate behaviors. They wanted methods for changing behavior. They were interested in behavior modification.

Other investigators began in the 1950s to explore how to apply findings and procedures discovered in learning laboratories to alleviate the kinds of problems faced by clinical psychologists and psychiatrists. Drs. A. Lazarus and Wolpe were two such persons. They began their clinical research in South Africa and both eventually came to the United States, where they continued their clinical research and writing. They too were interested in focusing on observable behavior. Since they were psychotherapists, they were responsible for treating their patients. As clinicians they had a natural interest in therapy. A combination of these two concepts produced behavior therapy.

Although early behavior therapists such as Lazarus and Wolpe seemed to emphasize the concepts of theorists such as Hull and Pavlov more than those of Skinner, there was no fundamental incompatibility in the approaches of the behavior modifiers and the behavior therapists. Behavior modifiers tended to be persons who had come out of operant conditioning laboratories. Behavior therapists tended to be persons who had trained and worked in mental health settings and then turned to findings from laboratory research for help in treating their patients more effectively.

Most contemporary behaviorally oriented psychological practitioners treat behavior modification and behavior therapy as synonyms. Whether they are talking about modification or therapy, the emphasis is placed on interventions and their outcome. In contrast, applied behavior analysis places the emphasis on analyzing what environmental variables control a given behavior rather than focusing primarily on outcome.

Strategies for Analyzing Behavior Change

Behavior analysts have developed a large number of strategies for evaluating the effects of environmental variables on individual subjects. The strategies are usually referred to as single-subject, $N = 1$, or intensive experimental designs. Hersen and Barlow (1975) have provided comprehensive descriptions and evaluations of most of these designs.

Perhaps the best known single-subject strategy is the ABAB design.

Each letter represents a treatment phase, with A usually indicating baseline or nontreatment conditions and B indicating treatment conditions. Each phase lasts a number of days, weeks, or sometimes months. The investigator records the subject's behavior throughout each phase. Normally at least five to ten observations are made within each phase. Following the initial baseline phase the investigator introduces a treatment for a period of time equal to the first baseline period. Assuming the treated behavior changes during intervention, the next step is to restore the original baseline conditions. Most typically the target behavior worsens during this third phase. The final phase is a return to intervention. If the applied researcher can systematically increase and then decrease the target behavior as the conditions are changed from phase to phase, experimental control is demonstrated and a controlling variable is identified.

Another widely used single-subject design is the multiple baseline strategy. For example, a behavior analyst may begin by observing three behaviors (such as on task, raising hand before speaking, and disruptiveness) in the same subject without applying any treatment. Then the investigator may apply an intervention to on task while keeping the other two behaviors on baseline conditions. If only on task improves and the other two behaviors stay the same, there is evidence that the treatment controlled the behavior. Next the analyst can apply the treatment to both on task and raising hand but not to disruptiveness. If raising hand then improves but disruptiveness does not, additional evidence accrues regarding the impact of the treatment. Finally, the investigator can apply the intervention to disruptiveness. If disruptiveness then improves, still more evidence is obtained about the power of the intervention.

A basic concept underlying the preceding designs is replication. Treatment effects are replicated within a single subject. Then those effects are replicated across many subjects taken one at a time. When the same effects can be repeatedly demonstrated within and across individuals, experimental control is demonstrated.

Applications

Interest in adapting the concepts and procedures of the experimental analysis of behavior to practical problems grew rapidly during the 1960s. This interest led to a new journal in 1968, *The Journal of Applied Behavior Analysis*. Its purpose as stated in the initial issue was "primarily for the original publication of reports of experimental research involving applications of the analysis of behavior to problems of social importance."

Applied behavior analysts have spent much time determining what factors enhance or hinder academic performance. They have investigated variables that control classroom behavior—sustained attention, disruptiveness, handwriting, hyperactivity, learning disabilities, doing homework, tardiness, truancy, and underachieving. Another focus has been health-related behaviors, including drug addictions, alcoholism, asthma, headaches, smoking, auto accidents, high blood pressure, pain, cerebral palsy, adjusting to deafness, diabetes, exercise, nutrition, obesity, rumination in infants, self-injurious behavior, recovery from head injuries, and chronic vomiting. A third area of exploration has been social and relational skills, including altruism, assertiveness, isolate behavior, marriage, parenting, oppositional children, cooperative play, sexual behavior, sexual deviations, and sharing.

Behavior analysts have identified ways to affect a wide range of personal problems, including aggression, anxiety, articulation disorders, autistic behavior, snoring, child molesting, excessive crying, delusions, enuresis, encopresis, echolalia, gambling, gender identity problems, head banging, homosexuality, incontinence, insomnia, phobias, stuttering, stealing, throwing tantrums, thumbsucking, tics, and difficulties in toilet training.

Applied behavior analysis has also been used to identify ways of promoting athletic performance, energy conservation, creativity, driver safety, personal goal setting, happiness, job interviewing skills, prayer, room-cleaning behavior, self-care, swimming, time management, and work output.

Effectiveness

Applied behavior analysis is not a set of treatment techniques. It is an approach to analyzing the impact of any environmental variable that might influence behavior. Psychological treatments constitute one broad category of environmental variables. Applied behavior analysis has been useful in evaluating the effects of a wide range of treatments. Behavior analysts have clearly demonstrated the possibility and value of experimentally analyzing which interventions are most effective for a particular type of psychological problem.

Applied behavior analysis bridges the gap between traditional laboratory research and clinical practice by merging experimental research with practical problem solving. The development of single-subject experimental designs has made it possible to do controlled research with individual subjects in their own homes, schools, playgrounds, offices, athletic fields, or hospital rooms. This particular approach seems to have some effect on most problem areas to which applied psychologists have paid attention.

Current Issues and Future Directions

The first two decades of applied behavior analysis involved primarily demonstrations of how various interventions could influence the targeted behaviors. The demonstrations were usually made with a limited number of subjects, on a limited number of problems, in a limited number of settings, and over a relatively short period of time. In contrast, the next few decades should see greater attention paid to a few major issues. One issue concerns generalization—that is, how to get primary treatment effects to generalize to untreated behaviors, untreated settings, and into the future. A second issue concerns how to increase the potency of available interventions so that they will not make impaired persons simply better but will make the suffering individual perform at the same level as "normals." A third problem is how to promote the assimilation of those treatment procedures which are validated by experimental analyses into the practice of all psychologists, psychiatrists, and other psychological practitioners regardless of their theoretical orientations. A final major problem is how to get society at large to adopt the approaches and programs which behavior analysts have demonstrated to have social value.

References

Hersen, M., & Barlow, D. H. *Single case experimental designs*. New York: Pergamon Press, 1975.

Sidman, M. *Tactics of scientific research*. New York: Basic Books, 1960.

Skinner, B. F. *The behavior of organisms*. New York: Appleton-Century, 1938.

Skinner, B. F. *Science and human behavior*. New York: Macmillan, 1953.

14

Assertiveness Training
Henry A. Virkler

The first systematic discussion of assertiveness training was by Salter in *Conditioned Reflex Therapy* (1949). Salter believed many psychological disorders were caused by excessive inhibition, and he prescribed assertive (his term was "excitatory") procedures as the treatment of choice.

For a variety of reasons Salter's views did not gain wide acceptance at that time, and it was not until the writings of Wolpe and A. Lazarus in the 1950s and 1960s that assertiveness training became accepted as a useful therapeutic technique. Since then several hundred articles, at least fifty books, and several assertiveness training inventories have been published. Assertiveness training has become widely accepted by both behavioral and humanistic clinicians as a useful adjunct to individual therapy.

Assertiveness can be defined as the ability to express disagreement, to defend oneself against unfair or inaccurate accusations, to be able to say "no" to unreasonable or inconvenient demands from others, and to ask for reasonable favors and help when these are needed. It also encompasses a number of friendship skills, including the ability to initiate, maintain, and terminate conversations, and to give and receive compliments comfortably. In all of these there is an emphasis on respecting the needs, feelings, and rights of the other person while expressing one's own.

Assertiveness, Passivity, and Aggression

Assertiveness can be differentiated from three other interpersonal styles: passivity, aggression, and passive-aggression. The passive life style is illustrated by the person who fails to stand up for his own thoughts, feelings, needs, or rights, or communicates these so ineffectively that others easily take advantage of him. People frequently adopt a passive life style because they fear they would be rejected if they were assertive. However, some Christians adopt this stance because they believe passivity is required by the biblical commands regarding humility and personal submission.

Aggressiveness is the opposite of passivity. While the passive person counts other people but not himself, the aggressive person counts himself without adequate regard for the rights or feelings of others. Aggressive people use physical or psychological intimidation in order to achieve their objectives. They often achieve their immediate goals, but repeated aggressiveness usually destroys any significant relationships they may have.

Passive-aggression, or indirect aggression, is an interpersonal style midway between passivity and aggression. Often the passive-aggressive person agrees to go along with something even though he does not want to, and then expresses his anger indirectly through silence, sarcasm, or cynicism. The recipient usually knows that *something* is wrong, but frequently is unaware of the issue that is actually causing the problem. Christians sometimes respond passively because they believe this is the biblical thing to do; but as their needs are repeatedly ignored, their frustrations build and they become passive-aggressive, often against their own wishes.

Training Process and Objectives

The process of assertiveness training is highly variable. Some people learn assertiveness in the context of individual therapy; others attend an assertiveness training group. Groups generally meet once or twice a week for three to twelve sessions. Topics covered usually include several of the following:

1. a theoretical understanding of assertiveness, passivity, aggressiveness, and passive-aggressiveness.
2. individual analysis of each person's typical mode of responding, either through self-analysis or one of the assertiveness inventories.
3. helping people identify the personal assumptions (often unconscious or preconscious) that cause them to respond passively, aggressively, or passive-aggressively.
4. modeling assertive interactions.
5. role playing assertive responses with feedback from the instructor and group.

Even as the format for assertiveness training is highly variable, so also are the skills taught in any given assertiveness group or book. Most assertive skills presently taught would fit into one of the following five categories: conversational skills, nonverbal assertive skills, methods for making initial assertive statements, methods for deflecting those who try to detour persons from following through on their initial assertive statements, and types of workable compromises.

Conversational skills include those behavioral skills needed to initiate, maintain, and close a conversation comfortably. They also include learning to give and receive compliments graciously.

Nonverbal assertive skills include learning to use eye contact, facial expressions, body posture, gestures, timing, voice tone, inflection, and volume to increase the probability that a person's message will be "heard" and acted on. Nonassertive people often invite rejection of their requests because of timid nonverbal behavior.

There are a number of models for making initial assertive statements, many of which use some combination of three components: affirmation, assertion, and action. The affirmation component includes some way of affirming the person, such as "I've appreciated the effort you've been making to clean your room recently." The assertion component specifies the problem behavior and indicates how the speaker feels when the problem behavior occurs. It avoids name calling or attacks on the other person's personality. Thus, instead of saying, "You're a slob!" or "You treat me as if I were your maid!" the individual would be coached to say, "There's one thing that still bothers me. After you finish showering you leave wet towels and dirty clothes all over the bathroom floor." The action component usually prescribes the specific action the person would like to have occur. This may involve an invitation to a talk about the issue or a proposal of specific behavioral change. If it specifies an action, the speaker may include a positive consequence (reward) if the person performs the requested behavior or a negative consequence if he does not.

Whenever a previously nonassertive person attempts to be assertive, it is common for someone in his environment to try to detour him back into his previous nonassertive style. These detouring attempts occur in various ways, such as put-off detours ("Not now"), distracting detours (picking up on some incidental part of the assertive statement and shifting the focus to that area), and blaming detours (blaming the speaker or someone else for one's behavior). In order to follow through on an initial assertive statement, people need to be taught how to evaluate such responses and how to deflect those detours that are purely manipulative.

A final set of skills included in some assertiveness training classes or books might be labeled workable compromises. Workable compromises are used if, after each person has expressed his or her thoughts and goals, the goals are dissimilar. Workable compromises include finding an alternative that includes both persons' wishes, developing a quid pro quo (this for that) contract, taking turns deciding, mutually agreeing to temporarily separate in order to accomplish both persons' goals, letting an involved third party decide, and positive yielding (yielding to the other person's wishes out of love or consideration).

Evaluation

There appears to be both a biblical basis for assertiveness and some biblical criticism of assertiveness. For example, Matthew 18:15–17 seems to recommend assertively attempting to restore broken relationships rather than allowing frustration to remain unspoken and build into resentments. "Speaking the truth in love" (Eph. 4:15) suggests a balance that is neither passive nor aggressive. Perhaps the strongest passage endorsing assertiveness is Ephesians 4:26–32, which says; "In your anger do not sin [don't be aggressive]. Do not let the sun go down while you are still angry [don't be passive]." Verse 31 then goes on to list the entire range of passive-aggressive emotions that are likely to result if persons fail to deal with their anger, and says that Christians are to put away all of these feelings. In addition, Proverbs contains indictments against angry (aggressive) behavior, and the New Testament clearly says that resentment and unforgiveness (the hallmark of the passive-aggressive person) are not to be part of the believer's life (Matt. 6:12–15; Mark 11:25; Eph. 4:32).

However, wholesale adoption of assertiveness is not appropriate for the Christian. The primary goal for the non-Christian is self-actualization; the Christian's primary goal is building God's kingdom in the hearts of people. Therefore the Christian may sometimes choose to suspend expression of his own needs or desires in order to be a testimony to the non-Christian (Matt. 5:38–48) or to build up a fellow believer (Rom. 14:1–21). Secondly, assertiveness often helps one become only a more polite narcissist. The biblical message is that we are to strive to become as concerned about the needs of others as we are about ourselves (Phil. 2:3–8). Finally, assertiveness rarely encourages people to examine their motives before being assertive. James 3:13–4:4 teaches that often our frustrations arise because we have selfish, self-centered motives. In these cases the biblical answer is not assertiveness but examination and modification of those motives.

Reference

Salter, A. *Conditioned reflex therapy.* New York: Creative Age Press, 1949.

Additional Readings

Bower, S. A., & Bower, G. H. *Asserting yourself.* Reading, Mass.: Addison-Wesley, 1976.

Faul, J., & Augsburger, D. W. *Beyond assertiveness.* Waco, Tex.: Calibre Books, 1980.

15

Aversion Therapy
Rodger K. Bufford

This therapy consists of a number of techniques utilizing a variety of stimuli. Common features include the use of unpleasant stimuli and the goal of weakening or eliminating undesirable behaviors.

There are two major groups of aversion procedures. First are punishment procedures, in which the frequency of a behavior is reduced directly through contingent presentation or removal of a stimulus. Second are aversive counterconditioning procedures, in which the undesirable response is changed indirectly through altering the functions of the discriminative and reinforcing stimuli. In practice this distinction is somewhat blurred, since most aversion procedures have both punishing and stimulus-altering effects.

Contingent Punishment

Although Skinner and others argue that punishment is ineffective and has undesirable side effects, there is a growing consensus that it is highly effective and that its side effects are beneficial rather than harmful. Punishment by electric shock has proven effective with excessive vomiting, self-mutilation, dangerous climbing, and sexual behavior such as transvestism and fetishism (Rimm & Masters, 1974).

Response cost contingency is another commonly employed punishment technique. This procedure involves withdrawing material reinforcers contingent on the occurrence of some undesirable behavior. Response cost procedures are effective in reducing verbal and physical aggression, stuttering, and obesity. Their effects are quite durable, and most investigators report few undesirable effects. One potential problem is incurring a debt such as might occur when monetary fines excced income; debt seems to reduce effectiveness of response cost.

Aversive Counterconditioning

In counterconditioning the discriminative and reinforcing stimuli that maintain the problem behavior are presented to the person and an unpleasant stimulus is presented simultaneously, so that discriminative and reinforcing stimuli acquire aversive properties through association.

Two basic forms of aversive counterconditioning are escape and avoidance training. Often escape training is used initially, then modified into avoidance training. A third form of aversion training involves presenting the unpleasant stimulus without permitting escape or avoidance.

In escape training the target stimulus is presented, then an unpleasant stimulus such as electric shock occurs. After brief exposure to the two stimuli the individual terminates the stimuli by making some specified response. For example, a transvestite is given an article of women's clothing to put on, then administered electric shock. When the clothing is removed, the shock is terminated.

In avoidance training the individual is presented with the target stimulus. If an avoidance response is made quickly enough, the unpleasant stimulus may be avoided entirely. Typically, the response is one in which the target stimulus is removed. In the above example, removing the article of clothing during the warning stimulus prevents receiving shock. The advantage of the avoidance procedure is that the client learns to be anxious in the presence of the target stimulus (women's clothing) and is negatively reinforced for actively avoiding it.

Covert sensitization is a form of aversive counterconditioning in which the client imagines an unpleasant event following the undesired behavior rather than actually experiencing aversive stimulation. For example, he imagines taking a large bite of hot fudge sundae topped with whipped cream and nuts, then imagines himself grossly fat, unable to fit into his clothes, and socially ostracized. In the avoidance phase he imagines becoming increasingly anxious as he approaches the ice cream shop. He then imagines turning away and experiencing immediate relief.

Stimuli used in aversion include drugs, electric shock, aversive imagery, and response cost. The ideal stimulus is one that permits sudden onset, prompt termination, controlled intensity, and rapid recovery so that repeated trials may be administered in a brief time. Electric shock is readily controlled in these ways but drugs are not. Drug administration also requires medical personnel, sometimes hospitalization, and is medically contraindicated for many individuals. It also may have side effects that impair conditioning. Shock is widely applicable except for persons with heart conditions. For these reasons shock has replaced drugs as the principal aversion technique.

Aversive counterconditioning has been found to be quite effective with transvestism and fetishism. Results with homosexuality are more modest; they are better for homosexuals voluntarily seeking treatment and for those with prior heterosexual experience. Although drugs have sometimes yielded promising results, shock is used almost exclusively with sexual behaviors.

Drug aversion continues to be used for alcohol abuse. Initially it is successful, but as time passes, an increasing percentage of clients resume drinking. Booster treatments reduce this frequency.

Research studies of covert sensitization have unfortunately produced disappointing results. Thus cognitive theorists such as Meichenbaum (1974) currently prefer stress inoculation.

Ethical Issues

Guidelines for aversion emphasize informed consent and minimal exposure to painful stimuli. Persons voluntarily seeking treatment respond better than those sent by the courts or family members. For both these reasons, use of aversion on reluctant patients is questionable (Bufford, 1977). Practically, the individual will avoid treatment if the experience is sufficiently unpleasant. Aversion to the target stimulus or elimination of the problem behavior must thus be accomplished without causing aversion to the treatment process.

Research evidence indicates that problem behaviors are most effectively eliminated when constructive behavioral alternatives are developed simultaneously. This raises two concerns. First, too often aversion techniques are used without establishing suitable alternate behaviors. Second, problems arise in selecting alternatives, especially for sexual deviances such as homosexuality, voyeurism, and transvestism. From a Christian perspective heterosexual activity outside of marriage is unacceptable. Alternate sexual behaviors which are morally acceptable are, then, often difficult to identify. The biblical concept of love suggests a direction for consideration. Learning to experience and express love, especially God's love, may be the alternative to the deviant sexual behavior. For those whose sexual behavior is motivated by seeking interpersonal closeness the alternative might be learning to experience the love of others. For those primarily motivated by desire for sexual gratification the alternative might be helping them learn how to express love in more acceptable ways.

Theoretical Issues

Covert sensitization is appealing for both theoretical and practical reasons (see Lazarus, 1976). However, lack of empirical evidence of treatment effectiveness raises doubt about the effectiveness of aversive imagery, and may suggest some practical limitations to the cognitive-behavioral approach.

There is considerable evidence that an aversion procedure combined with a specific alternative response works better than either procedure alone. Interestingly, Adams (1970) notes that a number of biblical teachings are consistent with the idea of replacing responses rather than simply eliminating them.

A promising suggestion by Lazarus is that it is important to match modalities of the aversive stimulus and the stimulus controlling the problem response. Thus, use of a whiff of ammonia might prove more effective than shock in controlling obesity and alcohol abuse because of the important role of taste and smell in these responses.

Finally, avoidance procedures are generally preferable to escape or unavoidable aversion procedures since avoidance is highly resistant to extinction.

Summary

Aversion therapy uses contingent punishment, aversive counter-conditioning, and covert sensitization to eliminate undesired behaviors. Research indicates contingent punishment and aversive counterconditioning are effective, but casts doubt on covert sensitization. Aversion procedures are generally more successful when coupled with procedures for establishing a desirable alternative behavior.

Electric shock therapy is now the preferred aversion therapy approach for a number of practical reasons, although theoretical considerations suggest that matching the aversive stimulus to the target behavior may be more effective.

References

Adams, J. E. *Competent to counsel.* Philadelphia: Presbyterian and Reformed Publishing, 1970.

Bufford, R. K. Ethics for the mass application of behavior control. In C. W. Ellison (Ed.), *Modifying man.* Washington, D.C.: University Press of America, 1977.

Lazarus, A. A. (Ed.). *Multimodal behavior therapy.* New York: Springer, 1976.

Meichenbaum, D. *Cognitive-behavior modification.* Morristown, N.J.: General Learning Press, 1974.

Rimm, D. C., & Masters, J. C. *Behavior therapy.* New York: Academic Press, 1974.

16

Behavior Therapy
Stanton L. Jones

This term is typically applied to an exceptionally broad group of approaches to enhancing human welfare. The terms *behavior therapy* and *behavior modification* are increasingly regarded as synonymous. For simplicity, only the former term will be used here.

History

The rise of behaviorism in the first half of the twentieth century set the stage for an application of this perspective to the clinical practice of psychology and psychiatry. The philosophy of behaviorism provided a view of persons as exclusively physical beings who necessarily acted in accordance with universal behavioral laws and a view of science which eschewed all knowledge not empirically verifiable. Applications of operationistic, quantitative, experimental scientific methods in psychology produced what were seen as remarkable advances in scientific knowledge about animal and human behavior.

The typical practices of clinical psychology and psychiatry at this time were also influential in the rise of behavior therapy because of their disparity with academic psychology. Kazdin (1982) called the predominant model at this time the "intrapsychic disease" approach. This approach tends to look for psychological disease processes underlying behavioral symptoms. Further, this view encourages the search for symptom syndromes (or clusters), implying a common underlying cause for each syndrome. Treatment approaches based on these conceptions (e.g., psychoanalysis) were preeminent during this period.

Kazdin (1982) has documented that many treatment methods essentially behavioral in practice had been used before 1900. For example, Lancaster in the early 1800s developed and used what was essentially a token economy system for the classroom, and Brissaud developed a precursor to systematic desensitization in the 1890s. Use of expressly behavioral methods of treatment began to increase steadily in the first half of the 1900s. Watson, Jones, and others worked at conditioning and deconditioning fear. The Russian psychologist Kantorovich and Americans Voegtlin and Lemere used aversive shock conditioning to treat alcoholics. In his *Conditioned Reflex Therapy* (1949) Salter proposed conceptualizations of and treatment methods for abnormal behavior which were based primarily on Pavlovian conditioning models of habit.

In 1952 Eysenck published his famous article in which he argued that there was no convincing evidence that psychotherapy as commonly practiced produced any benefits for clients above that which would normally accrue to them without formal treatment. This article scandalized the professional community and became a rallying point for the search for more effective (behavioral) methods for treating maladjustment.

Major developments began to emerge on three continents in the 1950s. In South Africa, Wolpe began to report his pioneering development of systematic desensitization for the treatment of anxiety-based disorders. In Britain, Eysenck, Rachman, and others at Maudsley Hospital in London were vigorous proponents of behavioral treatment methods similar to Wolpe's. In the United States an increasing number of applications of operant methods were reported. Ayllon, Lindsley, and Skinner worked with psychotic inpatients, and Bijou, Staats, and Ferster did pioneering work with disturbed children.

The behavior therapy movement has continued to grow. The character of the movement has evolved remarkably with its growth. The publication of Bandura's influential *Principles of Behavior Modification* (1969) marked an increased openness to the consideration of mediational variables (discussed below) and highlighted the diversity of views that might be called behavioral. Lindsley and Skinner in the United States and Lazarus in South Africa were the first to use the term *behavior therapy* in the 1950s. The first behavior therapy journal began publication in 1963; now over fifteen journals are devoted to that one topic and many others publish a substantial number of behavioral articles. A large number of books on the approach have been published. Most graduate schools of psychology teach specialized courses in the practice of behavior therapy, and several major national and international associations exist for the promotion of behavior therapy, the largest of which is the Association for the Advancement of Behavior Therapy. Given the relatively recent development, it is remarkable that Smith (1982) showed that behavioral and cognitive-behavioral orientations are together the most frequent orientation of practicing psychologists who identify themselves as adhering to a specific approach.

Distinctives

Erwin (1978) struggled to define behavior therapy and came to the surprising but compelling conclusion that "no such definition is possible because behavior therapies do not share a set of illuminating defining properties" (p. 38). He proposed rather that there is a group of characteristics that tend to be associated with what we call behavior therapy approaches. The more of these characteristics an approach exhibits, and the more clearly they characterize the approach, the more likely the approach is to be considered behavioral. The following list of characteristics is derived from Erwin (1978) and Agras, Kazdin, and Wilson (1979).

First, behavior therapy is fundamentally oriented toward the alleviation of human suffering and the promotion of human growth. Second, it is a psychological rather than biological form of intervention. Third, it is usually used to modify problem behaviors directly rather than to modify hypothesized psychological disorders. For example, the behavior therapist would attempt to modify a person's unassertive behavior directly rather than exploring a hypothesized inferiority complex. Fourth, behavior therapy emphasizes current determinants of behavior rather than historical antecedents. If a problem is shown to be clearly related to a series of childhood events, the behavior therapist would focus on how these events are still active in the person's life today rather than concentrating on retrospection. Fifth, behavior therapy can be used sequentially (i.e., different problems in the same person tend to be viewed as independent, thus allowing for different methods to be brought sequentially to bear on each problem). Sixth, assessment, problem conceptualization, and treatment are individualized. In behavior therapy diagnostic groupings are used at most for economy of communication; the behavior therapist tends to doubt that such categorizations are the best way to group disorders, questioning whether they represent real "species." Seventh, the therapist's role in relation to the client is that of behavior change consultant. Eighth, many behavior therapy techniques are closely related (at least on a metaphorical level) to classic learning theory research. Finally, behavior therapists are typically committed to an applied experimental science approach to clinical practice. Empirical confirmation of treatment effectiveness is emphasized and is the major criterion for judging the value of a technique.

Agras et al. (1979), noting that modern behavior therapy cannot be considered monolithic, differentiated four major perspectives on behavior therapy. The first they termed *applied behavior analysis*. This approach is most heavily influenced by Skinner's operant psychology. Its practitioners emphasize the alteration of the functional relationships between overt behaviors and their antecedents and consequences. Intensive analysis of individual cases is the major form of empirical investigation utilized.

The second school was labeled the *neobehavioristic mediational S-R model*. Typified by Eysenck, Wolpe, and Rachman, this perspective tends to emphasize classical conditioning processes (to which S-R refers) while also using operant methods. Neobehavioristic mediational refers to the willingness of its adherents (unlike the Skinnerians) to use hypothesized intervening psychological states in their conceptualizations (e.g., fear, anxiety). Their treatment techniques frequently assume the reality of mental events (e.g., systematic desensitization assumes that the person can really imagine a feared scene). These mental events are, however, viewed as being simply another type of causally determined behavior which operates according to the same laws of conditioning as all other forms of behavior.

The final two groups are dominant in contemporary behavior therapy. The third major group is the *social learning* group. Exemplified by Bandura and Mischel, this approach suggests that operant and classical conditioning processes occur primarily via cognitive mediation. Beliefs, thoughts, perceptions, and other cognitive processes are viewed as the major determinants of behavior. Modeling and other forms of vicarious learning (learning by indirect rather than direct experience) are emphasized. Humans are assumed to be capable of limited self-direction, in that people can exert some control over the environmental and cognitive determinants of behavior. The fourth major perspective is *cognitive-behavior therapy.* This perspective was inspired by Ellis's rational-emotive therapy. Mahoney, Meichenbaum, Beck, and others drew from Ellis the emphasis on cognitions as a major influence upon behavior, but attempted to develop more broadly applicable and less philosophically loaded methods for changing human cognition. The differences between these last two perspectives is primarily one of emphasis on thoughts and behavior, with this last group almost exclusively emphasizing the mediating cognitive variables that are frequently described as an "internal dialogue."

Practice of Behavior Therapy

In her or his relationship with the client the behavior therapist is primarily a consultant in behavior change who serves as a supporter and motivator in the process of change, as a resource in clarifying the problem and designing change strategies, and as a model of more functional behavior. Therapy usually begins with behavioral assessment, in which the attempt is made to understand the client's unique problems in light of their current psychological and environmental determinants. Treatment is carefully tailored to the results of the assessment process. Since client problems are frequently complex, treatment tends to be multifaceted.

The process of treatment varies with the specific orientation of the behavior therapist and the problems of the client. Applied behavior analysts are likely to use such techniques as material or social reinforcement, punishment, shaping, time-out, token economies, prompting, and contingency contracting. Applied behavior analysis seems to be most widely used with the retarded, children, and institutionalized populations. Neobehavioristic mediational S-R therapists utilize conditioning techniques such as systematic desensitization, flooding, covert sensitization, and aversive conditioning. The first two techniques are widely used with anxiety-based disorders (phobias, obsessive-compulsive disorders, impotence) whenever a stimulus for the anxiety can be identified. The latter two are used to create aversions to stimuli in order to decrease the occurrence of such problem behaviors as sexual deviations and drug or alcohol abuse.

Social learning therapists emphasize methods that utilize modeling and competency building—such as training in coping skills, social skills, assertiveness, and communication skills—to deal with social interaction difficulties, anxiety-based disorders, and depression. Self-control is also a focus in this model; it can be taught by teaching the skills of self-monitoring, self-evaluating, and self-consequating behavior. Cognitive-behavior therapists frequently use such exclusively cognitive methods as cognitive restructuring, problem solving, thought stopping, or covert sensitization. These cognitive-behavioral methods are used particularly in treating affective disorders (anxiety, depression, and anger), stress disorders, and pain; in children they are used to decrease impulsivity and increase academic skills.

There are few purists in any of these schools, and almost all the techniques listed for one group are used by practitioners in the other groups. The overall effectiveness of behavior therapy is difficult to judge. Some suggest that it is no better than other approaches. Reports suggest that it is extremely valuable in the treatment of specific anxiety disorders, behavior and cognitive disorders of childhood, interpersonal skill deficits, unipolar depression, sexual dysfunction, stress reactions, and schizophrenia (in tandem with pharmacotherapy). Lanyon and Lanyon (1978) provide a very readable introduction to the practice of behavior therapy.

Views of Human Nature

A major distinctive of a behavioral view of human nature is its emphasis on universal processes of human change, in contrast to other schools' emphasis on universal psychological structures, stages of development, or motivations. Because it is the "laws of learning" that are emphasized, there is greater readiness to appreciate the idiosyncratic nature of human life. Behavior therapists are less likely to emphasize commonalities of experience (e.g., Rogers's proposed tendency toward self-actualization) but rather to focus on the way in which learning can lead to the development of practically any pattern of human behavior imaginable, depending upon the person's learning history and biological potential. One implication of this is that behavior therapists tend not to employ a standard diagnostic nomenclature, which is judged to be rooted more in theory than reality.

Secondly, the behavioral view of humankind (except perhaps for the applied behavior analysis group) is interactional in nature; that is, it gives serious consideration to both personal and environmental (physical and social) determinants of human behavior. To the behavior therapist dynamic views of personality underemphasize the pervasive effect which external events have upon persons. They believe instead that behavior originates primarily from intrapsychic causes.

In the most general terms the behavior therapist views people in terms of their "person variables" (Mischel, 1973), their biological heritage, and their environment. Person variables (also termed organismic variables or learning history) include the person's acquired response capacities, expectancies, and the myriad of other cognitive variables. Biological variables include physical assets and deficits, physiologically based emotional responsiveness, and conditionability. Social and physical environmental variables must be considered at all levels, from the most immediate and specific (the parent reinforcing the noncompliant child's misbehavior with attention) to the most broad and indirect (e.g., culture and language). If the pressure cooker is a metaphor for understanding human behavior from a psychoanalytic perspective, then we might say that behavior therapists would use the computer as a metaphor for understanding the human person. Input (environmental variables) is processed through the software (person variables), which is built on the existing hardware (biological variables) to produce the behavioral output.

Most behavior therapists would argue that humans are basically hedonistic in nature. Behavior therapy, therefore, is maximally responsive to requests to end or decrease suffering and to promote growth toward greater pleasure and enjoyment of life. Behavior therapists have no a priori model of optimal human functioning toward which clients are led. On one hand, this allows them greater flexibility in attending to client complaints, since they have no prior commitments to a concrete definition of normality. On the other hand, this inevitably leads behavior therapy to be pathology oriented, especially in its research literature, because people typically come for treatment wanting relief from a specific problem or problem complex.

Conclusion

Erwin (1978) has suggested that behavior therapy neither needs nor is consistent with the philosophical behaviorism that was part of its ancestry. Many Christians reject behavior therapy on philosophical bases (i.e., the unacceptability of materialism, determinism, ethical relativism) that have little impact on its practice and effectiveness. The behavioral emphasis on the potential for beneficial change of one's thoughts and actions is consistent with a scriptural emphasis on similar changes as critical to sanctification (Rom. 12:1–2; Eph. 4:20–32). Biblical injunctions to avoid bad company (1 Cor. 15:33) and to build the community of believers (1 Thess. 5:11–22) show an environmental as well as intrapersonal focus of Christian faith. Habit is a theme of human life in the Scriptures (Heb. 5:13–14). On the negative side, the ever-present reductionism of behavioral analysis can undermine our understanding of such critical human capacities as love and will, as when the former is described in terms of reinforcement history and the latter as the possession of self-management skills. More fundamentally, the Scriptures suggest that both behavior and thoughts issue out of the heart, which is that central part of human life allied to or in rebellion against the Lord God. For the behavior therapist, thoughts and actions are purely functional; there is no human capacity akin to the biblical doctrine of heart. Overall, the behavior therapies warrant serious study by the Christian counselor.

References

Agras, W. S., Kazdin, A. E., & Wilson, G. T. *Behavior therapy: Toward an applied clinical science.* San Francisco: W. H. Freeman, 1979.

Erwin, E. *Behavior therapy: Scientific, philosophical, and moral foundations.* New York: Cambridge University Press, 1978.

Eysenck, H. J. The effects of psychotherapy: An evaluation. *Journal of Consulting and Clinical Psychology,* 1952, *16,* 319–324.

Kazdin, A. E. History of behavior modification. In A. S. Bellack, M. Hersen, & A. E. Kazdin (Eds.), *International handbook of behavior modification.* New York: Plenum, 1982.

Lanyon, R. I., & Lanyon, B. P. *Behavior therapy: A clinical introduction.* Reading, Mass.: Addison-Wesley, 1978.

Mischel, W. Toward a cognitive social learning reconceptualization of human personality. *Psychological Review,* 1973, *80,* 252–283.

Smith, D. Trends in counseling and psychotherapy. *American Psychologist,* 1982, *37,* 802–809.

17

Biblical Counseling
Rod Wilson

Developed by Lawrence J. Crabb, biblical counseling is an attempt at a biblically based theory of personality, psychopathology, and counseling. It received its first presentation in *Basic Principles of Biblical Counseling* (1975), where Crabb argued that man has two basic needs: significance and security. Difficulties stem from sinful thinking concerning how these needs can be met. Concurrently counseling focuses on the restructuring of these cognitive patterns. *Effective Biblical Counseling* (1977) develops the philosophical base of Crabb's approach, with particular emphasis on the integration of psychology and theology as well as a delineation of the etiology of personal problems. His most recent book, *The Marriage Builder* (1982), applies his model to the marriage relationship.

Crabb argues that, prior to the fall, man was loved and accepted (security) and regarded himself as worthwhile (significance). However, when man sinned and separated himself from God, his capacity for love was no longer filled and a need for security was produced. Similarly Adam lost his worth in terms of his relationship with God, and a need for significance was created. In his natural state, then, man develops beliefs about how his needs for security and significance can be met, sets goals in light of those beliefs, and lives accordingly. Operating constantly from deficit motivation the natural man strives to gain something that will meet his personal needs. The Christian, in contrast, does not operate from a deficit but from fullness, since his needs for significance and security are completely met in a relationship with Jesus Christ.

Crabb's understanding of the image of God in man is that we are personal beings who have a cognitive, volitional, and emotional component. Although the fall has distanced man from God, the image has not been lost completely. According to Crabb, man still has the capacity to think, choose, and feel. From this he concludes that true biblical counseling must be carried out with a recognition that man is composed of these various facets. This is presented in contrast to typical counseling models that tend to stress one or two aspects to the exclusion of the others.

Based on the foundation that man is created in the image of God, Crabb's model of counseling purports to take that into account. Because we are personal beings and have a need for security and significance, our natural tendency is to develop beliefs about how these needs can be met. When the belief has been established, behavior will be engaged in that will presumably fulfill this belief. So the wife who believes her security depends on her husband's love will always be trying to win his love. When his love diminishes, she will become frustrated because her need for security is not being met.

When this woman comes for counseling she will probably express feelings of resentment and reactive behaviors such as withdrawal of affection or angry outbursts. Crabb suggests that some Christian counselors would intervene at this level and ask her to confess her sinful response and change her behavior toward her husband. In contrast he argues that while clients tend initially to describe feelings and behavior, it is the task of the counselor to move to the identification of wrong thinking patterns. Why does this woman want her husband's unchanging affection? She believes that it will meet her need for security and its loss is deeply personal. The counseling process then moves from the identification of negative feelings and behavior to the identification of wrong thinking. Ultimately Crabb would contend that wrong thinking is anything that denies the fact that God is sufficient for meeting one's personal needs of security and significance.

After this three-step diagnostic stage, help occurs by promoting right thinking, planning right behavior, and identifying satisfying feelings. The crux of this lies in the changing of the assumptions.

The first step is the identification of their origin. The belief has been developed in the person's history and needs to be understood from that perspective. Also the counselor needs to help the client work through the feelings surrounding the cognitive assumptions and encourage him as he goes through the painful process of change. The real work of counseling, however, occurs when new cognitions or beliefs replace old ones. Crabb encourages clients to write out biblical assumptions on 3×5 cards and behave in accord with them. To the criticism that this may be hypocritical Crabb replies that behavior is not judged on the basis of whether our feelings are in accord with it but on the basis of whether it is biblical or not.

Crabb's overall counseling approach is based on an integration perspective that he has called "spoiling the Egyptians." Referring to the experience of the children of Israel in Exodus 12, he argues that the Christian can "spoil" (take from) the world (i.e. secular psychology) provided the principles are carefully screened through Scripture. In light of this Crabb freely acknowledges the influence of Ellis (importance of thinking), Mowrer (stress on responsibility), Frankl (meaning in life), Sullivan (social side of man), and Skinner (environmental influence) on his own thinking. Of these Ellis's contribution is clearly the most influential.

In sum, Crabb argues that the core of all psychopathology is our attempt to meet our needs independently of God, an attempt that is based on a satanically inspired belief (Crabb, 1981a p. 419). In articulating this approach Crabb seeks to be loyal to Scripture as it pertains to the nature of people, problems, and solutions. For this he is to be commended. However, two potential limitations may be noted.

Crabb (1981b) argues that many Christian counselors aspire to a "two-book view" of revelation and do not give the Scriptures the place they deserve. He suggests that ultimately this approach may weaken our view of the Bible and lead to a questioning of its authority. Three responses to this issue (Breshears & Larzelere, 1981; Ellens, 1981; Guy, 1982) raised questions about Crabb's view of Scripture, particularly in terms of its intent, and his lack of separation between biblical and theological inerrancy. This issue needs to be addressed in more detail, especially in light of the fact that Crabb's system purports to have a biblical base.

Another area of concern relates to the biblical substantiation for the basic security and significance needs. Crabb cites Paul's response to God's love in Romans 8 as an illustration of our need for security. Abraham's desire to find a city (Heb. 11:8–10) is used as an example of our need for significance. At a descriptive level these passages show one man who is responding to God's love and another who is responding to God's direction. The imputing of need, and the implicit message that these are the two basic needs do not appear to be well defended biblically. On top of that, the fact that these needs can be met only in Christ, and not in people, appears to deny the horizontal dimension of Christianity. While Crabb does argue that spouses may make us feel significant and secure, he adds that only Christ meets our needs in this area. Again theological backing for the distinction between being secure in Christ and feeling secure with others is not given.

References

Breshears, G., & Larzelere, R. E. The authority of Scripture and the unity of revelation. *Journal of Psychology and Theology*, 1981, *9*, 312–317.

Crabb, L. J. *Basic principles of biblical counseling*. Grand Rapids: Zondervan, 1975.

Crabb, L. J. *Effective biblical counseling*. Grand Rapids: Zondervan, 1977.

Crabb, L. J. Biblical counseling: A basic view. In J. R. Fleck & J. D. Carter (Eds.), *Psychology and Christianity: Integrative readings*. Nashville: Abingdon, 1981. (a)

Crabb, L. J. Biblical authority and Christian psychology. *Journal of Psychology and Theology*, 1983, *9*, 305–311. (b)

Crabb, L. J. *The marriage builder: A blueprint for couples and counselors*. Grand Rapids: Zondervan, 1982.

Ellens, J. H. Biblical authority and Christian psychology II. *Journal of Psychology and Theology*, 1981, *9*, 318–325.

Guy, J. D. Affirming diversity in the task of integration: A response to "Biblical authority and Christian psychology." *Journal of Psychology and Theology*, 1982, *10*, 35–39.

18

Bibliotherapy
Stanton L. Jones

Bibliotherapy refers to the use of literary materials as a treatment technique aimed at the reparation of a psychological disorder or the inducement of change toward growth. Discussions and research in this area almost always refer only to printed material (books, stories), but in this revolutionary age of media diversification it is quite likely that a discussion of books alone is too limited. There are innovative programs involving theater, movies, television, and other single or combined media presentations currently being used as adjuncts to or substitutes for therapy. These more innovative programs have not been explored thoroughly in the literature. Thus, bibliotherapy as the use of printed matter alone will be discussed here, but this discussion should hold for other forms of media as well.

Bibliotherapy has a long history. Sclabassi (1980) notes that the concept of growth through reading is an ancient one. Certainly the great moral writings of antiquity (e.g., the proverbs of the Hebrews, the ethical handbooks of the Greek Stoics) represent an attempt to codify rules for life conducive to enhancement of human welfare.

The concept of bibliotherapy as understood today dates back to the emergence of the mental health professions. Benjamin Rush in the early 1800s and Alfred Adler in the early 1900s were pioneers in the use of bibliotherapeutic methods.

There are two major approaches to bibliotherapy, the didactic and the catalytic, which can respectively be identified with more cognitive and behavioral approaches to therapy versus dynamic and humanistic approaches. The didactic approach attempts to facilitate change by providing information helpful in analyzing a problem being faced, formulating new approaches to problem resolution, and motivating the reader to implement and evaluate change procedures. Glasgow and Rosen (1979) have reviewed the self-help behavior therapy manuals that are but one subgroup of literature in this area. These works are generally intended to be used by the reader without professional help, but many behavior therapists use them on an adjunct basis during the process of behavior therapy. A survey of the self-help section of any bookstore reveals an incredible array of such materials. Didactic books have been developed in the areas of fear reduction, weight reduction, smoking cessation, enhancement of assertive responding and social skill, parenting and child management, physical fitness, sexual dysfunction, marital enrichment, depression, and problem drinking, among others. Unfortunately, writers of these works frequently do not document the effectiveness of their programs. Potential problems with such self-help works include extravagant claims for effectiveness, high noncompliance rates with the suggested techniques (one empirical study of such a manual failed to find a single subject who fully completed the recommended self-treatment procedure), and the negative impact which the reader's "failure" after following an "expert's" program might have on future commitment to and expectations for psychotherapy.

Catalytic bibliotherapy is substantially different, involving the use primarily of imaginative literature for the purpose of facilitating identification, catharsis, and insight on the part of the client (Sclabassi, 1980; Schrank & Engels, 1981). Identification with book or story characters can reduce the client's sense of isolation from others due to perceived uniqueness of his or her problems and can pave the way for catharsis. Catharsis, or therapeutic release of affect, can occur as the reader vicariously shares the powerful experiences of the literary characters. Finally, insight occurs as parallels between the reader and story characters are explored. There are few specific guidelines for method of presentation in this area, and there are no guidelines for choice of materials. Catalytic bibliotherapy has been used with children and adults, individually or in groups, as an elective adjunct to therapy and as a mainstay of the therapeutic content. Schrank and Engels (1981) reviewed the research in this area and concluded that positive recommendations for bibliotherapy far exceed conclusive demonstrations of its merit. But they feel that "catalytic bibliotherapy appears effective for developing assertiveness, attitude change, helper effectiveness, self-development, and therapeutic gains" (p. 145).

Atwater and Smith (1982) recently surveyed Christian psychologists, documenting their wide usage of bibliotherapeutic materials and providing an annotated bibliography of commonly used resources. Bibliotherapy is a potentially useful but underdeveloped approach to enhancing human growth.

References

Atwater, J. M., & Smith, D. Christian therapists' utilization of bibliotherapeutic resources. *Journal of Psychology and Theology*, 1982, *10*, 230–235.

Glasgow, R. E., & Rosen, G. M. Self-help behavior therapy manuals: Recent developments and clinical usage. *Clinical Behavior Therapy Review*, 1979, *1*(1), 1–20.

Schrank, F. A., & Engels, D. W. Bibliotherapy as a counseling adjunct: Research findings. *Personnel and Guidance Journal*, 1981, *60*(3), 143–147.

Sclabassi, S. H. Bibliotherapy. In R. Herink (Ed.), *The psychotherapy handbook*. New York: New American Library, 1980.

19

Bioenergetic Analysis
Clark E. Barshinger & Lojan E. LaRowe

Bioenergetic analysis is a form of psychotherapy founded by Alexander Lowen. Lowen was a student for many years of Wilhelm Reich, who was a contemporary of Sigmund Freud and the originator of body psychotherapy. Lowen continued the work of Reich in the analysis of bodily-muscular expressions of mental illness and in the development of techniques for releasing those tensions.

Bioenergetic Theory

In the theory of body psychotherapy it is believed that the person experiences the reality of the world primarily through the body (Lowen, 1975). The sense of individual identity stems from a feeling of contact with the body. To know who one is, an individual must be aware of what he or she feels. Without this awareness of bodily feeling and attitudes, a person becomes split into a disembodied spirit or mind and an increasingly inflexible, deadened body (Lowen, 1967).

The problem in mental health, according to body psychotherapy, is the tendency to repress or "implode" (i.e., to hold within and refuse to express) viscerally experienced feeling. The source of this repression of bodily experienced feelings is the growing child's desire to avoid the loss of love by conforming to what the child perceives to be the expectations of others. The child relies on his mind to figure out what is expected and then attempts to perform those behaviors that will ensure love. A result of this process is that the cerebral cortex struggles to gain control over the naturally experienced body emotion. The intelligence of the individual is funneled into ego, and the ego is increasingly split off from the needs and experiences of the body. This split is viewed as neurotic since mind (the cognitive functions) and body (the visceral feelings and responses) are one unitary process.

The result of long-term repression of bodily experience in favor of adaptation to the demands of society can be rigidification of the body. This is referred to as increasing muscular armor. Muscular armoring is accompanied by physical tension and the experience of deadness and isolation. Increasingly the cerebral cortex censors and controls as much of the experience of life as possible. Knowledge becomes increasingly intellectual, cut off from the inner depths of the person. Other personality characteristics include self-consciousness, self-doubt, competitiveness, conformity, striving and yet holding back, and frustration.

Control becomes the key in the life of such individuals. They are turned inward. Thoughts and fantasies replace feeling and action. Exaggerated mental activity substitutes for contact with the real world, and belief systems replace aliveness. Faith, hope, and love are increasingly superstitious, pietistic, legalistic, and/or authoritarian. Belief becomes objectified rather than experienced from within. Interpersonal relationships also suffer as other people become objects to be navigated around in life rather than persons to be intimately engaged. The rich inner life of emotions is squeezed to a trickle except for moments of sentimentally or vicariously experienced strong emotion such as through films, sports, and mass behavior. The individual relates more and more to his or her body as a machine to be used and pushed to its limits. The body is weighed, measured, and pushed to meet some idealized sense of proportion, rather than enjoyed for the feeling of aliveness and vitality for its own sake.

The healthy individual has the ability to adjust harmoniously to the demands of society while remaining open and responsive to needs, information, and experience coming from within one's own body (Lowen, 1970). Most individuals have trouble doing this. They lose touch with their inner experience. Bioenergetic analysis attempts to alleviate this alienation between ego and body and thereby assist individuals in their pursuit of faith and happiness. According to Lowen, faith comes from the heart, which is literally surrounded by flexible and nonrigid muscles. Thus, the pursuit of faith and happiness entails the releasing of energy throughout the body. The healthy individual experiences the freedom of thought and sensation that is rapidly and freely passed throughout the body without the resistance of chronically tight muscles inhibiting such an experience of vitalness.

Bioenergetic analysis also theorizes that different childhood developmental experiences result in different types of muscular armoring and thereby different personality or character types. Lowen devoted much attention to the analysis of and the therapeutic intervention with the different character types (Lowen, 1958). For example, very early life experience that is inadequate in nurturing love may result in what is called the oral character type. Such a person is characterized by feelings of deprivation, inner emptiness and despair, extreme fluctuations in mood, great dependency, and strong fear of loss of love objects. Another character type is the masochistic. The underlying quality of this person's life is the fear of self-assertiveness. Masochism is characterized by intense muscular tension, often resulting in muscle spasms and pain. Other character types include the hysterical, the schizoid, and the "rigid character structures" which include the phallic-narcissistic, the passive-feminine, and the compulsive. In each of these different character types childhood developmental issues differ, and the resulting muscular armoring, in both its intensity and location in the body, also differs. The different character types are treated therapeutically in often very different ways.

Bioenergetic Therapy

Therapy in bioenergetic analysis centers on increasing the internal unity of body and psyche in a context of safety, acceptance, and understanding. Body psychotherapy is a combination of physical exercises and more traditional verbal interactions. The physical exercises are aimed at stretching, relaxing, and opening the tensions in the body so that the deeper emotions and repressed memories of the individual can be reintegrated.

A safe environment is a key since the person in pain learned early that uncensored expression of feeling was fundamentally dangerous. Often the therapist will touch the patient in a nurturing way. At times he will encourage the patient to express some emotion strongly. This might take the form of pounding on a pillow with a tennis racket for the release of anger long denied expression. The expression of feeling in a physical and deeply honest verbal way begins the reintegrative process of allowing the ego and the body to once again communicate freely. To Lowen this is the beginning of faith and the emergence of the true self. Feelings are usually logical long before the intellect understands the rationality of the response. In other words, feelings may emerge that at first seem to be unjustified or irrational but which, upon closer examination and more information, become thoroughly understandable and logical.

One of the therapist's important functions in bioenergetic analysis is helping the patient to understand and accept the message of his feelings and body states. The final goal of body psychotherapy, then is a unitary, holistic response to life, where deep inner wells of being are free to be brought to bear on life. The heart is working in cooperation with the head and the head in cooperation with the heart. The individual is increasingly able to focus on life and its real problems rather than being self-absorbed.

Evaluation

One of the major strengths of bioenergetic analysis is its attempt to avoid the sterile and passive verbal reflections which have tended to characterize much traditional psychotherapy. The holistic goal of working with both body and mind often allows for a more vital sense of treatment and well-being. Body-orientated psychotherapies have proliferated recently. The popularity of these therapies could be argued to suggest that the inclusion of direct body movement and touch is experienced by the patient as more satisfying and releasing than traditional therapies which focus exclusively on verbal interchange.

One of the major criticisms of body psychotherapies is the tendency among some practitioners to be anti-intellectual. In such a case the client is often encouraged into emotional experiences and bodily movement without much sense of their purpose or meaning. The release of emotion in the therapy process is seen as an end in itself rather than a purposeful step in the unification of mind and body. Such an attitude can lead to the valuing of the expression of feelings regardless of the social context. The result is an insufficiently integrated and balanced individual. Such a person's credo is doing his or her own thing regardless of its impact on others.

Another criticism of body psychotherapy is that it often tends to create an unnecessary amount of confusion and disorientation in the patient. As the "de-armoring" process continues, there is a good deal of confusion and disorientation as the person attempts to get a new sense of who he or she really is. During this process it is important that a great deal of nurturance and support be given in order to provide the patient with a sense of trust and security.

Bioenergetic analysis and other body psychotherapies are fundamentally compatible with the teachings of Scripture. Throughout the history of Christianity there has been a tendency to disconnect the Christian faith from the body and to reduce the Christian message to abstract theology. A theology that flows only from a detached intellect is more likely to be a statement of the status quo than a compassionate, courageous spirituality. The Pharisees, for example, were condemned not for carnal sins of the flesh but for an egoistic perversion of the truth in which the letter rather than the heart of the law was worshiped. In the many scriptural references regarding the dangers of the flesh the reference is never to materiality and sensuousness as such, but to materialism and sensualism. In other words, it is not money and pleasure that the Bible condemns, but the lifting of these aspects of life to improper status within our lives. In short, the materialistic and sensualistic pursuit is fundamentally a *mental*, not a *material* process. It is the distortion occurring in hearts and minds that turns the body and its sensual pleasure from gifts of God to be enjoyed into sinful preoccupations.

Faith is the ability to surrender the more secure, predictable, and safe life of an ego-dominated existence in favor of an open responsiveness to the needs and desires of the true inner self. Faith and life become integrated because the person is integrated. Knowledge itself, Lowen reminds us, is a surface phenomenon and belongs to the ego, while truth flows through the whole being. We are advised in Ephesians 5 to know the love of God though it is beyond knowledge. Lowen postulates that knowledge becomes understanding when it is coupled with feeling. The Scriptures argue that the devil knows the truth and yet does not embrace it.

It is possible to argue that the problem of spirituality is knowing one's real needs. Most of us are unconsciously shaped to assume that our needs are related to consumption, status, and esteem. But our deepest needs are for touch, warmth, relatedness, and love. In its purest form bioenergetic analysis is committed to helping individuals become aware of these needs and then meet them in healthy ways.

References

Lowen, A. *Physical dynamics of character structure.* New York: Grune & Stratton, 1958.

Lowen, A. *The betrayal of the body.* New York: Macmillan, 1967.

Lowen, A. *Pleasure.* New York: Coward-McCann, 1970.

Lowen, A. *Bioenergetics and the language of the body.* New York: Coward, McCann & Geoghegan, 1975.

20

Cognitive-Behavior Therapy
L. Rebecca Propst

Cognitive-behavioral therapies have enjoyed an immense popularity these past 10 years as effective approaches to psychotherapy. Essentially, a cognitive-behavioral approach to psychological treatment is, as its name suggests, a combination of two treatments: the cognitive and the behavioral. Cognitive refers to the thoughts of the individual. A therapy treatment with a cognitive emphasis thus consists of an emphasis upon the modification of the individual's conscious thoughts about himself or his environment. The implication of this concept is that psychological disorders, and in particular affective disorders such as depression or anxiety, result from thinking the wrong kind of thoughts; this must then be corrected. Behavioral, on the other hand, refers to an emphasis on the individual's external behaviors. A behavior treatment for any disorder is usually focused on changing the individual's overt behaviors, with the assumption that the behavior itself is the problem. Cognitive-behavior therapy refers to the use of both behavior and cognitive techniques to change the way an individual thinks about himself or herself.

At present there appears to be ample evidence that one's thoughts have an impact on one's emotions (Kendall & Hollen, 1979). In addition, current theories of emotions suggest that while physiology may determine the intensity of the emotions, the content of the emotions (e.g., sad vs. happy) is determined by the cognitions or thoughts of the individual.

The behaviorism of cognitive-behavior therapy is not metaphysical behaviorism but methodological behaviorism. The distinction between these is crucial for the Christian. The former makes strong statements about determinism, and may imply in its more radical varieties an absence of responsibility and freedom on the part of the individual. Methodological behaviorism, however, implies only that there will be an emphasis on experimental rigor in the analysis of behavior. One will deal with publicly observable events such as behaviors in the discussion of changes in the individual.

The combination of the cognitive and the behavioral appears to have come about because, while on the one hand the efficacy of performance-based therapeutic procedures had been recognized, on the other hand behavioral explanation which defined change totally in terms of environmental contingencies did not seem to be sufficient. The internal thoughts and assumptions of individuals obviously mediate how they respond to the environment.

Philosophical Foundation

One underlying assumption of cognitive-behavioral therapists is the concept of *reciprocal determinism.* This implies a transactional approach to behavior, in which the individual is active in creating his own environment. For example, a person may perceive his environment in a distorted fashion, as is the case with depression. Such a person may then think negative thoughts about the environment and act on these thoughts. His actions may then engender certain changes in the interpersonal environment, which in turn will further influence his cognitions and subsequent behavior. This entire process is called reciprocal determinism because individuals' perceptions and thoughts about their environment or the environment they have constructed in their heads are in fact the environment they respond to. Thus they determine the environment. Likewise, the environment in the external world has an impact on their thoughts and behaviors.

Some more radical theorists have attempted to extend the notion of reciprocal determinism, to posit some sort of monism inherent in the universe. That is, because the individual determines his environment through his thoughts, the environment and the individual an identity. This is a reaction to the dualism that exists in rn psychology, which insists that not only are the individual's cognitions (mind) and his body totally separate, but so also are the individual and his environment. The distinctions become blurred, however, in cognitive therapy, because one's thoughts about the environment often make up the environment to which the individual responds.

For the Christian it is not necessary to move from complete dualism to monism (complete identity of everything). Not only does the Hebrew concept of the individual include both the physical and the spiritual (or mental), but there is also found throughout Scripture the theme of the unity of the world. Creation and the individual are inextricably bound up with each other. For example, because of the fall of the human race, "all creation groans, and waits to be delivered." Thus, the reality in which the individual finds himself is the reality which he has in some sense helped to create through his perspective.

Essential Characteristics of Cognitive-Behavior Therapies

Meichenbaum (1976) asserts that the basic postulate of the cognitive-behavioral therapists is that the final way to all behavior change is the internal dialogues in which clients engage. He further states that there are basically three stages in any cognitive-behavior therapy. The first stage involves teaching an individual skills in self-observation. There are two processes involved in this stage. First, individuals are given a conceptual framework in which they are told that indeed their thoughts have an impact on their feelings of depression and anxiety, and they need only change their thoughts in order to change their emotions. Essentially the idea communicated is that they can have some control over their emotions. The second process involved in this phase teaches individuals to monitor their thoughts. Essentially they are to ask, along with the psalmist (Ps. 42), "Why are you cast down, O my soul?" What are you thinking about that makes you seem so depressed? Individuals are usually given the assignment to monitor their thoughts when their mood changes.

The second stage of any cognitive-behavior therapy asks individuals to modify or restructure their thoughts. The way in which this is done usually varies with the therapist. Whereas Ellis in rational-emotive therapy may ask clients to realize why certain of their ideas are irrational, Beck (Beck, Rush, Shawn, & Emery, 1979) may ask his clients to present evidence that their cognitions are incorrect.

Clients may be challenged to change certain irrational thinking styles such as selective inattention to certain things in their environment or overgeneralization of a situation. In some cases clients may be given a behavioral assignment that will serve to actually disprove some of their negative thoughts. Some problem-solving therapies may ask the individual to substitute a problem-solving inner dialogue for an ongoing negative dialogue (e.g., "Let's see, after I do this first step, I must then do this next step . . ."). Finally, certain self-reinforcement therapies would encourage clients to monitor their performances in an area and then say positive things to themselves when certain behaviors occur.

An additional group of cognitive models are the covert conditioning models. These models consist of a number of techniques, such as covert counterconditioning, thought stopping, or covert sensitization. They posit the idea inherent in the classical conditioning model of pairing a negative stimulus (such as a negative thought) with a positive stimulus (such as a positive thought). For example, if an overweight individual continually thinks about food so that these thoughts represent a positive stimulus, certain therapists may ask the patient to imagine a negative scene every time he or she imagines food. One example of a negative scene is an image of getting sick and vomiting. Thought stopping may merely ask patients to verbalize the word *stop* every time they start to think something that they do not want to think, such as anxiety-provoking thoughts.

A number of cognitive techniques have a third stage wherein the individuals begin to look for underlying themes in their thoughts. After they have learned to monitor their thoughts and modify them, they then may be asked to review thoughts which they have recorded in order to look for the common theme. For the depressed or anxious individual, some of the underlying themes may be irrational and may consist of ideas such as "I must always be perfect." Meichenbaum, however, also emphasizes such ideas as idiosyncratic thought patterns that keep individuals from more effectively coping with their environment.

Treatment Efficacy

An important issue that must always be raised in evaluating any approach to therapy is treatment efficacy. Does the treatment do what it claims to do? Fortunately, cognitive-behavioral therapies fare better here than some of the more traditional approaches such as psychoanalysis because the efficacy of these cognitive-behavioral approaches has in fact been confirmed (Mahoney & Arnkoff, 1978).

In evaluating the efficacy of cognitive-behavioral treatments, all approaches can be divided into two large categories: the covert conditioning therapies and the cognitive learning models. The covert conditioning therapies do not fare as well as the cognitive learning models. The literature is mixed in its evaluation of both thought-stopping and covert sensitization techniques. Essentially, the effectiveness of both these techniques has yet to be demonstrated. Covert counterconditioning, however, seems to have some effectiveness. In this approach the individual is taught to relax and then asked to imagine progressively more aversive scenes or performances, such as speaking in front of a group, if that is a difficult problem for the individual.

Cognitive learning therapies have been shown to be fairly effective. This category includes cognitive restructuring therapies such as rational-emotive therapy, Beck's cognitive therapy (discussed above), and Meichenbaum's cognitive model. These approaches have been shown to be quite effective in the treatment of a number of disorders ranging from depression to childhood behavioral problems.

Also in this second category are the coping skills therapies. The distinguishing feature of these strategies is their emphasis on helping the client to master a repertoire of skills that will facilitate adaptation. Numerous procedures, such as training the patient to imagine the steps in solving a problem, have all been found to be effective. One procedure, which has been termed covert modeling, has been found to be especially effective with phobias and subassertiveness. A third type of approach in this category is the problem-solving therapy, in which patients are taught the rudiments of problem solving. A number of studies have reported the success of this therapy with various categories of individuals. Mahoney and Arnoff (1978) state that research support for the problem-solving therapy shows it to be one of the most promising of the cognitive-behavioral therapies.

Evaluation

The cognitive-behavioral therapies offer some exciting potentials for the Christian for two reasons. First, they have been found to be consistently effective. Second, their central notion, that the individual's intellectual construction of the world and his or her attitudes about that world are a major determinant of the individual's mental health, is a notion familiar to Christian theology. Certainly Scripture points out a close connection between thoughts and mental health (Prov. 23:7; Mark 7:20, 23; Phil. 4:4–9, 11, 13).

There are, however, two cautions in regard to cognitive-behavioral therapy. First, one must guard against baptizing any one approach to psychotherapy as the Christian approach. Also, while one's thoughts and perspectives are important for one's spiritual well-being, some theologies have held that the intellect can never be the central basis of a theology. A second caution is that some Christians tend to be too simplistic in their use of these therapies. Because the focus of these treatments appears to be on helping the individual gain a more healthy adaptive perspective on the world, many Christian counselors have felt that such a perspective could be gained by lecturing the individual or sermonizing during the therapy hour. However, cognitive therapy involves two processes which differentiate it clearly from simply lecturing to the client. First, the clients learn to monitor their own thoughts before they work on modifying them. Both counselor and client must be aware of what the client's thoughts are. Second, cognitive therapy places a larger emphasis on emotions than is usually realized (Beck, et al., 1979). Not only does the individual need to be tuned into his emotions, so that bad emotions or sudden changes in emotions become a cue indicating thought changes, but the counselor must continually make the link between the client's emotions and thoughts in the therapy session. If the above mentioned cautions are kept in mind, however, the cognitive-behavioral therapies can be effective and useful tools for the Christian counselor.

References

Beck, A. T., Rush, A., Shawn, B., & Emery G. *Cognitive therapy of depression.* New York: Guilford Press, 1979.

Kendall, P. C., & Hollen, S. D. (Eds.). *Cognitive-behavioral interventions.* New York: Academic Press, 1979.

Mahoney, M., & Arnkoff, D. Cognitive and self-control therapies. In S. L. Garfield & A. E. Bergin (Eds.), *Handbook of psychotherapy and behavior change.* (2nd ed.). New York: Wiley, 1978.

Meichenbaum, D. Towards a cognitive theory of self-control. In G. E. Schwartz & D. Shapiro (Eds.), *Consciousness and self-regulation: Advances in research.* New York: Plenum Press, 1976.

21

Coping Skills Therapies
Elizabeth M. Altmaier

Coping skills treatment is conceptually based in behavior therapy and owes its beginnings to a shift in emphasis within behavioral treatments from environmental control to self-control (Bandura, 1969). Coping skills treatments are oriented toward teaching the client a model for stress that emphasizes the role of the individual in coping with the stress and a set of techniques or skills for use in stressful situations.

Coping skills treatments are based in a model of disturbance that has three assumptions. First, it is assumed that humans develop both adaptive and maladaptive feelings and actions through the influence of cognitive processes. For example, our anxiety in a stressful situation comes about as we appraise the situation, think about resources that can be brought to bear on the situation, and decide whether we have sufficient or insufficient resources to cope, thereby determining whether the situation is a challenge or a threat (Lazarus, 1966). If we decide the situation is a threat, we will likely feel anxious and depressed, have thoughts that are fearful and avoidant of the task, and consequently have less adaptive behaviors.

The second assumption behind coping skills is that these cognitive processes (thoughts, feelings, beliefs) are learned according to the same laws of learning that govern the acquisition of behaviors. This assumption is the tie between the cognitive and behavioral theoretical backgrounds of coping skills. The third assumption is that the therapist's task is that of an educator or a trainer, who assesses clients' current levels of coping skills and provides education and direction in the process of altering present ineffective cognitive processes and acquiring new coping skills. Because of these assumptions, coping skills therapy is used in a preventive as well as a remedial context (Mahoney & Arnkoff, 1971).

There are several different treatment approaches which all fit under the label of "coping skills." These treatments all share a common goal of helping the client develop a repertoire of skills which will facilitate his or her adjustment to stressful situations. The four approaches most commonly considered coping skills therapies are covert modeling, coping skills training, anxiety management training, and stress inoculation.

The distinguishing feature of *covert modeling* is that the client mentally rehearses the desired behavior (e.g., making an assertive request) prior to the situation where the behavior will be used. This procedure is very common among athletes and has recently been employed with success in overcoming specific fears, such as interpersonal and social anxieties. Such covert, or imaginal, rehearsal is also an important feature of *coping skills training*, a variation of systematic desensitization in which the client is not instructed to stop visualizing a threatening scene when anxious, but is encouraged to maintain the image and cope with the anxiety by learning to relax it away. *Anxiety management training* uses clients' visualization of different scenes, some unrelated to the target fear, to develop generalization of the coping responses.

Perhaps the most fully articulated method of coping skills training is *stress inoculation* (Meichenbaum, 1974). Stress inoculation has three distinct phases: education, rehearsal, and application. In the education phase clients are presented a model which defines anxiety as having an affective component (feelings), a cognitive component (thoughts and beliefs about the stressful event), and a behavioral component (muscular tension, avoidance behaviors). Clients are also encouraged to view stress and their responses to it as a four-stage process: anticipation of stressor, confronting and handling the stressor, coping with being overwhelmed by the stressor, evaluation and reinforcement of coping. Clients are then taught a variety of coping skills during the rehearsal phase, with an emphasis on restructuring of thoughts and relaxation of tension. Lastly, during the application phase, clients are given opportunities to practice their newly acquired coping skills in controlled stressful situations.

The research on coping skills treatments has not yet included sufficient controlled outcome studies to allow a confident assertion of the effectiveness of these treatments. However, initial reports (see Jaremko, 1979 for review) suggest that the treatments are effective means of teaching coping skills to clients. The very nature of the treatment suggests that it is appropriate for clients with minimal degrees of pathology, who show ineffective behavior in certain aspects of their lives, and who experience depression and anxiety due to these situational problems.

The emphasis on cognitive processes as mediating the effects of the environment on the individual does not conflict with the biblical view of man as a rational person and, in fact, is an expression of the need to consider one's thoughts. Additionally, the emphasis on the individual's need to be an initiator of self-regulatory actions corresponds to a Christian emphasis on personal responsibility. In spite of many Christians' concerns over behavior modification (e.g., Kauffmann, 1977), there seems to be an acceptance of therapies more cognitive-behavioral in nature (e.g., McAllister, 1975). Given the promise of these therapies in general, and coping skills training in particular, such acceptance appears warranted.

References

Bandura, A. *Principles of behavior modification.* New York: Holt, Rinehart, & Winston, 1969.

Jaremko, M. E. A component analysis of stress inoculation: Review and prospectus. *Cognitive Therapy and Research,* 1979, *3,* 35–48.

Kauffmann, D. Behaviorism, psychology, and Christian education. *The Bulletin of CAPS,* 1977, *3*(3), 17–21.

Lazarus, R. S. *Psychological stress and the coping process.* New York: McGraw-Hill, 1966.

Mahoney, M. J., & Arnkoff, D. B. Cognitive and self-control therapies. In S. L. Garfield & A. E. Bergin (Eds.), *Handbook of psychotherapy and behavior change.* New York: Wiley, 1971.

McAllister, E. W. Assertive training and the Christian therapist. *Journal of Psychology and Theology,* 1975, *3,* 19–24.

Meichenbaum, D. *Cognitive behavior modification.* Morristown, N.J.: General Learning Press, 1974.

22

Crisis Intervention
Frances J. White

In recent years, short-term therapeutic help for emotional crises have become increasingly popular among mental health professionals. As practiced today, crisis intervention therapies have their roots in the work of Lindemann (1944), who developed a program to aid in the healthy resolution of the grief of the survivors and relatives of those who perished in the Coconut Grove nightclub fire of 1943. During the 1940s and 50s, when little professional attention was given to crisis intervention, Caplan (1964) and his colleagues followed up Lindemann's work, advancing the understanding of crisis and its healthy resolution. Since the middle 1960s—spurred by the community mental health movement, increased consumer demand, and limited professional resources—the helping professions have turned more and more to crisis intervention as an effective mode of providing care for those in emotional crisis.

In theory and practice crisis intervention is still developing. It is strongly eclectic, corralling insights and techniques from a variety of mental health disciplines. At the heart of its current theory and application is Caplan's (1964) concept of homeostasis. Borrowed

143

from physiology, the term, as understood in crisis theory, refers to the healthy balance between the emotional and cognitive experience and functioning of the individual, allowing him to relate effectively to his environment.

Each person has a homeostatic stability that is "normal" for himself. However, he constantly faces situations that disrupt that homeostasis. These "emotionally hazardous situations" (Caplan, 1964)—changes in environment, interpersonal relationships, or oneself that entail loss and are perceived as negative—give rise to painful emotions, sometimes accompanied by decreased cognitive ability. In the face of this stress the person calls forth habitual coping mechanisms (both conscious and unconscious) and problem-solving activities in an effort to restore homeostasis. If they fail to restore homeostasis, an emotional crisis may ensue.

Because individuals cannot tolerate stress indefinitely, emotional crises have a limited life span, usually resolving themselves, for better or for worse, within four to six weeks (Caplan, 1964). If the person receives help and learns new, effective coping skills, the crisis will resolve healthily, strengthening him for future events. In the absence of help or of acquiring effective coping skills, the crisis resolution will be maladaptive, leaving the individual more vulnerable to similar crises in the future.

Crises are a normal part of life and are not in themselves an indication of psychopathology. Everyone, even the well-adjusted, experiences emotional crises in stressful situations for which coping behaviors are weak or absent. Crises may be triggered by relatively predictable developmental events—life transitions such as birth, adolescence, and old age—and by the more unpredictable situational upsets such as illness, unemployment, divorce, or moving to a new home. Crises always involve either actual or symbolic conflicts with a significant other person. Developmental and situational changes lead to crisis when they reawaken unresolved conflicts and traumas from the past.

Because of the limited duration of crises, crisis intervention, to be effective, must take place as soon as possible after the precipitating event. The goal of crisis intervention is to restore the person as quickly as possible to at least a precrisis level of functioning, whether or not that level was ideal. Solving all the client's problems, restructuring personality, bringing about major changes, and resolving deep-seated, long-standing conflicts—goals common to long-term therapy—are outside the scope of crisis intervention. Any gains in those areas are considered a therapeutic bonus, not a goal to be pursued.

In crisis a person is more open than usual to receiving help and support from others and learning new ways of functioning. The therapist's role is to guide the client, over the four- to six-week duration of the crisis, toward an adaptive resolution. Unlike long-term insight-oriented therapy where the therapist may be passive and maintain a professional distance, crisis intervention calls for an active, personal encounter. The therapist must be direct and flexible enough to use a variety of techniques.

The therapist provides hope and support to the client, presenting himself as interested, caring, and willing to understand and help. Through empathy the therapist both communicates support and helps the client to ventilate and understand those negative emotions that are preventing him from coping with the situation, thereby restoring some cognitive mastery.

Since the goal of therapy is to restore the client's own functioning, the therapist, while supportive, does not foster dependency but seeks to mobilize the client's own internal strengths and external resources (e.g., family or friends) in defining the problem, identifying the event that precipitated the crisis, addressing and at least partially resolving the underlying conflict that has made the client vulnerable to that event, and planning ways of dealing with the situation. In the process the therapist seeks to help the client avoid learning or using maladaptive coping responses; learn new, adaptive coping skills; reconcile himself, both emotionally and intellectually, to the changes brought about by the crisis; and anticipate and plan for future similar situations.

The focus of therapy is the present situation, not the historical origin of the client's conflicts. Attention is given to past events only as they relate to the current crisis, helping the client to understand and act in his present situation. In the course of therapy the therapist gradually shifts responsibility for dealing with the problem to the client, building his hope, independence, and self-esteem. When crisis intervention is successful, the client's anxiety is replaced with genuine hope for the future as his supportive interpersonal relationships are strengthened and he gradually regains his capacity for independently planning ways to meet his needs.

Crisis intervention offers one way of answering Scripture's call to help those in need. Its balance between supportive help and encouragement of the client's own independent functioning is reminiscent of Paul's teaching that we are to bear one another's burdens, yet each is responsible to carry his own load when he is able (Gal. 6:2, 4–5). Its emphasis on hope is also consistent with Scripture's teaching on coping with difficulty (Rom. 5:3–5; James 1:2).

References

Caplan, G. *Principles of preventive psychiatry.* New York: Basic Books, 1964.

Lindemann, E. Symptomatology and management of acute grief. *American Journal of Psychiatry*, 1944, *101*, 141–148.

Additional Readings

Aguilera, D., & Messick, J. *Crisis intervention, theory and methodology* (4th ed.). St. Louis: C. V. Mosby, 1982.

Baldwin, B. A. Crisis intervention: An overview of theory and practice. *The Counseling Psychologist*, 1979, *8* (2), 43–52.

Ewing, C. P. *Crisis intervention as psychotherapy.* New York: Oxford University Press, 1978.

23

Existential Psychology and Psychotherapy
John G. Finch & Bryan Van Dragt

The word *existential* comes from the Latin *ex sistere*, meaning literally to emerge or to stand out. True to this emphasis, existential psychologists seek to understand human beings not as static, but always in the process of becoming or emerging.

The beginnings of existential philosophy are usually identified with the Danish philosopher and theologian Søren Kierkegaard. Kierkegaard argued that knowledge can only be discovered via existence, and existence is incapable of further reduction. His major protagonist was Hegel, who identified abstract truth with reality. Against this, Kierkegaard argued that truth cannot be found in abstract theory but only in existence. In contrast to Descartes's dictum, "I think, therefore I am," Kierkegaard answered, "I exist, therefore I think." Existence precedes essence.

Defining Characteristics

As a system of psychology the existential tradition stands in opposition to those approaches which view persons reductionistically.

147

Scientific psychology is viewed as treating people as objects rather than as human beings. Existential psychology rejects this subject-object cleavage. Rather than deal with human essence, the abstraction which has become the focus of traditional scientific psychology, existential psychology focuses on human existence. One's essence is one's existence; that is, the essence of man is his power to create himself.

In 1963 James Bugenthal, then president of the American Association of Humanistic Psychology, delineated five basic points which summarize the existential position:

1. Man supersedes the sum of his parts and cannot be understood from a scientific study of part-functions.
2. Man has his being in a human context and cannot be understood by part-functions which ignore interpersonal experience.
3. Man is aware and cannot be understood by a psychology which fails to recognize his continuous, many-layered self-awareness.
4. Man has choice and is not a bystander to his existence.
5. Man is intentional; he has purpose, values, and meaning.

This understanding of human nature, or ontology, puts a completely new light on psychotherapy. The goal is not to communicate with the other in terms of presuppositions and expectations, but rather to set aside our world and enter into the other's world as he lets us in. The therapist's concern and attention are focused on the phenomena themselves. In this way the therapist does not abstract himself or become objective about what is going on, but is very much involved in the process. Disclaiming the protective veneer of objectivity, the therapist is continually in the mainstream of the other's search for meaning and values. This might be described as a double-mirrored relationship. The therapist himself must be in quest of his destiny to better understand the process of searching.

Although existentialism is related to phenomenological psychology, most existentialists feel that the two traditions are separate. The Swiss psychiatrist Binswanger notes that while the existential therapist enters into the phenomena present before and with him, existentialism does not confine itself to states of withness. It includes the existence of the whole being. Binswanger likewise points to the conflicting "worlds" in which the individual lives as opposed to the phenomenologist's notion of the unity of the individual's inner world of experiences. Again, while phenomenology limits itself to the immediate subjective worlds of experience, existentialism takes in the whole existence of the individual. This is where the individual's history comes into play.

View of Persons

In order to better comprehend the whole person, Binswanger (1958) divided his concerns around three aspects of a person's existence, his mode of being in the world. He saw three worlds in which human beings live. These he termed *Umwelt, Mitwelt,* and *Eigenwelt.* By *Umwelt* he meant the biological world, including one's own body, the animal world, and, as a matter of fact, the entire physical existence. *Mitwelt* includes man in relation to other persons and emphasizes the more than biological interplay between persons. The aspect he termed *Eigenwelt* deals with the person in relation to himself—the self relating itself to its self and thus becoming a self. This is what Kierkegaard termed *spirit.*

In this understanding of persons several important factors stand out. Since man is seen as being, the implication is that he is moving toward becoming. This implies that man is a creature who is going in a certain direction to fulfill his destiny. On this journey he encounters certain distractions and diversions which attempt to mislead him in his questing. While his chosen strategies for dealing with the obstacles are rooted in his history, his ontology informs him, via anxiety, of his waywardness, and this reminds him of his responsibility to be himself in truth and to fulfill his destiny. This realization in turn implies that he has the freedom to choose. If he does not choose his destiny, he experiences guilt. Boss (1956) points out that guilt is not for things done or not done, but for who we refuse to be. Nor, says Boss, is guilt responsive to any other form of relief. Resolution of guilt comes about as the result of a change of direction in our lives toward the fulfillment of our destiny. In this view of personality symptoms are viewed as roadblocks that the human being throws up to avoid and evade his destiny. Psychopathology is a means of communicating. It is the purpose of the therapist to understand the language of the symptoms-symbols because symptoms are symbolic communications of what ails man.

Existential Psychodynamics

In his book *Existential Psychotherapy* Yalom points to death, freedom, isolation, and meaninglessness as the corpus of existential psychodynamics. He suggests these are the givens of existence and may be discovered by a "method of deep reflection. The conditions are simple: solitude, silence, time and freedom from the everyday distractions with which each of us fills his or her experiential world" (1980, p. 8).

Heidegger's (1962) discussion of death suggests that man lives on two levels: a state of forgetfulness of being and a state of mindfulness of being. To live in the former state is to live in continual distraction and diversion, in a preoccupation with things, abstractions, and impersonal concerns. Self-awareness is a very low priority in this existence. In the latter state one is continually aware of being. This awareness keeps one in touch with one's existence and the world of being. Living in awareness of one's being produces authenticity but is also fraught with anxiety. Anxiety increases when one who is aware of being is confronted with the reality of nonbeing, or death. An extraordinary sense of accountability is initiated with the realization of one's death. This limitation of time also urges one on to greater fulfillment or authenticity. Any experience that suggests a lessening of our individuality or a loss of our unique identity is in many ways reminiscent of our death, and this becomes a challenge to a fuller, more authentic existence.

The second major existential psychodynamic is freedom and its corollary, responsibility. The awareness of being has two dimensions, the awareness of our objective ego and the awareness of a transcending ego. This ability to transcend self not only reminds a person of his possibilities and his freedom, but it places on him the necessity to accept that responsibility. To be fully aware of this is what Kierkegaard describes as dizziness. Failure to accept and discharge our responsibility is what leads to guilt and a sense of groundlessness.

A third concern of the existentialist is isolation. This may be likened to a schizoid state—a condition in which a fundamental separation portrays the nonrelational character of the existent. Rogers describes this condition as the separation from one's own real wishes or desires. I am so unaware of who or what I am that I do not know who I am or what I want. All that confronts me is a sense of nothingness. Man is urged to discover his identity, his destiny. But this is the most awful calling of being separate and alone. On these twin possibilities man spends his entire life. Yalom (1980) describes this as the oscillation between life anxiety, the fear of self-affirmation and authenticity, and death anxiety, the fear of loss of autonomy.

The fourth major concern of the existentialist is meaning. This dimension opens up the whole world of values. Questions such as

"What is life all about?" "Why do we exist?" "What meaning in my life makes existence worthwhile?" are singularly and significantly relevant to existentialists. These are likewise most pertinent questions in therapy.

The elements of faith and commitment are both integral to the existentialist's notion of meaning. The question is, "Faith in what or whom?" The existentialist answer is that we begin with commitment to ourselves and our being, and only then do we find meaning. This is what is understood by reaching toward our destiny.

Yalom draws on Maslow when he speaks of the self-actualization process involving a person striving toward what most people would call good values—that is, toward kindness, honesty, love, unselfishness, and goodness. These values, according to Maslow, are "built into the human organism and . . . if one only trusts one's organismic wisdom, one will discover them intuitively" (Yalom, 1980, p. 438). Thus values and meaning are both seen to be rooted in existence.

Psychotherapy

While there is no single theory or approach to existential psychotherapy, May (1959) has summarized the major common elements in all existential approaches to treatment. He first points out that to look to existential psychology textbooks for techniques will be disappointing. The techniques used by existential psychotherapists are much like those used by other therapists. They are not, however, emphasized in existentialists' discussions of therapy. This is in reaction to the overemphasis on techniques in our Western culture, which is viewed as objectifying and "thing-ifying" persons.

According to May, the essential task of existential therapy is to "seek to understand the patient as a being and as being-in-his-world" (p. 77). Understanding a person is contrasted to analyzing an object. To understand a person means to relate to him as a person. The relationship of the therapist and patient is taken as a real one, not merely a professional role. Within this relationship the therapist attempts to help the patient experience his existence as real. The quintessence of existential therapy is to enable the person to become more fully aware of his existence. Involved in this is helping the patient develop an orientation to commitment. The patient must be brought to a decisive attitude toward existence. "The points of commitment and decision are those where the dichotomy between being subject and object is overcome in the unity of readiness for action" (May, 1959, p. 88).

Christian Existential Psychology

This section explores a Christian alternative to existential psychology and, as such, constitutes a critique of that psychology from a Christian perspective.

As noted above, existential psychology has largely abandoned any concern for an ultimate reference point for the spirit or self. Adopting a relativism that virtually rejects any unifying purpose or meaning to existence, modern existentialism has cut itself off from the vital taproot of which Kierkegaard spoke when he asserted that spirit must be grounded in Spirit. Christian existential psychology returns to this basic theme in Kierkegaard as its central tenet.

As a distinct system, Christian existential psychology has been developed in numerous articles and books over the past quarter century by Finch (1980b, 1982). These writings represent the meeting ground between his religious experience and his psychological awareness—a search that led him first into the pastorate and later into clinical psychology. Finch's approach represents an intentional integration of existential depth psychology and the Christian faith. The focal point for this integration lies in the Christian existential view of the nature of man.

Personality and psychopathology

In concert with other existentialists, Finch affirms that man is essentially what Kierkegaard called spirit. That is, man is not mere machine, as Freud and others proposed, but rather man has a definite potential and the freedom and responsibility to actualize that potential. But what is this potential? In Kierkegaard's terms, it is the "absolute of all that a man can be." The secular existentialist speaks of man's destiny. But to what do these terms refer? It is here that the Christian, in contrast to the logical positivist or "pure" scientist, is free to respond in absolute terms: the self, the absolute of all that a man can be, is defined by the *imago Dei*, the image of God in man.

Although made in God's image, man has allowed that likeness to be obscured by a network of defenses which, while purporting to protect the self, actually suffocates it. Enveloping the true, authentic self like a shroud, this "false self" prevents the spirit from coming to expression. The false self develops as a result of sin. Sin may be characterized as both a defense and a sickness, a sickness created by our egocentric tendency to assert that we are the captains of our fate, the masters of our souls. This act of pride cuts us off from the very Source of all life.

Man's spirit cannot be grounded or find meaning in itself, but only in the Spirit which created it. Freedom, responsibility, and the transcendent quality of the self have meaning only as they relate to God. It is this relation which is the core of Christian existential psychology, and it is in the life, death, and resurrection of Christ that this relation is elaborated most fully. It is therefore in the choice to invest oneself in the way modeled by Christ that one truly undertakes the task of becoming oneself. Finch recognizes that placing Christ at the center of psychology is a philosophical assumption. But he claims that his experience as well as that of innumerable others throughout the ages validates the assumption.

In fact, Finch asserts that following Christ is the supreme corrective to psychological disturbance. Insofar as man was created to be one with God, any deviation from this path creates an intolerable inner tension, for one is then at war with one's own being. This conflict must inevitably be expressed in physical and emotional distress. When one sets about becoming like Christ, one becomes aligned with one's ontology, the tension is eliminated, and the entire being—body, mind, and spirit—is once again integrated. This leads to another central theme in Finch's approach: the concept of anxiety.

Like other existential psychologists Finch sees anxiety in all its forms as demonstrating one's alienation from one's own being. Finch, however, puts the case even more unequivocally in his characterization of *all* anxiety as good. He sees anxiety as an inherent, positive, "creative directive to be oneself in truth, relentlessly" (Finch, 1980b, p. 154). When one makes life choices that are aligned with one's being as a child of God, anxiety is maintained at a creative level. However, when one violates one's nature, one blocks that creative flow and, like the waters of a dammed river, the pressure of anxiety intensifies and overflows into physical and psychological symptoms. By interpreting these symptoms and their causes biologically rather than ontologically or spiritually, we misconceive anxiety and increase it.

At the heart of anxiety we find the conscience. Where anxiety is "a nebulous power that activates and drives the being to fulfillment" (Finch, 1980b, p. 162), conscience is the focal point, the "eye of anxiety." Conscience may be defined as the spirit's potential for urging in one's consciousness its authoritative actualization in relation to Spirit. Conscience is ontological. That is, it is vital to man's being rather than contingent. It is not to be confused with the Freudian superego, which is the result of parental introjects and therefore potentially alien to one's ontology (consider the inner parental voice that may urge a woman "never to trust a man"), or with cultural norms or environmental influence, all of which conscience mediates and filters.

Failing to heed the call of conscience involves one in guilt. Viewed existentially, guilt consists not in what one has done or not done, but rather in one's failure to fulfill one's possibilities in the moment—that is, in one's refusal to *be*. Virtually all physical and mental or emotional disorders have their genesis in our attempts to avoid the reality of our guilt. The only way to dissipate guilt is to choose to be. This choice is the essence of repentance and forgiveness. When we choose to be authentic, "the whole order of things cooperates with us to annul the past which has produced the guilt, and to affirm the present." Here we are in the realm of grace—that divine, patient, loving "acceptance which both pulls and pushes our development, using every condition of existence to facilitate the emergence of the self" (Finch, 1980a, p. 249).

Human development.

Christian existential psychology views human development in terms of the struggle between the true and false selves. Already in the womb the fetus begins to react to parental anxieties by assuming a defensive posture. This defense eventually takes the form of an egocentric mistrust of and withdrawal from the milieu and an inner commitment to "go it alone," using everything and everyone for one's own ends—in short, a commitment to make the world good on one's own terms. This response is inevitable. It is one's foremost developmental task (and therefore also the work of therapy) to shed these defenses in order to be revealed *as one is*. It is only in the extremity of this openness and vulnerability that one relates genuinely to God.

Finch conceives the developmental process in terms of four stages. Progression through the stages is a lifelong journey marked by frequent setbacks.

The first stage is that of dependence, the authentic or natural state of the neonate and infant. As natural growth processes carry the self farther from the security of the womb, the dizzying freedom and responsibility of one's increasing abilities and possibilities create an anxiety from which the self tries to escape by contorting itself and distorting reality. All such tactics constitute an attempt to re-create the security of the womb by enticing (e.g., placation) or by coercing (e.g., tantrums) from the environment the nurturance one either does not trust to come freely or does not wish to procure in an honest fashion.

The second stage, that of independence, is actually a variation of the first stage. In it one seeks the privileges of freedom without the attendant responsibilities. Characterized by the bullying, pouting, blackmail, and other tactics typically associated with the adolescent's masquerade of selfhood ("I'm old enough to drive, but you'd better pay for the gas"), independence is actually a way of spreading anxiety to the environment so that it will allow one to be dependent. After an intense struggle one comes to the painful discovery that one's attempts to remain dependent only increase anxiety. As the self acts on this realization and gives up its vise-like grip on the defensive strategies by which it has imprisoned itself, the self is born in true freedom and responsibility. This is the stage of self-dependence, in which the self becomes self-caring, self-creating, self-affirming, and self-supporting.

Self-dependence is not to be confused with the idea of needing nothing. As Finch notes, we all need blood to survive. Self-dependence is analogous to producing one's own blood, while dependency is like receiving an endless series of blood transfusions because one's organism has lost the ability to produce its own. Nor is self-dependence to be confused with a schizoid withdrawal from, or inability to depend on, others. Rather, one functions in such harmony with oneself and the milieu that one is able to recycle and draw sustenance from what is offered rather than insisting on having things one's own way. Being in such spiritual harmony one is able to find meaning and value in even the harshest of life circumstances, even in the pain of a crucifixion or the irritations of an uncooperative spouse. This "selflessness" is possible because the self-dependent person is rooted both within and outside himself in God.

Finally, when two selves are able to relate to each other with "a mutuality and sharing that assumes full responsibility for oneself but no less responsibility for the other" (Finch, 1980b, p. 172), we reach the stage of interdependence or interrelation. In this stage anxiety is manifest in concern, and the source of motivation is a quiet inner serenity rather than a desire for satisfaction of one's needs at the other's expense.

One observes, then, that spiritual growth is marked by adoption of a mature *Weltanschauung*, or philosophy of life. This philosophy is not merely cognitive, but is rather inclusive of one's whole existence. The highest value of philosophy of life, asserts Finch, is expressed in the concept of *nishkamakarma*. Literally translated as "desireless action," this Sanskrit word conveys the idea of "doing one's duty with faith in God, without attachment to the fruit of the action" (Finch, 1982, p. 45). This stance of nonattachment (which is not to be confused with uncaring detachment) allows one to focus on the requirements of spirit rather than being pulled and pushed by the vagaries of time and circumstance.

Therapy

The fundamental task of Christian existential therapy is to facilitate spirit's encounter with Spirit. To this end the therapist seeks to dismantle, through loving confrontation, the strategies of the false self. The therapist guides the person into his anxiety rather than away from it, appeals to the individual's sense of responsibility, unclutters the conscience, and encourages a healthy perspective on guilt. The therapist's own values invariably become part of the therapeutic process as he enters deeply into the person's struggles. Because the relationship with the therapist becomes the vehicle by which the person experiences grace and a more mature *Weltanschauung*, it is critical that the therapist be actively engaged in his own search for authentic existence.

As the person's facade disintegrates and the props of dependency are removed, the individual experiences the dread associated with what has been called the *abyss*. This is a radical and ineffable confrontation with one's own being which becomes at the same instant an experience of the infinite love of God. For, having abandoned one's feeble attempts to constitute one's own universe and thus ensure one's own security, one finds that he or she is and always has been held. One does not fall, as one fears, *out* of existence, but rather *into* it.

Such a journey requires the most focused concentration. Integral, therefore, to Christian existential therapy is the concept of the monastic retreat for the purpose of spiritual direction. This retreat takes the form of a three-week intensive therapy, in which one lives alone and seeks oneself under God, with the therapist's direction. Writing and talking in absentia to one's significant others is one aspect of this process, which often resembles the primal therapies in its emotional intensity.

In conclusion, while existential psychology is not incompatible with a Christian world view, Christian existentialism asserts that it falls short of a complete understanding of man by virtue of its lack of a reference point for man's spirit. In bringing a theologically informed perspective to bear on this problem, Christian existential psychology finds this reference point in Spirit—that is, in God. And, giving fresh meaning to the doctrines of sin, guilt, grace, and forgiveness, an existentially informed Christianity offers new promise for healing in depth.

References

Binswanger, L. The existential analysis school of thought. In R. May, E. Angel, & H. Ellenberger (Eds.), *Existence*. New York: Basic Books, 1958.

Boss, M. "Daseinsanalysis" and psychotherapy. In J. H. Masserman & J. L. Moreno (Eds.), *Progress in psychotherapy*. New York: Grune & Stratton, 1956.

Finch, J. G. Guilt and the nature of the self. In H. N. Malony (Ed.), *A Christian existential psychology: The contributions of John G. Finch*. Washington, D.C.: University Press, 1980. (a)

Finch, J. G. The message of anxiety. In H. N. Malony (Ed.), *A Christian existential psychology: The contributions of John G. Finch*. Washington, D.C.: University Press, 1980. (b)

Finch, J. G. *Nishkamakarma*. Pasadena, Calif.: Integration Press, 1982.

Heidegger, M. [*Being and time*] (J. Macquarrie & E. Robinson, Eds.). New York: Harper & Row, 1962.

May, R. The existential approach. In S. Arieti (Ed.), *American handbook of psychiatry*. New York: Basic Books, 1959.

Yalom, I. D. *Existential psychotherapy*. New York: Basic Books, 1980.

24

Gestalt Therapy
David G. Benner

Developed by Fritz Perls in the 1940s, Gestalt therapy has rapidly evolved into an important and popular form of treatment. It attracts many because it represents a genuine alternative to more traditional insight-oriented approaches.

The major goal in Gestalt therapy is to teach the client to be more aware of what is happening both within and without. Perls thought that problems develop because people fail to maintain this awareness. Therapy attempts to restore awareness by focusing primarily on the here and now and by avoiding the twin traps of what Perls referred to as "obsessive remembering of the past" and "anxious anticipation of the future."

Theoretical Roots

Generally viewed as an existential-humanistic form of therapy, the approach has come to be considered a mainstream within humanistic psychology. Its roots reach beyond this orientation, however, and include three major systems: psychoanalytic psychology, Gestalt psychology, and existentialism.

Perls's training and early practice was as a psychoanalyst, and this system exercised considerable influence on his subsequent development. Though psychoanalytic roots are clearer in his early writings, they continue to show in his use of such concepts as superego, repression, introjection, and projection. While he believed he had completely abandoned his psychoanalytic heritage, classifying Gestalt therapy as an existential therapy, some still classify it as a form of psychoanalytic therapy.

As for the influence of Gestalt psychology, Perls initially intended to use the basic concepts of this movement as a foundation for a comprehensive system of personality, psychopathology, and psychotherapy (Perls, Hefferline, & Goodman, 1951). This ambitious goal went largely unfulfilled. He did borrow some of the basic concepts (most notably that of the figure-ground relationship) and the essential spirit of the movement (the desire to understand behavior and experience without analytic dissection), but he failed to do more than marry these to the other major concepts borrowed from psychoanalytic psychology and existentialism.

The third and perhaps most important influence was the existential movement in philosophy and psychology. Gestalt therapy's stress on such concepts as the expansion of awareness, freedom, the immediacy of experience, and the here and now all demonstrate its close relation to existentialism. Nowhere is this more clear than in the so-called Gestalt prayer: "I do my thing and you do your thing. I am not in this world to live up to your expectations and you are not in this world to live up to mine. You are you and I am I and if by chance we find each other, it's beautiful. If not, it can't be helped." (Perls, 1969, p. 4)

Basic Assumptions and Therapeutic Task

Proponents of Gestalt therapy begin with the humanistic assumption that individuals have within themselves all they need to achieve personal wholeness and live effectively. The essential ingredient missing from most people's lives is courage, the courage to become aware of their feelings and of the ways they characteristically avoid experiencing the present in its fullness.

Living fully in the present is most difficult. It demands choice and therefore responsibility. Human beings tend to avoid choice by limiting awareness and consequently limiting freedom. This results in anxiety and a suspension of personal growth.

The heart of the therapeutic task lies in increasing one's awareness. Gestalt therapy assumes that awareness mobilizes energy within the person and enables him to act. Until a person becomes aware that he is hungry, he does not seek food. The awareness of hunger leads naturally to action. Similarly, if a person is unaware of being angry, he takes no action. Awareness of anger makes action possible.

Acting on an awareness is described as finishing an experience. This produces a Gestalt, or a completed experience. Unfinished business results from failing to act on an important past awareness. Generally these experiences involve unexpressed feelings of anger, pain, guilt, and other negative emotions. Because they remain unexpressed, they linger on, continuously pressing for expression. Increasing awareness in the present not only stops the accumulation of unfinished experiences but allows the individual to act on those of the past that are the most pressing.

Gestalt therapy does not suggest, as some critics have alleged, that it is either possible or desirable to act on every awareness. Perls recognized that in any moment the individual is confronted with thousands of possibilities for awareness, only a small number of which can be followed by action. Selective awareness operates constantly.

Perls also recognized that action is sometimes inappropriate. Not every feeling of anger should be expressed, both to preserve social order and to achieve personal mental health. He assumed, however, that most people err on the side of too little awareness and consequently too little expression of feelings. He noted that we fail to be aware of those things within us which we wish were not there. Only after we become fully aware of them can they be changed.

This pursuit of heightened awareness requires the Gestalt therapist to function in an active manner, continuously calling attention to present experience. The therapist does this primarily through the use of *what* questions (e.g., What are you aware of now?) and *how* questions (e.g., How do you experience your fear?). He never employs *why* questions because they lead to rationalizations and intellectual rumination.

The goal is neither analysis nor understanding; it is integration. Lost parts of self are found when channels of awareness are reopened. Perls's dictum, "Loose your mind and come to your senses," captures well this sensory focus of Gestalt therapy. He believed clients must once again learn to use their senses fully if they are to grow.

Related to this is the emphasis on action rather than mere talk. Therapy techniques often require the behavioral involvement of the client. Sometimes the client will reenact an important past situation during which he failed to take the necessary action (e.g., crying at a parent's funeral). Other times he may portray a dream or fantasy in a role play. This emphasis on action is reflected in the designation of many therapy techniques as games. The most common of these include the game of dialogue, the rehearsal game, and the exaggeration game.

Gestalt therapy usually follows a group format. The therapist customarily works with one group member at a time, with individuals volunteering to take the "hot seat" and work on some issue. In the pure form of Gestalt therapy spontaneous interaction among group members is minimal. Members observe the therapist's work with one member and contribute only after completion of the therapeutic work. Other styles of Gestalt groups allow more spontaneous interaction. While the group has emerged as a favored medium and probably represents Gestalt's most potent context, individual therapy is also appropriate and commonly practiced.

Evaluation ↑

Because of the paucity of research on Gestalt therapy, gauging its overall effectiveness is difficult. The few studies that have been done have been generally encouraging. Foulds and Hannigan (1976) have shown Gestalt therapy to be effective in decreasing introversion and neuroticism; Nichols and Fine (1980), in increasing self-concept. These and most other existing studies, however, are therapy analogues conducted with student experimental subjects rather than clients seeking help.

Because Gestalt therapy has most frequently been applied to individuals who function relatively normally, little is known about its usefulness with more typical clinical populations. Most Gestalt therapists seem to agree with Shepherd that it is "most effective with overly socialized, restrained, constricted individuals—often described as neurotic, phobic, perfectionistic, ineffective, depressed, etc.—whose functioning is limited or inconsistent, primarily due to their internal restrictions" (1970, p. 235). She cautions against its use with psychotic or more severely disturbed individuals, and this caution seems sensible in the light of the degree of frustration and confrontation normally inherent in Gestalt therapy.

The most common criticism of Gestalt therapy is that it lacks a theoretical foundation. Initially Perls set out to develop an overall theory of personality, both normal and abnormal. He soon abandoned this pursuit, however, asserting that theoretical speculation interfered with creative clinical work. The theory that was developed consists of little more than a few hypotheses about psychopathology attached to one concept of normal personality development—the concept of awareness. The absence of a unifying theory reduces Gestalt therapy to an assorted collection of techniques with an overall philosophy of life. This theoretical deficiency constitutes a major weakness.

Related to this is the system's anti-intellectual bias. The mistrust of thinking, together with the consequent deemphasis on the cognitive factors in the therapy process, confines the therapist. It also conflicts with the biblical view that a person's thinking is an expression of one's heart or core (Prov. 23:7). Christian theology has historically understood rationality as one aspect of the image of God in which mankind was created. This suggests that a therapy system ought to take seriously the cognitive aspects of human functioning.

The biblical view of persons also stands in contrast to the strikingly independent person depicted as the healthy ideal of Gestalt therapy. The philosophy that "I do my thing and you do your thing" reflects an inadequate notion of our interdependence on each other. At least as described by Perls, Gestalt therapy denies our responsibility to others, and this fails to square with the Christian understanding of human relatedness to others and to God. The emphasis on personal responsibility and the refusal to accept helplessness as an excuse for not changing do reflect the Christian understanding of human nature. The emphasis on one's responsibility for oneself must also be joined, however, by an emphasis on responsibility to others.

References

Foulds, M. L., & Hannigan, P. S. A Gestalt marathon workshop: Effects on extraversion and neuroticism. *Journal of College Student Personnel*, 1976, *17*(1), 50–54.

Nichols, R. C., & Fine, H. J. Gestalt therapy: Some aspects of self support, independence and responsibility. *Psychotherapy: Theory, research and practice*, 1980, *17*(2), 124–135.

Perls, F. *Gestalt therapy verbatim*. Lafayette, Calif.: Real People Press, 1969.

Perls, F., Hefferline, R. F., & Goodman, P. *Gestalt therapy: Excitement and growth in human personality*. New York: Julian Press, 1951.

Shepherd, I. L. Limitations and cautions in the Gestalt approach. In J. Fagan & I. L. Shepherd (Eds.), *Gestalt therapy now*. Palo Alto, Calif.: Science and Behavior Books, 1970.

Additional Readings

Hatcher, C., & Himelstein, P. (Eds.). *The handbook of Gestalt therapy.* New York: Aronson, 1976.

Perls, F. *In and out of the garbage pail.* Lafayette, Calif.: Real People Press, 1969.

Polster, E., & Polster, M. *Gestalt therapy integrated.* New York: Brunner/Mazel, 1973.

25

Hypnotherapy
Vance L. Shepperson

Traditional hypnotherapy has emphasized the use of straightforward, direct suggestions to effect an altered state of awareness within a client. This can be done in either an authoritarian or permissive fashion. For example, an authoritarian approach to arm levitation would be: "Your arm is getting lighter and lighter, like a balloon tied to your wrist is pulling it up." A more permissive form of direct suggestion would be: "Isn't it delightful how you don't have to do anything but wait for that lightness in your arm to start it lifting up and up all by itself?"

In contrast to these direct approaches a more subtle means of suggestion was developed by Milton Erickson (Rossi, 1980). Indirect approaches, described in this chapter, employ an anecdotal or metaphoric format utilizing a number of techniques: embedded suggestions and commands, paraverbal shifts of tone, voice directionality, enunciation, syntax, and pacing; the use of truisms, binds, double binds, and other semantic variations derived from the field of neurolinguistic programming (Bandler & Grinder, 1979). Due to the subtle quality of indirection, a resistant, oppositional client—or merely a scared, unsure client—can be enticed more readily into cooperating with the therapist toward resolving whatever issues are problematic.

The indirect hypnotherapist also will capitalize on the attributes of universality and individuality in his metaphoric process in order to enhance the probability that his suggestions will be accepted and utilized by the client. *Universality*, as used in this context, refers to the process of relating anecdotes that tap experiences common to the average subject from a particular culture. *Individuality* refers to the process of tailoring a story in order to allow the client to utilize his own store of personal life experiences as he becomes more and more deeply absorbed in his inner reverie.

These and other principles of indirect hypnotherapy are illustrated in the induction to trance in Table 1. This metaphor is intended to facilitate arm levitation. Often the therapist will also use subtle nonverbal cues, such as gentle lifting of the wrist while talking. For purposes of illustration it will be assumed that the client in this example experiences his world primarily through kinesthetic sensory channels.

Throughout the induction procedure in Table 1 the metaphor was phrased in such a manner as to appeal individually to a kinesthetically oriented individual (e.g., feel, touch bottom, float, warmth, splash). Suggestions were also phrased in a manner that would tap common universal experiences in most individuals' memory banks. Combined with this induction were suggestions for deepening the level of trance at a pace with which the client felt comfortable (e.g., exploring deeper areas of the pool). Regardless of whether or not the client's arm actually levitated, the operator would probably have succeeded in inducing a light to moderate depth trance state.

Once the induction and some form of trance-deepening procedure has been accomplished, it is then up to the therapist to construct a series of suggestions that will indirectly address the client's problems. It is advised that the therapist first develop a metaphor that matches the client's problem statement and then bring in a resource that the client would find helpful in resolving his or her difficulty (see Gordon, 1978, for an excellent discussion of how one builds such a metaphor).

The example in Table 2 briefly illustrates the development of such a process in addition to all the earlier stated principles of indirect hypnotherapeutic suggestion. The client's problem is sexual frigidity. The client was the second of eight siblings in a poor rural family which offered her no privacy physically or emotionally. She married a highly driven man who attempted to apply the same high pressure

Table 1

Metaphor	Principles of Hypnotherapy Induction
Once, when I was quite young . . . and just learning . . . how to swim in the shallow end . . . of a warm pool of water . . . I had a most fascinating experience.	Evocation of childhood memories; suggestion to learn something new; introducing such learning as being safe; ideosensory suggestion to feel warmth; suggestion to build an expectancy set of curiosity.
I was spending my time playing, splashing, lightly floating. Every once in awhile I would touch bottom . . . just to make sure it was really there, as do most children. As I was exploring gradually deeper and deeper . . . areas of the pool . . . I began to feel more and more comfortable . . . with floating and didn't have to touch bottom quite so often.	Repetitious suggestion for levitation, experience of comfort and security and a trance. Suggestions for comfort and levitation in unspecified fashion. Embedded command to go deeper in trance.
I continued to drift quietly in the warm water for some time. . . . At some point in this period of drifting—and I don't know exactly when—I became consciously aware of something that had been happening outside of my awareness for some time.	Nonspecific suggestion for drifting into deeper relaxation; suggestion to feel warmth; building expectancy set for change; client given permission to proceed at his own pace.
As I had been floating so pleasantly . . . watching fleecy clouds to my right drift by in interesting, curious patterns . . . I had been playing intriguing little games in my mind, imagining shapes of birds or gliders or balloons in the clouds . . . as children are prone to do. During this time I had not been aware consciously that the arm on my right side had been slowly floating from down deeper . . . to the surface of the water. It was as if the arm had a mind of its own. What a pleasant surprise this was to me! I suppose this was when I first began to learn about trusting my own unconscious mind for new and different gifts.	Indirect suggestions for: developing a conscious-unconscious split; levitation of the right arm; dissociation of right arm from self (arm becomes object instead of subject); further work on maintenance of expectancy set for comfort and pleasure.

business principles that had allowed him to be very successful to his sexual life. His lack of gentleness and other earlier marital trauma between them had totally alienated his wife sexually. Both were committed, evangelical Christians. The metaphor in Table 2 was offered to them conjointly following a relaxation induction and a quiet, gentle, lulling period of trance deepening.

Table 2

Metaphor	Principle of Hypnotherapy Intervention
There was once a small clapboard church building out in the middle of nowhere, or so it seemed to the church. The people in the small town nearby mainly ignored the church unless they wanted her to somehow meet *their* needs. They came to her all in a rush to come and go away. . . . And no one ever knocked or asked her permission to come . . . in. It was kind of like she felt no one in the local *body* . . . of believers really respected her for what *she* had to offer.	Appeal to Christian beliefs; indirect reference to childhood loneliness and lack of attention; veiled reference to sexual intercourse and matching that reference with a set of equally negative feelings.
Everyone just seemed to rush in regularly and then pull out to go conduct business as usual. Well, very gradually, the small community prospered. And they gave her a new coat of paint; a new tall, proud steeple pointing upward; and they fixed the leaks in her roof so no one could see her tears on the inside. They even stuck in stained glass windows. Some of them had jewels in them so that people could press their eyes up close and get a really good look.	Reinforcement of the matching between the church and sexual intercourse with negative feelings; continued development of matching metaphor through indirect reference to prosperity, sexuality, a lack of privacy, and her husband still not understanding her emotional needs.
This went on for some time, . . . pretty on the outside but yearning for something more on the inside, . . . wanting to be a place of worship.	Reference to her need to be cherished and given free choice in sexual matters.
One day something strange happened. It was an unpredictable happening. Someone actually knocked. He knocked before coming in. It was the familiar face of an old admirer but with something different about him, something changed about his face. It was as though he really cared about her needs . . . *now*. . . . He came in and out, back and forth, taking care of all her needs that no one else had seemed to notice. He oiled the hinges on her doors; he ran his hands over her walls to make sure they were smooth and not rough; he straightened the candle on the high altar, and did all manner of caring things.	Introduction of resource metaphor. More explicit references to sexuality but in a changed, caring context with emotional insight and commitment.

Table 2 (contd.)

At first she was suspicious. But over time, as days went by and he continued to come to her and minister to her real needs, she began to look forward to his coming very much. Often when he walked by she felt like stretching out and coming to *him*. Often she didn't understand why she wanted him and his visits so badly. Yet, slowly, she just learned to accept the fact that consciously her spirit did not have to understand the changes going on inside of her . . . all the new feelings stirring within her . . . because after all she was just a simple country church being cared for deeply by a man who understood her and loved her in a new and different way. She thought often to herself about how the Holy Spirit worked in ways she didn't understand, and yet that was okay for her. She could just accept that and forget everything else, since it wasn't important anyway.	Indirect suggestion that change will take time. Development of a conscious-unconscious split in her awareness. Encouragement to just relax and accept change without questioning how or why it was taking place. Indirect connection of the Holy Spirit and her own spirit working together as a team; final suggestion for amnesia which was developed in subsequent suggestions.

This trance process was taped for them and they were asked to play it three or four times a week for several weeks. Following the intervention the couple reported an improvement in their level of emotional and sexual intimacy (as well as a greater enjoyment of church-related activities).

Christian Integrative Potential

This particular therapeutic style of intervention lends itself well to use by therapists who wish to convey to clients their own beliefs and values. By telling clients metaphors or parables in this manner the therapist communicates to the client on multiple levels of awareness. The method is similar to the style of speaking that Jesus used in communicating so effectively to the people of his day (Shepperson, 1981; TeSelle, 1975). Jesus aimed his messages at different levels of awareness. At one level of awareness a listener was having his physical needs attended; on another, his emotional; at still another, his spiritual needs. What he received depended on the relative press of his different needs or drives.

An example of Jesus' astute ability to communicate in this metaphoric manner is seen in his command to eat his flesh and drink his blood (John 6:54ff.). Some listeners were intrigued, some disgusted, some puzzled. The behavioral result was that some went away, some gained a significant insight into Jesus' primary intervention plan for their lives, and others shrugged their shoulders and waited for something they could understand.

The Christian therapist seeking to intervene on multiple levels in his clients' lives would do well to model the basic method Jesus presented in his work. The mechanics of this method are as follows. First, one must listen to the primary representational modalities used by a client (e.g., visual, auditory, kinesthetic, etc.) and talk his language back in the same modality (see Bandler & Grinder, 1979). Second, one must tailor one's metaphor to fit the specific aptitudes and interests of the client. When talking to a nature lover, speak in terms of the particular elements familiar to that person's environment. It is interesting to note in this regard that Jesus talked to crude sailors in terms of the sky and sea and wind. When dealing with scholars he moved to their intellectual environment, the Scriptures.

A further step toward effective metaphoric communication has to do with "seeding the unconscious." Basically this means just grazing an issue in passing with an indirect allusion to the insight one desires the client to reach at a later point when he is more ready to respond appropriately. This process of seeding was developed in more recent times by Erickson (Rossi, 1980). The technique may involve nothing more than a pregnant pause following a significant idea before one continues with the metaphor at hand. For example, if one wishes the client to go deeper into trance, a common seeding tactic might be a statement such as: "As he walked . . . *deeper and deeper* . . . into the woods he became more *self-absorbed.*"

These techniques allow a therapist to redefine or reframe the client's problem in such a fashion that a previously insoluble dilemma can now be viewed from a different, more workable perspective. The metaphor is essentially parallel to the client's life situation except in a few critical elements. These changes allow the client to recognize or develop resources within himself that were previously discounted or unavailable (Lankton, 1980). These resources can be spiritual, emotional, or relational. For example, one can be allowed to get in touch with the presence of one or more benevolent introjects from one's childhood through metaphor (e.g., "And so the little ragamuffin, hair all mussed and soot streaking her face, finally came to the startling realization that indeed she *was* a princess. All she had really been required to do was see her father pass by in the parade and call out as loud as she could, *Daddy!*").

Summary

Indirect hypnotherapy combines elements of neurolinguistic programming, traditional hypnotherapy, and an applied understanding of psychodynamic theory. It is recommended for those practitioners who have or wish to develop the gift of weaving therapeutic parables into the fabric of everyday life for both themselves and their clients.

References

Bandler, R., & Grinder, J. *Frogs into princes*. Moab, Utah: Real People Press, 1979.

Gordon, D. L. *Therapeutic metaphors*. Cupertino, Calif.: Meta Publications, 1978.

Lankton, S. R. *Practical magic: A translation of a basic neurolinguistic programming into clinical psychotherapy*. Cupertino, Calif.: Meta Publications, 1980.

Rossi, E. L. (Ed.). *The collected papers of Milton H. Erickson on hypnosis*. New York: Irvington Press, 1980.

Shepperson, V. L. Paradox, parables, and change: One approach to Christian hypnotherapy. *Journal of Psychology and Theology*, 1981, *9*, 3–11.

TeSelle, S. *Speaking in parables*. Philadelphia: Fortress, 1975.

26

Inner Healing
H. Newton Malony

I̶nner healing, a contemporary form of spiritual healing, is described by its advocates as a process wherein the Holy Spirit restores health to the deepest aspects of life by dealing with the root cause of hurts and pain. Basically it involves a twofold procedure in which 1) the power of evil is broken and the heritage of wholeness that belongs to the Christian is reclaimed, and 2) memories of the past are healed through prayer.

Forms of Healing

According to McNutt (1974), one of the leading figures in the field, inner healing is one of four forms of healing and is directed primarily toward the healing of memories. He concludes that there are three major types of sickness: sickness of the spirit caused by personal sin; sickness of the emotions caused by psychological hurts from the past; and sickness of the body caused by physical disease or accidents. Prayer can be directed toward any one of these. The prayer of repentance asks forgiveness for sin; the prayer for bodily healing is directed toward physical healing; and the prayer for inner healing is concerned with healing the effects of painful memories. There is a fourth kind of prayer mentioned by McNutt: the prayer for deliverance from demon oppression, or exorcism, in which symptoms of each of the other three sicknesses can appear.

Betty and Ed Tapscott, other leaders in this movement, agree with McNutt's model but do not include exorcism as one of the primary forms of healing (Tapscott, 1975). They suggest that "breaking the power of Satan" is the first step in any healing but feel that this is accomplished through spiritual healing, which means coming to know Jesus as personal Savior. This involves confession of sin, renunciation of occult power, being willing to forgive in the same manner that one has been forgiven, being honest, and being humble. Spiritual healing is the foundation for inner healing of the mind and physical healing of the body.

The other side of breaking the power of Satan is reclaiming one's Christian inheritance, according to the Tapscotts. This means reaffirming what was true in creation and what has been provided in salvation; namely, that God wants people to be whole and has given many spiritual riches to his followers if they will but claim them. These acts of renouncing evil and reaffirming faith in God's goodness become the basis for inner healing, which is accomplished by prayer for the healing of memories. They are also the foundation for physical healing, which occurs through prayer for God to make the body whole again.

Most, if not all, inner healers agree that the several types of sickness and their remediation often occur together. Therefore, even though they emphasize one form of healing (e.g., inner healing), they are aware of, and utilize, the other types as well.

Of special interest is their attitude toward secular healers such as physicians and psychologists. After noting that millions of dollars are spent each year going to physicians, psychologists, and psychiatrists, one writer suggests that divine healing is the best. The old adage, "Doctors treat but Jesus heals," is offered as an unquestioned truth. Removing symptoms (which doctors do) is not the same as healing the cause (which Jesus does through inner healing). This same writer praises God for Christian psychologists but concludes that "inner healing is psychotherapy, plus God!" Another writer puts it thus: "Psychiatrists bring a degree of healing by probing into the past and bringing understanding of our weak and vulnerable spots and our angry and fearful reactions, but only the Holy Spirit can move into these areas and remove the scars" (Stapleton, 1976, p. x).

Among contemporary inner healers only McNutt accords an equal place to secular healers such as physicians and psychiatrists. He states that he always prefers to work as a team with them rather than by himself. But even he qualifies this approbation by saying that whereas in the 1950s he, like so many priests, discounted his own abilities to heal and referred most psychologically disturbed persons to professionals, he has come to believe that psychiatry does not always help and that prayer for the healing of memories is often the treatment of choice (McNutt, 1974).

Techniques

Prayer for the healing of memories is the core of inner healing. Memories are the residues of experience. Practically everyone has memories from the past from which he or she needs release, even if these are only minor hurts or childlike fears. Others have memories of being unwanted or neglected, of evil deeds or unexpected accidents, or even of events that happened while they were still in their mothers' wombs. Breaking the power of unresolved and oppressive memories is a prime component of inner healing.

This understanding is the major diagnostic model for the prayer that releases persons from the tyranny of the past. It is presumed that the fears, guilts, lethargies, and depressions that result from oppressive memories are against the will of God and, as such, are susceptible to being remedied by him if the person is willing. Of particular import to inner healers has been Hugh Missildine's *Your Inner Child of the Past* (1963). Inner healers feel that they are talking sound psychology because many models of psychopathology put similar emphasis on past experience. They see themselves as legitimate, even though they insist that they do not pretend to be psychologists.

Although there is a basic similarity in approach among those who practice this form of healing, there are some distinctions. The specific approaches of three prominent practitioners—the Tapscotts, Francis McNutt, and Ruth Carter Stapleton—will be examined here.

The Tapscotts

The Tapscotts feel that memories can be healed by the individual himself as well as by the ministrations of another who has the power of healing. They encourage the person to begin with a prayer for the forgiveness of sins and a reaffirmation of Jesus as personal Savior. They suggest that the person next renounce all the forces of evil or Satan that have become a part of his life, asking the Holy

Spirit to reveal these forces. At this point the person is to trust the Holy Spirit to bring to mind the images and memories that are handicapping. Even though no release is apparent, the person is to vocally renounce the power of these memories and images. Then he is to ask Jesus to fill the void that is left if the memories should leave. Jesus is asked to give his peace, his joy, and his love.

It is important to note that up to this point persons will quite likely have experienced no healing. Instead they are restating their faith and asking for God's power in their lives. Then they are requested to visualize Jesus walking hand in hand with them back through every moment of their lives. As the Holy Spirit lifts up memories of unpleasant situations, they are to take Jesus into these events. Jesus will redeem the painful memories, set the person free from them, and heal the past. The person is asked to thank God in advance for the miracle that will be worked through inner healing.

The Tapscotts provide printed prayers to be used with or by persons at every stage of the process. Although they do not say so, they seem to imply that these are once-for-all events. However, they recognize the possibility that the release from such experiences might fade, and they prescribe a set of acts designed to keep the inner person healed. These include daily prayer and Bible reading, conscious praise, regular commitment to the Lord, dedication of one's home to God, standing firm against Satan, becoming part of a spirit-filled fellowship, finding a prayer partner, and constantly forgiving others.

Francis McNutt

McNutt begins with the assumption that the basic need of life is for love; if we are ever denied it at any time in our lives, our ability to love and trust others may be seriously affected. The wounds resulting from loss of love fester and handicap us. The first step in inner healing is for Jesus to heal these wounds. The second step is for Jesus to give us the love we want and thus to fill the empty spaces once they have been healed and drained of the poison of past hurts and resentment. Whenever the person becomes aware of fears, anxieties, resentments, hates, or inhibitions, that is the time to seek inner healing.

Before the prayer for healing is offered, two questions are explored with the person. First, when can you remember first feeling this way? Second, what was happening that caused you to feel this way? If the person cannot remember an incident, then God is asked to reveal it. After the time and place of the hurt has been identified, a prayer for the healing of the hurt is offered. In as imaginative and childlike manner as possible, the healer prays that Jesus will go back into the experience and heal the person of the wound that resulted from it. McNutt states, "Jesus, as Lord of time, is able to do what we cannot. . . . The most I was ever able to do as a counselor was to help the person bring to the foreground of consciousness the things that were buried in the past, so that he could consciously cope with them in the present. Now I am discovering that the Lord can heal these wounds . . . and can bring the counseling process to its completion in a deep healing" (1974, p. 187).

After the memories have been healed, the person prays God to fill the void in his life with love. Because of the basic need for love, full healing cannot occur until the person is given what he has been missing, namely love. McNutt notes that this part of inner healing is often more difficult than the healing of the wounds of the past. The person is so accustomed to being without love that he does not know how to receive it. If the person says he does not feel the love of God, Jesus is asked to speak to the person at the depth of his soul and to call him by name. Since the nature of the wounds is known to the healer, he or she prays that God will provide the specific kind of love that the person did not have. Again, the prayer is very childlike and imaginative.

Ruth Carter Stapleton

Of note is Stapleton's emphasis on inner healing as a process, not a one-time event. Her accounts are replete with long-term relationships in which the person returns to the healer again and again. In only a few cases does she report immediate results. Further, she places an emphasis on the fact that inner healing is something more than sound doctrine or even insight into traumatic events. She suggests that most people act as though they want help when they do not really want to change.

Stapleton suggests that the desire to be whole often comes as a result of some inspirational experience with an evangelist or healer. After this the motivation toward healing changes and becomes the basis on which inner healing can occur. She postulates an "inner child" that lives in most of us and has an insatiable need for approval and love. This inner child needs to be "revealed and healed." Although she agrees with other healers that there are real past traumas that need to be faced and healed, there are in many people fantasized hurts grounded in the child within us. Thus, she seems to have an implicit model of evil which must be faced or revealed in the healing process. Finally, she emphasizes group experiences of inner healing much more than do others. Members of the group were often used in role play of other members' situations and much mutual insight occurred.

Stapleton's term for the process of inner healing is *faith imagination therapy*. In this process she recommends that persons visualize as vividly as possible Jesus coming into the experiences that have been identified as troublesome. They are encouraged to allow Jesus to respond to the situation and to take over their own behavior. She contends that forgiveness lies at the heart of all inner healing, and she encourages persons to use each situation as an opportunity to forgive and build. As Jesus dominates the visualization, persons are encouraged to allow themselves to develop into the persons God intended them to be.

Although Stapleton relies heavily on intuitive insights given her by the Holy Spirit, she leaves to the person the task of filling in the details of the visualization. In this process of faith imagination with Jesus at the center, healing deep inside the person occurs. The final step in the process is when the individual ceases being too proud or too self-depreciatory to begin some kind of ministry of service to others. As noted, for Stapleton this process is one that requires prolonged contact over an extended period of time.

Relationship to Guided Imagery

The psychotherapeutic technique most similar to the procedures in inner healing is that of guided imagery (Leuner, 1969). Stapleton is in accord with many practitioners of this technique in asserting that faith imagination is a way of inducing positive changes deep within the mind. According to Leuner guided imagery attempts to replace regressive and defensive mental habits with more mature, adaptive ego functioning. The core method in both guided imagery and faith imagination is that of suggestion. Several aspects of these procedures should be noted.

Initially the role of the therapist or healer is definitely an active one. Although many inner healers listen long and empathically (as would many psychotherapists using guided imagery), when they begin to treat the person they become very active. They are not client centered in their approach or their presumptions. They act on a great deal of intuition, and once they intuit a dynamic, they assertively lead the individual in a fantasy designed to induce healing.

However, it would seem that neither inner healers nor therapists employing guided imagery exert quite the control that hypnotists do, although their methods are similar. Neither faith imaginations nor guided fantasies are hypnotic suggestions. They have more fluidity to them. In many hypnotic situations the hypnotist provides most, if not all, the details. In inner healing and guided imagery the individual is encouraged to imagine the action and elaborate the basic situation in fantasy.

There is yet another similarity in the two methods that should be noted. They both use archetypal personages in their fantasies. Guided imagery as a psychotherapeutic technique usually relies on Jungian understandings of psychic structure and dream analysis. For example, roads are life lines, mountains are ambitions or problems, crossroads are decision points, caves are suppressed memories or fears, witches are denied impulses, and old men are inner wisdoms. Inner healers confine themselves to two figures in the Trinity—the Holy Spirit and Jesus Christ. They encourage the individual to allow the Holy Spirit to reveal the incidents that provoked trauma and to allow "Jesus" to be present in the reliving of those events and to heal them.

One could say that the inner healer's Jesus is most like the "old man" of guided imagery. However, there is a radical difference. The guided imagists assume that the old man is the source of inner wisdom, which was there all along but which had been denied due to the pressures of living and to defenses against trauma. The inner healers make a different assumption. Although they rely heavily on reclaiming the inheritance of the image of God in creation, they emphasize much more the gifts of salvation that have been made available through the cross of Christ. Furthermore, Jesus is not inner wisdom but transcendent personal power. He exists outside the person and is much more than denied power. He brings insight and healing that are unavailable to personal resources no matter how suppressed. He is a person, not simply an insight.

Finally, there is a common presumption among inner healers and guided imagists that something more than insight is needed for healing to occur. Both groups are action therapists in the sense that they agree that reexperiencing is the prime means of psychological change. In this they resemble both Gestalt therapists and psychoanalysts, although their presumptions of the dynamic processes involved are somewhat different. Gestalt therapists are more inclined to induce the reexperience of past processes, such as feelings, while psychoanalysts are committed to a spontaneous working through of the transference with the therapist.

Guided imagists and inner healers deal with total events, although the former typically induce standard classical fantasies while the latter encourage reliving of actual personal situations. Yet in both, the participation of the person in present experiencing is the vital component of healing. However, it should be said that here again the inner healers assume that inner resources will not, in and of themselves, accomplish the task. What is needed is the presence and power of the living Christ, who will do for the person what he could not do for himself—namely, heal the memories and heal the person so that he can live anew.

Critique

Several critiques of inner healing have been given. The most recent is that of Alsdurf and Malony (1980), who have analyzed a number of the assumptions underlying the work of Stapleton. Although inner healers differ in some crucial ways, the Alsdurf and Malony critique seems to apply to all in general.

Initially Stapleton is accused of engaging in a simplified psychotherapy, although she denied this. In fact, she claimed that her approach is not counseling in the sense that this word is used among mental health professionals. Yet it is hard to deny that she was indeed engaged in such when one examines her accounts of her work. She met with persons in periodic sessions over extended periods of time. She led group meetings that included sharing, role playing, guided fantasies, and interpersonal catharsis. In spite of her denial she seemed to evidence a cavalier reliance on serious psychodynamic theorizing and an overreliance on semipopular authors such as Missildine.

While her basic presumption that Jesus can heal quickly and deeply allowed her to expect miracles, she used many standard psychotherapeutic methods without acknowledging them. Furthermore, she seemed naïvely free from the caution that most psychotherapists have in approaching some problems optimistically while recognizing great difficulties inherent in others. Again, her too easy acceptance of one model, Missildine, caused her to assume an almost photographic memory of the past while almost reifying a psychic structure, the inner child of the past, that most theorists would find problematical.

Perhaps the basic problem is that while Stapleton provided fairly intensive psychotherapy, she did not seem to acknowledge the manner in which students of psychopathology have come to understand these issues. To deny this reality is to remain free from self-criticism while evoking the discount of those who know better. This is not to say that her (and other inner healers') basic belief in the power of Jesus to heal needs to be subjected to such analysis by secular theory. It does not. It is to say that this tradition of healing would be strengthened if inner healers could be better informed about how human beings function and what causes them to be as they are.

Another critique, which may be more attributable to Stapleton than to other inner healers, is that she lacked a thorough doctrine of sin. In some comments made to secular groups of therapists, it seems as if she were willing to identify her approach too simplistically with holistic healers who may be operating under Eastern presumptions that do not include a basic propensity toward evil. Thus, while using Christian terminology she may be implicitly utilizing basic assumptions more like secular therapists who have concluded that humans have the resources for self-healing. It should be noted that McNutt and the Tapscotts put great emphasis on the importance of the forgiveness for sin in their methods and that Stapleton denies any such omissions when confronted with this critique. However, her words in certain settings belie this denial and denote a possible naïve reliance on a methodology that seems to bypass the need for the individual to face personal evil in an effort to affirm the power of Jesus to heal hurts resulting from traumatic past events.

All in all, however, inner healing should be looked upon as a unique and powerful form of therapy currently held in wide respect by a large part of the Christian world. Christian psychotherapists should study it deeply and attempt to learn from its bold use of Christian resources in the helping process.

References

Alsdurf, J. M., & Malony, H. N. A critique of Ruth Carter Stapleton's ministry of "inner healing." *Journal of Psychology and Theology*, 1980, *8*(3), 173–184.

Leuner, H. Guided affective imagery. *American Journal of Psychotherapy*, 1969, *23*, 4–22.

McNutt, F. *Healing*. Notre Dame, Ind.: Ave Maria Press, 1974.

Missildine, W. H. *Your inner child of the past*. New York: Simon & Schuster, 1963.

Stapleton, R. C. *The gift of inner healing*. Waco, Tex.: Word Books, 1976.

Tapscott, B. *Inner healing through healing of memories*. Houston: Tapscott, 1975.

27

Integrity Therapy
David W. Brokaw

Integrity therapy is a moral approach to psychotherapy that places a critical emphasis on the interrelationship between mental health and behaviors concerned with honesty, responsibility, and involvement with others. Its fundamental principles were formulated by O. Hobart Mowrer, who is best known for behavioristic research on learning theory. He proposed that emotional disturbance is a symptom of concealed guilt, which in turn emerges from violations of the individual's conscience. In Mowrer's view a return to psychological well-being requires confession of one's moral failures to significant others and subsequent acts of restitution. This approach is distinguished from more orthodox deterministic therapies by its insistence on the individual's personal responsibility for his or her psychopathology.

Integrity therapy is an innovative synthesis of diverse clinical and philosophical traditions. Its principal roots include Sullivan's interpersonal psychiatry, the Judeo-Christian religions, and behavioral psychology.

Mowrer's core assumption is that "human personality is primarily a *social* phenomenon" (1972, p. 22). Since we are social creatures by nature, our moral and psychological integrity depends on community with other persons. Mowrer holds, as do the interpersonalists, that psychopathology and mental health are intimately related to the quality of one's relationships with others.

A second major root is found in the Judeo-Christian tradition. Mowrer finds in the early Christian church an excellent model of healing; in it he identifies precedents for the form, process, and goal of integrity therapy. In terms of form, Mowrer's group format is modeled after the intimate house churches of early Christianity. The therapeutic process involves Mowrer's accommodations of spiritual disciplines such as confession of sin and penance (restitution). As for the goal, group members are called to strive toward moral ideals compatible with the Judeo-Christian ethic.

Behavioral psychology makes up a third root of integrity therapy. Paraphrasing an E. Stanley Jones aphorism, Mowrer endorses the behavioral principle that "it is easier to *act* yourself into a new way of feeling than to *feel* yourself into a new way of acting" (Drakeford, 1967, p. 116). Mowrer's theory of neurosis, attributing emotional disturbance to specific transgressions of social norms, draws heavily from learning theory (London, 1964). His technique of cure—that is, prescribing acts of restitution—clearly involves the learning and reinforcement of new behaviors, leading some to describe the integrity approach as an action therapy.

The integrity philosophy of neurosis and treatment may be contrasted with psychoanalytic theory. Freudians maintain that anxiety is partially a result of an overly strict conscience, termed the superego. Treatment is thus directed toward reforming the superego along less punitive lines. Mowrer, on the other hand, posits that anxiety reflects the moral "dis-ease" of an appropriately guilty conscience, driven by fear of community reprisal. From his perspective treatment must facilitate personal growth, such that the individual behaves more responsibly vis-à-vis the reality demands of conscience and society.

Mowrer further postulates that neurotics are alienated from others as a consequence of breaking societal rules. He insists that treatment must therefore facilitate the individual's return to community. This process occurs within the context of a subcommunity or therapy group. Such groups offer the added advantage of holding individuals responsible for their misbehavior and rewarding more mature life choices.

Integrity therapy specifies a clearly delineated technique of cure involving two primary client activities: confession and restitution.

The former requires the client to accept personal responsibility for wrongdoing and is distinguished from complaining or blaming. Confession is directed toward the significant others who have been wronged.

The technique of restitution follows from Mowrer's contention that symptoms reflect the punishment of a guilty conscience. Integrity therapists insist that guilt must be resolved through restorative actions. This action principle includes giving up one's current misbehavior, rectifying past injustices, and serving others. Mowrer emphasizes that confession without restitution is simply cheap grace and is ineffective for dealing with real guilt.

In addition to confession and restitution Mowrer encourages emotional honesty. This involves activities such as verbalizing feelings or physically touching other group members. Such practices serve to facilitate emotional release and to promote greater interpersonal involvement.

Due to the scarcity of research on the results of integrity therapy, its benefits are difficult to assess. Practitioner observations suggest that integrity techniques are applicable to a wide variety of psychological problems, including marital conflict, anxiety, and depression. Three groups in particular, however, appear nonamenable to this approach: antisocial (psychopathic) personalities, paranoid personalities, and persons whose emotional difficulties are due to physical causes.

Apart from the issue of treatment efficacy, integrity therapy may be assessed in terms of its compatibility with biblical principles. Despite Mowrer's frequent use of religious terminology his approach to persons is clearly nontheistic. For example, words such as *sin, confession,* and *forgiveness* have no transcendent referent: these terms refer exclusively to the horizontal dimension—that is, what persons do to one another. Mowrer clarifies his humanistic emphasis: "Our assumption is that our first obligation is to be good human beings . . . and that in pursuing that end we cannot be displeasing whatever Higher Power or Divine Intelligence one may or may not believe to exist" (1972, p. 11). Although Mowrer rightly points out the individual's responsibilities to other persons, his perspective ignores biblical teachings that: 1) individuals are ultimately responsible to God; 2) moral failures involve transgressions of divine standards; and 3) forgiveness comes from God through Christ.

On the other hand, many concepts and principles of integrity therapy appear compatible with Christian thought: the importance of community (Heb. 10:25), confession (James 5:16), honesty (Exod. 20:16), and restitution (Lev. 5:16). Mowrer's emphasis on acting out moral behaviors is not inconsistent with the exhortation in James 2 that believers demonstrate faith through good actions. Integrity theory is also consonant with Christianity in advocating some crucial Judeo-Christian standards of right and wrong. Because of these areas of convergence, this approach may be accommodated to a biblically based therapy approach (cf. Drakeford, 1967).

References

Drakeford, J. W. *Integrity therapy.* Nashville: Broadman, 1967.

London, P. *The modes and morals of psychotherapy.* New York: Holt, Rinehart, & Winston, 1964.

Mowrer, O. H. Integrity groups: Principles and procedures. *The Counseling Psychologist,* 1972, 3(2), 7–33.

Additional Readings

Mowrer, O. H. *The crisis in psychiatry and religion.* Princeton, N.J.: Van Nostrand, 1961.

Mowrer, O. H. *The new group therapy.* Princeton, N.J.: Van Nostrand, 1964.

28

Jungian Analysis
John A. Sanford

At the turn of this century Jung and Freud independently developed their ideas about the reality and importance of the unconscious. Freud, the older man, was the first to publish some of his findings, and Jung was greatly impressed by Freud's work. The two met and enjoyed a close working relationship and friendship from about 1906 to 1913, when personal and theoretical differences drove them apart.

After he left Freud, Jung worked alone and developed his own depth psychology, which he called analytical psychology to distinguish it from Freud's psychoanalysis. Jung agreed with Freud on the idea of libido or psychic energy, on the existence of the unconscious part of the mind, on repression, and on the importance of dreams. However, Jung believed the unconscious contained not only repressed or forgotten memories and emotions that were personal to an individual but also typical patterns of energy and behavior that were common to everyone. These patterns Jung called archetypes. He called the latter strata of the unconscious the collective unconscious or objective psyche to distinguish it from the personal unconscious.

Jung also observed in people an innate urge toward wholeness. He distinguished between the ego and the self. The ego he regarded as the center of consciousness, while the self was the center of a total personality that embraced both the conscious and the unconscious. He believed the self to be the whole personality that exists from the beginning as a potentiality and strives to be realized through a developmental life process in which the ego must participate. Jung called this process individuation. In this process the center of the personality shifts from ego to self, and as the ego becomes more conscious of the self, the range of consciousness greatly expands.

Process and Style

The cornerstone of Jungian analysis is the individuation process. The Jungian analyst tries to help this process take place in his client in the belief that as a person individuates he becomes more whole and therefore finds healing and a creative solution for his difficulties.

Jung did not prescribe any set treatment methodology. For one thing, he perceived that people are psychologically different. Some are extraverts (more oriented to outer reality), and some are introverts (more oriented toward inner reality). In addition there are four psychological functions: thinking, feeling, sensation, and intuition. Each person uses one of these functions as his or her main function, and this determines one's particular approach to life. For this reason a therapist of one personality type may work differently than a therapist of another type. A therapist may also work one way with a client who is an introverted thinking type, and a different way with a client who is an extraverted feeling type.

In addition, Jungian psychology as it is practiced today is not a monochromatic system. Some Jungian analysts tend to pattern their therapy after Jung's own approach. Others are more eclectic in their approach and may combine Jungian methods with methodologies from other schools of psychology. Still others have altered Jung's original ideas so much that they refer to their psychology as archetypal psychology to distinguish it from Jung's original analytical psychology. In addition, Jungian analysts come from varied professional backgrounds, and this also may influence how they work as therapists.

Techniques

Nevertheless, there are certain typical methods and procedures widely used in Jungian analysis. While Jungian analysts can and do function as marriage counselors, family counselors, and group therapists, the main thrust of Jungian analysis is individual therapy. Because all Jungian analysts are trained first as psychotherapists, generally accepted psychotherapeutic procedures are usually followed. However, in addition there is an attempt to work with unconscious material as it emerges in dreams, fantasies, slips-of-the-tongue, etc. It is the use of unconscious material that distinguishes analysis from therapy or counseling. Viewed in this way all analysis is a form of therapy, but not all therapy is analysis, since a great deal of therapy deals only with the ego.

Dreams are frequently especially important in Jungian analysis. Dreams are seen as manifestations of the unconscious that tend to compensate inadequate or one-sided ego attitudes. They are regarded as emanating from the self, and for this reason they tend to illuminate and heal when they are recognized, contemplated, and (when possible) understood. The language of dreams is symbolic. This means that they use something known and familiar in the everyday world of consciousness to represent something that is unconscious and therefore not yet known. In this way unconscious contents can approach consciousness and thus enlarge and creatively alter a person's conscious viewpoint.

Dreams are pertinent to particular people at specific times in their lives. For this reason no single theory of the meaning of dreams is always applicable. Jung rejected Freud's narrow interpretation of dreams as always symbolic of repressed sexual urges. Instead of imposing a meaning on the dream from some theoretical structure, the Jungian analyst tries to listen carefully to the structure and symbolism of the dream to see what the dream itself is expressing.

Because dreams are, like a tailor-made suit of clothes, so highly individual, one needs to know who the dreamer is and what that person's life circumstances are before a dream can be understood. When a client presents a dream, he is often encouraged to express his associations to the various dream symbols and images. Sometimes the analyst may also amplify the dream by pointing to similar archetypal motifs in myths and fairy tales. It is as important to explore the dream as a living experience as it is to interpret the dream along the lines of psychological theory.

Dream images, and other manifestations of the unconscious as well, may be further developed by the process of active imagination. In this process a person who is fully awake and alert interacts with images that have arisen from the unconscious. For instance, a figure who appeared in a dream may be brought back to consciousness and a dialogue with that figure may develop. By concentrating on dream figures and images they may begin to have a life of their own, and the ego can then interact with the enlivened psychic image. Sometimes a whole story may develop, the dream or fantasy being continued in this way and allowed to evolve. This method allows consciousness and the unconscious to approach each other, and permits the self, as a function of the psyche transcending and uniting them both, to bring about a process of inner unification. Because active imagination requires a certain amount of psychological maturity and development, it is not a recommended procedure with everyone and often is utilized only in later stages of analysis.

Jungian analysis also regards creative expressions of the psyche as important for the healing process. Dancing, painting, sculpting, and writing are often found to be helpful ways to express and integrate the unconscious. When these methods are used, the point is not to become a good dancer or artist, but to use nonintellectual ways of contacting the vital energy of the self. It is also often recommended that a client keep an informal notebook called a journal in which he or she can record and contain dreams, fantasies, thoughts, creative inspirations—in fact, anything that crosses the screen of consciousness.

The Analytic Relationship

Jung regarded the relationship between therapist and client as especially important. It was his belief that in the process of therapy the personality of the therapist could beneficially affect the personality of the client. If this is to happen, the therapist must be a relatively conscious, mature, and ethical person. Because Jung felt the relationship of therapist and client was so important, he rejected Freud's idea that the client should lie on a couch and the therapist sit behind him. Instead he worked with his clients face to face so there could be a direct and equal interaction.

The relationship between therapist and client is called the transference. The transference may be a relatively simple matter of rapport, a warm relationship in which the concerns of the client can be talked over in a friendly and understanding atmosphere. The transference also includes the hopes and expectations that the client brings into the relationship, plus the interest in the client that the therapist brings. But sometimes the transference may include the transferring to the therapist of reactions that come from childhood. For example, the client may unconsciously see in the therapist the figure of the mother or father and repeat patterns of relating that were learned in childhood. The transference may also include the projection onto the therapist of unconscious archetypal images. For instance, the savior archetype may be projected onto the therapist, or the archetype of the anima or animus (the contrasexual side of a man or woman).

Projection is an unconscious mechanism that results in vital aspects of one person being seen in the other person. When projections occur in the transference, it is helpful, and often necessary, to analyze them in order to make conscious the projected images. In this way the client can withdraw his projections, taking them back into himself so to speak, and thereby enlarge the scope of his personality.

Of course, it may also work the other way around, and the therapist may project contents of her own onto the client. This is called the countertransference. It is expected that with the help of her extensive personal analysis the therapist will be aware of this when it happens and will integrate what is taking place within herself.

One reason for the importance of the relationship between the therapist and the client is that it provides a container for the client's personality. Their relationship has been likened to an alchemical vessel in which the various components of the client's psyche can be contained and gradually transformed: projections can be recognized and withdrawn, dreams can be remembered and reexperienced, emotions can be freely expressed and integrated, all within the "closed vessel" of the analytical relationship.

Training

Since so much in the process of Jungian analysis depends on the personality of the therapist, Jungian training programs place a heavy emphasis on the therapist's individuation. The wholeness, consciousness, and integrity of the therapist are thought to be as important as the acquisition of techniques of doing therapy. For this reason the cornerstone of training to be a Jungian analyst is the continuing analysis of the therapist, although many other things are also involved.

Training is undergone at Jungian Institutes in major cities throughout the United States and Europe. While requirements for admission to training programs vary from one institute to another, all require that a person is or will soon be a licensed psychotherapist, and that he have a considerable amount of personal Jungian analysis. Psychiatrists, psychologists, marriage and family counselors, specially licensed social workers, and sometimes clergy may all be eligible for training programs that lead to certification as a Jungian analyst.

Jungian Analysis and Other Traditions

Jungian analysis can be compared to other psychological approaches and to Christianity. As indicated, Jung agreed with many of Freud's ideas, but saw the psyche in a much broader light than Freud and never insisted upon a specific treatment methodology. Like Rogers, Jung believed the psyche was self-healing and that the true "doctor" was in the patient; but unlike Rogers, Jung emphasized the importance of integrating unconscious material. Jungian psychology sees the emphasis transactional analysis places upon the interaction of parent-child-adult as the exploration of an important archetype (that is why it is so universally applicable), but understands that personality includes many other archetypes in addition to this one. Where Gestalt psychology has little personality theory, Jungian analysis rests on an extensive theory of personality. Gestalt therapy also frequently utilizes an extraverted group approach, whereas Jungian work usually is individual and frequently more introverted.

The concepts of analytical psychology can both enrich and challenge the Christian viewpoint. For instance, Jung's theory of the collective unconscious can be viewed as giving a scientific basis for the biblical view of the objective existence and reality of a spiritual world. Likewise, Jung's idea of individuation corroborates and vitalizes the Christian premise that the life of the individual has a meaning. On the other hand, Jung's idea that Christ is a symbolic representation of the self may enrich the Christian doctrine of Christ as the Son of God, but it also challenges the Christian idea of a unique revelation in Christ, since Jung saw the self represented in many different religious traditions. Finally, Jung's treatment of the nature of evil, and its relationship to the self and to individuation, may also prove problematical to the Christian.

Yet some of the methods frequently used in Jungian analysis can be helpful to the Christian counselor or spiritual director. Jung's emphasis on the importance of dreams, for instance, finds ample support in the view of the Bible and early church, where dreams were universally regarded as an important way in which God spoke to people. Jung's symbolic approach to the unconscious also finds a fruitful parallel in the parables of Jesus, for Jesus also taught in the "as if" language of symbols. The Bible also contains several excellent instances of active imagination—for example, Ezekiel's vision of the dry bones and Isaiah's vision of Yahweh.

29

Life Skills Counseling
Elizabeth M. Altmaier

Traditional counseling methods have, for the most part, failed to be effective with clients who are from disadvantaged backgrounds. This failure is especially pronounced when the counseling method employed is one where discussion of feelings is stimulated by an ambiguous or nonstructured relationship between counselor and client. Adkins (Adkins & Wynne, 1966) developed a counseling approach, based on his experiences with a vocational training program, which emphasizes the use of a structured format to help disadvantaged adolescents and adults learn skills related to employment, interpersonal adjustment, and citizenship. He used three criteria for designing this program. First, the counseling should be centered on problems related to living and working in a city environment. Second, the skills that clients brought to counseling should serve as a foundation for newer skills. Third, the program should allow for both group interactions and personal attention.

Adkins worked with counselors to formulate a task analysis of the skill requirements for successful relationships within work, family, and community settings. On the basis of this analysis he developed a list of fifty common life problems, which were then grouped into five areas: developing oneself and relating to others; managing a career; managing home and family responsibilities; managing leisure time; and exercising community rights, opportunities, and responsibilities. Each of these areas, which are titled curriculum tracks in the program, was divided into smaller units (Adkins, 1973). For example, representative units of the managing a career area are (1) interviews, tests, and application blanks; (2) relating to one's boss; and (3) pay check deductions. These units represent competencies or skills needed to succeed in the larger area.

Adkins also developed a process for teaching these skills that was targeted to the needs of his audience. Since he had noted in his work with disadvantaged clients that nondirected group discussions tended to be unfocused and nonproductive, he developed a four-stage process to teach life skills. This process is based on "a fundamental notion . . . that experience followed by reflection, followed by goal-setting, followed by further exploration, reflection, and so forth" (Adkins, 1970, p. 111) was the most productive method for encouraging self-directed change. His four-stage process, therefore, begins with a stimulus, moves to evocation, then objective inquiry, then to application.

During the stimulus stage the counselor presents a problem using a tape recording, a movie, or an interview and thus stimulates the group's interest and involvement in the topic. Once the group begins to discuss the problem, the counselor's objective is to draw from each group member what he or she knows about the problem—the evocation stage. The group's ideas are written on a blackboard or newsprint, and discussion continues until interest lags. Then the ideas are categorized and questions are developed. The third stage, that of objective inquiry, involves having group members obtain relevant information. The counselor uses prepared multimedia kits to direct the members' information-seeking activities both within and outside the classroom. Once the relevant information has been obtained and presented to the group, the group selects one or several aspects of the problem to work out in the application stage. During this stage projects that allow for the development and application of new skills are devised and completed.

The life skills approach is meant to be flexible. Thus, a counselor might focus on one area in particular (e.g., employment) and spend several sessions going through the four stages, or may choose to cover every curriculum track at a less specific level of involvement. This flexibility is a major advantage of the approach. Another advantage is that the emphasis on life problems and skills translates counseling goals into specific behavioral objectives rather than insight-oriented affective and cognitive outcomes. Transfer of learning from life skills counseling to real-life problems would therefore be heightened. Maintenance of change would also be likely as the newly learned skills would be incorporated and used successfully after the counseling had ended. Finally, the learning process is learner centered rather than teacher oriented. Thus, motivation for learning, as Adkins (1980) reports, is usually high.

In summary, life skills counseling is an alternative counseling approach designed to teach coping skills to underserved populations (people who need but do not make use of traditional counseling services). Both a program design and a learning process model have been developed. Since the research evidence to date is scanty, the effectiveness of this approach must be demonstrated through use and evaluation. However, Adkins (1980) reports on several research projects in progress which indicate that learners and counselors find the program to be effective.

For a Christian counselor this approach may represent an excellent method for education and development among his or her clients. Although conceived as a remedial intervention, life skills counseling could easily be adapted for use in a preventive context and for life problems, such as marriage and parenting, which seem to be frequent client concerns.

References

Adkins, W. R. Life skills: Structured counseling for the disadvantaged. *Personnel and Guidance Journal*, 1970, *49*, 108–116.

Adkins, W. R. Life skills education for adult learners. *Adult Leadership*, 1973, *22*, 55–58; 82–84.

Adkins, W. R. Life skills counseling. In R. Herink (Ed.), *The psychotherapy handbook*. New York: New American Library, 1980.

Adkins, W. R., & Wynne, J. D. *Final report of the YMCA youth and work project*. Contract 24–64, Department of Labor. New York: YMCA of Greater New York, 1966.

30

Logotherapy
Darrell Smith

Logotherapy is an approach to psychotherapy developed by Victor Frankl (1962, 1969, 1978). The term is derived from two Greek words, *logos* (word or meaning) and *therapeia* (healing). Logotherapy, then, is providing or experiencing healing through meaning. Logotherapy can be subsumed under existential psychiatry and psychology. Frankl at one time referred to his approach as *Existenzanalysis*, but has subsequently preferred logotherapy in order to distinguish his work from that of Boss and Binswanger, who have also created existential analytic approaches. As do existential orientations logotherapy views the individual as being free, responsible, unique, and holistic. In the therapy process the client is challenged to become decisive in using his or her freedom in order to discover meaning in life.

Frankl views the individual as a self-determining and self-actualizing person. Thus a human being possesses the innate capacity to transcend environmental factors, be they biological, psychological, or sociological. The transcendent ability is possible because of spiritual freedom that characterizes human beings and distinguishes them uniquely from the animal world. This spiritual freedom is not so much freedom from oppressive forces as it is the potential for discovering, deciding, and actualizing one's existence. Such freedom cannot be taken from the individual, and it is this dimension that makes life meaningful and purposeful.

Human personality is a unity composed of three intermeshing realities: the somatic (physical), the mental (psychological), and the spiritual (noölogical). The combined interaction of the physical and psychological components forms what might be called the psychophysicum. Each dimension of the personality is indispensable, but it is the spiritual dimension that gives meaning. The primary motivation in human behavior is the will to meaning. This is in contrast to Freud's idea of will to pleasure and Adler's concept of will to power or superiority. This will to meaning involves a set of ideals and values that pulls rather than pushes an individual in life. It is a fulfillment of spiritual needs in the process of choosing and deciding.

Like Adler, Frankl thinks it is necessary for an individual to first solve some basic life tasks before finding meaning and purpose in life and thus being fully actualized. These tasks include discovering the meaning of love, the meaning of work and mission, and the meaning of death and suffering. Only then can the meaning of life itself be found.

Problems in living can be discussed under three classifications: neuroses, noögenic neuroses, and psychoses. The neuroses are psychogenic and are experienced either as some type of anticipatory anxiety or an obsessional disturbance. The noögenic neuroses have a spiritually based etiology and are manifested as existential boredom and frustration, a vacuum existence, and a loss of meaning and purpose in life. The psychoses are organic or physically based. A diagnosis always seeks to differentiate these three basic types of problems. Most problems, however, tend to be mixed in nature, and seldom does one problem have a single causation and unitary symptomatology. Accurate differential diagnosis work does indicate the appropriate form of therapy. A neurosis is treated with psychotherapy, a psychosis with physical medicine, and a noögenic neurosis with logotherapy.

The relationship between the logotherapist and the client is characterized by warmth and closeness with a consistent concern for scientific objectivity. An ultimate goal of logotherapy is to help the individual accept responsibility for himself through using spiritual freedom to make personal choices and decisions in the discovery of meaning in and to life.

A variety of methods and strategies are used in the practice of logotherapy. Logotherapy in the purest sense consists of Socratic-like dialogue. Another mode of intervention is logodrama, in which the client is guided in narrating and experiencing the events and meaning of his life. A third strategy is paradoxical intention. This involves asking the client to intend that which he fears. The technique is designed to help individuals overcome anticipatory anxiety or hyperintention. The final major strategy is dereflection. This counteracts obsessive ideation or hyperreflection by helping the client stop thinking about the problem. Both paradoxical intention and dereflection are based on the individual's capacity to detach himself from absorption with personal problems. They have a cognitive behavior emphasis but were developed before cognitive behavior approaches existed.

Logotherapy is the most systematic of all the existential approaches to counseling and psychotherapy. It offers a clear perspective on the nature of the human being, a useful theory of personality, a multidimensional answer to the nature and cause of problems in living, a well-articulated set of procedures and processes to follow in doing therapy, and a body of clearly defined techniques. Much of Frankl's thinking is compatible with historical Judeo-Christian theology (Tweedie, 1961).

References

Frankl, V. E. *Man's search for meaning*. Boston: Beacon Press, 1962.

Frankl, V. E. *The will to meaning*. New York: World Publishing, 1969.

Frankl, V. E. *The unheard cry for meaning*. New York: Simon & Schuster, 1978.

Tweedie, D. F. *Logotherapy: An evaluation of Frankl's existential approach to psychotherapy*. Grand Rapids: Baker, 1961.

31

Neurolinguistic Programming
Clark E. Barshinger & Lojan E. LaRowe

A recent development in psychotherapy founded by Bandler and Grinder (1975, 1976), neurolinguistic programming is a compilation of their studies of particularly successful psychotherapists. Bandler and Grinder, after analyzing these other methods and techniques, developed a model that focuses on how the client processes information and on how to utilize this "internal strategy" for producing desired changes.

Representational Systems

Fundamental to this model are the representational systems—that is, the ways of experiencing and processing the world. There are three major representational systems: auditory, visual, and kinesthetic. The dominant system employed by an individual is indicated by both eye patterns called accessing cues and linguistic patterns. Bandler and Grinder report that as you face other persons, their eyes will look up and left when they are accessing remembered images visually, up and right when they are visually constructing

197

images, down and right when they are accessing feelings and other kinesthetic sensations, down and left when they are listening to internal auditory sounds such as internal dialogue, level left for remembered auditory sounds, and level right for constructed auditory sounds.

For example, if you were to ask a person with a visual representational system when she last saw a movie, her eyes would move up and left as she searches for a visual representation of herself the last time she attended a movie. Similarly, if you were to ask a person with an auditory representational system when was the last time he heard Handel's *Messiah*, his eyes might well go level and left as he searches for the memory of that experience auditorily. If you ask a person with a kinesthetic representational system when was the last time he felt angry, he very likely would look down and to the right to access that feeling and retrieve that memory kinesthetically.

The other way of determining a person's representational system is through the linguistic patterns they use. For example, persons with a visual representational system tend to use words that are visual (e.g., picture, vague, bright, flash, perspective). Persons with an auditory representational system use words that are auditory (e.g., scream, screech, hear, amplify, harmonize). Individuals with a kinesthetic representational system use words that are kinesthetically oriented (e.g., handle, feel, grasp, warm, tight, rough).

Knowledge of an individual's representational system makes it possible to establish rapport with the individual. For example, if an individual is looking up right and left while talking (using visual linguistic patterns), responding to that person with visual linguistic patterns (looking up left and right oneself) can put the individual at ease since both persons are experiencing the world in the same way. Rapport is also increased by mirroring nonverbal communications. For example, sitting in the same position, using the same voice volume and tone, and employing the same gestures as the client facilitates the sense of rapport that exists in the communication.

Techniques

Having established rapport, the therapist is now ready to use the techniques for intervention. One technique is *overlapping,* the process of connecting a representational system that is ordinarily not used by the client with one that is regularly used. The result is that the client is gradually enabled to use the new representational system.

Another technique is *anchoring.* Based on the principles of classical conditioning, anchoring is a process whereby some behavior of the therapist is connected to an experience for the client. For example, while a client is remembering a very powerful, confident moment in his or her past, the therapist may lean over and lightly touch him or her on the hand. In the future whenever the therapist wishes to bring the resources of that memory into the client's awareness, he or she need only reach over and touch the client in exactly the same way. Anchoring can be used to change negative memories and to create previously unavailable possibilities by mobilizing resources that were previously out of the individual's awareness.

Another tool in neurolinguistic programming is *reframing*. Reframing is based on the principle that every behavior, both internal and external, has some useful and meaningful purpose. Reframing aims to make the client aware of the positive intention of some behavior previously perceived as negative. Perceiving the positive intention of the problem behavior allows the individual to find more constructive ways of fulfilling this intention. Reframing can also refer to simply looking at the problem in a new way and thereby accepting it with more ease.

Neurolinguistic programming makes significant use of *metaphor*. The value of metaphor is that the telling of a parallel story to the problem situation of the client allows the person to change without really trying. Often people's conscious efforts to change actually end up interfering with their ability to change. The use of metaphor allows a hidden example to become available to them so they can follow the lead of the metaphor and resolve their problems without consciously trying so hard.

Two other tools of neurolinguistic programming are *meta model* and *strategies*. The meta model deals primarily with linguistic patterns that in one form or another overgeneralize or distort external reality. The meta model consists of questions aimed at clarifying hidden limitations individuals place on themselves by accepting inadequate information. For example, one category in a meta model is deletion. To the statement, "I'm afraid," a helpful response is, "Of what or whom are you afraid?" To the statement, "He's the best player," the response might be, "He's the best player among whom?" Through a series of such questions the neurolinguistic programmer is able to help a client understand himself better.

Strategies on the other hand put the emphasis on eye patterns. For example, when asked why he can't study a person might look quickly up and to the left (visual recall) and then, looking down and right, say, "I just can't feel confident." The client might be unaware of the visual picture from the past that flashes through his or her mind just before the feeling of discouragement. This strategy can be improved by bringing the picture from the past into the client's awareness and thereby counteracting some of its negative impact.

As with so many of the other newer therapies, research on the effectiveness of neurolinguistic programming is lacking. Because of the absence of a theory of personality or of psychopathology, the approach seems more a collection of therapeutic strategies and techniques than a comprehensive system of psychotherapy. Many of these appear to be very useful, and a number of them are regularly incorporated into family therapy and hypnotherapy approaches.

References

Bandler, R., & Grinder, J. *The structure of magic.* Palo Alto, Calif.: Science and Behavior Books, 1975.

Bandler, R., & Grinder, J. *The structure of magic II.* Palo Alto, Calif.: Science and Behavior Books, 1976.

Additional Readings

Bandler, R., Grinder, J., & Satir, V. *Changing with families.* Palo Alto, Calif.: Science and Behavior Books, 1976.

Lankton, S. R. *Practical magical: Translation of basic neurolinguistic programming into clinical psychotherapy.* Cuppertino, Calif.: Meta Publications, 1980.

32

Nouthetic Counseling
John D. Carter

Nouthetic counseling is a theory formulated by Jay E. Adams (1970) based on the Greek word *noutheteō*, translated as "admonish." Adams's most systematic work on counseling appeared in 1973 as *The Christian Counselor's Manual*, and in 1979 he began a theology of counseling, *More than Redemption*. Seminary trained, Adams has a doctorate in speech. After a pastorate and three years of teaching speech, he became professor of practical theology at Westminster Seminary, where he continues a part-time affiliation.

Personality Theory

Nouthetic counseling can be described in terms of its theory of human nature, view of pathology, and model and process of counseling. Nouthetic theory stresses the overt aspects of human nature. Adams maintains that God describes love in attitudinal and behavioral terms in defining it as commandment keeping (John 14:15). Hence nouthetic counseling focuses less on how clients feel than on how they behave. In addition, voluntary changes in behavior are a function of intelligent decisions and affect the emotions as a result, thus reaching the whole man. "People feel bad because of bad behavior: feelings flow from actions" (Adams, 1970, p. 93).

To Adams the sequence is clear: God's commands deal with behavior and attitudes. The individual chooses to behave consistently or inconsistently with these commands, and good or bad feelings follow accordingly. Somehow the result is communicated to the whole person, but what the whole person means for Adams is never defined. Behavior is defined as responsible conduct. An attitude is a habitual pattern of thought which strongly influences actions.

Attitudes may be changed more easily than feelings, which Adams defines as the perception of a bodily state, either pleasant or unpleasant. He views other emotional responses of the body as "*responses* to judgments made about the environment and oneself" (1974, p. 112). They come in two kinds, good and bad.

Psychologically, the thrust of Adams's theory is that behavior is central and has fundamental significance. Attitudes are second and interior, but as habitual thought patterns they have an external behavioral focus. Feelings are the most internal and least accessible. They follow or are caused by behavior. Adams maintains this sequence is clearly the biblical ideal (1973, p. 135).

Theologically Adams holds a dichotomous view of man, maintaining that the soul and the spirit are used interchangeably in the Bible. The image of God in man is of more central importance in nouthetic theory than is soul or spirit. This image is moral and cognitive. In the fall the image became a "reflection of the father of lies" (Adams, 1970, p. 128). The Christian is described as restoring the image by eliminating disorder and confusion (1973, p. 342). The fall, Adams says, was a fall into loss of control over the environment, and God calls the Christian to master his environment. "In this way he may once again reflect the image of God by subduing and ruling the world about him" (Adams, 1970, p. 129). The focus for the Christian is on behaviorally confronting the environment. The cognitive aspect of the image would appear to be related to the attitudinal or judgment process that mediates feelings, though Adams does not integrate his psychological and theological descriptions of man.

View of Psychopathology

The title of chapter 14 of *The Christian Counselor's Manual* summarizes Adams's view of pathology: "Sin is the problem." The chapter begins, "Christian counselors should not need to be reminded that they have been called to labor in opposition to the world, the flesh and the devil." This is elaborated as, "sin, then, in all its dimensions, clearly is the problem with which the Christian counselor must grapple." In his analysis of the fall described in Genesis 3 Adams views the basic temptation as the satisfaction of desire rather than obedience to God. The same choice exists today.

According to Adams the choice is between two ways of living: "the feeling-motivated life of sin oriented toward self" or the "commandment-oriented life of holiness oriented toward God" (Adams 1973, p. 118). The choice is reduced to love or lust, God's commandments or the client's desires. In nouthetic counseling feelings appear to be equated with desire, and desire is tied to sinful actions (Adams 1973, p. 120). Hence feelings are not to be attended to or trusted. However, nouthetic theory maintains that feelings do not necessarily lead to sinful actions since commandment living is called for in spite of feelings. God is not opposed to good feelings, but Adams says they always come from him. How this can occur is not explained.

In addition to sin as a cause of pathology, organic disease and demon possession are also possible causes, though the latter, according to Adams, is not really possible in the believer. According to Adams there is no such thing as mental illness or emotional disorder—that is, there is no pure or partial psychological cause of pathology since there is no such thing as mental illness. Thus sin is the cause of problems (pathology) when there is no demonic or organic problem.

Three levels of problems exist: presenting problems ("I'm depressed"), performance problems ("I haven't been much of a husband"), and preconditioning problems ("I avoid responsibility when the going gets tough"). Presentation problems are often presented as a cause when actually they are an effect. Performance problems are often presented as an effect when actually they are a cause. Preconditioning problems are often presented as an effect when actually they are the underlying cause (Adams, 1970, p. 148). Adams goes on to emphasize that the preconditioning problem is a habitual response which, as the root problem, often clarifies the relationship between the other two problems. Consequently his theory of pathology is consistent with his view of man. Both have a strong behavioral orientation; listening to feelings (desire) leads to sinful action, while obedience to God's commandments leads to good feelings.

Counseling Process

The model of nouthetic counseling is based on the Greek *noutheteō*, which is translated thirteen times in the New Testament as "admonish" or "warn." Since Adams recognizes that there is no one-word English equivalent, he speaks of "nouthetic confrontation" and uses this phrase as his model.

The model has four basic characteristics. First, confrontation in counseling is viewed as inseparable from pastoral authority. Second, the goals of nouthetic counseling are stated to be the same as the goals of Scripture. "Nouthetic confrontation is, in short, confrontation with the principles and practices of Scripture" (Adams, 1970, p. 51). Third, nouthetic counseling was originally conceived to be team counseling, though the emphasis on the use of a team of counselors with a single client has not been stressed in Adams's later writings. Fourth, nouthetic counseling has a strong similarity to legal counseling—that is, it is directive, gives advice, and imparts information.

The process of counseling that unfolds from this model is grounded in Adams's basic assumption that people need meaning or hope in their lives. He feels that one way to raise hope is by taking people seriously when they talk of sin (1973, p. 46). Adams also uses Matthew 18:15–29, which he calls the reconciliation/discipline dynamic, to give hope. If a brother transgresses against you, go to him; if he won't hear, take one or two with you; if he still won't hear, go to the church, which he must heed or discipline will result. Counseling is helping the client apply this dynamic correctly.

In addition to these general methods Adams uses the Personal Data Inventory, listed in an appendix of the *Christian Counselor's Manual*, to gather a client's history and to assess the client's present problems. The early sessions may also involve further history gathering. However, by the sixth session the major issues should be clear, and by the eighth to tenth session the problem should be well on its way toward solution (Adams, 1973, pp. 233–234). Adams does not specify the exact length of therapy, but it appears to be relatively short.

The main focus of nouthetic counseling is on *what*, not *why*. The counselor directs his attention as needed to the presentation, performance, or preconditioning problem. He imparts information, gives advice, and focuses on problems in a confrontive manner. The assignment of increasingly difficult homework relevant to the client's problem is another method used. A frequent technique is restructuring all areas of a client's life and pressing for change in each so as to prevent relapses.

According to Adams the Holy Spirit is the real Counselor. "Ignoring the Holy Spirit or avoiding the use of Scripture in counseling is tantamount to an act of autonomous rebellion" (1973, pp. 6–7).

Counseling is only truly nouthetic when the counselee is a Christian. Adams maintains that every Christian is called to be a counselor, but counseling is the special calling of the pastor. There is no legitimate place for a psychiatrist or clinical psychologist, since there is no such thing as a psychological or nonorganic psychiatric problem. Adams is absolutely insistent on this point throughout his writings. Consequently he maintains that a good seminary education is more appropriate for a counselor than medical school or clinical psychology training.

Finally the nouthetic counselor cannot listen to or accept the client's sinful attitudes or ventilations, since the "acceptance of sin is sin" (1970, p. 102). Acceptance or support is passive, hence it is wrong for three reasons: (1) the counselor must never support sinful behavior; (2) support is harmful because it acknowledges and approves of the client's handling of his problems; and (3) there is no biblical basis for passively "being" but not "doing" or "saying" (1973, p. 154). Nor is there any room for empathy that is not problem oriented. Admonishing is the evidence of love, since love, for Adams, is responsible behavior (1970, p. 55).

Evaluation

Since Adams has asked to be evaluated biblically, this is a good place to begin. In his strong emphasis on responsibility Adams has underscored a biblical stress on responsible action. However, what he has omitted is the Bible's focus on the heart as the source of actions, whether good or evil. The New Testament uses the word *heart (kardia)* over 150 times to describe the internal source, the deepest level of human nature or cause of actions. From the heart flows good (Matt. 12:35), evil (Matt. 15:19), doubt (Mark 11:23), conviction (Acts 2:37), and belief (Rom. 10:9). Adultery can be an internal desire not yet an overt act (Matt. 5:28). However, Adams ignores not only the specific passages using *heart* but also this whole inner dimension of human beings which is so central to the Scriptures. In spite of its significance heart is only mentioned twelve times in his first two major works. Equally absent are the related internal concepts of soul, spirit, and flesh. These concepts are so central to the Bible that no model of human nature or counseling can claim to be biblical without them.

A second major weakness in Adams's theory is his failure to justify on biblical grounds why *noutheteō* (admonish) should be the basis for a theory of biblical counseling. He does note the relation-

ship between *noutheteō* and *didaskō* (to teach). He argues that since
the pastor is called to teach, he is also called to admonish, which he
interprets as counseling. However, the problem is not just the selection of one biblical concept without a rationale, but the omission of
other more biblically central concepts—for example, *parakeleō*,
translated "comfort," "console," or "exhort" seventy times in the
New Testament. In addition *parakeleō* is a gift given to the church
for ministering to the body of believers (Rom. 12:7). Hence *parakeleō*
clearly makes a better concept on which to build a biblical theory of
counseling.

A third weakness in Adams's theory is his omission of biblical
thought that is in conflict with his views. Thessalonians 5:14 describes three types of relating to three kinds of problems: admonish
(*noutheteō*) the unruly, encourage (*paramutheō*) the fainthearted,
help (*antexō*) the weak. Yet Adams argues for the use of one approach—admonish—with everyone, contrary to this passage of
Scripture. In addition, nouthetic counseling is in conflict with the
whole point of the Book of Job: sin is not always the cause of disaster and suffering. While Adams (1979) specifically recognized that
Job's problems were not a result of sin, his whole theory asserts that
sin *is* the problem.

Another weakness is Adams's failure to understand the psychologists he most severely criticizes, Freud and Rogers. At one point he
attributes the concept of transference to "Rogerians and other Freudians" (1970, p. 101). Psychologically, Rogers and Freud are very
dissimilar. No serious psychological analysis has ever viewed them
as similar. Nor does Rogers discuss transference or make it a part of
his therapy. Adams also states, "The Freudian viewpoint boils down
to this, that God is to blame for the misery and ruin of man" (1970,
p. 214). Since Freud was an atheist, this is a blatant misrepresenta-
tion of his theorizing. Adams's failure to understand psychologists is
not surprising, since a glance through the pages of his books shows a
striking absence of references to the major works of the psychologists he criticizes, though there are many popular and secondary
source references.

References

Adams, J. *Competent to counsel.* Philadelphia: Presbyterian and Reformed
Publishing, 1970.

Adams, J. *The Christian counselor's manual.* Grand Rapids: Baker, 1973.

Adams, J. *More than redemption.* Phillipsburg, N.J.: Presbyterian and Reformed Publishing, 1979.

Additional Readings

Carter, J. D. Adams's theory of nouthetic counseling. *Journal of Psychology and Theology*, 1975, *3*, 143–155.

Carter, J. D. Nouthetic counseling defended: A reply to Ganz. *Journal of Psychology and Theology*, 1976, *4*, 206–216.

Ganz, R. L. Nouthetic counseling defended. *Journal of Psychology and Theology*, 1976, *4*, 193–205.

Oakland, J. An analysis and critique of Jay Adams's theory of counseling. *Journal of the American Scientific Affiliation*, 1976, *28*, 101–109.

33

Object Relations Therapy
William L. Edkins

Object relations therapy is a psychoanalytic treatment associated with object relations theory. Treatment of emotional disorders from an object relations model focuses on the mental representations or objects the patient has construed of himself and of significant others in his life.

Object relations theory was developed by psychoanalysts. Although some of them—for example, Fairbairn and Guntrip—have significantly deviated from classical psychoanalytic theory, they have for the most part retained psychoanalysis as the method of treatment. Klein would be the most significant exception in that her treatment does come in conflict with various aspects of mainstream psychoanalytic treatment.

As developed by Freud, classical psychoanalytic therapy was primarily geared to the treatment of problems associated with failure to resolve the oedipus complex. However, through the work of psychologists such as Anna Freud, Hartmann, Spitz, Mahler, Jacobson, and Kernberg, as well as through the findings of object relations theorists who are more on the fringes of psychoanalytic orthodoxy such as Klein, Winnicott, and Fairbairn, the psychoanalytic understanding of the preoedipal years of life has greatly increased. This has enabled psychoanalysts to diagnose and treat more primitive pathologies that have their roots in the breakdown of preoedipal relationships. This treatment of earlier, more primitive disorders entails a focus on the dyadic mother-child object relationship and all the related issues of intense attachment and dependency, separation and autonomy, and fundamental identity. Guntrip (1968) describes this domain of object relations therapy as the unfolding and treatment of the patient's infantile self, which is terrified, retreating from life, and hiding in an inner citadel of his personality.

Object relations therapy is based on the assumption that units of object relations exist within everyone. These are composed of stable and enduring representations or images of the self linked to images of objects by intense affects. For example, a positive internal object relation might consist of a mental representation of the person's self as a vulnerable and trusting child relating to a strong, caring, and nurturing parent, linked together by an affective experience of love and warmth. On the other hand, a negative internal object relationship unit might be characterized by the hatred and rage a victimized child would feel toward a sadistic parent. These images account for why different individuals would experience the same situation in entirely different ways. Thus, the person who has internalized a predominantly benevolent object relating to a healthy self will experience a blow to his self-esteem quite differently from someone who has a basic identity as a victim suffering under a cruel object.

The goal of psychoanalytic therapy from an object relations perspective is to bring these foundational units of personality to the surface so that they can be exposed to further learning and adaptation and be integrated into the entire adult personality in a more healthy way. This is closely related to the classical psychoanalytic concept of transference. Freud noted that in the course of treatment repressed attributes of parental objects that involved intense conflicts would surface and be unconsciously transferred to the analyst. The analysis of this transference would form the kernel of treatment. The transference relationship remains a primary focus of treatment in object relations therapy. However, object relations therapists view the transferred material not merely as aspects of repressed conflicts but as internal self and object representations. Thus the analysis of the transference yields the clearest available information about the patient's internal object relations world.

Actually these repressed infantile relationships, or the more primitive split objects, can surface in all relationships. Sutherland, a noted British object relations therapist, notes that "all kinds of people are made the pegs on which the object of repressed relationships are hung" (1963, p. 119). He goes on to explain that this surfacing continually recurs as people attempt to work through bad relationships and to become whole persons. What makes psychoanalytic treatment distinct from all the other relationships in which a patient transfers or projects these infantile objects and needs is that the therapist is a trained observer who can penetrate the trappings of the patient's false self and can allow contact and participation in these repressed relationships. In this analytic relationship the patient can allow himself to reexperience the repressed or split-off aspects of himself so that he might find an object now, in the therapist, who does have the ability to understand and relate to his intense needs and affects. This provides the opportunity for the patient to internalize his therapist so that he can then provide these necessary functions for himself.

The difficulty with this kind of treatment is that it typically requires a three- to five-year period of at least twice weekly therapy in order to effect significant change in the internal object world. On the other hand, it does offer treatment and hope for the seriously disturbed.

Like psychoanalysis this method of treatment is not based on an absolute moral and ethical foundation, in contrast to Christianity. In fact, certain analysts deal with God for the most part as simply another internal object, without existence in reality (e.g., Milner, 1969). However, the overall process of development and growth which characterizes this approach is quite consistent with the biblical model of sanctification, which is based on an internal relationship, namely "Christ in you."

References

Guntrip, H. J. S. *Schizoid phenomena, object relations and the self.* London: Hogarth, 1968.

Milner, M. *The hands of the living God.* New York: International Universities Press, 1969.

Sutherland, J. D. Object-relations theory and the conceptual model of psychoanalysis. *British Journal of Medical Psychology*, 1963, *36*, 109–124.

34

Pastoral Counseling
Creath Davis

Relatively new in its modern form but not in its purpose, the care and cure of souls is as old as the believing community itself.

The beginning of the modern pastoral counseling emphasis is identified with men such as Anton T. Boisen, who himself was hospitalized three different times for short-lived but acute mental problems. In 1925 Boisen, who was chaplain at Worcester State Hospital, Massachusetts, began bringing theological students into the hospital for three months of study and work. He viewed the pastor's study of "living human documents" as superior to academic research alone. Having been a patient himself, he realized the necessity of the helper understanding the plight of the one he attempts to help, and he saw how quickly medical trainees could gain knowledge for their task by being involved with patients. Thus the clinical pastoral education movement began with a medical model. Boisen's work gave rise in 1930 to the Council for Clinical Training, and his methods soon became part of the curriculum of many seminaries.

Other pioneers in the field include Russell L. Dicks, chaplain, and

Richard C. Cabot, chief of staff, at the Massachusetts General Hospital. Dicks's personal experience with hospitalization and surgery gave him added sensitivity to human needs. He describes his struggle with pain; his personal doubts, apprehensions, and fears; the horror of the anesthetic; the confusion of hospital routine; the different attitudes of various doctors and nurses; and the effect this all had on him. Also in the pioneering forefront of the contemporary developments in pastoral counseling are Carroll A. Wise, Seward Hiltner, Paul Johnson, Wayne E. Oates, and Charles Holman. In Great Britain, Leslie Weatherhead was a major figure in pastoral care and pastoral applications of psychology. By 1935 he had established a clinic at the City Temple, London, for those needing psychiatric treatment as well as pastoral help.

Basic Functions and Formative Concepts

Clebsch and Jaekle (1964) have identified four pastoral care functions from the pages of church history:

1. healing—"a pastoral function that aims to overcome some impairment by restoring the person to wholeness and by helping him to advance beyond his previous condition."
2. sustaining—"helping a hurting person to endure and to transcend a circumstance in which restoration to his former condition or recuperation from his malady is either impossible or so remote as to seem improbable."
3. guiding—"assisting perplexed persons to make confident choices between alternative courses of thought and action, when such choices are viewed as affecting the present and future state of the soul."
4. reconciling—seeking "to reestablish broken relationships between man and fellow man and between man and God" (p. 33).

These functions were shaped by four germinal ideas that were influential in the 1940s and 50s during the formative period of contemporary pastoral counseling (Clinebell, 1966). The first of these was the formal structured counseling interview coming directly from the psychotherapeutic interview (appointments, definite time limits, a private meeting place with the label "counseling" attached).

Second, the client-centered, or person-centered, method was seen as the normative and often exclusive methodology. Based on the work of psychotherapist Carl R. Rogers, it holds that each person has the capacity to understand himself and his problems and initiate change in the direction of psychological growth and maturity, providing he is treated as a person of worth. The counselor's function is to assume, insofar as he is able, the internal frame of reference of the client and to communicate this empathic understanding to the client. It is an attitude of complete willingness on the part of the therapist to have the center of evaluation and responsibility remain with the client. The counselor's role stresses attitudes and ways of relating rather than techniques. The assumption is that the creation of a climate of warmth, understanding, and freedom from attack will enable the client to drop his defensiveness and explore and reorganize his lifestyle (Rogers & Becker, 1952). This approach is nondirective, with the greatest emphasis being placed on listening.

Third, new insight was viewed as the central goal of counseling. This emphasis represented a giant advance over the advice-giving or merely problem-solving approaches. Finally, the interlocking concepts of unconscious factors in the motivation of behavior and the childhood roots of adult behavior were both accepted as major influences in personality. Man was seen as not totally the master of his psyche. The more emotionally disturbed a person is, the more pervasive the domination of his behavior by unconscious impulses, conflicts, and repressed memories. The genetic emphasis held that present behavior could be understood only by exploring the complexities of a person's early relationships with the need-satisfying adults in his life. These relationships shaped the individual's basic personality structure and profoundly influenced all his relationships, including his relationship to God.

Uniqueness

While psychotherapists look primarily to the healing forces of life within their patients for recovery, pastoral counselors depend on the power of God present in the midst of life for constructive changes (Brister, 1964). All healing forces are seen as God-given; and unless these are released within the person and his relationships, there will be no healing. The counselor is simply a catalyst in a process which he does not create but which he has learned to facilitate. The pastoral counselor's effectiveness depends on an awareness that healing and growth take place through the relationship rather than as a result of psychological cleverness.

Oates (1962) describes pastoral counseling as being more than simply focusing on specific problems that must be solved. It certainly includes problem solving, but even this takes place either implicitly or explicitly within the commonwealth of eternal life as it is known in Jesus Christ. Our past experience, our present needs, and our future destiny all come into focus in the pastoral conversation. The essence of pastoral counseling is to make the Christian faith effective in the lives of people.

Genuine acceptance is essential in effective counseling. Only when love (*agape*) is experienced will growth occur. Accepting the person is not synonymous with accepting irresponsible behavior. A pastoral counselor's accepting love implies, not ethical indifference, but discriminating awareness of human sin, divine judgment, and the need for the mercy, grace, and love of God.

Acceptance or rejection is communicated both verbally and nonverbally in attitudes, voice tones, and facial expressions. The counseling interview will be influenced greatly by the presence of kindness or sternness, sincerity or superficiality, perceptivity or dullness regarding the person's situation. The person who experiences acceptance from his counselor can express his feelings of helplessness, admit his anxiety or hostility, confess his sin, offer his prayer for divine wisdom, and be assured all the while that he is not alone in his struggle.

The pastoral counselor recognizes the physical, spiritual, emotional, and intellectual dimensions of human life as interrelated parts of the whole of personality. Each affects all.

One of the most distinctive elements of pastoral counseling is its theological base. Pastoral counseling is not limited to scientific knowledge for its understanding of persons but brings a perspective that science alone cannot provide. This perspective is derived from the rich heritage of biblical revelation and the Judeo-Christian tradition, which presents clearly the nature of God (the infinite personal God whose character is revealed as love, righteousness, and truth, Exod. 34:6–7); the nature of human beings (created in the image of God with significance and freedom and by willful choice guilty of sin—rebellion acted out in attempting to live apart from God, Gen. 1–3); the nature of the world (God's handiwork that has been affected by man's fall, Gen. 3); and the redemptive drama (God's promise fulfilled in Christ, who "hath borne our griefs and carried our sorrows" and given us his gracious gift of love, forgiveness, reconciliation, and deliverance, Isa. 53:4; Eph. 2:13–16). These are but a few of the theological perspectives that inform the pastoral counselor.

The pastoral counselor seeks guidance from the Scriptures but does not use them or other religious resources in a mechanical or legalistic fashion. This would result in the exchanging of one form of bondage for another. The very essence of these resources is the dynamic interchange (relationship) between God and the pastoral counselor and between the counselor and the people of God. It is God who works (directly and indirectly through other people) through prayer, Scripture, and other religious experiences and through counseling relationships and procedures to bring wholeness. The pastoral counselor is Christ's representative, who enables a person to sense the caring presence of God and to trust him, which is the essence of the Christian life.

Pastoral counseling aids in discovering one's identity. People must tell their own stories if they are to discover themselves and understand their own history, handicaps, emotions, and gifts. A second, deeper look at life, beyond the primary experience of living it, gives people a perspective on its passages, perils, and privileges. The counselee is a learner who narrates his story to a teacher sent from God, who in turn interprets and assists the counselee in gaining meaning from experience. One's identity and destiny are thus linked to a community of promise, expectancy, and fulfillment.

The pastoral counselor has unique resources available for dealing with human brokenness and guilt. True guilt comes because one has violated God's moral law, the greatest of which is to love God with our whole being and our neighbor as ourself. False guilt or neurotic guilt comes from feelings of inferiority, projected rejection of oneself by others, or from a supersensitive conscience that registers all criticism by others as true. The authority inherent in the symbolic role of the pastoral counselor makes him or her uniquely fitted for helping the counselee find forgiveness for true guilt and release from false guilt.

Similarly the pastoral counselor has a unique perspective to bring to the tragedies and sufferings of mankind. Suffering is an undeniable part of the human scene, and will not be permanently avoided by any of us. Yet the difference between Christian faith and unbelief in dealing with suffering is great. The pain and the anxiety may not be lessened, but what becomes of us as we struggle with life's problems will reveal the mystery of a benevolent God who not only uses our suffering to enlarge our capacity for life, but who also participates in our suffering. Suffering can create a fellowship, or an intimacy, that no other experience in life affords, especially an intimacy with God. Nowhere in all the world is the agony and pain that we feel felt as deeply or as keenly as it is in the heart of God, and the promise of the living Christ is never to leave us.

It is this realization that enables us to believe that there is redemptive purpose in our suffering even if we cannot identify or articulate clearly what that purpose is. It helps enormously to know that our suffering is not simply blind happenstance in a cold, impersonal universe.

Goals

The basic goal of pastoral counseling is to put people in touch with God. Life experiences can become so overpowering that unless one can establish a grace/faith relationship with the God who created him and who intervenes in history and in human life, there may be little or no hope. Regardless of how impossible the human equation looks, when God is added to it, hope flourishes.

The pastoral counselor knows from biblical revelation that God in his infinite wisdom, purpose, and love acts uniquely in each person's experience. Sometimes God intervenes in such a way as to rescue us from our difficult situations; at other times he enables us to work through those difficulties and to come out on the other side as better persons. There are also times when he simply enables us to endure a situation that will not change. Thus we can experience his grace as a miraculous deliverance, as a life-changing process, or as the strength to endure. The pastoral counselor does not tell people the particular way God will intervene in any situation, but that God will intervene as one comes to him in faith.

Pastoral counseling also helps one understand and relate properly to himself. The pastoral counselor brings the gift of objectivity along with a perspective of the significance and value of human personality and human life to the counseling process. No person can really know who he is until he understands his origin (created in God's image) and his destiny (the eternal purpose for life and the choice to respond to or resist the claims of God on one's life). The pastoral counselor understands that inherent within Christ's command to love your neighbor as yourself is the mandate for a proper love of one's own self. Christianity affirms life and personal identity and furnishes a genuine basis for self-acceptance and for a healthy egoism.

Pastoral counseling gives balanced attention to both value issues and emotional/interpersonal dynamics. Psychological problems involve value confusions just as frequently as they involve straightforward emotional and interpersonal dynamics. The pastoral counselor works out of a context where clarification and stabilization of value issues are as prominent a factor as any other.

Another goal of pastoral counseling is to improve the quality of one's relationships. In reality a person is as rich or as poor as the quality of his personal relationships. Every maladjusted person is a person who has not made himself known to another human being and in consequence does not know himself; nor can he be himself. More than that, he struggles actively to avoid becoming known by another person. The journey toward wholeness must include healthy relationships.

Pastoral counseling also seeks to help one assume responsibility for himself and to make decisions and commitments courageously. To see oneself as being at the mercy of external circumstances and/ or internal urges is to be caught in the psychological posture of a helpless victim. It is true that life confronts us with many circumstances over which we have little or no control, and the same may be true of some inner urges, but as human beings we are far from being helpless victims. We can choose our attitudes and our responses to these pressures and can, by the grace of God, do something redemptive with them.

Yet another goal is to help people learn "burden-bearing" involvement as the means for participating in the process of reconciliation—of healing the wounds of loneliness and grief, and of loving and forgiving in the context of truth and grace. The Christian experience was designed by God to be a community experience.

Pastoral counseling seeks to facilitate growth in the counselee who desires spiritual wisdom and strength for constructive character change. It also seeks to give support to individuals who need to mobilize their resources for life during some crisis. Such support enables persons to work through their pressing problems and not be overcome by them.

In summary, the goal of pastoral counseling is to relate the biblical resources to every human circumstance. Pastoral care is thus viewed as personal and social, preventive and therapeutic, supportive and confrontive. The object of care is nothing less than the person in the full range of his existence. Care does more than operate in crises. Care aids human development and growth and assists in life's transitions as well as in serious spiritual problems.

Methods Employed

Leaders in pastoral counseling are reluctant to identify themselves with any particular method of counseling and generally resist labeling their own approach. The goals listed above show something of the breadth of approaches used. Most attempt to correlate biblical wisdom and psychological insight in an effort to strengthen persons for life, death, and destiny. A disciplined eclecticism that draws on various sources of wisdom in the practice of pastoral counseling is an appropriate model.

The client-centered, or person-centered, approach has helped to rescue pastoral counseling from the overdirectedness of advice giving and has demonstrated the importance of disciplined listening and responding to feelings. But there is a place for the use of one's authority selectively in sustaining, guiding, feeding (emotionally and spiritually), inspiring, confronting, teaching, and encouraging persons to function responsibly in their relationship with God and with others. In the pastoral counselor's interaction with the counselee he will express empathy as he seeks to identify with the counselee. He will invite personal self-disclosure, reflect the counselee's feelings back to him for thought or clarification, affirm what has been said, and help to effect transitions from one pattern of thought to another. When appropriate he will confront the person with Christian truth or with possible consequences of his feelings or plan of action. Finally he will provide support for dealing realistically with the difficulty faced.

A person's guiding values and the resulting behavior should be examined, not just in terms of how one feels about these matters (although this is important), but also how they influence his relationships and sense of worth and what can be done to help one live more constructively.

It is important that the counselor accept his or her own humanity as a rich resource for counseling effectively. Being a real person when encountering others is most essential for establishing a healing relationship. Whatever approach is taken, the pastoral counselor maintains a vision of spiritual wholeness rooted in the promise of the Christian faith.

References

Brister, C. W. *Pastoral care in the church.* New York: Harper & Row, 1964.

Clebsch, W. A., & Jaekle, C. R. *Pastoral care in historical perspective.* Englewood Cliffs, N.J.: Prentice-Hall, 1964.

Clinebell, H. J., Jr. *Basic types of pastoral counseling.* Nashville: Abingdon, 1966.

Oates, W. E. *Protestant pastoral counseling.* Philadelphia: Westminster, 1962.

Rogers, C. R., & Becker, R. J. A basic orientation for counseling. In S. Doniger (Ed.), *The best of pastoral psychology.* Great Neck, N.Y.: Pastoral Psychology Press, 1952.

35

| Person-centered Therapy |
| Harry A. Van Belle |

Developed by Rogers in the 1940s, person-centered therapy (originally called client-centered therapy) is probably the first typically American system of therapy ever formulated. Like all other forms of therapy it is of course historically dependent on psychoanalysis; thus it is not free from imported European influences in its constitutive parts. But the distinguishing characteristic of this approach to therapy as a whole is that it is made in America for Americans.

Philosophical Roots

More than any other form of therapy, person-centered therapy embodies the early American faith in the primacy of the individual. Early American culture held that if individuals are left to themselves, they will naturally exercise their capacity to realize their fullest potential. It insisted on the necessity of allowing individuals the freedom to choose their own course of action. Person-centered

219

therapy reiterates this theme in therapeutic language when Rogers states that the therapist should rely on the client for the direction of movement in the therapeutic process (Rogers, 1959). Rogers's adherence to this cultural notion of the primacy of the individual is responsible for the individualistic stamp of person-centered therapy as well as for the typically nondirective character of its earliest formulation. It represents the influence of Rogers's view of human beings on his approach to therapy.

Rogers is often seen as a spokesperson for that theoretical orientation in psychology called third force or humanistic psychology. For that reason person-centered therapy is frequently characterized as a phenomenological approach to therapy—that is, an approach that shows unqualified respect for the client's perception of reality. While this characterization has some validity, it is one-sided and superficial because it neglects the other, much deeper dimension of Rogers's thought: his emphasis on growth. Ultimately Rogers's reverence for growth is deeper than his respect for individuals. For that reason also it is more correct to call his person-centered therapy a growth therapy rather than a phenomenological therapy.

This emphasis on growth in person-centered therapy is due to the fact that for its theoretical-philosophical roots, it hails back to a typically American philosophy rather than to some European import. Pragmatism rather than phenomenology or existentialism forms the philosophical backdrop of this approach. There exists a particularly close affinity between Rogers's person-centered therapy and Dewey's pragmatism. Dewey elevated the notion of change and growth to the central characteristic of living existence. Person-centered therapy does the same. Structure is always dependent on process in Dewey's pragmatism. This holds for person-centered therapy as well.

To be sure, there is also a difference between Dewey and Rogers at the human level of functioning reality. For Dewey change requires human forming, or experimentally guided (re)construction, to become growth. For Rogers change is growth. If allowed, growth occurs naturally and has its own formative power. We can obstruct it or surrender ourselves to it, but we can never induce it or (re)form it. Dewey takes a culturally formative attitude to growth. Rogers takes an actively receptive attitude toward it. This makes Dewey the father of all eclectic forms of therapy and Rogers the father of all nondirective, person-centered forms of therapy. However, both forms of therapy are united in their common emphasis on change and growth.

Evolution of Theory.

Because of this dynamic emphasis it is difficult to give a systematic description of person-centered therapy. Those systematic descriptions that do exist tend to describe it in terms of one of the stages of its development. For example, strictly speaking it is incorrect to characterize the approach to therapy developed by Rogers as "person-centered" therapy. Person-centeredness is only one of its formulations. At least two other formulations can be distinguished. In order to do justice to the developing character of Rogers's views on therapy, as well as to the dynamic character of his thought, we need to understand person-centered therapy systematically in its development. The central theme running through this developmental description is a movement from fixity to fluidity.

First formulation.

Rogers's first formulation of therapy is nondirective (Rogers, 1942). It states in essence that therapy is an autonomous process in the sense that it occurs entirely within the client. The therapist can either facilitate its release or obstruct the occurrence, but he can never cause or induce it. For that reason Rogers repeatedly warns the therapist against interfering with the life of the client. Such intervention would be therapeutically counterproductive.

Instead, he enjoins the therapist to free the process by creating a warm relationship that is maximally permissive of the expression of feeling. By focusing on the feelings of the client, the therapist brings to open expression all the conflicting feelings that the client has regarding himself and his situation. This yields a process of catharsis, or emotional release, in which these feelings are resolved.

The inevitable and spontaneous result of this catharsis is the achievement of insight on the part of the client. Again, this second movement of the process cannot be given to the client by any form of direction or education. It is the inevitable and spontaneous consequence of the first, cathartic movement because it is entirely brought about by the growth forces inherent in the client himself. To be genuine, such insight must be a working insight. It necessarily involves a process of choice and action on the part of the client. For that reason also the client must earn or achieve this insight himself. It cannot be given to him by the therapist.

Since the therapeutic process is autonomous and thus driven entirely by the growth forces within the client, the only stance that the therapist can possibly take is a nondirective, nonauthoritarian, permissive one. The main aim of therapy in this conception is to avoid obstructing the growth process.

Second formulation

In his second formulation of therapy Rogers moves from nondirectiveness to person-centeredness (Rogers, 1951). In doing so he also gives a richer description of the therapeutic process. The fundamental attitude of the person-centered therapist is one of active trust in the client's capacity for self-help. This attitude of trust must be unconditional because it itself forms the condition for therapy. It makes therapy therapeutic. It must also be pervasive. It cannot be a technique that one tries out on the client and modifies or discards depending on the client's response. Herein lies the essential difference between eclectic and person-centered therapy. The attitude of the eclectic therapist changes depending on its effect on the client. But the active trust that characterizes the whole of the person-centered therapist's attitude lasts for the duration of therapy, irrespective of the changes that occur in the client. To be sure, techniques are not without their usefulness for the person-centered therapist. They serve to communicate his attitude of trust to the client. But this also exhausts their function. As a result of this person-centered attitude in therapy the client gradually becomes more and more aware of his potential for helping himself. Thus it leads the client toward a sense of personal autonomy.

The process that elicits this awareness is essentially that of disorganization and reorganization of the client's self-concept. The self-concept of a person who has no need for therapy is, by and large, internally consistent with what he daily experiences and perceives. Yet even such a person is occasionally bound to have experiences that are incongruent with his self, and these tend to threaten the internal consistency of the self. However, a congruent person normally defends his self against these experiences by denying them access to his awareness. When these incongruent experiences become so powerful or numerous that he can no longer keep them from awareness, the person enters therapy.

As the client begins to explore himself in therapy, he is likely to discover even more attitudes, feelings, and experiences that are incongruent with his self-concept. This tends to further threaten his self until he moves into the amorphous state of no longer having an organized self-concept. Emotionally this disorganization process tends to be extremely disturbing for the client. With every new discovery he is forced to ask himself anxiously what this will do to the basis of his life. The actively and unconditionally trustful attitude of the therapist allows him to continue his self-exploration process in spite of his emotional upheaval. The therapist demonstrates his unconditional and pervasive trust in the client by actively following him, without fear, in any direction and toward any outcome that he may determine. If supported by the therapist, this process of self-disorganization will inevitably result in the growth of an enlarged and reorganized self. This self now can much more comfortably include all those experiences that were previously denied.

The sense of growth further forms the backdrop for the despair that the client experiences in therapy, thus making it possible for him to continue the process to its completion. The outcome of this therapeutic process is a reorganized self-concept that now is much more congruent with his experience. As the process of reorganization occurs, the client begins to feel himself more and more in action. In effect, he discovers that by relinquishing his hold on experience, he has gained more control over experience. Once again, however, the force driving this therapeutic process is not the structuring or interpreting efforts of the therapist but the forward-moving growth forces of life inherent in the client himself. Once released in therapy, these forces make the client aware that he is not the mere product of outside influences but in some real sense the maker of himself, his own product.

Third formulation

While Rogers's first and second formulations of therapy deal with the attitude and action of the therapist, his third and final formulation focuses almost exclusively on the therapeutic process. In this conception therapy is that process through which the client becomes a fully functioning person (Rogers, 1961). In therapeutic terms, to become a fully functioning person means to become the therapeutic process which, as a result of therapy, is released in the client. This third formulation differs from Rogers's person-centered description in that the outcome of therapy is now no longer an enlarged, reorganized self but rather the process of therapy itself. The end result of therapy is no longer openness to, and congruence with, experience but rather an identification with the dynamic living experience that a person is.

This process entails first of all that the client lose all control over his experience. He must surrender himself to his organism (which Rogers largely identifies with experience). Rather than impose meaning upon his experiential organism, the client must let it tell him the meaning that it has. This will happen only if he becomes nondirective and receptive toward his own organic experience. The self as thinker about experience must diminish in order for the growth forces of the experiential organism to bear fruit. When this occurs, the client's self is no longer the watchman over experience but an inhabitant in living dynamic experience.

From the point of view of Rogers's third and most mature formulation, therapy is a process that moves the client from fixity to changingness. Since the organism is a perpetual process of change or actualization, dynamic changingness is the inevitable result of becoming one's experiential organism. For Rogers this dynamic changingness is the hallmark of a mentally healthy person. It means that the client's self is at its best when it functions as a fluid Gestalt that changes with the experience of the moment. As a result of this therapeutic movement the client begins to live existentially, literally changing from moment to moment, ever and anew transcending himself. Finally, instead of having a set of values he becomes a valuing process.

This dynamic changingness is not random movement, however. It is constructive movement in a positive direction. It is also realistic because it is open to all the client's impulses and experiences. Thus the client has access to a maximally possible amount of information. For that reason he is in a position to make the best possible choices for himself so that he can live as fully as possible. The change for the better which the client obtains according to this conception of therapy is that he becomes an experiential organismic process and therefore also a more fully functioning person.

Evaluation

For the neurotic client who is torn apart by conflicting feelings and internal inconsistencies, person-centered therapy offers a sense of emotional relief and a renewed sense of personal wholeness and competence. It helps the client become himself more comfortably, and it helps him change himself more freely.

But this enhanced sense of personal autonomy is not without its cost, because it condemns the client to a life of perpetual change, with no chance of anchoring himself to abiding structures either outside or inside himself. The picture of the fully functioning person that emerges at the end of therapy is that of a person who is thrown back upon himself for the task of maintaining his personal integrity and who is driven by a compulsion to grow. It evokes a sense of intense restlessness about human life. The fully functioning person cannot find rest in his dependence on his fellows or on the Person who is the source of his being, nor on the created structures in terms of which he lives and moves and has his dynamic being. To do so would be a violation of his personal autonomy and of the internal growth principle which, according to this conception of humanity, forms the essence of a person's being.

This state of being is the direct result of Rogers's fixation on growth, as exemplified by his lifelong simultaneous preoccupation with the autonomy of persons and the centrality of dynamic growthful experience in human life. The following statement illustrates Rogers's basic intent: "Experience is, for me, the highest authority. The touchstone of validity is my own experience. No other person's ideas and none of my own ideas are as authoritative as my experience. It is to experience that I must return again and again; to discover a closer approximation to truth as it is in the process of becoming in me. Neither the Bible nor the prophets—neither Freud nor research—neither the revelations of God nor man—can take precedence over my own direct experience" (Rogers, 1961, p. 23).

The central thrust of Rogers's view of therapy is decidedly anti-Christian. At the same time, his system of therapy contains many valuable insights that Christians can gratefully use in their own approach to therapy. Such notions as the respect and care for persons together with an emphasis on human freedom are reflections of important biblical themes, albeit that because of their secularized character they are pale reflections. However, in utilizing these moments of truth we do well to carefully re-form them in order to make them conform to the revealed will of the Lord.

References

Rogers, C. R. *Counseling and psychotherapy*, Boston: Houghton Mifflin, 1942.

Rogers, C. R. *Client-centered therapy*. Boston: Houghton Mifflin, 1951.

Rogers, C. R. A theory of therapy, personality, and interpersonal relationships, as developed in the client-centered framework. In S. Koch (Ed.), *Psychology* (Vol. 3). New York: McGraw-Hill, 1959.

Rogers, C. R. *On becoming a person*. Boston: Houghton Mifflin, 1961.

Additional Readings

Kirschenbaum, H. *On becoming Carl Rogers*. New York: Delacorte Press, 1979.

Van Belle, H. A. *Basic intent and therapeutic approach of Carl R. Rogers*. Toronto: Wedge Publishing Foundation, 1980.

36

Primal Therapy
Bryan Van Dragt

Primal therapies embrace the traditional notion that psychological illnesses are the result of repressing, or removing from consciousness, the feelings surrounding traumatic life experiences. Healing involves reexperiencing and integrating these repressed feelings in as totally uninhibited a fashion as possible. The screaming that often accompanies the release of these powerful emotions has earned the primal therapies their reputation for being a radical treatment approach.

The primal therapies have a complex ancestry that can be traced to the cathartic method of Breuer and Freud (see Swartley, 1979, for primal therapy's family tree). In 1897 Freud first used the term *primal* or *primary* to denote psychological processes that ignore reality and attempt to gratify every wish either by simple motor activity (such as eating or sexual intercourse) or by identifying with the source of previous satisfaction (such as mother's breast). In contrast, secondary processes take external reality into account when seeking to satisfy a wish. Psychodynamic theorists now use the term *primal* (meaning first in time) for a memory or scene from early childhood that is apparently the first stage in the development of a neurosis.

Freud initially attempted to release and work with these primal experiences directly through free association and hypnosis, but he later abandoned this task as too difficult and as potentially damaging to both therapist and patient. Others, however, have resumed where Freud left off, and in 1972, under the leadership of William Swartley, the International Primal Association was formed. Among contemporary versions of primal-type therapy, Janov's primal therapy has drawn the most attention, both for the coherence and breadth of the theory and for its somewhat sensational presentation in his book, *The Primal Scream* (1970).

After seventeen years of practicing standard insight therapy as a psychiatric social worker and psychologist, Janov encountered a baffling clinical situation that forced him to change his theories of neurosis. During an otherwise ordinary group therapy session Janov invited a patient to call out, "Mommy! Daddy!" in imitation of a scene from a play which had fascinated the young man. The patient complied and was soon writhing on the floor in an agony that finally ended in a piercing, deathlike scream. This ordinarily withdrawn person was as puzzled as Janov about the experience and could only report, "I made it! I don't know what, but I can *feel!*" (Janov, 1970, p. 10). Analysis of this and similar clinical experiences led to Janov's theory and therapy, which would regard the young man's scream as a product of the primal pains that reside in all neurotic individuals at all times.

Janov believes that all neurotic behaviors and most physical symptoms derive from a single common source: the suppression of feeling. This suppression begins early in life when the child's basic needs go unmet for any length of time. The pain that results from this deprivation continues until the child either gets his parents to satisfy him or shuts off the pain by shutting off the conscious awareness of need.

The thousands of parent-child interactions that deny the child's needs make him feel that there is no hope of love when he is really being himself. The child therefore begins to act in the expected manner rather than out of his own real needs and desires. The primal scene for Janov is the critical point at which the child shifts from being more real to being more unreal. At this juncture the child is said to be neurotic, and the unreal behavior soon becomes automatic. The real, feeling self is locked away behind layers of defense.

What is crucial here is that the child does not eliminate the need simply by splitting off from it. When excessive pain causes needs to be buried, the body goes into a state of emergency alert, which is experienced as constant tension. Because one's real needs have been removed from consciousness, one must pursue the satisfaction of these needs symbolically. Thus, an incessant smoker who was weaned too abruptly or too early may be symbolically expressing the need to suck his mother's breast. This, for Janov, is the essence of neurosis: the pursuit of symbolic satisfactions. And because the satisfaction is only symbolic, there is no end to the pursuit.

The ultimate goal in primal therapy is a tensionless, defense-free existence in which the individual experiences internal unity and is freely and deeply himself. Janov believes that this state is impossible for the neurotic to achieve without eliminating (i.e., experiencing) primal pains. When one feels fully the pain of one's basic unmet needs, when one finally *wants* what one *needs*, the struggle for love is resolved and the unreal self is destroyed. The patient is then said to be normal.

The primal therapist's objective is therefore to dismantle the patient's defenses in order to destroy the barrier between thoughts and feelings. The therapeutic milieu is carefully contrived to facilitate this. For the first three weeks of treatment the patient is seen daily in individual sessions lasting as long as the person needs (usually two to three hours). For at least the first week the individual stays alone in a motel room. Isolation, sleeplessness, and elimination of tension-relieving activities weaken defenses and keep the patient focused on himself.

During therapeutic sessions the patient lies spread-eagle on the couch. He is encouraged to relive early situations that evoke strong feelings. Defensive maneuvers such as intellectualization are confronted immediately and forbidden, so that one comes at last to experience one's feelings and pain—to "have a primal"—rather than simply to discuss these things. The therapist is thus "the dealer of Pain, no more, no less" (Janov, 1970, p. 247).

After the third week the person is placed in a postprimal group composed of people who have been through the treatment. The function of this group is to stimulate its members into new "primals." The patient usually stays in the group for twelve to fifteen months.

Many primal therapists reject Janov's "busting" technique, preferring gentler methods such as massage or music to move the person into primal experiences. The role of pain in neurosis is also controversial. Some therapists observe that pleasure is sometimes more assiduously avoided.

The primal therapies usually last from one to two or more years, depending on the patient's readiness to allow his or her chaotic primal feelings into awareness. These therapies should not be used in their radical form with individuals who have fragile ego structures. The experience of primal hurts carries with it the potential for harmfully disrupting the psychotic or near-psychotic personality. Great skill is required of the therapist to avoid what Swartley calls the "insidious accumulation of side effects" (1979, p. 209) in either therapist or patient.

Though Janov has been criticized for going too far, perhaps the most salient critique from the Christian perspective is that he does not go far enough. For although Janov follows his patients into the primal experiences of birth and even intrauterine trauma, he stops short of the final abyss; his reductionistic view of persons as essentially biological entities forces him to consider neurotic those experiences that arise out of one's spirit dimension. For example, Janov sees the experience of "oneness with God" as irrational and interprets it as a "loss of reality" (1970, p. 222). For the Christian, however, such a transcending experience is the truest expression of the true self, for God is the very ground of reality. Anxiety calls one to reckon not only with repressed childhood feelings but also with one's responsibilities and commitments, both immediate and ultimate. In the oft-quoted words of Augustine, "Thou hast made us for thyself, and our hearts are restless till they find their rest in thee."

Christian alternatives to Janov's primal therapy include Osborne's (1976) primal integration and Finch's Christian existential psychology (Malony, 1980). Though developed independently of Janov, primal integration uses essentially the same concepts, terminology, and techniques, but in a context that is accepting of religious experiences and values.

Christian existential therapy uses many primal techniques, including a three-week intensive therapy which the patient spends in isolation. However, Finch's approach goes beyond "emptying the well" of childhood hurts to an exploration of what lies beneath the well itself, namely, God. Finch views persons as essentially spirit— created in God's image, by God, and for God. Until one comes to know God experientially, as he is revealed in Christ, one is not truly oneself. In such a context primal therapy finds a responsible, holistic, deeply Christian expression.

References

Janov, A. *The primal scream*. New York: Putnam, 1970.

Malony, H. N. (Ed.). *A Christian existential psychology: The contributions of John G. Finch*. Washington D.C.: University Press of America, 1980.

Osborne, C. G. *The art of learning to love yourself*. Grand Rapids: Zondervan, 1976.

Swartley, W. The new primal therapies. In A. Hill (Ed.), *A visual encyclopedia of unconventional medicine*. New York: Crown, 1979.

37

Problem-solving Therapy
Elizabeth M. Altmaier

Solving the practical problems of everyday life is an especially relevant topic for counselors, who are often approached by clients when the clients' problem-solving abilities are inadequate. In fact, D'Zurilla and Goldfried (1971) noted that "much of what we view clinically as 'abnormal behavior' or 'emotional disturbance' may be viewed as ineffective behavior and its consequences, in which the individual is unable to resolve certain situational problems in his life" (p. 107).

Although problem solving might appear to be a unitary process, and therefore easily acquired through counseling, it actually consists of five separate stages (Heppner, 1978). Stage 1 is a general orientation, or "set." An optimal problem-solving set is one in which the person acknowledges the existence of the problem and behaves as though an effective resolution is possible, neither acting impulsively nor retreating from the problem. Stage 2 involves formulating an accurate and specific description of the problem. This description is necessary for alternative responses or solutions to be generated, a process which constitutes stage 3. Making a decision by selecting one action from a number of alternatives is stage 4. Finally, stage 5 involves testing the effectiveness of the chosen alternative against some criterion or standard.

Mahoney (1977) compares a client's problem solving to that of a scientist and argues that the scientist's logical skills are applicable in the client's day-to-day situations. Thus, in his "personal science" approach the client is taught steps of problem solving contained in a sequence represented by the mnemonic SCIENCE: Specify general problem; Collect information; Identify causes or patterns; Examine options; Narrow options and experiment; Compare data; Extend, revise, or replace.

Until recently problem solving was studied by using predefined laboratory-type problems such as mazes, anagrams, and puzzles. However, present research is better contributing to our understanding of the role that problem solving plays in normal adjustment by examining events affecting how people solve real-life personal problems. Spivack and his colleagues (Spivack, Platt, & Shure, 1976) have studied problem-solving processes among preschool children, emotionally disturbed children and adolescents, and hospitalized psychiatric patients. In general their findings indicate that "normal" and "deviant" populations show significant differences in problem-solving ability. For example, emotionally disturbed adolescents generated fewer solutions to hypothetical problems than did their normal peers; in addition, their options often had a distinct antisocial (e.g., physically aggressive) character to them.

Recently Heppner (1982; Heppner & Peterson, 1982) has developed and tested a personal problem-solving inventory that allows assessment of three major aspects of problem solving: personal confidence, approach-avoidance style, and personal control. He used this inventory to distinguish between successful and unsuccessful problem solvers in a college student population. Further study of these two groups revealed that successful problem solvers had fewer symptoms of depression, had more of a tendency to enjoy cognitive activities, were more positive in their self-concept, and utilized coping styles that were less blameful and more problem focused in comparison to unsuccessful problem solvers.

It seems clear that successful problem solving is related to better social adjustment. In thinking about training individuals in such skills, it is clear that several questions need to be addressed: Can such thinking skills be taught? Would learning these skills impact the individual's level of adjustment? Would the effects of such training last over time?

Resolving real-life problems, which usually involves a major interpersonal component, involves a series of skills (Spivack et al., 1976). The first of these is an awareness of the variety of interpersonal and other problems in human existence and a sensitivity to their occurrence. Second is the skill of generating alternative solutions to problems. A third skill, which is emphasized in the work of Spivack and his colleagues, is that of means-ends thinking. This skill includes both spelling out the step-by-step means by which a resolution would be achieved and recognizing the obstacles that must be overcome for the means to work. A fourth skill is that of anticipating the consequences of one's actions on others and on oneself. These skills need to be present for successful problem solving to occur. Their absence may be the result of insufficient learning (the person has not been exposed to these skills or has not learned them adequately) or of the situation (the problem-solving situation may engender emotions that inhibit problem-solving success).

A considerable amount of research evidence suggests that these skills can in fact be taught and that their acquisition does impact behavioral adjustment. Many of the problem-solving training programs described by Spivack et al. (1976) incorporate games and dialogues whereby problem-solving skills are acquired in the context of everyday activities. For example, Shure (1981) discussed a training project in which parents and teachers were taught, when children experienced problems in playing with their peers, to elicit the child's view of the problem (e.g., Sally stole my truck), how each child feels about the problem, the child's description of the problem, and alternative solutions. In her study children who were engaged in these dialogues were rated, compared to no-treatment controls, as having learned both solution and consequential thinking and as having improved adjustment behavior after the training period. Follow-ups at six months and one year revealed that these gains were maintained. For example, of the group of children trained in problem solving, 83% were rated as adjusted immediately after training, 86% six months later, and 77% one year later (decrease not significant). For the untrained children the corresponding percentages were 41%, 42%, and 30%.

Mahoney & Arnkoff (1978) suggest that "among the cognitive learning therapies, it is our opinion that the problem-solving perspectives may ultimately yield the most encouraging clinical results" (p. 709). These approaches seem particularly valuable for two reasons. First, they include both a coping and a restructuring orientation, a blend that will help the client control his or her inappropriate responses while operating on the environment to achieve desired goals. Second, problem-solving therapies allow, in fact demand, that individual differences be recognized and utilized in treatment. These approaches therefore show unique promise for the Christian practitioner because they emphasize a built-in individuality of treatment that might include prayer, seeking advice from others, and so on, as problem-solving alternatives for Christian clients. While there are certain clients and psychological disorders for which these approaches would not be suited, they do have particular promise and are a feasible choice for many kinds of developmental concerns.

References

D'Zurilla, T. J., & Goldfried, M. R. Problem solving and behavior modification. *Journal of Abnormal Psychology*, 1971, *78*, 107–126.

Heppner, P. P. A review of the problem-solving literature and its relationship to the counseling process. *Journal of Counseling Psychology*, 1978, *25*, 366–375.

Heppner, P. P. A personal problem-solving inventory. In P. A. Keller & L. G. Ritt (Eds.), *Innovations in clinical practice: A source book*. Sarasota, Fla.: Professional Resource Exchange, 1982.

Heppner, P. P., & Peterson, C. H. The development and implications of a personal problem-solving inventory. *Journal of Counseling Psychology*, 1982, *29*, 66–75.

Mahoney, M. J. Personal science: A cognitive learning theory. In A. Ellis & R. Grieger (Eds.), *Handbook of rational-emotive therapy*. New York: Springer Publishing, 1977.

Mahoney, M. J., & Arnkoff, D. B. Cognitive and self-control therapies. In S. L. Garfield & A. E. Bergin (Eds.), *Handbook of psychotherapy and behavior change: An empirical analysis* (2nd ed.). New York: Wiley, 1978.

Shure, M. B. Social competence as a problem-solving skill. In J. D. Wine & M. D. Smye (Eds.), *Social competence*. New York: Guilford, 1981.

Spivack, G., Platt, J. J., & Shure, M. B. *The problem-solving approach to adjustment*. San Francisco: Jossey-Bass, 1976.

38

Psychoanalysis
S. Bruce Narramore

Developed by Freud from the mid-1880s through the 1930s, psychoanalysis was the first truly psychological form of therapy for the treatment of mental and emotional maladjustments. It is considered the most in-depth approach to psychotherapy because of its frequency (four or five times weekly), its length (three to five years), and its focus on the reconstruction of early childhood experiences and mental functioning.

As a form of psychotherapy, psychoanalysis grows logically out of the psychoanalytic theory of personality development and psychopathology. This theory holds that maladjustments develop out of conflicts between biologically based drives such as sex and aggression, which arise from a group of processes known as the id, and the repressing forces of the personality, the ego defense mechanisms. Psychoanalysis is designed to identify these conflicts and overcome them. By becoming aware of previously hidden wishes and conflicts that were too threatening or anxiety provoking to be faced, patients are enabled to confront them more maturely, give up inappropriate defense mechanisms, and develop a balanced functioning between their instincts (id), their reality-judging functions (ego), and their moral standards (superego). Since conflicts between impulses and defenses were developed in the context of intimate relationships with parents and siblings, psychoanalysis places a strong emphasis on the healing nature of the therapeutic relationship.

According to psychoanalytic theory, anxiety-provoking wishes and feelings have been repressed because the ego was too weak to face them. Awareness of them would generate excessive anxiety because of the fear they would get out of control or because key people in the environment would react to them with punishment, rejection, or disapproval. Because the child's ego was too weak to cope with these psychic realities, the person had to rely excessively on defense mechanisms such as repression and projection. Although these defenses help avoid painful or frightening wishes and memories, they also use up a great deal of emotional energy and result in a denial or avoidance of some aspects of reality. Pathological symptoms are a kind of compromise between the repressed wish and the defenses in which the wish is consciously avoided but finds a substitute expression through the symptom. Repression of one's anger, for example, may enable the person to avoid the conscious awareness of being an angry person. But the repressed anger may show up in disguised form as self-hatred and depression. Until these previously avoided conflicts can be found and faced, the person cannot develop the ego strength to face reality, be honest with his or her emotions, and function efficiently and congruently.

Both the quality of the therapeutic relationship and a number of specific techniques are utilized to bring these previously repressed conflicts to the surface so they can be analyzed, understood, and resolved.

The Role of the Analyst

The psychoanalyst's role can be roughly divided into two parts. The first is the offering of a sensitive, caring relationship in which patients feel free to explore the painful psychic material that is at the root of their personality disturbance. This real relationship is the context for all psychoanalytic work, but it lies somewhat in the background as a necessary but not sufficient cause of effective analytic work. It includes the analyst's ability to hear and understand the patient's struggles without anxiety or condemnation as well as the ability to comprehend the meaning of previously repressed material. This role is that of deeply sensitive listener who hears both the conscious and unconscious mental processes of the patient.

The second part of the analyst's role consists of his or her technical procedures. These technical procedures are the analyst's actions
or techniques. They comprise what analysts do as they listen empathically to their patients. These procedures center around encouraging the patient to free associate and interpreting the meaning of
these associations. They also include the analyst's use of silence,
dream interpretation, and the interpretation of resistances and
transference.

Free Association

Since the psychoanalytic theory of pathology sees the roots of
maladjustment in the conflict between the largely unconscious impulses and wishes of the id and the evaluative control functions of
the ego, the techniques of psychoanalysis are aimed at resolving and
reworking these conflicts. The basic rule of psychoanalysis is that
the patient tells the analyst everything that comes to mind during
the analytic hour. The purpose of this is to help patients go beyond
their conscious, rational, ego-controlled thoughts in order to become
aware of previously repressed wishes, thoughts, feelings, and experiences.

By saying everything that comes to mind, no matter how embar-
rassing, irrelevant, or painful it may seem, the psychoanalytic patient gives the analyst a full view of his or her psychological life. By
listening carefully to the patient's free associations the analyst is
able to sense painful areas, contradictions, or defenses patients are
using to avoid facing aspects of their lives.

Resistance

Although patients seeking treatment consciously desire to
change, psychoanalytic theory proposes that at an unconscious
level they do not want to give up the defenses that hide painful or
unacceptable feelings and wishes because they know of no other
way of handling them. In psychoanalysis all the patient's efforts
(both conscious and unconscious) to avoid these anxiety-provoking
thoughts and feelings by continuing the defenses are called resistance. Resistance is simply the use of defense mechanisms during
psychoanalytic treatment. Since it is the inappropriate use of defense mechanisms that keeps patients from facing the conflicts giving rise to their maladjustments, the analysis of resistances is one
of the major therapeutic activities of the psychoanalyst. Common
resistances include not talking, censoring one's thoughts, talking in

a highly intellectual manner that avoids feelings, missing appointments, talking only of present concerns (rather than both the past and the present), and acting out one's hidden conflicts in pathological or defensive behaviors.

Psychoanalysts begin to help patients overcome their resistances and become aware of hidden conflicts by pointing out and demonstrating how the patient is resisting. They may observe, "It is interesting that each time we talk about your father you miss your next appointment," or, "When you mention your brother's death you seem to pass over it very quickly and change the subject." Once patients become aware they are resisting, the analyst helps them explore what memories, feelings, or wishes are being pushed from awareness and why. In each case it is some painful emotion such as fear, guilt, shame, or anger.

As patients become aware of what and why they are resisting, the analyst helps them explore the sources of these conflicts. If the patient consistently avoids any semblance of angry feelings in talking about experiences that normally prompt anger responses, the analyst encourages the patient to explore his family dynamics in order to learn why the patient is so fearful of experiencing angry feelings. By repeatedly analyzing these resistances and helping patients face upsetting emotions and memories, the analyst hopes to open the patient to finding better ways of coping. As this is done, the patient's ego grows progressively stronger and able to cope, and his id impulses are more maturely integrated into the total personality.

Interpretation

The psychoanalyst's primary therapeutic activity is interpretation. Interpretation consists of making previously unconscious mental processes conscious. This is done in conjunction with the analysis of resistances, since it is the resistances that keep these processes out of awareness during the analytic hour. Interpretations, however, go beyond analyzing resistances to explore in depth the meaning, cause, and dynamics of a psychological process or experience. In formulating interpretations that help patients understand their dynamics, analysts rely heavily on dreams and free associations to piece together a picture of the conflicts the patient has been avoiding.

For example, in the same or succeeding sessions a patient may discuss an aggressive colleague at work, a policeman he believes mistreated him, and a dream he had about his father. The analyst will see a pattern in which the patient is tending to view most of the significant men in his life as threatening to his masculinity. By asking the patient to give associations to these men, the reason for the fears will usually become apparent. In line with psychoanalytic theory, one hypothesis might be that the patient harbors competitive and resentful feelings toward male authority figures growing out of his childhood desire to replace his father as the object of his mother's love (the oedipus complex). By slowly uncovering resistances, making interpretations, and tying different bits of psychological experience together, analysts help patients gradually explore the roots of their current adjustment struggles and conflicts.

Transference

Another cornerstone of psychoanalytic technique is the process of transference. In transference patients experience (transfer) feelings or reactions toward a person in the present that are really a reliving of childhood reactions to other significant people. Although everyone transfers some reactions and feelings from childhood figures (such as parents and siblings) to adult social relations (such as spouses and employers), the psychoanalytic situation is set up to maximize this process so that the patient will relive and resolve earlier conflictual relationships. The frequency of sessions, the use of free association, the use of the couch (which prevents usual social interaction and encourages exploration of one's inner feelings), and the focus on dreams and past significant relationships are all designed to promote regression to earlier, more primitive psychological levels of functioning and transference. Within the transference patients experience their fears, guilt, sexual and aggressive wishes, and their defenses against these thoughts and feelings much as they did in childhood. This time, however, they experience them with a person (the analyst) who is not threatened and who can help them understand and accept their wishes and feelings and handle them in mature ways.

Psychoanalytic theory holds that as patients react to their analysts, earlier maladaptive relationships are brought into focus and can be understood and altered. Along with free association and interpretation, then, the transference relationship is one of the major procedures for uncovering repressed feelings and experiences.

The transference relationship is also a key to keeping the analysis from simply serving as an intellectual excursion into the past. By actively experiencing transferred feelings with the analyst the patient is able to struggle with difficult emotions on a firsthand basis. In this way the analyst in part becomes a substitute parent who is able to help patients cope with difficult wishes and feelings they felt they could not handle with their real parents.

Evaluation

Although many Christians have dismissed psychoanalytic theory because of Freud's stress on sexuality and the belief that psychoanalysis promotes acting out of sinful impulses, a closer evaluation indicates that at least some aspects of psychoanalytic theory are congruent with scriptural teachings and with careful observation of human functioning. From a biblical perspective it seems that many aspects of the broad structure of psychoanalytic theory are consistent with a biblical view of human nature, while much of the specific content is questionable or in conflict.

Freud's stress on the existence of unconscious mental processes, for example, is supported by phenomena such as dreams and hypnosis, which demonstrate the activity of thoughts we are not consciously aware of. It is also consistent with scriptural passages that speak of the human personality's complexity and tendency to self-deceit (e.g., Jer. 17:9). Psychoanalysis' understanding of the role of defense mechanisms in warding off unacceptable wishes and feelings goes beyond scriptural descriptions of how we avoid facing painful reality but is consistent with that scripturally described process.

The psychoanalytic assumption that all behavior is purposeful and motivated is consistent with a biblical view of human nature that sees individuals as intelligent, self-determining, social persons created in the image of God. So is the assumption of the continuity of childhood and adult experiences. Parents, for example, are instructed to train children properly so the parents can have assurance that their children will follow that way in adulthood (Prov. 22:6). The psychoanalytic belief that there is a reciprocal relationship between the individual and his or her environment is also consistent with scriptural teaching on the role of both personal and societal responsibility.

When we come to the specific content of Freud's theory, particularly his view of motivation, we encounter serious problems. Although Scripture has a great deal to say about human sexuality, it certainly does not give it the prominent motivational role that psychoanalysis does. In fact, the Bible rather clearly describes humanity's drive to be autonomous and godlike as the major motivating force behind human maladjustment. Similarly, Freud's theory of neurosis appears inadequate. Although the broad outline of conflicts that motivate defenses, which in turn produce neurotic symptoms, is widely accepted, most theorists question the central role Freud gave to the oedipus complex in this process. Broader social motivations and dynamics appear to be closer to both clinical observations and scriptural revelation.

Even given the compatibility of some of psychoanalytic theory with a Christian view of human nature, psychoanalysis leaves us with a truncated view of personality. Freud and his followers have provided a depth technique for exploring the dynamics of human personality. As such, psychoanalysis can provide a good deal of understanding of human functioning. However, it remains for Christians to thoroughly evaluate psychoanalytic theory in light of the biblical view of human nature, motivation, and growth. Even when that task is completed, psychoanalysis will not provide a full picture of human nature. Like all theories of personality, psychoanalysis gives only one perspective or way of looking at human personality. It is limited by the finitude of the theorist, the selection of methods of observation, and the complexities of the subject matter.

Summary

Although some critics claim that psychoanalysis encourages people to act out their sexual and aggressive drives, this is not the case. The issue for analysts is being aware of one's wishes and drives so that one can face them and make mature, conscious choices that take into account one's wishes, the demands of reality, and one's own moral valuations.

During the last forty years a wide variety of therapeutic alternatives to psychoanalysis have been developed. Most of these are of shorter duration, less expensive, and more focused on specific symptoms. Psychoanalysis itself has also been evolving as analysts place greater stress on the importance of the child's very earliest interpersonal relationships (first four years of life) and on the role of aggression in the development of maladjustment, and less emphasis on Freud's biological views of instincts. In spite of the variety of therapeutic approaches today, however, psychoanalysis continues to be one of the few depth therapies that attempt to make fundamental alterations in the structure of the patient's personality.

Additional Readings

Freud, S. *Therapy and technique.* New York: Collier Books, 1963. (Papers originally published between 1888 and 1937.)

Greenson, R. R. *The technique and practice of psychoanalysis.* New York: International Universities Press, 1967.

Menninger, K. *Theory of psychoanalytic technique.* New York: Harper & Row, 1958.

39

Psychoanalytic Psychotherapy
S. Bruce Narramore

Psychoanalytic psychotherapy is an intensive method of therapy based on psychoanalytic personality theory but differing somewhat from the technique of classical psychoanalysis. It is sometimes called psychoanalytically oriented psychotherapy or psychodynamic psychotherapy, although the latter term actually includes a number of insight-oriented therapies other than psychoanalytic psychotherapy (e.g., Gestalt and Adlerian therapy). Psychoanalytic psychotherapy was developed as a modification of psychoanalysis due to the inability of some patients to handle the intensive self-exploration of analysis and because of the desire to find a shorter, less expensive treatment that could be utilized with a greater variety of individuals.

Like psychoanalysis, psychoanalytic psychotherapy assumes that adult personality maladjustments grow out of conflicts between one's wishes or drives and forces that cause repression. It sees the roots of adult maladjustments in childhood experiences; stresses the role of sexual and aggressive drives; and conceptualizes maladjustments in terms of conflicts between the id, ego, and superego. It also shares its major therapeutic techniques with psychoanalysis, as well as its terminology of resistance, defense, transference, and interpretation.

While the understanding of personality development and psychopathology held by psychoanalysts and psychoanalytic psychotherapists is identical, the therapeutic goals and the course of therapy are slightly different. Traditional psychoanalysis is generally carried out on a four or five times a week basis for three to five years. The goal of this extensive therapy is a major restructuring of the total personality. By contrast, psychoanalytic psychotherapy involves between one and three sessions weekly for a period of one to three years. It is oriented more to eliminating symptoms and solving problems than to a radical restructuring of the personality.

In psychoanalysis patients are encouraged to follow the fundamental rule of free association and verbalize anything at all that comes to their minds during the analytic hour. Coupled with the analyst's nondirectiveness this promotes the exploration of every area of the patient's life, including those that at first seem irrelevant to the presenting problem. In contrast, psychoanalytic psychotherapy limits its focus more to issues surrounding the presenting problems and their development. In line with this more limited goal psychoanalytic psychotherapy does not rely as heavily on free association. While psychoanalytic psychotherapists do encourage patients to discuss everything that comes to mind, the psychotherapy is structured in a way that is frequently more focused and problem centered and does not result in true free association.

In psychoanalysis the therapist-patient relationship is the main focus of therapy. By encouraging the development of transference the psychoanalyst hopes to activate the main features of the patient's pathology within the patient's relationship to the analyst. In contrast, psychoanalytic psychotherapy does not focus as intensely on the transference, and the therapist endeavors to help the patient gain insight into conflicts, struggles, and problems without necessarily fully reliving them in the present relationship.

In both psychoanalysis and psychoanalytic psychotherapy the therapist's primary task is twofold: first, to provide an atmosphere or relationship that encourages self-exploration; and, second, to help patients become aware of previously unconscious wishes, feelings, conflicts, and experiences through the technique of interpretation. In psychoanalysis interpretation is usually seen as the only significant therapeutic technique. Analysts listen carefully to patients' dreams and free associations in order to identify the patients' resistances and the warded-off wishes, feelings, and experiences. Any technique that would hinder the process of free association and the interpretation of resistance is viewed as countertherapeutic. By contrast, psychoanalytic psychotherapists may occasionally make careful use of advice or guidance, and they may even encourage certain neurotic defenses if these will further the patient's adaptation to the environment. Such techniques are considered inappropriate in psychoanalysis because they encourage dependency and may reinforce repression, whereas in psychoanalytic psychotherapy they are viewed as appropriate if they will help the patient achieve a higher level of functioning.

A final distinction between psychoanalysis and psychoanalytic psychotherapy is the depth of the patient's regression to primitive levels of thought and feelings. In psychoanalysis the reclining position, frequent sessions, use of free association, and relative anonymity and nondirectiveness of the analyst encourage patients to reexperience their emotional conflicts with the analyst. This regression to primitive or infantile levels of functioning is encouraged in order to understand the sources of adult maladjustments and rework them. In psychoanalytic psychotherapy, by contrast, the less frequent sessions, the shorter length of treatment, and the greater focus on symptoms and present conflicts mean that patients do not typically undergo such a deep regression. This reexperiencing of infantile feelings and reactions is not always viewed as crucial in the more problem-oriented approach of psychoanalytic psychotherapy.

Although it is generally agreed that psychoanalytic psychotherapy is significantly different from psychoanalysis, those differences are not clear-cut, and these two forms of therapy are best seen as different points on the same continuum. Both therapies stress the uncovering of repressed memories, wishes, and feelings; and both utilize transference, interpretation, and dream analysis. The difference is more in degree than kind. The more frequent the sessions, the greater the use of interpretation, the more the focus on transference and dream interpretation, and the deeper the patient's regression, the more the therapy can be considered psychoanalysis. The less frequent the sessions, the greater the focus on presenting and environmental problems, and the greater the therapist's reliance on techniques other than interpretation, the more appropriate the label *psychoanalytic psychotherapy* becomes.

Additional Readings

Fromm-Reichman, F. *Principles of intensive psychotherapy.* Chicago: University of Chicago Press, 1950.

Langs, R. *The technique of psychoanalytic psychotherapy* (2 vols.). New York: Aronson, 1973.

40

Psychodrama
James H. Vander May

Psychodrama is a form of psychotherapy based on the philosophy and theoretical principles of Jacob L. Moreno. A client, or "protagonist," acts out situations to resolve creatively conflicts in himself and with others. This is usually done in the context of a therapeutic or educational group. Psychodrama is an action-oriented approach that restores the individual's lost spontaneity, or ability to live creatively and wholeheartedly, through the use of dramatic interactions.

Historical Development

Moreno was born in Bucharest, Romania, in 1892. His early work in psychodrama was with children in the gardens of Vienna. He would assist them to act out their fantasies and problems. Moreno continued to develop his emerging theoretical system in work with Viennese prostitutes. It was in these brothels that the Moreno version of group psychotherapy was conceived. In 1921 he created the "theater of spontaneity," a totally new version of theater in which

244

professional actors took on roles from newspaper accounts and enacted the stories.

In 1925 Moreno came to the United States. He founded a private psychiatric hospital at Beacon, New York, in 1936. Psychodrama was the primary therapeutic method. Within the next eleven years Moreno, although ridiculed by his peers, developed a unique group treatment that continues to flourish today. His ideas have permeated the encounter and human potential movements of the last 20 years.

Basic Instruments of Psychodrama

Moreno (1978) describes psychodrama as having five instruments. The stage is the first. Many therapeutic stages are circular in design, modeled after Moreno's circular, three-tiered stage with overhanging balcony and lights. The top level of the stage represents the highest level of involvement—the area wherein one places the agonies and ecstasies of life. Lower levels represent the steps of warming up—the periphery or external aspects of existence. These intricate designs are not necessary for a productive psychodrama but are helpful.

The second basic instrument is the protagonist, the individual who receives primary focus in the psychodrama. The protagonist recreates situations from past, present, and future, portraying them with dramatic realism so that new behaviors may be learned and new cognitive patterns established. The protagonist acts as a representative of the group, often exploring a theme that the group has identified as meaningful to them.

A third instrument is the auxiliary ego. Auxiliary egos are representations of the protagonist's significant others. As the protagonist moves into action, he or she chooses group members to represent those individuals who are part of the scene being played. These roles are often parents, spouses, parts of the self, etc. The auxiliary becomes the other in the drama after having been given the necessary information to play the role.

Another type of auxiliary ego is the psychodramatic double. The double helps the protagonist to express thoughts and feelings that would otherwise remain suppressed. The double mimics the protagonist's bodily posture and mannerisms so that the highest level of identification may occur.

The group is considered a fourth instrument. Although psychodrama may be conducted individually in an office setting, it is generally applied as a group treatment. The group is strategically involved in the selection of the protagonist so that the issues to be explored are relevant to the lives of group members. The group members assist through becoming auxiliary egos and in their sharing and support following the psychodrama.

The process is guided by the fifth instrument, the director. The director assists the group in the selection of a protagonist, directs role reversals and scene setting, and acts as the overall coordinator of the drama. The director challenges the protagonist to achieve new insights and new behaviors—those that lead to healthier living. The whole process of the initial group warm-up activities, the enactments of the protagonist, and the verbal closure is guided by the director.

Therapeutic Process

The process of the psychodramatic session is threefold. The initial warm-up phase serves to lessen the social tensions and offers group members an opportunity to identify their feelings and needs. The warm-up is often an activity suggested by the director. Activities range from group interaction exercises to verbal sharing of concerns.

A group theme often becomes the criterion for the selection of the protagonist. The action phase then not only becomes a psychodramatic portrayal of an individual's private concern but represents the overall concern of the group. Common themes are returning to the community; handling anger, grief, marriage and family tension; and loss of self-esteem.

The protagonist, guided by the director, develops scenes that depict the conflict. Auxiliary egos are chosen to represent significant others in the scene, and role reversals are conducted to determine the characters of the significant others. The action, whether past, present, or future, is dramatized in the here and now. Once maximum insight and catharsis occur, the intensity diminishes and sharing begins.

The group becomes the central focus of the sharing-integration phase. They share their common humanity with the protagonist. They relate the scenes portrayed on the stage to their own lives and to significant others. A group healing occurs, one relating to the initial group concern.

Theoretical Principles

Moreno's basic principles are sociometry, social atom, tele, roles, and spontaneity. *Sociometry* is the measurement of one's feelings of attraction, repulsion, and indifference to others on the basis of a specific criterion. Generally this is done in a therapeutic group or school classroom. A criterion could be "With what group members would you be willing to share a secret about yourself?" The sociogram is the basic measuring instrument. Haskell (1967) suggests several examples of sociometric tests.

Moreno used the concept of the *atom* to illustrate the relationship of the individual to significant others. It represents the smallest social unit where significant emotional relationships occur. Usually the social atom is represented as an illustration placing the individual at the center with lines reaching out like spokes to significant people. The content of the relationship—such as attraction, repulsion, or indifference—is then measured through sociometric techniques.

Tele refers to a feeling that is transmitted from one individual to another. Tele, however, is based on the assumption that one sees others clearly and without transference. Transference is a one-way projection of feelings toward another individual (such as the husband who unconsciously transfers feelings about his mother onto his wife). Tele assumes reciprocity. Both individuals have positive feelings such as mutual empathy. It is a two-way process of attaining and maintaining realistic relationships. Tele is the substance of significant relationships, the glue that cements the social atom and encourages it to expand.

Roles and *role playing* are important aspects of Moreno's thinking. A role is the characteristic function and contribution of the individual as well as the expected behavior and position defined by the group for the individual. Conflicts occur between the individual and societal demands, as can be seen in the conflicting roles of women in our culture. Role confusion is exhibited by adolescents who are developing and learning new roles. In these situations role training is a useful function of psychodrama. The individual explores role conflicts and develops new skills in these areas.

Spontaneity is a most important concept in psychodrama. Moreno considers spontaneity as self-initiating behavior, usually in response to some life situation. It requires novelty and adequacy. Without spontaneity the individual will display stereotypic robotlike behaviors. Pathological spontaneity occurs when the individual is being novel but demonstrates little competency or appropriateness in the situation. Such a response is psychosis.

The application of spontaneity to the psychodramatic enactment is very important. The protagonist is challenged to create novel roles and perceptions. Spontaneity for the passive individual could be the act of risking the expression of feelings or of developing more open and intimate relationships with others. For another who is extremely opinionated it may be a sincere attempt to listen to and respect the views of others. Spontaneity is seen by Moreno as basic to all forms of productive creative acts.

Applications.

Psychodrama is applicable to three areas: therapy, training, and education. Most often group treatment lends itself well to this modality, especially in inpatient and partial hospitalization settings. Outpatient groups may also benefit. Another therapeutic use is known as psychodrama "a deux," or the application of psychodrama techniques to individual therapy.

Psychodrama is usually conducted as sociodrama when introduced into the educational system. This form is more familiarly known as role playing. It employs the use of stories and situations acted out for the affective and attitudinal learning of the students. Several other agencies use psychodrama techniques for training. The FBI trains its staff in hostage negotiation with psychodrama as do several police departments. Medical students treat trained auxiliary egos playing roles of patients whom these future doctors will be treating.

View of the Cosmos.

Moreno believes that the God of the Hebrews and the Christ of the New Testament are no longer suitable supreme beings in our society. His new focus is on the "I-God," the infinitesimal part of the Universal Self that each person represents. "Every self is identical with the self of God. All have taken part in the creation of themselves and in creating others. Thus, we can become not only a part of the creation but a part of the creator as well. The world becomes our world, the world of our choice, the world of our creation" (Moreno, 1941, p. xv).

Even amid speculation that Moreno was poetically describing a psychodramatic God, there was an unexpected reaction by others who condemned him as a megalomaniac. However, it seems that his intent was to encourage and invite each individual to search the fullest dimension of himself and others and to assume full responsibility for his own creating.

Moreno rates Christ as an extremely gifted psychodramatist. Christ is the Son of God only as we are all sons of a God. The

Scriptures are viewed as a fallible record of events and not as a holy revelation of God.

It is important at this point to separate the invention from the inventor in this therapeutic modality. Psychodrama itself is neither Christian nor unchristian. It is an instrument, a psychotherapeutic scalpel which, in the hands of the Christian therapist, can assist in bringing about healing and integration for a client.

Many of the biblical guidelines for living are enhanced by psychodrama. Role reversal may produce a new understanding of one's relationship with another and therefore promote forgiving, healing, and loving. Role training assists the Christian in practicing more Christ-like behaviors in simulated situations. Psychodrama as a therapeutic treatment or educational modality is compatible with a biblical Christian perspective.

Reference

Haskell, M. *An introduction to socioanalysis.* Long Beach: California Institute of Socioanalysis, 1967.

Additional Readings

Moreno, J. L. *Words of the father.* New York: Beacon House, 1941.

Moreno, J. L. *Who shall survive?* (3rd ed.). New York: Beacon House, 1978.

Moreno, J. L. *Psychodrama* (Vol. 1) (3rd ed.). New York: Beacon House, 1964.

Moreno, J. L., & Moreno, Z. T. *Psychodrama* (Vol. 3) (3rd ed.). New York: Beacon House, 1969.

Moreno, J. L. *The theatre of spontaneity* (2nd ed.). New York: Beacon House, 1973.

Starr, A. *Psychodrama: Rehearsal for living.* Chicago: Nelson, 1977.

41

Rational-Emotive Therapy
Jeffrey M. Brandsma

Rational-emotive therapy is a treatment approach developed in the 1950s by Albert Ellis after he became disenchanted with the convoluted theory of, and the passivity required in, classical psychoanalysis. Ellis claims that his basic premise can be traced to the Greek Stoic Epictetus and is stated most clearly by Marcus Aurelius: "If thou art pained by any external thing, it is not this thing that disturbs thee, but thy own judgment about it. And it is in thy power to wipe out this judgment now."

Ellis has had an extremely productive career, and has done extensive work in the field of sexology. His major psychotherapeutic statement was *Reason and Emotion in Psychotherapy* (1962); since then his approach has been summarized in many different publications (e.g., Ellis & Harper, 1975). This approach has provided a broad and flexible framework for, and was a forerunner and part of, the cognitive-behavioral approach to psychotherapy that became very popular in the 1970s. It has had great impact on the whole field of psychotherapy and has produced many new applications and spin-offs (Wolfe & Brand, 1977). Indeed, there can be a rational approach to any human problem, as its various proponents continue to demonstrate. Maultsby (1975), among others, has been an important popularizer by making this approach more concrete, specific, and behavioral. He has written several self-help books.

The Concept of Rationality

Rationality has a long history of meanings and definitions of which these present-day proponents, characterized by an ahistorical approach to behavior and philosophy, have little or no awareness. Ellis defines rationality in terms of four basic values: survival, maximizing pleasure (and avoiding all except internal, prosocial pain), being part of a social group, and attaining intimacy with a few of that group. Maultsby is more specific and sets up five criteria. Rational behavior and thinking:

1. is based on objective, consensual reality.
2. is self-protective and life-enhancing.
3. enables goal achievement.
4. prevents significant conflict with others.
5. prevents significant personal, emotional conflict.

To be "rational" one must fulfill the first two criteria and at least one of the latter three.

The ABC Theory of Emotions

In connection with their definition of rationality, rational therapists have a theory of how emotions work (cf. Russell & Brandsma, 1974). The ABC theory is employed as a useful device to explain emotional response and distress. This theory postulates that all emotional responses are the result of cognitive processes, and the invariant sequence is:

(A) perceptual processes—situational determinants.
(B) cognitive processes—thinking, evaluating, self-talk.
(C) physiological responses—feelings.

It is implied in this sequence that thinking, or self-talk, is crucial in creating and maintaining emotional responses, and the important cognitive processes can be verbalized (with some effort) in simple declarative sentences. Thus, the talking to self that one does in evaluating complex stimuli is the root cause of emotional disorder.

The C responses can be produced by B alone. They can also become conditioned or habitualized to A stimuli with little or no intervening consciousness B. The former is called a belief, and the latter an attitude or "thought shorthand." These processes can be either adaptive and efficient or disordered, depending on how well they match up with the criteria for rationality.

Rational Psychotherapy

Therapy leads clients to ask four basic questions:

1. What am I saying to myself?
2. Is it true?
3. What is the evidence for my belief?
4. What is the worst that could happen if . . . ?

Clients are taught, often by written homework assignments (Maultsby, 1971) or by persuasive argumentation, to separate As from Bs from Cs, facts from opinions, thoughts from feelings. An appropriate A section will pass the "camera check"; that is, all statements there can be verified by a camera with sound equipment. If they cannot pass the test, they belong in B. When all important beliefs have been identified and the person's feelings and behaviors are accounted for B, patients are taught to identify their irrational ideas, their "sane" versus "insane" statements. Assuming a statement to be relevant to A, there are many kinds of irrational statements. The most common are positive and negative exaggeration, rationalization, catastrophizing, absolutistic statements, meaningless metaphors, lies, rhetorical questions, nonsequiturs, denial-minimizations, and overgeneralizations.

After these statements are identified and labeled, the client is taught to apply the logicoempirical method to his or her personal statements and hypotheses (as in the previous four questions and criteria for rationality). This is the D, or disputation, part of the ABC theory. Some proponents add an E section to specify a desired outcome in terms of feelings and behavior. Ellis has identified twelve major irrational ideas, but by far the four most common ones, with their rational alternatives, are those in Table 3. By argumentation and direct teaching the client is taught to challenge and replace his irrational thinking with rational alternatives. Then the client is given the homework assignment to visualize himself thinking and acting on the basis of his new cognitions and the desired outcomes. This is called rational-emotive imagery (REI) and is practiced sev-

Table 3

Irrational Idea	Rational Alternative
It upsets me.	Reality just is. I upset myself by how I think about it.
I have to . . .	I don't have to do anything. I will consider only my long-term best interests. "Musturbation" is self-abusive.
I should get what I want.	Everything is exactly as it should be. I may wish for, want, or desire what I want, but it is only *unfortunate* if I don't get it—not awful or a catastrophe!
My self-worth is defined by my behavior.	Behavior is only a small part of my total self. I can rate performances, in order to increase my efficiency, but it is illegitimate to even attempt to rate myself.

eral times each day, usually for specific problem situations. After this internal preparation behavioral techniques such as assertion training, role playing, and practicing are used to further imprint the new cognitions. Specific activities may be prescribed by the creative therapist to help the person test out experientially the irrationality of his position. Rational therapists differ in the extent to which they emphasize and apply various aspects of this process, but the above is a general outline of their approach.

Critical Perspective

The ability to think, abstract, and make sense out of reality is one of the greatest blessings that human beings have. Rational therapy is excellent in helping people to separate classes of problem behavior and to evaluate their own thinking, thus to be more responsible, make better choices, and stop whining. The thrust toward critical thinking and autonomous functioning is commendable. However, the strength of this approach is also its weakness. The implied view of persons is rather mechanical, overly cognitive, and exceedingly individualistic. Rational therapists translate everything into cognitions, including motivation, and assume that all cognitive processes can be easily verbalized and are available to awareness. They do not emphasize the interpersonal nature of the individual or his enmeshment in various systems (family, cultural, etc.).

The view of reality taken by most rational therapists is quite limited from a Christian perspective because they make the mistake of assuming that scientific methodology and principles define the universe. They often slip into scientism by transmuting legitimate methodological naturalism into illegitimate ontological naturalism; that is, they confuse a useful method with the nature of reality. Paradoxically the ones who most strenuously dispute the "religion" of Freud, Rogers, and any form of theism then proceed to set up their own religion based on empiricism and scientific method. It follows that ethics are always situational, since there are no absolutes except perhaps avoidance of social chaos and harm to others, and the attainment of one's personally defined goals—that is, the values of rationality.

Rational therapists (with only a few notable exceptions) tend to have a negative orientation toward feelings. Their interest is not in integration of feelings but rather in controlling or eliminating them. On the whole, rational therapists do not emphasize listening carefully or empathic understanding. They are interested in words and semantics, not experiences or meanings. Thus they tend toward premature attacks on language, they do not hear or understand deeper meanings, or see and understand nonverbal communication. This system is an excellent example of the advantages and pitfalls of a philosophy of science taken from the first half of the twentieth century. Christians would do well to use many of its insights to discipline their own thinking and behavior, but retain a critical posture toward several of the deficits in technique and, more importantly, its underlying assumptions and philosophical mistakes.

References

Ellis, A. *Reason and emotion in psychotherapy*. New York: Lyle Stewart, 1962.

Ellis, A., & Harper, R. A. *A new guide to rational living*. Englewood Cliffs, N.J.: Prentice-Hall, 1975.

Maultsby, M. C. *Help yourself to happiness through rational self counseling*. Boston: Malborough House, 1975.

Maultsby, M. C. Systematic, written homework in psychotherapy. *Psychotherapy: Theory, Research, and Practice*, 1971, 8, 195–198.

Russell, P. L., & Brandsma, J. M. A theoretical and empirical integration of the rational-emotive and classical conditioning theories. *Journal of Consulting and Clinical Psychology*, 1974, 42, 389–397.

Wolfe, J. L., & Brand, E. (Eds.). *Twenty years of rational therapy*. New York: Institute for Rational Living, 1977.

42

Reality Therapy
Richard D. Kahoe

Developed by Glasser (1965), reality therapy is a reflection of the mid–twentieth-century reaction against psychoanalysis and the medical model of pathology and therapy. In contrast to psychoanalysis, reality therapy emphasizes rationality and thinking over emotions, the present and future over the past, health and possibilities over illness. It projects the commonsense psychiatry of Adolf Meyer, and its emphasis on behavior reflects contemporary behavior therapy. When Glasser, late in his psychiatric residency, questioned established psychoanalytic premises, he found ready support from his teacher, G. L. Harrington (credited as a cofounder of reality therapy). Harrington had studied in the 1950s at the Menninger Clinic with Hellmuth Kaiser, who stressed the importance of interpersonal contact between the two parties in therapy (Barr, 1974). Glasser's thinking was supported by contemporary critics of prevailing psychiatric dogma, including psychologist O. H. Mowrer (who wrote the foreword to *Reality Therapy*) and psychiatrist Thomas Szasz.

Like Szasz, Glasser rejects the concept of mental illness and the

255

general use of psychiatric labels, seeing all functional pathology as irresponsible learned behavior. Reality therapy teaches clients to act responsibly to meet their human needs. The past is not scanned for reasons ("excuses") for the irresponsible behavior, but in the warm, supportive relationship plans are made to act in more responsible ways.

Glasser controls training in reality therapy through his Institute for Reality Therapy. His Educator Training Center similarly promotes the tenets of reality therapy in administration and teaching in elementary and secondary schools.

A View of Humanity

The basic concepts of reality therapy constitute a theory of human nature, both normal and disturbed. People behave in whatever ways they can to meet their needs. If their learning, situation, or resources are inadequate to meet their needs, they will be unfulfilled and miserable, and may be seen as disturbed or needing psychiatric care.

The essential human needs are the same in all cultures and situations. Physiological needs are rarely involved in psychopathology. Mental health professionals are concerned with two sets of basic needs: "the need to love and be loved and the need to feel that we are worthwhile to ourselves and to others" (Glasser, 1965, p. 9). The two-way need for love is both intrinsic and instrumental. People need at least one close relationship in order to meet their needs, including the need to feel worthwhile. Implicitly those who go to therapists do so because they lack other human involvements through which they can meet their needs. Glasser is not cynical when he says that paying a therapist is only "buying a friend."

Therapeutic assistance may also be needed when one loses an established object or source of love. Inability to love can be so painful and threatening to one's self-esteem that the person withdraws from efforts to relate and to meet socially dependent needs. The abilities to love and be loved are subject to a person's perception; a depressed or suicidal client may complain of unbearable loneliness, despite being surrounded by apparently devoted family and friends.

The ability to feel worthwhile to ourselves and to others resembles the common concept of self-esteem. In reality therapy it has distinctive bases. Although abundant love usually produces a sense of worth, unconditional love may not do so. "The child knows the difference between right and wrong behavior and is frustrated because receiving love for behavior that he knows is wrong does not allow him to feel worthwhile" (Glasser, 1965, p. 10). Morals and values are intricately related to self-esteem in reality therapy. Thus it is that disturbed behavior is identified as irresponsible and based on inferior standards (not on an overly strong superego, as psychoanalysts may aver). Furthermore, responsible, mentally healthy behavior must not only meet one's own needs, but it also must not interfere with other people's meeting their own needs.

Reality therapy seems compatible with the biblical view of humanity in many ways. (Glasser professes Judaism, and he reports that Harrington is a Christian.) Glasser's emphasis on loving and needing involvement recalls Scripture, ranging from "it is not good for the man to be alone" (Gen. 2:18 NIV) to "the greatest of these is love" (1 Cor. 13:13). Self-worth is not so obviously a biblical doctrine, but we are made "a little lower than the heavenly beings" (Ps. 8:5), and God loved us so much "that he gave his one and only Son" (John 3:16). Of course, ethical standards and responsible behavior receive stronger biblical imperative. Reality therapy's most explicit moral bases are more humanistic than theocentric, but it rejects ethical neutrality and relativity, and views some behaviors as inherently wrong.

The Reality Therapist

Reality therapists represent many helping professions—for example, social work, school administration, clinical psychology, guidance counseling, the ministry. Full-fledged reality therapists are certified by the Institute for Reality Therapy. Among 415 clinical and counseling psychologists in the American Psychological Association surveyed by Smith (1982), 1 percent identified with reality therapy.

If the reality therapist serves as a paid friend to the client, the friendship offers a tough love, with notable objectivity, firmness, and persuasiveness. The therapist assumes certain responsibilities for the involvement and makes them clear to the client, but he or she never assumes responsibility for the client's behaviors.

Reality therapy teaches clients (by model, exhortation, and practice) to meet their needs responsibly, respecting others' needs and rights. Techniques used to solve immediate problems are generalized to other situations so that clients become increasingly independent of therapy.

Sometimes the principles of reality therapy are oversimplified, suggesting that anybody can become a reality therapist. While the techniques can be succinctly stated, at several points the therapist's intuitive art and strength of personality are sorely tested. People who attempt to become reality therapists without careful training and supervision may be led astray by one or another idea taken out of context.

The Therapeutic Process

Glasser originally (1965, p. 21) identified three therapeutic procedures: involvement, rejecting unrealistic behavior, and teaching better ways to fulfill the client's needs. His training materials in the 1970s and a later essay (1980) identified the more familiar eight steps of reality therapy.

The first, make friends, includes the willingness to reveal one's own values and limitations and to become emotionally involved with one's clients—to be affected by their problems and suffer with them. Although Glasser downplays emotions, an emotional involvement requires the therapist to convey some empathy for the feelings clients express. The therapist must understand human behavior well enough to fathom the client's behavior and not be disgusted by it, however deviant. Each step of reality therapy is built on all preceding steps, and amateur attempts at reality therapy may fail most often by slighting Step 1, through the therapist's inexperience or eagerness to change the client's behavior.

Step 2 asks the clients, "What are you doing?" This focuses on clients' behaviors, to persuade them that they choose to act as they do. Unlike rational-emotive therapy, reality therapy does not stress that clients also choose how they feel; it just ignores the debatable issue of emotions altogether. While the therapist may listen to feelings offered, the second step shifts the focus toward behavior, which is probably affecting the feelings anyway.

Step 3 follows by asking, "Is what you are doing helping you?" Clients evaluate their own behavior and come to recognize the ways it is unrealistic, irresponsible, or simply not meeting their major goals. The question departs significantly from Glasser's original second step—rejecting the unrealistic behavior. This earlier strategy invited misunderstanding in that the therapist more or less abruptly changed from unconditional friendship to critical rejection (Frazier & Laura, 1972). Almost surely Glasser rarely operated that way. Nonetheless, the therapist must make judgments, challenging a glib response like, "Sure; it makes me feel good to cuss out my teacher!" While making friends the therapist learns the client's needs and goals well enough to turn "Is it helping?" toward more fundamental or long-term goals.

Step 4 helps the client make a plan to do better. While clients should make substantial contributions to the plans made in therapy, the therapist may have to make suggestions, to proffer alternative plans, to modify plans to make them more realistic and readily attainable. However it is developed, the plan must be one the client will accept.

Step 5 gets a commitment to the plan. The commitment may be sealed with a handshake or in a written contract. The timetable usually involves having at least part of the plan completed by the next session, with scheduled evaluation points for the other parts.

The next two steps refer to the follow-up on the commitment. Step 6 is to accept no excuses. If the commitment has not been kept, the therapist may say, "Yes, but you didn't do it, did you?" Then the commitment is renewed or the plan revised. Step 7 does not provide for punishment, but neither does the therapist interfere with natural consequences of the lapse. If an alcoholic client breaks a pledge of abstinence, the therapist would not upbraid or withhold therapy, but neither would he or she plead mercy from the client's spouse or judge.

Step 8 is never give up. The therapist's commitment involves sticking with therapy as long as the client is willing to work on the problems. If a plan fails, therapy picks up at the appropriate prior step and tries again. If a client resists even the mild, implicit confrontation of "Is it helping?" the therapist falls back to maintaining the friendship. So reality therapy may continuously recycle through the eight steps until clients themselves can accept and evaluate their behavior, assume responsibility for their plans, and make commitments to proper conduct.

Reality Therapy (1965) described applications in a residential treatment center for delinquent girls, a mental hospital chronic ward, public schools, and private practice. Glasser's next book, *Schools Without Failure* (1968), explicitly stressed the public school system, to which he devoted considerable attention. Besides California's Ventura School for Girls, where reality therapy was forged, other residential treatment programs for youths use reality therapy. Frazier and Laura (1972) described a church application, which failed because the minister did not follow the principles outlined above.

Evaluation

Two decades of development by a cohesive group of therapists from various backgrounds have honed reality therapy into a coherent and effective treatment for a wide variety of psychological problems. That cohesion could perpetuate blind spots. Conventionally trained therapists may charge that glossing over emotions fails to resolve underlying emotional problems. Techniques from rational-emotive therapy, when appropriate, could avert this criticism and still maintain the spirit of reality therapy. Then, nondirective therapists may challenge a therapy that even implicitly presumes to define reality for its clients.

It is not absolutely true, as often charged, that the principles of reality therapy are simple to understand and the therapeutic techniques easy to master. This therapy requires considerable insight into human behavior and artful applications to concrete personal situations. Still, reality therapy could be more widely adopted in pastoral counseling. Specific training in the therapy should not substitute for graduate education in psychology or clinical pastoral training, but reality therapy can be an effective tool for clerical counselors. Both the implied view of humankind and the therapeutic methods seem well suited to ministerial counseling roles.

Possibly the major limiting factor in widespread use of reality therapy, by ministers and other counselors, is its continued "ownership" by Glasser's organizations. While control over orthodoxy of the system has merit, if reality therapy were taught in other counselor-training programs, its apparent values could find wider application.

References

Barr, N. I. The responsible world of reality therapy. *Psychology Today*, 1974, 7(9), 64; 67–68.

Frazier, S. L., & Laura, R. S. Reality therapy: A critical examination. *Pastoral Psychology*, 1972, *23*, 39–49.

Glasser, W. *Reality therapy*. New York: Harper & Row, 1965.

Glasser, W. *Schools without failure*. New York: Harper & Row, 1968.

Glasser, W. Reality therapy. In N. Glasser (Ed.), *What are you doing?* New York: Harper & Row, 1980.

Smith, D. Trends in counseling and psychotherapy. *American Psychologist*, 1982, *37*, 802–809.

43

Short-term Therapies
Vance L. Shepperson

S hort-term, or brief, therapies have traditionally been viewed as sorts of stop-gap interventions that one resorts to if one does not have an adequate amount of time or expertise to do anything else. However, the current mainstream perspective has shifted and short-term therapies are today viewed with more respect. It is being recognized that significant intrapsychic and interpersonal change can be accomplished in a short period of time if one is willing to try something different.

Gurman (1981) adopts a perspective supportive of this new emphasis on briefer therapies. He maintains that a high percentage of all psychotherapy patients terminate treatment in less than 12 sessions, and thus the emphasis on briefer therapies is new only by design.

Brief therapies in general have a number of common ingredients. They tend to concentrate on just one or two salient issues or themes. They require the therapist to be relatively more active and directive than a traditional longer term therapist would be. The therapist has to be willing to assume more responsibility for what happens during each session without infringing on the client's autonomy or treating him like an infant.

The therapies requiring a short period of time have a significant number of differences from each other. These differences center around basic theoretical assumptions regarding the mechanism of change, criteria for patient selection, and therapeutic style and strategy. Approaches to these differences can be reasonably grouped into two major camps: brief individual therapies (psychodynamic and behavioral) and brief systems therapies.

Brief Psychodynamic Therapies

Theoretical assumptions

The basic curative element postulated by psychodynamic therapists practicing brief therapy is still insight. The client's insight into his own intrapsychic process is facilitated primarily by active clarification and interpretation of his resistance and transference, in roughly that chronological order. A highly focused beam of emotional energy is brought to bear on the defined issue at hand. This issue will typically vary across patients and therapists. Sifneos (1979), Wolberg (1965), Malan (1976), and to a lesser degree Davanloo (1978) tend to focus primarily on oedipal issues to the exclusion of what they view as themes of lesser importance. Particular attention is paid to evidence of oedipal struggles within the therapy relationship. Mann and Goldman (1982) take a distinctively different approach. They tend to pursue individuation-separation issues as a central theme. This pursuit is ensconced in a theoretical framework that is very time conscious: the very fact that one has so little time to work together is used as a powerful lever to push the client into the separation-individuation arena.

Criteria for patient selection

In general dynamic briefer therapists have relatively stringent requirements for allowing patients to work in a brief therapy format. Most of the theorists cited above will require all of the following qualities in a patient: resilient ego strength, a focused presenting problem, fair to good capacities for attention, relatively high motivation, a history of at least one past successful relational attachment, a better than average capability for insight, no prior suicide attempts, and no evidence of psychosis or borderline psychiatric conditions. Mann and Goldman (1982) claim to have a much lower criterion; namely, good ego strength as demonstrated by the patient's ability to tolerate loss adequately in the past. If the above criteria are not met, the therapist will tend to switch therapeutic modalities from dynamic to supportive therapy. Sifneos refers to this as moving from short-term anxiety-provoking therapy to short-term anxiety-suppressive therapy.

Treatment strategy and techniques

Most brief dynamic theorists are stage oriented. The length of these stages is dependent on both therapist and client variables. The most important therapist variable is whether or not a predetermined termination date is part of the treatment plan (e.g., Mann sees all clients for only twelve sessions; the other theorists cited above vary their treatment length from eight to forty sessions, with twelve to fifteen weekly sessions being modal). Although different descriptive terminologies are used to define treatment stages, the concepts are relatively similar. The initial stage is characterized by a bright, optimistic expectancy, the establishment of a supportive alliance, and the development of a positive transference. The therapist is actively assessing, defining, and clarifying the central issue with the client while establishing a trust base that will support the negative effect aroused later in treatment. This phase typically lasts from one to three sessions.

The second phase of therapy is initiated by a higher frequency of confrontive interpretations on the part of the therapist. The client's defenses and transferences are actively confronted in such a way as to arouse anxiety; the client may also be challenged to engage in a variety of different therapeutic activities (e.g., Wolberg, 1965). This is followed by a shift in the client's mood from buoyant expectancy of magical change to a potpourri of negative emotions. If the client does not leave treatment at this point, the prognosis for significant short-term change is enhanced. This stage lasts from four to twenty sessions, depending on the particular theorist's orientation and the severity of the client's disorder. The final stage of therapy finds the therapist pushing the client to integrate new ideas, feelings, and activities into his daily life. Most brief therapists will also work to help clients process their separation anxiety in a more healthy manner than they have been able to do in the past.

Brief Behavioral Therapy

Theoretical assumptions

Traditionally the subgroups within the behavioral school have emphasized the crucial importance of environmental factors in the change process. Classical and operant conditioning using a stimulus-response model was the accepted method of change. More recently cognitive behavior modification approaches have flourished. These approaches are more compatible with a social learning perspective in which cognitive mediating variables are accepted as causal in the change process. An excellent example of a broad-spectrum behavioral approach is the multimodal behavioral therapy of Lazarus (1976).

Criteria for patient selection

The primary benefit of brief behavior therapy is that one may tailor a particular behavioral approach to the level of intelligence, insight, judgment, and ego strength of each individual. The treatment door is wide open to the poor-functioning chronic schizophrenic as well as the bright, high-functioning neurotic (Wilson, 1981).

Treatment strategy and techniques

The initial step in this approach is to carry out a detailed behavioral assessment of a well-defined problem. The therapist then contracts with the client, either verbally or in writing, a specific agreement detailing the procedures they will follow, the number of sessions they will work together (most often eight to twelve sessions to begin with for mild to moderately severe difficulties), and a contingency plan for dealing with any foreseeable difficulties. Typically if the patient appears to have more than one problem, the least difficult will be addressed first. Along with establishing the rewarding feeling of mastering one difficulty the behavioral brief therapist will often arrange for external positive reinforcements in order to enhance motivation. Thus, difficulties are addressed in a step-wise fashion, with the therapist functioning as a benevolent teacher-coach.

Brief Systems Therapies

Theoretical assumptions

Brief systems (marital and family) therapists assume that:

1. change can and will take place even without insight if the system is willing to follow the therapist's prescriptions;
2. change is cybernetic and follows principles of circular rather than linear causation.

3. many problems in living that individuals bring to therapists are the result of a lack of coping skill rather than an excess of backlogged emotional garbage; that is, most psychological problems have pedestrian origins.

Criteria for patient selection

The systems therapist will typically include all of the significant individuals within the identified patient's current primary social grouping, whether they are related biologically or not. A central concern for most brief systems therapists, regardless of the nature or severity of the presenting problem, is to redefine the problem in such a way that the therapeutic system (therapist and family) can avoid getting enmeshed in nonproductive interpersonal clutter. Depending on the aptitude, interests, and resilience of the particular systems therapist, an extremely broad range of difficulties can be treated using this modality.

Treatment strategy and techniques

The primary tool of the strategic brief therapist is directive rather than interpretation (Haley, 1976). Directives typically focus on how members within the system interact with one another and the sequence and structure of their interactional process.

Directives can be either compliance based or defiance based (Papp, 1980). When working with a cooperative system the therapist will frequently exercise his "expert authority" to involve as many members of the family as possible in an activity. This activity can be either within or between sessions. The therapist can direct this activity based on a straightforward or more indirect, metaphoric conceptualization of the problem. The effect of this intervention is to relabel or redefine a few strategic areas of the system's sequence of interaction; eventually this change in sequence will calcify into a structural change in the system. When the oppositional tendencies within the system are such that compliance-based directives are rendered impotent, the brief strategic therapist will move toward the use of defiance-based directives. This has become known as paradoxical intervention, and the art of understanding and effecting such directives has received much attention in recent years.

Systems therapists are less stage oriented than are dynamic brief therapists. Some will tend to conceptualize intermediate phases in therapy that are viewed as necessary "halfway houses" to the desired restructure of the system (Haley, 1980).

The average length of treatment is usually between twelve and twenty sessions. The Milan group conducts what they have referred to as long brief therapy; typically they see a family for only 12 sessions, but each session is one month apart (Palazzoli-Selvini, Boscolo, Cecchin, and Prata, 1978). They contend that the system requires that amount of time to digest their carefully planned strategic interventions. This group is also distinctive in that they have used a "Greek chorus" concept in which an anonymous panel observes through a one-way mirror and sends in interventions which the co-therapist team can choose to be puzzled by, disagree with, passively acknowledge or actively applaud. This unique technique allows for a spatial representation of the ambivalence toward change present within most systems. The Greek chorus can push hard for transformation, while the co-therapists can express doubts and vote for homeostasis.

Summary

Some of the contrasts made between the major camps of brief therapy are in practice more theoretical than real, since many brief therapists are eclectic by disposition. For example, an individual might be seen alone, but treatment might flow from a systemic conceptualization of the client's problem, with both interpretations and directives being used as the therapist deems appropriate. The continued development of brief therapies is highly likely given the current economic and political climate. The use of these active, high-leverage treatment tactics is an area of conceptual and operational potency that the average clinician cannot afford to be without.

References

Davanloo, H. (Ed.). *Basic principles and techniques in short-term dynamic psychotherapy.* New York: Spectrum, 1978.

Gurman, A. Integrative marital therapy: Toward the development of an interpersonal approach. In S. H. Budman (Ed.), *Forms of brief therapy.* New York: Guilford, 1981.

Haley, J. *Problem solving therapy.* San Francisco: Jossey-Bass, 1976.

Haley, J. *Leaving home: The therapy of disturbed young people.* New York: McGraw-Hill, 1980.

Lazarus, A. A. *Multimodal behavior therapy.* New York: Springer Publications, 1976.

Malan, D. H. *The frontier of brief psychotherapy.* New York: Plenum, 1976.

Mann, J., & Goldman, R. *A casebook in time-limited psychotherapy.* New York: McGraw-Hill, 1982.

Palazzoli-Selvini, M., Boscolo, L., Cecchin, G., & Prata, G. *Paradox and counterparadox: A new model in the therapy of the family in schizophrenic transaction.* New York: Aronson, 1978.

Papp, P. The Greek chorus and other techniques of paradoxical therapy. *Family Process,* 1980, *19,* 45–57.

Sifneos, P. E. *Short-term dynamic psychotherapy: Evaluation and technique.* New York: Plenum, 1979.

Wilson, G. T. Behavior therapy as a short-term therapeutic approach. In S. Budman (Ed.), *Forms of brief therapy.* New York: Guilford, 1981.

Wolberg, L. R. (Ed.), *Short-term psychotherapy.* New York: Grune & Stratton, 1965.

44

Supportive Psychotherapy
Bethyl J. Shepperson

Supportive psychotherapy is a type of psychological treatment that utilizes various techniques directed toward symptomatic improvement and reestablishment of a client's usual adaptive behaviors.

Distinctives and Objectives

In general, psychotherapy is a psychological treatment assisting people with emotional problems. The treatment may be one of three different kinds: supportive, reeducative, or reconstructive (Wolberg, 1977). The differences between these kinds of treatment center on their objectives and approaches. The many, varied schools of psychotherapy find their preference in one of these three kinds of treatment. An example of each is guidance (supportive), family therapy (reeducative), and psychoanalytic psychotherapy (reconstructive).

As suggested by its name, supportive therapy aims to *support* clients, strengthening their defenses and preventing them from getting worse during the healing process. This treatment works to bring a client to a place of emotional equilibrium as soon as possible; its intent is to bring about an improvement of the symptoms so

268

that the client can resume a level of functioning close to his or her norm. Briefly, this therapy has three goals:

1. to strengthen existing defenses.
2. promote a level of functioning in the individual adequate to meet the demands of his or her environment.
3. to reduce or remove the detrimental external factors that prompt the stress.

These somewhat modest goals are not intended to change personality structure, although sometimes constructive alterations occur on their own once restoration is made and the successful new adaptations have been achieved.

Supportive measures may be used in two ways: as a primary treatment or as an adjunct to reeducative or reconstructive psychotherapies. Wolberg (1977) suggests four reasons for using support:

1. as a temporary necessity for basically sound personality structures that are momentarily overwhelmed by transient pressures the person is unable to handle.
2. as a primary, extensive means of maintaining borderline and characterologically dependent clients in homeostasis.
3. to promote ego building, so that an individual can subsequently lend his or her efforts to more reconstructive psychotherapeutic work.
4. as a temporary resting place during more intensive therapy when anxiety becomes too great for one to cope adequately.

Those who seem to benefit most from supportive psychotherapy are people who are experiencing an acute crisis and need temporary encouragement. Also, chronically disturbed individuals can function quite adequately when receiving ongoing support.

Supportive therapy is contraindicated in situations where authority issues are so predominant that the client becomes competitive and depreciating, and seeks control of the therapeutic process by aggressive or hostile means. This form of therapy is also contraindicated in situations where the client detaches and becomes helpless; in this instance supportive therapy only serves to encourage the pathologic dependency.

Therapeutic Approach and Techniques

Supportive therapy views the client as an individual capable of change. Furthermore, it is not assumed that insight is necessary for

such change to occur. A more crucial curative ingredient is hopeful-
ness; an individual will weather the necessary difficult times when
he believes there is hope, even if that hope must be temporarily
borrowed from the therapist. Therapeutic optimism is therefore an
important qualification for the supportive therapist. He or she
should also have, and be able to communicate, a concern for and
nonjudgmental acceptance of the client. The therapist should also
be flexible, as supportive therapeutic work typically draws on a
broad range of techniques. The most important of these are described below.

Directive guidance

The giving of advice or guidance is a technique that must be
carefully regulated to the needs of the client. Specific recommendations are suitable for anxious and disorganized individuals but not
for those capable of making their own decisions. In general, advising
a client in areas of life changes that may be irreversible should be
avoided.

Nondirective guidance

This technique avoids some of the dangers of directive guidance
yet still provides guidance. Here the therapist listens carefully and
offers the client a summary of the problems he or she has described
along with several approaches for resolution. The therapist assumes
the person is capable of good judgment and places the responsibility
for decisions on the client.

Environmental intervention

This technique consists of initiating stress-reducing changes in
the environment when a client is unable to take action to improve
his or her own life situation. Examples might be a phone call to an
employer or to a medical facility for an appointment, or suggesting
a change of housing or a vacation. This technique must be used
carefully with those clients who easily become dependent.

Ventilation

Allowing a client to express previously suppressed emotions and
thoughts often results in a noticeable reduction of emotional tension
and the capability to think more clearly. This method should be
used selectively. It should not be employed if tension escalates rapidly or disorganized thinking and behavior increase.

Reassurance

Encouragement can often be beneficial, particularly after the client has thoroughly expressed his or her feelings concerning a situation. General, pat statements, such as "Everything will be all right," are not supportive and usually shut down further communication.

Education

After the client's problems are determined, the therapist's participation can often have an educative component. The focus may be on providing the client with the information and experience for learning better ways to solve problems.

Diversion

This tactic redirects a client's thinking and/or behavior away from disturbing topics to less intense and more therapeutic ones. Diversion is used primarily with clients who become so absorbed in personal problems that they neglect other important areas of their lives. It is particularly useful for those who are medically ill or experiencing chronic pain.

Other techniques

Other supportive measures include tension control such as self-relaxation, self-hypnosis, meditation, and biofeedback; milieu therapy, which includes environmental manipulation, home treatment, day treatment, occupational therapy, music therapy, dance therapy, and social therapy; pressure and coercion; persuasion; confession; chemotherapy; and inspirational self-help group therapies such as Alcoholics Anonymous or Parents United.

Biblical Evaluation

A basic theme of Scripture is growth and restoration. Central to life is the phenomenon of growth, the capacity to change, and the restorative process. The biblical message is that while pain, hurt, pathology, and sin exist, there is still hope for healing and wholeness.

Christ teaches us through his parables and discerning dialogues that people hear and respond at varying levels, depending on their circumstances and personal development. Children, adults, men, women, disciples, and Pharisees all heard the same message, but each responded quite differently. Depending on the situation, Jesus used a variety of approaches, such as guidance, instruction, encouragement, acceptance, and protection.

There is a similarity between some approaches of supportive psychotherapy and the approaches Jesus took. The directive approach is clear in such passages as "Go home to your people and report to them what great things the Lord has done for you, and how he had mercy on you" (Mark 5:19). Reassurance and encouragement are given as people hear a message of hope: "I am the way, and the truth, and the life" (John 14:6). Education is masterfully illustrated by, "He who has seen me has seen the Father" (John 14:9). "He that is without sin among you, let him be the first to throw a stone at her" (John 8:7) is a superb diversion tactic.

Supportive therapy therefore seems to be an important mode of psychological treatment, broadly compatible with Christ's own style of relating to people. Either as an adjunct or alternative to more reconstructive approaches, supportive techniques are clearly the treatment of choice in many situations.

Reference

Wolberg, L. R. *The technique of psychotherapy* (Vol. 1) (3rd ed.). New York: Grune & Stratton, 1977.

45

Transactional Analysis
H. Newton Malony

Transactional analysis is viewed by its advocates as a theory of personality, a view of psychopathology, a mode of psychotherapy, and a philosophy of life. In each of these the primary data for consideration are observable ways in which persons interact with each other. These interpersonal interactions are called transactions, and it is the belief of this approach that an analysis of these transactions is the prime means for understanding and changing persons.

As a theory of personality transactional analysis assumes that those behaviors, attitudes, and styles that charaterize persons are habits they have developed in efforts to obtain "strokes" from other persons with whom they interact. "Stimulus hunger" is seen as the basic motivation of life. This term refers to the innate desire to interact with the world, and most of all the desire to interact with other people. Personality is therefore a style of interacting with others from whom one seeks recognition, status, and intimacy. Personality does not result, as Freud suggested, from an individual need for pleasure but from a social need for others. In this regard transactional analysis is more like ego psychology than psychoanalysis.

As a view of psychopathology transactional analysis assumes that persons are born innocent and trusting. They yearn for intimacy, and they reach out confidently to others. Over time two events commonly occur. People become stereotyped and they become defensive. They give up on experiencing intimacy—that for which persons have a need—and settle for the types of interpersonal relationships (or transactions) that lead to isolation and negative self-images. These types of transactions are called games, and they always end in bad feelings for both persons involved. Games are those types of interactions that always result in negative endings and reinforce a person's bad feelings.

As a mode of psychotherapy transactional analysis assumes that if persons become aware of the self-defeating, intimacy-destroying, isolation-producing ways in which they are interacting with others, and they decide to change these into more fulfilling manners of relating, they can. Transactional analysis affirms the capacity of people to recognize and analyze and alter their behavior. As contrasted with psychoanalysis, which is pessimistic about persons' abilities to become aware of their dynamics because of its presumption that psychopathology is determined by the unconscious, transactional analysis is optimistic about the ability of persons to gain such insight because it presumes that the origins of these problems is in conscious and subconscious ego states that are available for introspection.

As a philosophy of life transactional analysis affirms the potential and possibility of intimacy in human relationships. It is prescriptive, not just descriptive, of what human life ought to be, and it has ideal states toward which it feels society ought to be committed. For example, in Steiner's *Scripts People Live* (1974) a significant section is devoted to a critique of the type of society that promotes isolation and competition. Transactional analysis is optimistic and realistic at the same time. It is idealistic in terms of what human life was meant to be, and it works with persons and with institutions to make them more humane in the sense that they better induce intimacy among people.

Background

While transactional analysis includes a number of contemporary theorists (e.g., Harris, Steiner, Jongeward, James), it evolved from the ideas of one man, Eric Berne. Berne was a psychiatrist who practiced most of his life in the San Francisco area. He had gone through several years of training to be a psychoanalyst prior to being told he would not be approved in 1956. It has often been assumed that because of this disappointing experience Berne decided to create his own theory in contrast to psychoanalysis. This is only partially true; Berne had begun much earlier to state his opinions about the need for a shorter form of treatment than psychoanalysis and for a view of personality that emphasized the ego rather than the id. These ideas germinated during his experience of growing up in the home of a father who was a physician to the poor in Toronto. While a United States army psychiatrist, he published five papers on clinical intuition.

In the late 1950s Berne began to conduct weekly seminars for professionals in his San Francisco office. This led to the publication of *Transactional Analysis in Psychotherapy* (1961), which is said to be the formal beginning of the movement. Many of the recent leaders of the International Transactional Analysis Association and writers in the *Transactional Analysis Journal* were participants in Berne's weekly seminars. There they became stimulated by his "social psychiatry" (a label often ascribed to transactional analysis) and went on to make significant theoretical contributions of their own.

In his seminars Berne placed great emphasis on simple language. He discounted fancy verbiage and cautioned professionals not to use incomprehensible technical jargon. He was interested in finding easy-to-understand terms that patients could fathom and could use in their own effort to get well. He reportedly said after listening patiently to an elaborate case presentation replete with jargon, "That is all well and good. All I know is the patient is not getting cured" (reported in Steiner, 1974, p. 14). In spite of the fact that some professionals criticized transactional analysis for its use of colloquial, folksy, undignified terms such as "games," "trading stamps," and "fairy tales," Berne was unapologetic in his insistence that theory should be shareable and usable.

Basic Concepts

Among these terms were the ones used by Berne to denote ego states. It was his conviction that behavior was a function of the role persons perceived themselves to be playing in transactions with other persons. These perceived roles are determined by the state of mind, or ego state, of the person at a given time. Although he recognized that people's mental states were complex and unique, Berne suggested that they could be grouped under three major types: the "parent," the "adult," and the "child" ego states.

Parent ego states are those in which a person experiences directive, nurturing, critical, prescriptive, and/or protective inclinations. Transactional analysis distinguishes between critical and nurturing parent ego states and suggests that these attitudes and feelings are usually derivatives of people's experiences with their own parents.

Child ego states are those in which a person experiences impulsive, accommodating, fearful, enthusiastic, pleasureful, intuitive, hurtful, and/or gleeful inclinations. Transactional analysis distinguishes between the free and adapted child ego states and suggests that these feelings, too, are derivatives of people's experiences with others from whom they have learned these childlike attitudes. Further, transactional analysis sees the child ego state as the repository of natural, innate energy and self-affirmation. The "little professor" component of the child ego state is that unlearned wisdom with which children are endowed and upon which persons can draw for unlearned wisdom.

Adult ego states are those in which a person experiences pragmatic, rational, realistic, functional inclinations leading toward problem solving and cooperation. Transactional analysis perceives the adult ego state as energized by the child ego state and influenced by the parent ego state. It suggests that the adult should dominate life and that problems ensue when persons interact with each other on the basis of the prejudgments of the parent or the impulsiveness of the child. However, the hyperrationality characteristic of those who have blocked off their parent or their child ego states presents an equal problem. The optimal state of affairs is one in which there is a free-flowing relationship between the three ego states with the adult dominating.

Relationship to Psychoanalysis

This model of psychic structure illustrates transactional analysis's similarity to as well as its difference from psychoanalysis. Both theories contend that inner personality structure is important, although their terms for the components differ and their presumptions about levels of consciousness are dissimilar. The terms *id*, *ego*, and *super-ego* seem similar to *parent*, *adult*, and *child*. Psychoanalysis assumes that the id is unconscious and that the ego and superego operate in unconscious, preconscious, and conscious states. Transactional analysis, in contrast, contends that they are all conscious ego states.

Furthermore, whereas psychoanalysis concludes that the ego and superego are structures that evolve from the id, transactional analysis feels that the parent and adult ego states coexist with the child from an early time in a person's life. From this point of view the ego (of which the parent, adult, and child ego states are parts) exists as a psychic structure along with the id almost from the very beginning of life.

Moreover, these ego states exist in the conscious or preconscious mind and are available to the person for reflection. This is a critical difference from psychoanalysis, which believes that much of the personality is unconscious and available to awareness only through such procedures as free association and dream analysis. Transactional analysis is very hopeful about people's attempts to understand themselves. In this sense the psychoanalytic model of personality as an iceberg of which only a small part can be seen above the water is turned upside down by transactional analysis. Personality is like an inverted iceberg where most of the ice is above the water and can be seen.

Both psychoanalysis and transactional analysis assume that personality structure develops through life experiences. However, whereas psychoanalysis contends that memories become distorted and repressed, transactional analysis is convinced that past memories have been stored in the mind just exactly as they happened and can be recalled. The mind is like a phonographic and photographic recorder that stores experiences and later expresses itself through the several ego states to which the person has access through introspection.

The final difference between psychoanalysis and transactional analysis regards the nature of neurotic behavior. Both are learning theories that emphasize habits. Both emphasize the uncanny tendency of persons to repeat behavior that is self-destructive and unproductive. Pathology for both is continuing to give old answers to present problems. Two emphases are distinctive in transactional analysis, however.

First, transactional analysis is larger in structure and in concept than psychoanalysis. Freud was primarily concerned with the tendency to repeat behavior that held down the repressed anxiety associated with anger and sex. Transactional analysis agrees with this, but in addition is concerned with total life goals and the person's orientation to the world. Thus, it talks of life positions that underlie the living out of life scripts which extend across a lifetime.

The second distinctive of transactional analysis is the nature of the motivation that underlies the repetition compulsion which characterizes psychopathology. The psychoanalytic understanding is grounded in the fear of a negative consequence—that is, a repressed impulse getting out of control. In contrast, transactional analysis sees repeated unproductive behavior (i.e., games) as based on the avoidance of a positive consequence. Human behavior, as noted, is the result of the instinctive urge to relate to others. Optimal relating involves intimacy—free, spontaneous, trustful, energized transactions. However, intimate relationships are unpredictable, risky, and therefore frightening. Persons are attracted to intimacy and afraid of it at the same time. Because of the exhilaration it evokes, they long for it; but because of its lack of sureness, they settle for less than intimacy and construct games to guarantee it will not occur. They do not trust themselves to be intimate. This is quite different from the psychoanalytic point of view.

The Therapy Process

The transactional analyst works on a threefold model: analysis, experience, decision. The first step is structural analysis, in which clients are led into an analysis of the dominant ego states that characterize their interactions with others. Then they explore the genesis of these relative emphases in relationships with parents and in other significant experiences. They then attempt to analyze the transactions they are having with important persons to assess patterns and to ascertain the nature of games that may be present. Through depth reflection the person is led into intuitions about life scripts and basic life positions.

In the experience part of therapy the client is led through recreations of important events and significant interactions. Reexperiencing is encouraged because it is assumed that insight by itself is not healing. Insight provides the basis for change, but change comes through reexperiencing and redecision. Many procedures are utilized to facilitate such experiencing. The transactional analyst is an active therapist and engages in intentional interventions to evoke the involvement of the client emotionally as well as cognitively.

Ultimately the transactional analyst is convinced that change comes by redecision. The therapist assumes the role of the nurturing parent and encourages the client in thinking that life can change. Although premature decision, which is not based in emotional reexperience, is abortive, in the final analysis change will never occur unless individuals determine to courageously try to be different. Transactional analysts believe that people can take control of their lives and that healing can occur provided such decisions are grounded in depth insight.

Evaluation

There are a number of underlying assumptions in transactional analysis that Christian counselors would do well to consider. Examples of such assumptions are that persons are born with a trusting, open, intimacy-seeking attitude (the I'm OK, You're OK life position) but lose it in the process of living and that healing means a rediscovery and reassertion of that basic attitude toward life. Christians would agree with this and would call it being created in the image of God. Yet Christians would not agree that other life positions (I'M OK, You're Not OK; I'm Not OK, You're OK; I'm Not OK, You're Not OK) are only misperceptions. They too are real. The issue for the Christian is not wrong attitudes or incorrect perceptions, but sin. In fact, the Christian assumes that the most correct statement of reality is I'm Not OK, You're Not OK. As the Bible states, "All have sinned and come short of the glory of God" (Rom. 3:23). Transactional analysis does not have a serious enough doctrine of the human condition from the Christian point of view.

Another issue has to do with what happens when persons affirm their OK-ness. It is not simply a change of attitude or the making of a new decision, as transactional analysis would contend, but a recognition that sin is present and only God can make it right. No effort or insight can return persons to the I'm OK, You're OK position. The Christian gospel says that God in Christ has done this for us (cf. Rom. 8). He has forgiven our sin and restored us to a position of OK-ness. Thus, the Christian corrective to transactional analysis is I'm Not OK, You're Not OK, but That's OK. This is redemption as well as healing.

Transactional analysis makes very sound assumptions that can be used by Christian counselors if they keep in mind that it is based on humanistic presuppositions which need supplementing by the affirmations of the Christian faith.

References

Berne, E. *Transactional analysis in psychotherapy.* New York: Grove Press, 1961.

Steiner, C. *Scripts people live.* New York: Grove Press, 1974.

Part 3

Couple, Family, and Group Therapies

46

Behavioral Marital Therapy
Stanton L. Jones

$\mathbf{M}$arital therapy is a relatively recent development within the field of behavior therapy, with behavioral marital therapy increasing dramatically in its influence and sophistication during the late 1970s. In the late 1960s behavioral marital therapy typically involved teaching spouses to reward (through attention or tokens) those behaviors they desired from their partners. While the basic theoretical conceptualizations behind behavioral marital therapy are consistent with those of early researchers, the theories have been better elaborated and the therapeutic techniques rendered much less artificial and mechanical.

Generally, behavioral marital therapy contends that each person's behavior can best be seen as a function of that person's social environment and past learning history. Since one's spouse is a powerful part of one's social environment, it follows that marriage "is best thought of as a process of circular and reciprocal sequences of behavior and consequences, where each person's behavior is at once being affected by and influencing the other" (Jacobson & Margolin, 1979, p. 13). This conceptualization has received some empirical support. Because of their belief that each spouse's behavior in the marriage will be in part a function of the behavior of the other spouse, researchers predicted and demonstrated that marriages are characterized by reciprocity—that is, the tendency for spouses to exchange positive (rewarding) and negative (punishing) behaviors at about the same rate. Spouses tend to treat each other in similar manner over time, though this should not be taken to imply an immediate reciprocity in a reflexive sense.

Behavioral marital therapists view marriage as being rule governed, with the relationship rules (implicit and explicit expectations regarding roles, duties, acceptable behavior, etc.) serving to structure and define the exchange of positive and negative behaviors. Change is inevitable in marriage relationships. Unfortunately, many persons are more likely to influence their spouses to change through aversive means than positive means. Aversive control techniques (nagging, yelling, threatening) are more successful in producing immediate behavior change (compliance) than positive means (compromise, praise, reason). However, the aversive means create complicating problems by their very use. Behavioral marital therapy is directed at developing positive change patterns in a dissatisfied couple.

Marital distress is viewed as occurring for a variety of reasons. Spouses may lack positive behavior change skills such as basic communication and problem-solving skills. The "reinforcement value" of each spouse for the other can decay over time, so that one spouse seems to have little or nothing to offer the other. This may occur due to a gradual buildup of grievances or a failure of each person to grow and develop, thus bringing fresh life to the relationship. There may also be undiscussed rules or unresolved expectancy conflicts in the marriage. Finally, situational changes (e.g., a new job, new social or romantic relationships) may undermine motivation to put necessary time and work into the relationship.

Behavioral marital therapy is almost always conducted with both partners present. It tends to be brief, more directive than many forms of marital therapy, and maintains a strong focus on specific changes that must occur in the relationship. Critics suggest that it is mainly a group of techniques without a good theory of the overall conduct of the therapeutic process. While this criticism seems overdone, it is undoubtedly the case that the techniques are the main focus of behavioral writers. The other less specific aspects of the therapy process are more difficult to conceptualize behaviorally.

There are three major forms of behavioral marital therapy interventions, each of which has numerous variations. The first class of interventions, probably the most widely used, focuses on increasing the clients' positive change skills. This most often takes the form of communication skills training. One variant is training in problem-solving or negotiation skills. Spouses might also be taught active listening skills to facilitate understanding, or possibly new skills for clearly expressing affection and emotions. In the process of learning these skills spouses come to see more clearly the impact they have on each other, thus setting the stage for the start of positive change in the relationship.

The second general class of interventions are those which serve to structure and increase the couple's positive interactions, thus serving to increase relationship satisfaction. These techniques might be useful where spouses have gradually habituated to each other or where situational factors (lack of time, money, etc.) have prevented them from sharing pleasant interactions. The most common form of this intervention is for the therapist to negotiate with clients to observe special days or periods of time when they strive to dramatically increase their positive interactions, either on a unilateral or bilateral basis. Writers term these times "love days" or "caring days." There are numerous other techniques for increasing positive interactions.

The final major class of interventions are the contracting methods which aim to make explicit the expectations and rules affecting the marital relationship. Behavioral therapists once emphasized the use of quid pro quo contracts, which specifically link the behavior of the spouses in an "if I do this for you, then you do that for me" fashion. Because of the numerous difficulties with this approach, therapists are now much more likely to use good faith contracts, which mainly serve the purpose of clarification of expectations.

At this time there are numerous studies documenting the beneficial effects of behavioral marital therapy in increasing marital satisfaction. The approach has not been shown, however, to be significantly more effective than other therapies. Behavioral marital therapy research has been criticized as having been conducted with atypical couples (e.g., those responding to newspaper advertisements) and for lacking long-term follow-ups of treated couples to verify the stability of the treatment gains.

Behavioral marital therapy's strengths include its directness, specificity, action orientation, and apparently shorter time span of treatment. The directness of scriptural injunctions for changes in marital relationships may suggest the frequent suitability of such direct approaches with many couples. The focus on relationship patterns rather than personal problems frequently helps clients be nondefensive and receptive to change. One prominent Christian author and marriage counselor (Wright, 1981) feels that the cognitive-behavioral framework is largely compatible with revealed truth.

Behavioral marital therapy suffers from all the limitations inherent in the field of behavior therapy. The approach has an inadequate philosophical groundwork of materialism and strict determinism. This gives it a somewhat mechanistic flavor. Its basic principles (reinforcement, punishment) are defined tautologically, and there are very real problems with reducing all interactions into either reinforcers or punishers. Also, the limited number of documented interventions could lead the naïve therapist to push clients through a standardized treatment package rather than individualizing the approach. It should also be noted that most of the approaches classified as behavioral marital therapy were in existence under other names before being labeled as behavioral techniques. Finally, a major problem with behavioral marital therapy is its lack of a model of healthy marriage. Overall, the approach promises to enrich the field of marital therapy. However, as it currently stands it is very likely inadequate as an overall model of marital therapy.

References

Jacobson, N. S., & Margolin, G. *Marital therapy.* New York: Brunner/Mazel, 1979.

Wright, H. N. *Marital counseling.* Denver: Christian Marriage Enrichment, 1981.

47

Conjoint Family Therapy
Dennis L. Gibson

Developed by Satir (1967), conjoint family therapy is a model of therapy in which a therapist sees family members together when just one of them, usually a troublesome child, is identified as the one needing help. Satir took her training in social work, which has a larger-than-the-individual emphasis. In 1959 she brought that perspective to the Mental Research Institute in Palo Alto, where she collaborated with Jackson, Bateson, Watzlawick, and others associated with the communications theory of psychopathology and family systems functioning. Sullivan's earlier work on interpersonal theories of personality significantly influenced this group's leading force, D. Jackson.

Satir identified with the optimistic, experiential humanism referred to as the "third force" in midtwentieth-century American psychology. She was one of three remarkable therapists (with Perls and Erickson) studied by the founders of neurolinguistic programming, Bandler and Grinder. These two astute observers reduced Satir's effective actions to descriptive terms. *Changing with Families* (Bandler, Grinder, & Satir, 1976) semantically analyzed key verbal sequences that Satir used to clarify communications between members of a dysfunctional family system.

In her view of human nature Satir emphasizes that all behavior, no matter how distorted, aims at preserving and enhancing self-esteem. Virtually synonymous with self-esteem is a person's sense of being esteemed, validated, welcomed, and responded to congruently by others. Therefore, behavior that society regards as "sick, crazy, stupid, or bad" is really a message signalling distress and requesting help. Everyone can learn to communicate feelings more effectively and thus escape his or her psychic prisons.

Satir calls her model of therapy a growth model, in contrast to the medical model and the sin model. She caricatures the latter as a critical, moralistic model; it lacks the element of good news that the Bible announces for persons whose values, beliefs, and attitudes make them incongruent with the blueprint by which a loving God created them.

Satir is evidently antichurch, since she sees Christianity causing more guilt than is good for people. She regards pathology as dysfunctional communication by individuals within families and cultures. In this she comes close to the profound insight expressed by an Old Testament prophet: "I am a man of unclean lips and live among a people of unclean lips" (Isa. 6:5).

Illness in a person derives from inadequate methods of communicating in that person's intimate relationships. It follows that the goal of therapy is to improve those methods. That means putting into clear, direct words messages that have been delivered in the past by unclear and indirect nonverbal gestures and nuances. Most of these transactions have been outside the awareness of the participants, so they could never talk about them. Therapists make the covert overt.

One of the primary topics that people can learn to talk about is differentness. Therapists work to immunize family members against the jarring effects of discovering that loved ones think, feel, perceive, and desire in ways different from themselves. A therapist "raises their capacity to give and minimizes their sensitivities to painful subjects, thereby decreasing the necessity for defenses" (Satir, 1967, p. 165).

The conjoint therapist concentrates especially on reducing the threat of blame, so as to build "a safe, understanding framework within which child and mates will be able to comment on what they see and hear" (Satir, 1967, p. 132). Achieving this safety is a primary step toward uncovering the root of all family problems—discord in the husband-wife relationship.

In her role as therapist Satir actively manages the sessions. She structures the first two to four sessions by taking a family chronology. She questions relentlessly and specifically, often repeating her questions as if a little slow to catch on. This repetition simplifies and clarifies what had previously been to the family confusing, overwhelming aspects of their lives.

Absolutely opposed to any hint of faultfinding, Satir speaks of the identified patient's "pain" and says that the whole family hurts. She thus shifts the investigative aspect of therapy from that of a policeman seeking to arrest a villain to that of a curious child seeking to solve a puzzle. She spreads ownership of the problem to the family. She further fosters a "we" orientation in positive ways by citing the strengths of the family, especially the storms they have already weathered in their history. She highlights the relationship-seeking intention behind even the most hurtful actions. At the end of the first interview she assigns each family member to make it known when pleased by what another member does.

Conjoint family therapy is primarily a means for fostering more enjoyable and productive relationships among persons living or working together in systems. Management relations, marriage enrichment, and premarital counseling increasingly use concepts that Satir and her colleagues advocate.

References

Bandler, R., Grinder, J., & Satir, V. *Changing with families*. Palo Alto, Calif.: Science and Behavior Books, 1976.

Satir, V. *Conjoint family therapy* (Rev. ed.). Palo Alto, Calif.: Science and Behavior Books, 1967.

48

Contextual Family Therapy
Hendrika Vande Kemp

This approach understands human existence in the context of human relationship, emphasizing the covenantal relationship based on having received and having to reciprocate. It is strongly rooted in the Judeo-Christian tradition, and its proponents have sought to integrate family theory and the biblical theologies of both Old and New Testaments. Other roots lie in object relations theory, which emphasizes the internal images of significant others developed during the earliest years of life.

The first major systematic presentation of the contextual perspective was by Boszormenyi-Nagy and Spark (1973). These authors stress the loyalty commitments in families, invisible fibers holding together the relationship network. Each family member keeps track of his or her perception of the balances of give-and-take in past, present, and future. Affirming the work of Erikson, these authors assert that an environment worthy of trust, the ideal childhood environment, inevitably engenders indebtedness. If the child cannot repay the benefits received, an emotional debt will accumulate. Ultimately several generations of personal relationships may be necessary to build a family environment characterized by an adequate balance of trust and mistrust. When loyalty debts are heavy, the adult child may be unable to transfer loyalty from the parents and the family of origin to a new relationship. Thus, marital commitment will continually be in tension with loyalty to the family of origin. In the future the marital commitment is likely to be in conflict with loyalty to the offspring as the unbalanced relationship ledger seeks to balance itself in the new generation. Vertical loyalty commitments tend always to conflict with horizontal ones, so that the loyalty owed to previous or subsequent generations (to parents, grandparents, and children) will conflict with loyalty owed to husband or wife, brothers and sisters, friends and peers.

The contextual family therapist takes into account four dimensions while assessing the family's dynamics:

1. facts, which are those aspects provided by destiny and include such things as ethnic identity, adoption, survivorship, illness, sex, and religious identity.
2. psychology, which refers to those things occurring within the person, thus affirming the psychodynamic dimensions of drives, psychic development, object relations, and inner experience.
3. transactions or power alignments, those aspects examined especially by the structural and systems family theorists.
4. relational ethics, concerned with the "balance of equitable fairness between people, . . . the long-term preservation of an oscillating balance among family members, whereby the basic interests of each are taken into account by the others" (Boszormenyi-Nagy & Ulrich, 1981, p. 160).

It is this emphasis on relational ethics that is most distinctive to the contextual approach. Entitlement and indebtedness are among the existential givens of life, and relationships are trustworthy only to the extent that they allow these ethical issues to be faced.

The most basic of the existential givens is the fact of one's birth. We do not ask to be born, yet we are born into a family which inherits the invisible loyalties of countless preceding generations. Another given which the therapist must take very seriously is the wish of every family member to establish trustworthy relationships. The assumption of adversary relationships within families violates the basic urge toward relational justice. The family is strengthened by moves toward trustworthiness and weakened by moves away from it. Thus, high levels of individual merit, accumulated by supporting the interests of others, contribute to the health of the whole family.

The concept of legacy relates to the family's bookkeeping system and has two ethical components. The first is based on the debts and entitlements contributed by legacy, to which the child must adapt his or her life. One's actual entitlement is composed both of one's natural due as parent and child, and of what one has come to merit. That the legacies ascribed to different children in one family may be unequal is another existential given. Legacy expectations are perceived by family members as ethical imperatives. Thus, they are perceived as things one *ought* to do rather than things one would *like* to do. The currency in which one's relational debts are paid is also dictated by the family, so that options available to a member of one family may not be available to a member of another. Enlarging the range of options may be one of the tasks of the contextual family therapist.

A situation of grave concern to the contextual family therapist is that of split loyalty, in which the child can offer loyalty to one parent only at the expense of the other. It is imperative for the mental health of the child that in a situation of divorce and remarriage the child not be asked to renounce loyalty to the noncustodial parent. Also damaging to the child are parents who are unwilling to accept payments on the debt owed by the child. When nothing is acceptable as repayment, the child enters into new relationships with no emotional energy available for the relationship. That which is given to the mate or friend will be regarded as stolen from the parental account. The tragic component of legacy is that "patterns shall be repeated, against unavailing struggle, from one generation to the next" (Boszormenyi-Nagy & Ulrich, 1981, p. 166). Accounts can only be settled in those relationships where they were engendered, and thus it is critical that one's "unfinished business" with parents and brothers and sisters be completed before one enters into a marital relationship, where the same dynamic repeats itself.

In this context family pathology is regarded as the result of exploitation in the realm of relational ethics. Examples of exploitation are the secret marriage contracts in which each partner serves to act out the negative aspects of the other; the scapegoating of a child, in which the child bears the family's pain; the parentification of a child, in which the child tries to give to its parents the nurturance they never received from their parents; and relational corruption, in which one person believes that he or she is entitled to be unfair to anyone, because he or she has never been on the receiving end of a truly nurturing relationship.

In contextual family therapy the goal is always to move the marital partners and family members in the direction of ethical relationships. By involving members of the extended family the chains of invisible loyalty and legacy can be loosened, allowing individuals to give up symptomatic behavior and open up new options. However, individual goals are always considered in the context of all family members, since "no family member can alone judge whether the ledger is in balance" (Boszormenyi-Nagy & Ulrich, 1981, p. 164).

Integrative efforts focusing on this approach have come primarily from Krasner and her co-workers (Krasner & Shapiro, 1979). Krasner's work, drawing on the rabbinic tradition, has focused on such issues as trust building in religious communities, the idea of a "no-fault" world, forgiveness, and other implications of relational justice. Boszormenyi-Nagy and his colleagues also address the loyalty conflicts inherent in the traditional psychotherapeutic situation, where the therapist challenges the client's loyalty to the parents. Contextual family therapy adds a psychodynamic perspective to God's words that "the iniquity of the fathers shall be visited on the children," and reminds us that the ethical dimension of relationships cannot be escaped.

References

Boszormenyi-Nagy, I., & Spark, G. M. *Invisible loyalties*. New York: Harper & Row, 1973.

Boszormenyi-Nagy, I., & Ulrich, D. N. Contextual family therapy. In A. S Gurman & D. P. Kniskern (Eds.), *Handbook of family therapy*. New York: Brunner/Mazel, 1981.

Krasner, B. R., & Shapiro, A. Trustbuilding initiatives in the rabbinic community. *Conservative Judaism*, 1979, *33*(1), 3–21.

49

Family Systems Therapy
Robert R. Farra

Family systems therapy is an approach to the treatment of families most often associated with the work of Murray Bowen. Bowen began his work in the early 1950s in association with the National Institute of Mental Health. Working first with severely disturbed children, he was struck by the ways in which patients were assigned psychiatric diagnoses that were not at all helpful in the treatment of these patients. Additionally, Bowen was not satisfied with the psychiatric definition of schizophrenia, which held that the emotional disturbance of this disorder was contained within the individual.

As Bowen treated schizophrenic children, he became aware of an emotionally close relationship between the patient and the patient's mother. He observed that this relationship had taken on a symbiotic quality that seemed to rob the patient of a solid identity. As his theory developed, Bowen saw that this relationship between the patient and mother provided the inadequate mother with a great deal of power over the patient. Further, there appeared to be an emotional struggle between mother and child. Whenever the child attempted to break away from the symbiotic relationship, the mother would become extremely anxious and the child would, in turn, give up attempts to become autonomous.

As Bowen further developed his family theory, he began to look at the father's relationship to the mother and child. He observed that the father seemed removed, cut off from the highly emotional relationship between mother and child. Bowen discovered that parents of schizophrenic children were unable to achieve authentic emotional closeness in the marital relationship. Instead, this relationship was marked by undifferentiation (inability of couples to be emotionally separate) or pronounced marital fusion which, according to Bowen, manifests itself in one of three ways: intense marital conflict, sickness or dysfunction in one spouse, and the projection (triangulation) of unresolved marital problems onto one of the children. Bowen discovered that if therapeutic attention was focused on the parents of schizophrenic children and if the couple began to address their unresolved conflicts, through a process of differentiation of self, the patient's psychotic symptomatology disappeared.

Later Bowen found that children achieve varying levels of differentiation of self from the family ego mass in their families of origin. Differentiation is similar to Erikson's (1963) concept of identity. Individuals marry others of equal level of differentiation of self. If individuals possess low levels of differentiation of self, emotional fusion is likely to manifest itself in the marital relationship.

Key Concepts

Differentiation of Self Scale

This scale is an effort to classify all levels of human functioning, from the lowest possible levels to the highest potential level, on a single dimension. The lowest score, which is 0 on the scale, indicates total undifferentiation and 100, the highest score, indicates the greatest degree of differentiation.

Differentiation of self

This is the degree to which an individual will negotiate and compromise his basic beliefs and convictions in order to gain approval or increase position in relationships, particularly in the marital relationship. Individuals who possess low differentiation of self regard feelings and subjectivity as dominant over the objective reasoning process (Bowen, 1972). Individuals who possess high differentiation of self "have an increasing capacity to differentiate between feelings and objective reality" (Bowen, 1978).

Fusion

This concept refers to the emotional "stuck togetherness" of a family. According to Bowen, the level of differentiation of self determines the degree of emotional fusion. There are three areas in which fusion is expressed in the nuclear family: in marital conflict, in dysfunction in one spouse, and in projection to one or more children.

Triangle

Triangle refers to the most basic unit of any emotional system. A two-person emotional system is unstable in that it forms itself into a three-person system or triangle under stress. As tension increases in the dyad, it is common for one person to "triangle in" another to relieve some of the tension. This shifts the focus of tension away from the first two and onto the third, and this prevents the resolution of conflict in the dyad.

Family projection process

This occurs when parents fail to deal effectively with their marital conflict and triangle in one of their children. This shifts the focus from the marriage and projects it upon the child. The child exhibits the marital conflict by developing psychological problems.

Multigenerational transmission process

This concept describes the pattern that develops over multiple generations as children emerge from the parental family with higher, equal, or lower basic levels of differentiation than the parents. According to the theory the most severe emotional problems, particularly schizophrenia, result from the lowering levels of differentiation of self over multiple generations.

Emotional cutoff

This concept refers to the process by which individuals handle their unresolved emotional attachments to their parents.

Therapy

According to Bowen, the overall goal of therapy is to help individual family members rise up out of the emotional togetherness (fusion) that binds them and to help the motivated family member to take even a small step toward a better level of differentiation.

Bowen identified nine therapeutic techniques that promote differentiation. First, the therapist serves as a coach rather than as a traditional therapist interpreting behavior. He constantly questions one spouse, then the other. The purpose of such questioning is to temporarily inhibit emotional responsiveness, thus allowing each spouse to hear the other. Second, the therapist serves as a model by using "I" statements. This provides an example for an individual, couple, or family. Third, the therapist avoids becoming triangled by refusing to take sides. Fourth, the therapist encourages each family member to work toward a greater level of differentiation from his or her own family of origin. Fifth, the therapist uses a coaching model rather than a model based upon transference.

Sixth, the therapist avoids emotionality. Bowen suggests that the more the therapeutic relationship is endowed with high emotionality, the less likely it is to be long-term. The lower the emotionality and the more the relationship deals in reality, the more likely the change will come slowly and be solid and long-lasting.

Seventh, the therapist works with the strongest person in the family or couple. Eighth, the therapist avoids the emotionality of a crisis and refuses to be pulled into the conflict of a crisis. Finally, the therapist uses reversals and humor to detoxify an emotional situation, to allow the family to look at their own dysfunctional behavior, and to permit a family member to get "unstuck" from what seemed to be an unchangeable position.

References

Bowen, M., Toward the differentiation of a self in one's own family. In S. L. Framo (Ed.), *Family interaction: A dialogue between family researchers and family therapists.* New York: Springer Publishing, 1972.

Bowen, M. *Family therapy in clinical practice.* New York: Aronson, 1978.

Erikson, E. H. *Childhood and society* (2nd ed.). New York: Norton, 1963.

50

Family Therapy: Overview
Robert J. Salinger

D uring the past fifteen years the treatment of whole families in emotional crisis or conflict has become an established clinical procedure. This chapter will review basic aspects of family dynamics and consider some biblical concepts that relate to family structure and function.

Basic Concepts of Family Therapy

Family therapy differs from individual therapy in several important respects. Instead of an individual with a problem, the therapist focuses on the individual within his family and defines the problem as a relational one. The therapist relates to the whole family rather than to one member of the family and observes the interaction of the family members rather than relying on the report of one member. Therapy is directed toward changing the structure of the family. This in turn leads to changes in the behavior and the inner experience of all the members of the family. These changes include changes in the ways the members relate.

Family therapy is such a new field that theories and techniques of treatment have been tremendously diverse, with a large number of schools of treatment. These have been grouped into four basic approaches by Gurman and Kniskern (1981): psychoanalytic and object relations, intergenerational, systems theory, and behavioral. There are several theories and techniques within each of these approaches.

The family itself is not a static entity. It is a constantly evolving system with its own set of developmental phases. The family can be seen as adjusting to the presence of young children, as coping with the emergence of adolescent members, or as working through the empty nest syndrome. Each of these developmental tasks requires changes in the pattern of the members' interactions with one another and threatens the personal security of each member.

The interactional style of the family will determine the way these developmental problems are resolved, depending upon the freedom of the family members to communicate stress to one another and resolve conflict. High stress and poor conflict resolution ability may result in the precipitation of psychiatric or medical symptoms in one of the members. Stress may come from contact of one or more members with extrafamilial stressors, a natural transitional phase in development, or an idiosyncratic problem in a member.

A family is defined as a psychobiological group of people with a boundary that separates them from the other people in their environment. Families are divisible into structural (e.g., marital or sibling) and functional (e.g., parental) subsystems—that is, groupings of family members designed to meet certain needs or carry out their functions. It is possible for a man to be an effective husband in his functioning in the spouse subsystem and an ineffective father in his function in the parental subsystem.

The ability of a member of a subsystem to develop the skills necessary for effective functioning in the family depends on that member's freedom and the freedom of the whole subsystem from interference by other subsystems. When the boundaries around various subsystems are not clearly defined, confusion within the family will result. Members of the various subsystems will not know what is expected of them, and they will not be able to achieve competency in the various tasks required of them.

All families have power and authority hierarchies. Parents and children have different levels of authority in the family. In a normal generational delegation of authority, parents in general have authority over their children, and there is a complementary function between the husband and wife in an interdependent relationship. In pathological families power patterns almost invariably differ from this. Identified patients generally tend to wield a great deal of covert power in their families.

Family members develop a predictable set of responses to interactions between other family members. The basic pattern involves at least three members of a family and is called triangulation. In the presence of anxiety any two-person system will tend to involve the closest vulnerable other person to form a triangle. In addition, when the tension in a triangle is too great for a threesome, it will involve others, forming a series of interlocking triangles. Eventually the interactions stabilize and anxiety is passed through the family along predictable channels. This process of triangulation is the process of symptom formation. Usually the person least able to pass on the emotional tension in the most stable triangle develops a symptom or expresses overt conflict with the other involved members of the triangle.

General systems theory posits the development of an equilibrium with a certain range of tolerated variability in any system. When behavior or interactions occur which deviate beyond the threshold of tolerance of the system, the distress level of the system rises. Corrective mechanisms will also be invoked to restore equilibrium. Given the levels of stress in our society and the tasks that face the family developmentally, it is inevitable that the family's interactional pattern will be frequently confronted with the necessity for change. This change may occur in an adaptive or maladaptive way depending on the freedom of the system to be flexible. General systems theory also posits an inherent resistance to change in the system because it is set up to maintain itself in equilibrium.

The family exists to provide support for its members. It is intended to function as a shelter from impinging forces outside it, all of which make various demands on family members. It is the site of the growth and development of its members, both children and adults. In order for growth to occur, family members must experience two things. They must develop a sense of belonging, initially to one other person and later to other family members, and they must be able to individuate and establish a sense of separateness within the context of belonging. Throughout life the individual must develop competent responses to the variety of situations encountered in life. These situations present constant challenges to self-esteem and personal security. A sense of belonging is necessary in order to risk adaptive behavior. The freedom to be separate is critical in order to succeed adaptively outside the family of origin.

Biblical Concepts of Family Functioning

The model of family functioning and development discussed above is consistent with biblical concepts of family functioning. The Bible provides clear guidelines for family structure and function, and a model for relationships that mitigates against triangulation. Biblical values foster personal responsibility, growth, and individuation in the context of belonging to a family group.

Structure and roles

Paul delineated the basic concepts of family structure in his letters to the churches at Colossae and Ephesus. Each marital partner makes a covenantal commitment to the other. There is an ordered mutuality in the marital relationship, one which is intended to transcend convenience and personal satisfaction. The man is the spiritual, emotional, and administrative head of the family. Husbands are encouraged to relate to their wives as equals, participants with them in the grace of God (1 Peter 3:7). The analogy of the marital unit to the union of Jesus and the church reflects both the intensity of investment required in the marital relationship and the high regard given to the marital relationship by God (Eph. 5:25–30).

Having established the marital pair, Paul goes on to delineate parental authority over children. In addition, the subsystems are given different tasks. Children must learn obedience, a lifelong socialization process. The family is the source of learning about the necessity for negotiation and compromise between the needs and desires of the individual and the needs and desires of those around him. The parental subsystem has the task of providing a sense of belonging and personal value and setting necessary limits in such a way that children do not become overly frustrated or resentful and alienated from the family.

Both parents are to provide discipline, instruction, and affection, not leaving child rearing to mothers alone. Discipline here refers to a consistent pattern of training for the imparting of certain skills, not merely punishment. Parents are able to teach their children social skills, housekeeping skills, skills in having fun, and to provide practical spiritual instruction, teaching them about God and his ways.

Triangulation and conflict resolution

Application of basic scriptural values to family relationships will release forces in the family that promote growth, individuation, cohesiveness, and stability. These forces mitigate against triangulation and scapegoating. Every member of the family stands equal before God (Acts 10:34). There should be a growing awareness of God's concern for and valuing of each member of the family. It is difficult to continue to blame someone and to consistently attribute negative qualities to them when one realizes that the person is highly valued by God and is his creation. Furthermore, everyone in the family falls short of God and has his or her own problems to be solved (Matt. 7:1–5; Gal. 6:1–5). Families are a place where people should not need to hide for fear of being rejected, judged, or criticized.

Jesus gave instructions for conflict resolution in the church (Matt. 18:15–16). He prescribed honest confrontation between the two parties involved in the conflict, with a bona fide attempt to resolve the conflict before involving another party. When an outside person is involved, the involvement should be forthright and open, with a chance for each party to speak and be heard. The purpose is to move to an open expression and resolution of the conflict. Triangulation occurs when an outside person is brought into the relationship to detour the conflict and avoid a confrontation. For example, a mother will tell her daughter about her husband's criticisms of her. She may then feel better, but her daughter's relationship with her father has been undermined. The daughter may act out her mother's anger and be labeled a "brat" by her parents.

The scriptural solution to this situation requires the wife to honestly confront her husband about his criticisms, despite the anxiety that might be provoked by such a confrontation. Should the two of them be unable to reach a resolution, they could agree to go together to seek an outside opinion. This maintains the mutuality of the relationship, keeps the tension in the dyad, and enables the outside party to be used for conflict resolution rather than tension reduction. Tension reduction will follow clear discussion of differences and resolution of conflicts.

Biblical injunctions to forgive do not mean that one must overlook intolerable situations, deny conflict, or minimize interpersonal stress. In fact, the call to forgiveness often uncovers long-suppressed conflict requiring a confrontation with self and others. Often this is more difficult than continuing the resentment. The willingness to forgive is a statement of concern for the other, a realization that the relationship is more important than who is right or wrong.

Boundaries

Adam's attempt to blame Eve for his own disobedience is the first example of many recorded attempts to avoid accountability. Accountability to God means one must be willing to be an individual in one's own family despite strong emotional forces in other directions at times. There is a call to personal integrity in the midst of the intense emotional pressures of family life. Jesus showed his willingness to withstand these pressures at the same time that he honored his family (John 19:25–27).

Jesus was careful to point out that an undue tie with one's family (i.e., the lack of individuation) is a serious obstacle to serving God. God must be seen as even more important than one's parents and children. One must be willing to accept the possibility of conflict in order to be faithful to the call of God (Matt. 10:34–39). The conflict will be a tension of priorities.

In addition, Christians are called to extend their involvement beyond family boundaries. The church is a sharing community, with its members involved in an unusually intensive way with one another beyond the limits of family boundaries. This biblical pattern of stressing the importance of family along with extrafamilial involvement is also reflected in Christ's own extension of his personal family boundaries to all who love and obey God (Matt. 12:50).

Summary

Biblical concepts of family functioning are consistent with current family theory and clinical practice. There are clear guidelines for family structure, including a firm marital coalition and generational boundaries. These provide guidelines for a Christian therapist and for a family seeking God's order, which transcends cultural and individual idiosyncrasies. Furthermore, scriptural guidelines for the resolution of interpersonal conflict, coupled with respect and valuing of all family members, provide strong forces against triangulation and scapegoating processes. Scriptural values of openness, caring, and sharing in the midst of order and structure are those traits which the research of Lewis, Beavers, Gossetl, and Phillips (1976) found to be associated with optimal families. Healthy Christianity should be a force toward increased family cohesiveness as well as individual growth of family members, thus adding a potent force for change to the family system.

A family therapist dealing with a religious family must consider the influence of religious values on both family structure and family functioning. These values may be serving the family in either healthy or dysfunctional ways. A Christian family with problems may be involved more fully in a therapeutic endeavor by engaging the healthy aspects of its religious system. Distorted values that are hindering the growth of the family can be addressed as trust in the therapist develops.

References

Gurman, A. S., & Kniskern, D. P. (Eds.). *Handbook of family therapy.* New York: Brunner/Mazel, 1981.

Lewis, J. M., Beavers, W. R., Gossetl, J. T., & Phillips, V. A. *No single thread: Psychological health and family systems.* New York: Brunner/Mazel, 1976.

51

Functional Family Therapy
Christine V. Bruun

This therapy (Alexander & Parsons, 1982) has been used chiefly in the treatment of families with a delinquent member. Developed from theory, research, and clinical experience, the model focuses on the specific relationships ("functional outcomes") that family members are seeking from each other. Adaptive behaviors are substituted for "inefficient," problematic ones to achieve the same relational goals. For instance, adolescents seeking independence (relational distance) are trained to negotiate with their parents for this outcome rather than to engage in delinquent behavior to gain it.

This model combines systems theory with a behavioristic approach. From a systems perspective behavior is meaningful in the ways it is linked to the behavior of all the other family members, rather than individual stimulus-response sequences. The behavioral emphasis is seen in the concept that individual actions are rewarded by producing desired relationships with others in the family. Specifically, each person in the family chooses behaviors that are reinforced for him or her by relational distance or intimacy.

Functional family therapy differs from traditional orientations, which regard the individual as responsible for his actions and behavior as good, bad, or healthy. Instead, the model makes the assumption that all behavior is adaptive in terms of its functional relationship properties. This means that behavior is not inherently good or bad, or even healthy or sick. Behavior is simply a vehicle for producing and maintaining specific outcomes from interpersonal relationships. These outcomes are conceptualized as distance, intimacy, or a moderated combination of both. To illustrate, an adolescent's running away is an inefficient, rather than an unhealthy, method to gain the outcome of distance.

Criteria for ideal functioning are not used in functional family therapy. Instead, maladaptive processes in delinquent families are altered to correspond more closely with the adaptive, problem-solving capacities of nondelinquent families. As nondelinquent families have been shown to communicate with more reciprocal supportiveness and less reciprocal defensiveness, have less silence, more equal talk time, and more constructive interruptions for feedback and clarification (Alexander, 1973), these specific processes are targeted for intervention.

A complete assessment is considered essential for successful treatment. In particular, three critical levels of analysis are necessary:

1. relationships among all family members which result in regular, ritualized sequences of behavior.
2. the functional "payoffs" (distance or intimacy) that each member receives in the behavioral sequence.
3. individual strengths, weaknesses, and behavioral styles.

"Functional family therapists must understand how the behavior change of an individual must be embedded within the powerful processes of family relationships, and how these behavior or other changes will consistently meet each family member's outcomes or functions" (Barton & Alexander, 1981, p. 417).

Intervention consists of therapy and education. Therapy prepares the family members for behavioral change by redefining the negative views that they hold toward each other. The therapist accomplishes this "reattribution" by addressing each person (rather than focusing on the identified patient), speaking in nonjudgmental terms, and helping the family understand how their actions are interdependent. Another powerful tool of reattribution is relabeling objectionable behavior, putting it in a more acceptable framework. For example, a truant teenager may be described as "seeking his own way to be independent" and a possessive mother may be recast as an "involved" parent.

Education implements the behavior change strategies. The therapist selects behavioral techniques consistent with the family's interpersonal and individual styles. The new behavior modality must fit (1) the relational outcomes that individuals were previously seeking (i.e., the outcomes stay the same, but the means of achieving them change) and (2) the reattributions of the therapy phase. For instance, an "independence-seeking" adolescent would be better served by the flexibility of negotiating a behavioral contract with his parents than having a contingency management program closely monitored by them.

Research data (Alexander, Barton, Schiavo, & Parsons, 1976) have shown that a key factor in family change is the therapist's interpersonal skills. Therefore, Barton and Alexander emphasize that the functional family therapist must possess relationship and structuring skills. Relationship skills include the ability to link the feelings of family members with their behaviors, the use of nonblaming language, interpersonal warmth and humor, and self-disclosure. Structuring skills, necessary to implementing change, include directiveness (coaching and modeling effective communication), self-confidence, and clarity.

The functional family model has been shown to be particularly effective with families of delinquent adolescents. A comparison of delinquent families in treatment using this model with the delinquent member treated individually or receiving no treatment showed an improvement in family communication processes when the functional model was used (Alexander & Barton, 1980). When compared to psychodynamic and client-centered family therapy, recidivism rates for delinquents treated by functional family therapy were significantly lower (Parsons & Alexander, 1973); and in a follow-up study several years later, sibling delinquency rates in the families of the same treatment groups were also significantly lower for the functional therapy group (Klein, Alexander, & Parsons, 1977).

This model of family therapy diverges from Christian thought in the positions that, first, the individual is not considered responsible for his behavior since behavior is a message about relationships rather than being "good" or "bad" in itself, and, second, "the therapy process in the functional family model is admittedly very manipulative and does not reflect 'reality' or 'truth'" (Barton & Alexander, 1981, p. 423). Both these positions provide a relativistic view of behavior and personal responsibility. However, the intent of this approach seems to be to give persons an acceptable perception of themselves in order to help them attain goals they have chosen as important to them. This intent is congruent with the Christian faith's respect for the integrity of the person.

References

Alexander, J. F. Defensive and supportive communication in normal and deviant families. *Journal of Consulting and Clinical Psychology*, 1973, *40*, 223–231.

Alexander, J. F., & Barton, C. Intervention with delinquents and their families: Clinical, methodological, and conceptual issues. In J. P. Vincent (Ed.), *Advances in family intervention, assessment, and theory*. Greenwich, Conn.: JAI Press, 1980.

Alexander, J. F., Barton, C., Schiavo, R. S., & Parsons, B. V. Systems-behavioral intervention with families of delinquents: Therapist characteristics, family behavior, and outcome. *Journal of Consulting and Clinical Psychology*, 1976, *44*, 656–664.

Alexander, J. F., & Parsons, B. V. *Functional family therapy*. Monterey, Calif.: Brooks/Cole, 1982.

Barton, C., & Alexander, J. F. Functional family therapy. In A. S. Gurman & D. P. Kniskern (Eds.), *Handbook of family therapy*. New York: Brunner/Mazel, 1981.

Klein, N. C., Alexander, J. F., & Parsons, B. V. Impact of family systems intervention on recidivism and sibling delinquency: A model of primary prevention and program evaluation. *Journal of Consulting and Clinical Psychology*, 1977, *45*, 469–474.

Parsons, B. V., & Alexander, J. F. Short-term family intervention: A therapy outcome study. *Journal of Consulting and Clinical Psychology*, 1973, *41*, 195–201.

52

Group Psychotherapy
William G. Bixler

The practice of persons forming into groups for purposes of mutual protection, support, and understanding is as old as mankind itself. However, the scientific investigation and utilization of the healing powers of groups is less than a hundred years old.

The beginning of modern group therapy can be traced back to 1905 when Joseph Pratt, a Boston internist, set up special classes for tuberculosis patients. These "classes" not only involved instruction to the patients about the treatment of their common malady, but it also provided them opportunity for interpersonal support and encouragement. As Pratt increased his work with these patient groups, he came to realize the psychological benefits that resulted from them.

Pratt's work became known to psychiatrists, including Edward Lazell and L. C. Marsh, who in the 1920s and 30s adapted the group method for use with psychotic patients. Although they were methodologically unsophisticated, these men helped awaken the mental health professions to the therapeutic value of working with the psychologically disturbed in group settings.

The first group therapists were psychoanalytic in theory and technique. However, they were soon challenged by nonanalytic clinicians who saw this particular treatment modality fitting well with their own psychotherapy theories and methodologies. Thus the models of group therapy began to proliferate, with many, such as psychodrama and Gestalt group therapy, moving far afield from the psychoanalytic approach to groups.

The proliferation of group therapy models became a veritable explosion in the late 1960s and 70s, with a new form of group therapy seeming to spring up almost daily. Despite the faddishness often associated with such groups, it could not be denied that many persons experienced emotional and psychological healing by participating in therapy groups.

This same period saw the emergence of the encounter group movement, which emphasized the use of groups for enhancing the emotional growth of psychologically healthy people. Groups were no longer considered useful only to mentally ill persons; rather, they could be used to teach principles of group dynamics, increase interpersonal intimacy, help persons get in touch with their emotions, etc. While encounter, or growth, groups have many adherents and are often used in businesses and industry, group therapy remains the primary focus for most mental health professionals who work with the psychologically disturbed.

It is somewhat of a misnomer to speak of group therapy in the singular, given the vast number of models in existence. These models often differ markedly in their methodology and theory, and in their understanding of human nature. Despite these differences, almost every type of group therapy can be defined at its most basic level as treatment of "several emotionally disturbed people who meet with the therapist as a group for the purpose of helping find a more comfortable and effective adaptation" (Halleck, 1978, p. 387).

Major Models of Group Therapy

Psychoanalytic

That the first group therapists were psychoanalytic in orientation may seem paradoxical, given Freud's emphasis on understanding and treating the individual psyche. However, pioneering therapists such as Burrow, Wender, and Schilder recognized that many of Freud's concepts were applicable not only to individuals being treated by classical psychoanalysis but also to persons in therapeutic groups.

Psychoanalytic group therapy uses traditional Freudian concepts and treatment techniques, modifying them for use in a group context. Therapists engaging in this form of treatment see their patients as suffering from psychological problems due to conflicts experienced at various developmental stages. Not only are these conflicts unconscious, but the patient resists their emergence into awareness.

The group therapist asks the members to comment on any and all things said and done in the group, similar to the technique of free association in individual analysis. During this process the therapist attempts to help the various members understand their resistance to unveiling internal conflicts. This is accomplished by the therapist pointing out to the member the defense mechanisms he is using as these are manifested in interactions with other group members and with the therapist.

The relationship between an individual group member and the therapist leads to transference. This transference of feelings from a parental figure to the therapist is not only permitted but encouraged by the therapist, based on the assumption that insight into the historical reasons for transference will free a person from its grip. Often a group member will also manifest transference toward other members. This "multiple transference" provides more opportunities for interpreting the transference to the patient than would be the case in individual analysis. Also, the numerous interactions between members will highlight the defense mechanisms habitually used by each participant.

While not ignoring group dynamics, psychoanalytic group therapy primarily focuses on the unconscious intrapsychic experience of individuals within the group. It moves from the level of interpersonal interaction to that of investigating unconscious motivation. Because of this individual focus Wolf and Schwartz (1962) prefer to call it "psychoanalysis in groups" rather than psychoanalytic group therapy.

Group dynamic

Group dynamic theorists do not deny the validity of psychoanalytic theory when applied to individuals. However, they argue that an individualistic perspective is not adequate to fully understand what occurs in a therapy group. Thus they look to social psychologists, such as Lewin, to help explain precisely what happens when patients meet together for therapy. Lewin held that all elements in a social field, or environment, whether persons, motivations, drives, etc., could not be fully comprehensible apart from their context.

Thus from the standpoint of group dynamic theory the individual words and actions of each group member are no longer conceptualized as being independent of the group process. Rather, all behavior in the group is seen as embedded in the context of the group, with the group viewed and treated as if it were an organism with its own peculiar traits and characteristics.

A representative example of a group dynamic model of therapy is that of Whitaker and Lieberman (1964). They hold that seemingly independent and unrelated behaviors of group members actually refer to an implicit here-and-now concern. There is thus an underlying coherence to members' verbalizations which is unconscious even to the members.

The covert concern or theme of the group is conceptualized by Whitaker and Lieberman as always taking the form of a conflict, termed the focal conflict. This is usually a conflict between a wish motive and a fear motive. For example, one group's focal conflict may be between a shared wish to gain the attention and approval of the therapist and a fear that gaining the attention would result in feelings of rejection by other group members (Yalom, 1975).

The group will experience tension when confronted with the focal conflict. They will then work toward a group solution that will allay the fear while allowing for partial satisfaction of the wish. In the example cited above, the group might share their desire for approval from the therapist with each other, while supporting those in the group who are most fearful of rejection.

The group therapist has the task of dissipating unrealistic fears of members of the group that they will be rejected by him. Another responsibility is to increase the group's sense of psychological safety while helping them to circumvent restrictive solutions to the focal conflicts.

Each individual group member becomes increasingly involved in the group as more of the group's focal conflicts touch on his or her own unresolved emotions. Although the conflicts are frightening, a certain amount of security is provided as consensually arrived-at solutions emerge that promise to keep anxiety and conflict at manageable levels (Shaffer & Galinsky, 1974).

Existential

Existential psychology blends the thinking of philosophers such as Sartre, Heidegger, and Kierkegaard with the therapeutic approaches of men such as Binswanger and Boss. The first sympathetic presentation in the United States of existentialism as a movement relevant to the mental health professions came in 1958 with the publication of *Existence*, edited by May, Angel, and Ellenberger. The aim of existential psychology is to understand a person in his total existential reality, which includes his subjective relationship to himself, to his fellow humans, and to the world (Misiak & Sexton, 1973).

The subjective, phenomenological experiences of each member of an existential therapy group are held in the highest regard and are generally not viewed as needing to be interpreted or analyzed for deeper, hidden meanings. The explicit denial of psychic and biological determinism carries with it an emphasis on the ultimate responsibility of each person for his own meaning in life. Life has no inherent meaning; mankind is free and responsible to make choices; thus meaning must be chosen and created by each person.

Psychopathology is viewed as stemming from inauthentic modes of being. Inauthenticity may come from fear of responsibility and from not acting, even in the face of the ultimate absurdity of one's finiteness and eventual death.

Existential group therapy provides its members with many and frequent opportunities for I-thou encounters, relationships which reflect authenticity and "beingness." The group therapist is to live the therapy rather than do it; that is, he is to be himself without role or façade. Group members are treated as subjects to be experienced rather than as objects to be analyzed. There is no attempt on the part of the therapist to force his own world view on the group, for this would be treating the members as objects to control, change, or manipulate. The group provides support for its members as they struggle to relate to one another more authentically, to create their own sense of meaning in the universe, and to take absolute responsibility for their own actions.

Nondirective

Nondirective, or group-centered, group therapy takes its theory and methodology from the work of Rogers, who asserts that a therapist must manifest nonpossessive genuineness and empathy to provide the proper therapeutic environment for change on the part of the patient or client.

In the same way, a nondirective group provides an atmosphere of acceptance, openness, and empathy for its members so that they can then mobilize their own inner resources to help them change. Since each member enters the group with anxiety due to an inability to relate effectively with others, the proper group atmosphere will lessen the anxiety and accompanying defensiveness.

The group provides opportunity for self-discovery and self-disclosure. More positive and satisfying ways of relating to others are highlighted as each member becomes increasingly free and adept at self-examination, with assurances that the group will not condemn or reject. Persons who are blind to positive aspects of themselves gain clarity of self-perception, and with it an increase in the sense of self-worth.

The therapist models genuineness, empathy, and warmth for the group with no attempt to coerce or persuade members to change their value system. Members are exposed to values other than their own as they interact in the group; however, they are responsible for themselves in choosing and changing their values or beliefs. Thus the therapist, while maintaining a nondirective role, is nevertheless quite active as he responds to group members in a way that will help them to become increasingly aware of their deep feelings. The group usually deals with whatever problems come up in a session; there is no particular agenda or attempt to analyze beyond the level of emotional expression.

Here-and-Now/Process

This model is not associated with any one method of individual psychotherapy, as is the case with psychoanalytic and nondirective group therapy. Despite the handicap of not having a parent therapy, it is one of the most widely used models of group therapy. It is presented by Yalom in his widely read text, *The Theory and Practice of Group Psychotherapy* (1975).

Yalom argues that the therapeutic power of a group resides in two "symbiotic tiers," here-and-now activation and process illumination. In the first tier the group members must focus their attention on their feelings toward one another, the therapist, and the group as a whole. The immediate events in the session thus take precedence over events both in the distant past and in the current outside life of the members. This here-and-now focus enhances the development and emergence of each member's social microcosm; it also facilitates feedback, catharsis, meaningful self-disclosure, and the acquisition of socializing skills. The vitality of the group is greatly intensified, and each member becomes deeply involved in the session.

However, the second step, process illumination, is necessary for any real therapeutic gain. The group must recognize, examine, and understand process—that is, it must understand itself, study its own transactions, transcend pure experience, and apply itself to the integration of that experience.

The group lives in the here and now, and then doubles back on itself in order to examine the here-and-now behaviors that just occurred. The therapist steers the group into the here and now while guiding the self-reflecting process. The group can assist the therapist in focusing on the here and now, but the self-reflection, or process commentary, remains the responsibility of the therapist (Yalom, 1975).

Psychodrama

Psychodrama is one of the oldest models of group therapy extant. Jacob Moreno, credited with coining the term *group therapy*, began to develop this treatment modality in the 1920s. Despite its long history psychodrama has not been as widely accepted and utilized as its creator hoped it would be. However, many of the techniques used in psychodrama, such as the empty chair technique and role reversal, have been adopted by individual and group therapists of diverse theoretical orientations.

Psychodrama emphasizes action or behavior rather than mere verbalization. Instead of talking about life problems, group members are asked to act them out in spontaneous dramatization. The dramatization, or psychodrama proper, takes place on a stage in front of an audience consisting of group members and assistants to the therapist, who is called the director.

In order to emotionally prepare the audience to benefit from the psychodrama, the director engages in preliminary warm-up exercises to decrease the various levels of anxiety and defensiveness found in the members. Once the group is warmed up, a group member is chosen to be the protagonist, the central character in the psychodrama. The director helps the protagonist determine the problem to be dramatized; as much information as possible is obtained in order to get an accurate picture of the problem and of the significant persons in the protagonist's life who are part of the problem. Auxiliary egos are chosen from the other group members or from the director's assistants to play the significant persons in the protagonist's life, to play intrapsychic elements of his psyche, or to play the protagonist himself.

The purposes of the spontaneous dramatization are to help the protagonist achieve an emotional catharsis or total emotional release, to break down emotional blockages due to repression and suppression, to desensitize the protagonist to intense expression of affect, and to help the protagonist become comfortable with new ways of responding behaviorally to old conflictual situations.

The session often ends with a wrap-up time in which the audience is provided opportunity to be supportive to the protagonist while also sharing how they benefited via identification with the various characters in the psychodrama.

Gestalt

Gestalt therapy, created by Fritz Perls, became an exceedingly popular form of group therapy in the late 1960s and early 70s. Like psychodrama it emphasizes action rather than words. Gestalt group therapy may take two forms. In the first, therapeutic work is done between the therapist and one participant within the group setting. The other group members are encouraged to observe and experience what is going on without interaction until the work is over. After the work is complete, they are free to interact and share what they experienced during the one-to-one work. The second method involves all participants interacting within the group.

The methods and techniques of Gestalt group therapy find their source in the philosophy and psychology of its founder. The major focus is on the enhancement of awareness of the group members. Being in touch with one's flow of awareness is considered an essential aspect of a Gestalt therapy group. However, the object of this awareness is not facts or cognitions but sensory data, feelings, and emotions. Talking about the past, asking questions, making psychological interpretations are all considered futile exercises that cannot help persons change their behavior.

Numerous techniques are used to enhance awareness and decrease intellectualizations. For example, group members are asked to turn questions into first-person statements, to talk to persons directly rather than talking about them, and to eschew discussion of their personal histories.

The Gestalt group therapist holds that each person is solely responsible for his own behavior, and that behavior is only in the here and now. Each group member has the potential for greater self-reliance and for therapeutic change if the blockages to self-awareness, such as intellectualizing, can be removed (Greenwald, 1975).

Encounter groups

The term *encounter group* is a generic label for a wide variety of experiential, humanistically oriented groups. T-groups, sensitivity groups, personal growth groups, marathon groups, truth labs, and human relations groups are all considered encounter groups (Yalom, 1975).

The encounter group movement began in the 1950s with the human relations training established by the National Training Laboratory. The basic skill training groups, or T-groups, were created to teach persons about interpersonal behavior, to explore group dynamics, and to discuss group members' problems in their home organization. Gradually the emphasis moved away from group dynamics to group work for the sake of self-fulfillment and self-realization. Encounter groups became, in essence, group therapy for normals.

Goals within encounter groups are often vague and ill-defined, but are usually shaped by a belief that even psychologically healthy people experience a certain degree of isolation and alienation from others and from themselves. Thus, these groups will strive for goals such as increased emotional intensity, heightened sensory awareness, increased self-disclosure, and a reexamination of one's basic life values.

There are a number of important differences between encounter groups and therapy groups. Encounter group members are generally psychologically healthier than group therapy members. They are able to communicate better, learn more quickly, and to apply what they have learned to life situations. Group therapy members, on the other hand, are usually fearful, suffer low self-esteem, are pessimistic about their ability to change, and desire safety rather than growth as a primary goal.

The encounter group leader is perceived as a guide or facilitator for the group. The group usually does not hold the leader in awe, tending to see him as a peer. Group therapy members, however, deal with the distortions in relationships that are symptomatic of psychological disorder. Transference reactions toward the group therapist are unavoidable. For better or worse, the therapist is most often seen as a healer, someone to be looked up to for guidance, insight, and safety.

Lastly, the atmosphere of encounter groups is usually less tense and disquieting than that of therapy groups. Encounter group members look forward to learning more about themselves and others in the group; they eagerly anticipate getting more "in touch with themselves." Group therapy members often fear and loathe the idea of getting to know themselves better; they may be suspicious of other group members and resistant to change.

Research

Yalom (1975) has done a considerable amount of research attempting to identify the therapeutic aspects or elements common to all the group therapies regardless of their theoretical or methodological differences. He has divided these common elements or "curative factors" into eleven primary categories:

1. Instillation of hope—the creation of a sense of optimism and positive expectation.
2. Universality—decreasing each group member's sense of being alone in his misery and psychopathology.
3. Imparting of information about mental health and illness.
4. Altruism—the creation of a group climate of helpfulness, concern, support, and sharing.
5. Corrective recapitulation of the primary family group—helping group members to see that their interactions in the group recapitulate their interactions with primary family members.
6. Development of socializing techniques—increasing group members' ability to relate to one another in positive and mature ways.
7. Imitative behavior—helping group members to change via observation of functional, mature behavior on the part of the therapist and other group members.
8. Interpersonal learning—utilizing transference, corrective emotional experiences, and insight to assist members in changing themselves.
9. Cohesiveness—the sense of togetherness that causes a group to see itself holistically rather than as a collection of individuals.
10. Catharsis—the open expression of affect within the group process.
11. Existential factors—dealing with such issues as personal responsibility, contingency, basic isolation, and mortality.

The curative factors of group therapy are not static or autonomous, but can be influenced by a variety of forces. Different types of groups may emphasize different clusters of curative factors, depending on the methodology of the group and the leadership style of the therapist. Also, various factors may be more salient at one stage of therapy than at another. For example, instillation of hope and universality may be more important in the early stages, whereas catharsis and the corrective recapitulation of the primary family group may be much more therapeutically valuable in the later stages of treatment.

Orlinsky and Howard's (1978) comprehensive review of research comparing the efficacy of group therapy versus individual therapy found that a majority of studies showed no significant difference in outcome between the two modalities. A few studies found group to be more effective than individual treatment, while other research found the combination of both types of treatment to be superior to individual therapy alone. Two studies indicated that persons in individual therapy sometimes had better outcomes than those who had only group therapy. However, group treatments have been shown often to be effective in helping people achieve more healthy, positive evaluations of themselves and others, as evidenced by instruments measuring self-concept assessment, attitude change, and positive personality development (Bednar & Kaul, 1978).

The available research data do not strongly support the notion of differential effects or superiority of any one type of group therapy. This lack of confirmation does not eliminate the possibility that some types of groups are more effective. The problem may lie with the research tools and methodologies, which may not be precise enough to separate out differential effects. Further research may discover that significant differential effects do, in fact, exist.

Biblical/Theological Perspectives

A critique of group therapy per se will not be found in Scripture, since the Bible was not written as a psychotherapy textbook. However, the assumptions and goals of the group therapies need to be critically examined from a biblical perspective.

One of the basic working assumptions of all group therapies is that human relationships are not only important but essential for healthy functioning. This assumption is shared by Scripture; in Genesis it is the impetus for the creation of Eve. Adam's isolation was declared "not good," implying the goodness of the husband-wife relationship and, by extension, all human relationships. The goodness of relationships is confirmed throughout Scripture, from the story of David and Jonathan to Paul's plaintive lament that "no one supported me, but all deserted me" (2 Tim. 4:16).

Further, the doctrine of common grace would support the notion that psychological healing can occur via group therapy as a function of God's general care and concern for all humanity. God, who causes rain to fall on the just and the unjust (Matt. 5:45), may also send penultimate healing via group therapy relationships, without diminishing the ultimate healing that is effected by faith in Christ.

Still it is necessary to critique and reject unbiblical assumptions and goals that are associated with certain therapies. A Christian world view stands in opposition to the existential notion that man creates his own meaning in a meaningless universe. The psychodrama goal of achieving godlike autonomy is likewise antithetical to a biblical understanding of man as dependent on the Creator. Also, the Freudian notion that religious beliefs are nothing more than neurotic projections must be summarily rejected.

Despite these criticisms the emphases of group therapies on honesty, empathy, individual responsibility, mutual support, and personal integrity cannot be gainsaid. While group therapy is not a substitute for Christian fellowship, there are many fearful, anxious, insecure Christians who may benefit greatly from it.

References

Bednar, R. L., & Kaul, T. J. Experiential group research. In S. L. Garfield & A. E. Bergin (Eds.), *Handbook of psychotherapy and behavior change* (2nd ed.). New York: Wiley, 1978.

Greenwald, J. A. The ground rules in Gestalt therapy. In F. D. Stephenson (Ed.), *Gestalt therapy primer*. New York: Aronson, 1975.

Halleck, S. L. *The treatment of emotional disorders*. New York: Aronson, 1978.

Misiak, H., & Sexton, V. S. *Phenomenological, existential, and humanistic psychologies: A historical survey*. New York: Grune & Stratton, 1973.

Orlinsky, D. E., & Howard, K. I. The relation of process to outcome in psychotherapy. In S. Garfield & A. E. Bergin (Eds.), *Handbook of psychotherapy and behavior change* (2nd ed.). New York: Wiley, 1978.

Shaffer, J. B. P., & Galinsky, M. D. *Models of group therapy and sensitivity training*. Englewood Cliffs, N.J.: Prentice-Hall, 1974.

Whitaker, D., & Lieberman, M. *Psychotherapy through the group process*. New York: Atherton, 1964.

Wolf, A., & Schwartz, E. K. *Psychoanalysis in groups*. New York: Grune & Stratton, 1962.

Yalom, I. *The theory and practice of group psychotherapy* (2nd ed.). New York: Basic Books, 1975.

Additional Readings

Kaplan, H. I., & Sadock, B. J. *Comprehensive group psychotherapy*. Baltimore: Williams & Wilkins, 1971.

Naar, R. *A primer of group psychotherapy*. New York: Human Sciences Press, 1982.

53

Marital Contract Therapy
Arlo D. Compaan

Developed by Clifford J. Sager, a psychoanalytically trained psychiatrist, marital contract therapy is a therapeutic approach to marital dysfunction based upon the concept of contracts (Sager, 1976). According to this approach each spouse has an individual, unwritten contract for the marriage. It is the set of expectations and promises, conscious and unconscious, he or she has for the relationship. A third contract, the marital contract, develops as a consequence of the marital interaction. It is the operational, interactional contract created by the marital system and the unconscious and conscious ways the two spouses seek to fulfill their individual contracts.

Sager groups the various individual contracts into seven different types: equal, romantic, parental, childlike, rational, companionate, and parallel. The combinations of the individual contracts become the forty-eight different marital contracts, or marital types, described by him. Marital discord results from contractual disappointments when the expectations of one spouse are not being met by the other. Most often these expectations have not been clearly expressed and may be largely unconscious.

Therapy primarily seeks to clarify the terms of the two individual contracts and those of their interactional contract. This begins with helping each spouse explain the expectations they have but have not clearly verbalized. It also involves helping each to become more aware of the unconscious expectations they have for the marriage. This process of making conscious what is unconscious requires considerable clinical skill. Finally, once clarification of the contract has been obtained, agreement on its terms must be reached in order for marital satisfaction to continue.

The identification of individual contracts, the diagnostic phase of therapy, is made by collecting information from three categories. First is the expectations each spouse has for the marriage (e.g., my mate will be loyal and devoted, or marriage will be a respectable cover for the expression of my aggressive drive). Second is the intrapsychic and biological drives of each spouse. Sager identifies thirteen basic parameters useful in evaluating each spouse (e.g., independence-dependence, closeness-distance, and dominance-submission). The reciprocal nature of contracts is particularly operative in this area: "I want so-and-so and in exchange I am willing to give such-and-such." The third source of information is the external manifestations of marital problems, the problems often presented as the reasons for seeking therapy (e.g., poor communication, sexual dysfunction). These symptoms, according to Sager, are secondary manifestations of problem areas originating in the other two areas.

In examining each of the above three sources of information, three levels of awareness must be considered. The first is the conscious and verbalized level. These are the expectations and needs that both spouses have talked about in their marriage. The second level is conscious but not verbalized. This includes expectations and needs that the spouses know they have, but for a variety of reasons have been unwilling to tell each other. The third level is the needs and expectations that are present and that influence behavior but are beyond the awareness of both spouses.

The interactional contract is the behaviors followed by each spouse in trying to fulfill his or her individual contract. According to Sager, "much of therapy consists of making the interactional contract and the partners' behavior in it more conscious, and of using the consciousness to work toward a new single contract that provides the basis for healthier interactions" (p. 29).

Contract therapy incorporates many methods proposed and utilized by other therapists. What is distinctive is the focus on expectations and the relationship of these expectations to underlying biological and psychological needs. The implications for assessment and diagnosis of mental dynamics are also a significant contribution.

Marital contract therapy is psychoanalytic in its emphasis on the levels of awareness and intrapsychic needs. However, systems theory has influenced the concept of interactional contracts and expectations of marriage. Learning theory has also influenced the approach in its use of behavioral observation in order to identify the interactional contracts of the marriage. In the absence of research, it would appear that the approach may be useful for persons with good ego strength, observational abilities, and verbal abilities. It also provides many helpful concepts and techniques that would fit within virtually any other approach to marital therapy.

Marital contract therapy has some basic similarities to the Old Testament concept of the covenant in that it focuses on promises and expectations in the relationship between two contracting or covenanting parties. Problems in the relationship of God to man and woman result from the breaking of covenant, just as marital discord results from unmet contracts. Sager makes clear that such making and breaking of contracts in marriage (as in our relationship to God) occurs significantly at unconscious and unverbalized levels in the relationship.

Reference

Sager, C. J. *Marriage contracts and couple therapy.* New York: Brunner/ Mazel, 1976.

54

Marital Therapy: Overview
Brian L. Carlton

M arital therapy is a specialized area of therapy that evolved from the general field of psychiatry. As early as 1931 papers were presented to the American Psychiatric Association describing the sequential analysis of married couples (Sager, 1966).

Because psychoanalysis has traditionally concerned itself with the internal dynamics of the human psyche, it seemed heretical to examine any relationship except the patient-therapist relationship. Freud seemed to feel that it was counterproductive and dangerous for an analyst to become involved in working with more than one member of the same family (1943). Consequently, marital therapy did not gain credence among psychoanalysts until the early 1960s. Jackson (1959) coined the term *conjoint therapy* to describe a therapist meeting conjointly with a husband and wife.

In the 1960s and 1970s marital therapy seems to have been incorporated into the more broadly based family therapy movement under the conceptual umbrella of general systems theory. There appear to be negligible systemic differences in working with a married couple as opposed to the entire family. Some theorists have argued that the differences between marital therapy and family therapy are semantic rather than conceptual (Gurman & Kniskern, 1979).

Marital therapy is founded on the epistemological premises of general systems theory, which differ significantly from the individually oriented, intrapsychic, insight therapies. Based on the medical model, psychodynamic theories assume the Aristotelian notion of linear causality (A causes B). The therapist searches for cause-effect relations, focuses on intrapsychic dynamics, and views symptoms as unresolved intrapsychic conflicts.

In contrast, systemic marital therapy originated from the fields of cybernetics and communications theory, which assume a feedback cycle of circular causality (A causes B, which in turn causes A). The marital system is composed of two subsystems, husband and wife. The behavior of each marital partner creates an interactional pattern or symptom maintenance cycle. The work of the therapist is to join the couple and actively devise interventions that will rearrange the dysfunctional patterns of interaction.

Necessarily when one shifts to the study of the two-person system, one is entering the field of communication. The therapist must describe the individual in terms that apply to the exchange of communicative behavior between two or more people. Symptoms, then, are seen from a communicative rather than intrapsychic point of view, and the individual is best described as a person in communication with others. Communication theory conceives of a symptom as a nonverbal message. Moreover, the client's symptoms are perpetuated by the way he himself behaves and by the influence of other people intimately involved with him.

Intrapsychic therapists generally assume a passive or nondirective role in the therapeutic process. Internal mental processes are inferred from behavior, and change is believed to occur through increased self-awareness.

Because distressed marriages are frequently repetitive, resolution-resisting systems, the therapist cannot afford to remain passive. He must be active and must strategically direct the flow of communication if he is to effect change. Communication theorists question the plausibility of nondirective therapy. As Haley points out, "Actually nondirective therapy is a misnomer. To state that any communication between people can be nondirective is to state an impossibility. Whatever a therapist does not say to a patient as well as what he says will circumscribe the patient's behavior"(Haley, 1963, p. 71).

In contrast to psychodynamic theories, marital systems theories postulate that change occurs as a product of the interpersonal context of client and therapist. It is furthermore suggested that exploration of the human psyche or increased self-awareness may be irrelevant to therapeutic change. To be effective change must occur in the overall system, between both partners.

Behavior therapy has also made significant contributions to marital therapy. The theoretical underpinnings of behavior therapy as a strategy for treating couples evolved from behavior exchange theory, which addresses the interdependency of marriage (Jacobson & Margolin, 1979). Exchange theory assumes that couples constantly emit stimuli that have reinforcing or punishing effects on the partner. Each possible combination of behavioral exchanges yields an outcome for each partner. These outcomes collectively determine one's tendency to emit rewarding behavior in future encounters, one's level of satisfaction in the relationship, and one's general tendency to continue in the relationship.

One factor that determines the outcome of a particular interaction is the receiver's appraisal of his or her potential outcomes in alternative relationships or the outcomes accruing as a result of being alone. The more positive each spouse estimates his or her options outside of the relationship to be, the more positive the outcomes in the relationship need to be in order to justify continuance of the relationship (Jacobson & Margolin, 1979).

It should be acknowledged that marital therapy, like systems theory, is still evolving from its conceptual infancy. It would therefore be premature to offer a critique of marital therapy at this time. However, it is fairly clear that marital therapy has arisen from a need to explain and treat marital distress where psychodynamic theories have failed or proven inadequate. If it is true, as Kuhn (1962) postulates, that progress in science evolves from paradigms that better explain phenomena, then systems theory has altered our conception of human problems in much the same way as the theory of relativity altered our conception of the universe.

References

Freud, S. *General introduction to psychoanalysis.* Garden City, N.Y.: Garden City Publishing, 1943.

Gurman, A. S., & Kniskern, D. P. Marriage and/or family therapy: What's in a name? *American Association for Marital and Family Therapy Newsletter,* 1979, *10*(1), 5–8.

Haley, J. *Strategies of psychotherapy.* New York: Grune & Stratton, 1963.

Jackson, D. D. Family interaction, family homeostasis, and some implications for conjoint family therapy. In J. Masserman (Ed.), *Individual and familial dynamics.* New York: Grune & Stratton, 1959.

Jacobson, N. S., & Margolin, G. *Marital therapy: Strategies based on social learning and behavioral exchange principles.* New York: Brunner/Mazel, 1979.

Kuhn, T. S. *The structure of scientific revolutions.* Chicago: University of Chicago Press, 1962.

Sager, C. J. The treatment of married couples. In S. Arieti (Ed.), *American handbook of psychiatry* (Vol. 3). New York: Basic Books, 1966.

55

Premarital Counseling
H. Norman Wright

The first mention of premarital counseling as a valued service occurred in a 1928 article in *The American Journal of Obstetrics and Gynecology*. Then, and until the mid-1950s, most writing in the area of premarriage concerned physicians and the premarital physical exam. In the 1950s religious literature began to focus on premarital counseling and writings from the mental health profession.

Historical Development

Traditionally there have been three main groups who provide most of the premarital counseling: ministers, physicians, and mental health professionals. Physicians are most concerned about the physical exam and have little time for long-term counseling. Most mental health counselors have received little or no training in the field of premarital counseling and actually see fewer couples than do those in the ministry. Since minsters are involved in performing the ceremony, they have a greater opportunity to prepare couples for marriage, and most couples tend to seek out ministers for this service. Ministerial involvement in this form of counseling arose as an expansion of the pastoral counseling movement in the 1940s and 1950s.

During the early years of premarital counseling the emphasis appeared to be on troubled couples or individual pathology. Then the role of the minister as a screening agent emerged in the literature of the 1950s and 1960s. Johnson (1953) stated that he saw the minister as being responsible for the continuing growth of a couple's marriage. The role of the minister as an examiner of the emotional readiness and maturity of couples for marriage was emphasized by Stewart (1970) and Rutledge (1966).

In order to challenge the ever-expanding divorce rate, some states have become involved in encouraging premarital preparation. California and several other states have passed legislation requiring persons under eighteen to obtain not only parental consent but also a court order giving permission to obtain the marriage license. The Superior Court of Los Angeles County, along with courts in many other counties, mandated premarital counseling as a prerequisite for obtaining a marriage license by minors. Many churches and public health agencies offer their services to young couples seeking permission to marry. In 1972, of the 4,000 couples who applied for marriage licenses in Los Angeles County, 2,745 turned to ministers for their counseling. Many of the other couples used community health services.

Even though the law and the program are relatively new, initial conclusions indicate that couples generally found the experience helpful, and many return for counseling after marriage. The findings reinforce the conviction that premarital counseling is a valuable means of offering primary prevention of common problems of marriage.

Many ministers now receive intensive training in premarital counseling in various seminaries throughout the United States. Organizations such as Prepare (Minneapolis, Minnesota) and Christian Marriage Enrichment (Santa Ana, California) are conducting nationwide seminars for the purpose of training ministers and counselors in premarital preparation.

Objectives

There is little uniformity amongst those conducting premarital counseling. Traditionally ministers were concerned with the wedding ceremony and the spiritual relationship of the couple. In the past decade there has been a new trend emerging. This involves: (1) a very thorough preparation program of several sessions prior to the wedding; (2) premarital counseling as mandatory and not an option for the couple; (3) an intensive homework schedule accompanying the sessions with the couple.

Typically there are several basic objectives to be achieved during premarital counseling. One goal is to make arrangements for the procedural details of the wedding ceremony itself. The couple can express their desires, and the minister can make suggestions and provide guidelines. Premarital counseling is an opportunity for the minister or other counselor to build an in-depth relationship with the couple, which could lead to a continuing ministry in the future.

Providing information is another goal. Probably more teaching occurs in this type of counseling than in any other. Part of this teaching involves helping the couple to understand themselves and what each one brings to marriage, to discover their strengths and weaknesses, and to be realistic about the adjustments they must make to have a successful relationship.

Another goal is providing correction. Correction of faulty information concerning marriage relationships, the communication process, finances, in-laws, and sex will be a regular part of the counseling for most couples. One of the main purposes is to help the couple eliminate as many surprises as possible from the impending marriage. By eliminating these and helping the couple become more realistic about the future, marital conflict will be lessened.

The counselor must have expertise in many areas, because the couple is looking to him or her as the conveyor of helpful information. This is an opportunity to provide an atmosphere in which the couple can relieve themselves of fears and anxieties concerning marriage and settle questions or doubts they may have. This may also be a time in which strained and severed relationships with parents and in-laws will be restored.

The final purpose for counseling could be one of the most important goals. This is a time to assist the couple in making their final decision: Should we marry? They may not come with that in mind, but engagement is not finality. Research indicates that between 35 percent and 45 percent of all engagements in this country are terminated. Many people do change their minds. Perhaps during the process of premarital counseling some couples will decide to postpone their wedding or completely terminate their relationship. On the other side, there will be some cases in which a minister will decide that he cannot, in good conscience, perform the wedding because of the apparent mismatch or immaturity of the couple.

Format and Techniques

The structure or format of premarital counseling varies considerably. Many couples are seen by the minister or counselor for several sessions. Other programs involve a combination of conjoint sessions with several group sessions. A third alternative is to conduct all sessions on a group basis. One example of this third alternative is the Engaged Encounter Movement, an outgrowth of the Marriage Encounter Movement. Many are using the combination approach of conjoint and group sessions, which can provide a couple with between ten to twelve hours of preparation. The ideal and most productive of approaches appears to be either the conjoint or the combination of conjoint and group program. The personal involvement and interaction of a guide with one couple for several hours is an element that a group experience cannot produce.

In most premarital settings various evaluation instruments are used. This is done to assist the couple to gain a better understanding of themselves and their relationship. The various approaches to personal and couple assessment cover a broad range of devices, including personality inventories, psychological tests, rating scales, questionnaires, and personal data forms. Instrumentation helps to promote a strong level of couple involvement in the counseling process. It also assists the counselor or minister in obtaining information that otherwise might be missed. Some of the most frequently used tools are the Taylor-Johnson Temperament Analysis, Prepare, Family History Analysis, Myers-Briggs Indicator, and the Premarital Counseling Inventory.

One of the newest trends developing in the field of premarital counseling is an emphasis on each person's family of origin and the ensuing effect upon the couple's forthcoming marriage. Couples are assisted in determining if they have completed the parental separation process and if there is any unfinished business existing between them and their parents. This approach also helps them understand the kinds of marital models they have for their own marriage. This approach is involved in Stahlmann and Hiebert's (1980) Dynamic Relationship History and Wright's (1981) Family History Analysis.

The content of premarital counseling varies, but the comprehensive multisession approach typically covers numerous significant topic areas. Content areas usually include the following: the effect of courtship, the quality of love, the purpose and meaning of marriage, sexual knowledge and expression, timing for marriage, reasons for marriage, fears and concerns of marriage, family background, family dependency, family closeness, separation from family, personality characteristics, self-image, emotions, spiritual relationship and life, anticipating a future together, expectations, needs, roles, goals, decision making, communication, conflict resolution, in-laws, finances, leisure and friendships, and children.

Evaluation

Research on premarital counseling has been very limited. What is needed is long-term follow-up studies of couples who received premarital counseling versus those who did not. Such studies will need to control for the number of sessions couples receive and the approach taken in the sessions. Proper instrumentation must also be established for the purpose of pre- and post-testing.

In the absence of such research anecdotal reports are the only available data as to the effectiveness of premarital counseling. Numerous ministers and organizations attest to very positive results from premarital counseling. These responses are based on self reports from couples, simple evaluation responses from couples, and personal observations and contact with previously counseled couples. A much lower than average national divorce rate has also been used as a criterion.

There does seem to be some evidence that the more sessions couples attend, the greater the results. These results are reflected in the reports of couples on the value of the counseling, the lower number of divorces, and the number of couples who decide to not marry during the process of premarital counseling (Wright, 1981).

Future research will be important in this relatively new field of preventive counseling. However, the potential for increased effectiveness and for the stabilizing of future marriages appears good through carefully conducted premarital counseling.

References

Johnson, P. E. *Psychology of pastoral care*. Nashville: Abingdon, 1953.

Rutledge, A. L. *Premarital counseling*. Cambridge: Schenkman Publishing, 1966

Stahmann, R. F., & Hiebert, W. J. *Premarital counseling*. Lexington, Mass.: Lexington Books, 1980

Stewart, C. W. *The minister as marriage counselor*. Nashville: Abingdon, 1970

Wright, H. N. *Premarital counseling* (Rev. ed.). Chicago: Moody Press, 1981.

56

Problem-centered Family Systems Therapy
Christine V. Bruun

Problem-centered family systems therapy has evolved out of several decades of research and clinical work on the part of Nathan Epstein and his colleagues. It provides a clear, systematic means of understanding and treating the troubled family. Much emphasis is placed on clarifying the major, sequential steps of therapy ("macro" stages) as contrasted with the specific interventions and strategies ("micro" stages) that vary with therapists' preferred styles. Problems are seen as coming from a blockage in one or more of the three basic functions that a family needs to perform for its members:

1. providing survival needs such as food, shelter, and money.
2. managing developmental stages (individual and family).
3. giving support in stressful situations and crises.

Although Epstein originally took a psychoanalytic position in adult and child psychiatry, his present approach treats the whole family from a systems perspective, incorporating communication, transactional, and learning theory. This shift occurred when his research (Westley & Epstein, 1969) indicated that the emotional health of adolescents reflected the organizational and transactional patterns of their families.

Therapy Process

The focus of the therapy process is on current family problems. Past issues are given minimal attention. Treatment generally requires six to twelve sessions. Family members are enlisted as active collaborators in the problem-solving process. The family provides most of the momentum in the treatment process by identifying its own strengths and weaknesses and by devising means to solve its own problems. The therapist serves mainly as a catalyst, clarifier, and facilitator.

The major intervention steps of Epstein's model are assessment, contracting, treatment, and closure. Each step begins with an orientation by the therapist, who explains that particular phase and secures the family's permission to continue. Each step contains substages in which the family and therapist gather and clarify information, decide how to use this material, and then implement their decision. The hallmark of this model is the emphasis on the family's participation and capacity to be aware of its own problems and to act on them. At the end of each step the therapist summarizes his or her views and seeks a consensus with the family and their permission to proceed, a position that shows respect for the family members and reduces resistance to therapy.

Assessment is the most detailed step of this model and includes all family members living at home. Epstein regards a thorough and comprehensive diagnostic survey as the critical factor in the success of therapy. Six dimensions are investigated to give an overall picture of family functioning: problem solving, communication, roles, affective responsiveness, affective involvement, and behavior control. Each of these dimensions is carefully explored to gain understanding of the family's strengths and weaknesses as well as the level of effectiveness at which the family is functioning.

Problem solving concerns the family's ability to identify and discuss problems and to explore and implement alternatives. Communication involves the family's ability to speak clearly and directly to the appropriate person. Roles are predictable patterns of behavior for family members. The family is assessed as to how well the necessary role functions are performed, how appropriately roles are assigned, and how accountable persons are for their responsibilities. Affective responsiveness measures the degree to which the full range of human emotion, positive and negative, is experienced in the family and the level of appropriateness to the situation. Affective involvement explores the level of participation in the interests of other family members, from the extremes of no involvement to over-involvement. Behavior control concerns the ways the family monitors and sanctions its members' behavior. Styles of control range from effective, flexible control to rigid and chaotic control.

These six dimensions are also used in a careful assessment of the presenting problem. Additional problems concerning individuals (physiological and psychological) are also assessed, as well as those concerning the family and wider social systems (school, church, extended family). The assessment stage is completed when both therapist and family agree on a list of family problems.

Contracting is the second major step. The therapist helps the family decide whether they would like to work alone on their problems or continue in treatment. If the latter, the family specifies what changes they expect from each other and sets concrete goals. Each person in the treatment process, including the therapist, commits himself to meeting these goals by signing a contract agreement.

The third major step is *treatment*. The therapist gives the initiative for action to the family, including identifying problems with the highest priority and the tasks that move toward meeting the goals. Tasks are distributed among the family members and progress towards goals is evaluated. If goals are met, further tasks are assigned. If a task is not completed, or even attempted, in three successive sessions, Epstein advises either outside consultation or termination.

Closure is the final step. Therapist and family summarize what they have learned in treatment, discuss how they can adapt these gains to future problems, and establish long-term goals. A future follow-up session is planned to monitor the family's progress.

Evaluation

Although more research regarding the effectiveness of this approach needs to be conducted, Epstein and Bishop (1981) consider it particularly effective with acute disturbances in previously well-functioning families. It also appears that it may be more effective with single-parent families having a child six to twelve years old and with families in which this is the first experience in therapy.

Epstein explicitly states that the underlying value system of this approach is the Judeo-Christian ethic. The individuals in the family are respected for their capacity to generate productive, healthy solutions to their problems, and emphasis is given to the optimal development of each human being. The therapist is not considered as all-knowing and omnipotent but as a co-worker with the family. This approach of regarding the family as the primary experts on themselves seems to restore the dignity the family may feel it has lost by revealing its problems and weaknesses. The humility of the therapist's stance and the belief in the worth of the individual are both consistent with the biblical perspective.

References

Epstein, N. B., & Bishop, D. S. Problem-centered systems therapy of the family. In A. S. Gurman & D. P. Kniskern (Eds.), *Handbook of family therapy.* New York: Brunner/Mazel, 1981.

Westley, W. A., & Epstein, N. B. *The silent majority.* San Francisco: Jossey-Bass, 1969.

57

Psychoanalytic Family Therapy
Hendrika Vande Kemp

The basic assumption underlying the psychoanalytic approach to family therapy is the reciprocal relationship between conflict among family members and conflict within the mind of any one member (Ackerman, 1966). The two levels constitute a circular feedback system; interpersonal conflict affects intrapsychic conflict, and vice versa.

According to Ackerman interpersonal conflict in the family group generally precedes the establishment of fixed patterns of intrapsychic conflict. Symptom formation is a late product of the processes of internalization of persistent and pathogenic forms of family conflict. Potentially, symptoms are reversible if the intrapsychic conflict can once more be externalized and placed into the field of family interaction where a new solution can be found. The psychoanalytic family therapist is, therefore, much more interested in historical family relationships than is the family therapist with a systems orientation. Current interactions are of interest only as they reexternalize issues that have become internalized in one or more family members.

At the beginning of the family's life cycle this approach stresses the unconscious factors in mate selection. Inevitably when two people marry they replicate in some way the relationship of their parents and re-create what is sometimes called the childhood emotional pattern. A mate is chosen who reduces one's anxiety and re-creates the warmth of the original parent-child relationship. The dynamics of romantic love allow for the denial of the more negative characteristics of the mate, which also mirror the pattern of the parents. In order to live with the tension of the partner's combined negative and positive characteristics, both spouses collude in the denial of these aspects and attempt to make the partner into exactly the kind of person who will meet one's innermost needs. When two partners are both healthy, well-adjusted individuals, these dynamics produce a healthy marriage. When the partners are poorly adjusted, the marriage will manifest greater difficulties, creating problems for the children born into the family.

In psychoanalytic family theory this process of inducing problems in the child as a result of marital distress is known as scapegoating, a concept borrowed directly from the biblical scapegoat, which carried the sins of the people Israel into the wilderness. As Framo describes this process (Boszormenyi-Nagy & Framo, 1965), it requires the existence of a group (the family) whose members feel threatened by some hint of evil (an undesirable characteristic or personality trait) and who agree to use some other person (a family member) to personify that evil, which can ultimately be eliminated by destroying the scapegoat (through a serious physical or emotional illness that takes him or her away from the family). In treatment the scapegoat is not held personally responsible for the symptoms thus induced by the family, and therapy will focus on finding a way to take the person out of the scapegoat role.

The scapegoating process, along with healthier processes that create the family's self-image, is often maintained by the formation of family myths. These involve patterns of mutually agreed upon, but distorted, roles for family members resulting from compromises between all family members so that each individual's self-identity and defenses are maintained through the myth. Collusion among family members allows the family to see itself as living up to its ideal image and avoiding other repudiated images. Children are recruited into the maintenance of family images first defined in the parents' unconscious marriage contract. When parents see in themselves characteristics that contradict the family myth, they may delegate a child or adolescent to resolve the issues for them, thus often reinforcing various kinds of undesirable behavior by which they themselves are unconsciously tempted. Such a child may then be expelled from the family in order to maintain its ideal image. Other children may be bound to the family, unable to leave because their loss would create an unbearable blank in the family's image.

The maintenance of the family myth inevitably leads to the creation of family secrets. Secrets may involve actual facts or events known by one family member and kept secret from others, such as a mother's abortion that is not shared with the children. They may also involve events or conditions known by all family members but simply not talked about, such as a father's alcoholism. Such secrets constitute a taboo. Other secrets involve shared or individual fantasies that are not talked about, such as incestuous feelings. Bringing such secrets into the open and discussing their impact on the family may be an important focus of family therapy.

Ghosts and skeletons in families are also emphasized in this approach. Skeletons are the facts that embarrass family members and may include such historical events as imprisonment, institutionalization in a mental hospital, defection from the military, or an illegitimate pregnancy. Because they constitute the family's darker side, skeletons often become secrets as well. Ghosts in the family are created when members of past generations continue to be psychologically present. Their presence is dysfunctional when unfinished business remains. Often ghosts result from unmourned deaths in the family. The mourning process is not an automatic one, and professional assistance may be needed to facilitate it. When the ghost is a living family member, family therapy may involve bringing this person into the therapeutic process.

Psychoanalytic family therapy is often indicated for serious, longstanding emotional problems that have resisted treatment from a structural, functional, or strategic perspective. It tends to involve long-term rather than short-term treatment and generally will involve several generations of family members.

References

Ackerman, N. W. *Treating the troubled family.* New York: Basic Books, 1966.

Boszormenyi-Nagy, I., & Framo, J. L. (Eds.), *Intensive family therapy: Theoretical and practical aspects.* New York: Harper & Row, 1965.

Additional Readings

Box, S., Copley, B., Magagna, J., & Moustaki, E. (Eds.). *Psychotherapy with families: An analytic approach.* Boston: Routledge & Kegan Paul, 1981.

Skynner, A. C. R. *Systems of family and marital psychotherapy.* New York: Brunner/Mazel, 1976.

Stierlin, H. *Psychoanalysis and family therapy: Selected papers.* New York: Aronson, 1977.

58

Social Network Intervention
E. Mansell Pattison

In terms of social anthropology, social network is a construct of social relations. It involves an analysis of patterns of linkages between persons and the manner in which an individual is linked to the larger social structure. Three levels of analysis exist. The micro-level of analysis is linkage of the individual to intimates, family, extended kin, and close friends. The macro-level is community, social, and cultural organization, analyzed in terms of impersonal collectives. The mezzo-level is social network analysis: the personal linkages between persons (direct linkages) and through persons to others (indirect linkages).

The social network paradigm (Leinhardt, 1977) represents a conceptual schemata for mapping the mezzo-level of social linkages. Consider a Persian rug. A macro-level analysis considers the overall type of rug. A micro-level analysis involves the structure of any one square inch. A mezzo-level analysis traces how each color thread is tied to another thread to produce patterns. The threads are the content of social links; the knots are personal contacts.

Consider threads in terms of content (golf interest, political influence, dental skill). A dentist may be linked to persons in his life space who are dentists, politicians, or golfers, or some of each, or people with all three themes (direct linkages). The same dentist may have a political interest but know no politicians. Yet he may influence politicians via conversation with his golf partners who have political connections (indirect linkages). If the person has single theme links (he only knows dentists), the network will be sparse and simple in content and have few interconnections. If a person embodies many themes, he will link directly and completely to more persons. At the same time there will be more interconnections among the people in the network, thus indirectly linking him to many others (e.g., the dentist has golf friends who know his political friends).

A community, like a rug, is composed of many intersecting social themes that link different people directly and indirectly to each other. Thus a person does not have one social network. Rather, he participates in many different social networks, which indirectly interconnect. Social network analysis may focus on themes—for example, rumor networks, political networks, community assistance networks. Or analysis may focus on persons—the connections an individual has to others (egocentric analysis). Social network analysis is applied in mental health to both theme analysis, such as family or assistance networks, and to individual analysis (Gottlieb, 1981).

From the standpoint of individual analysis a person is linked to approximately 1,500–2,000 persons—the finite limits of one's personal community. These persons can be arranged in zones. Zone 1 (personal) consists of family you live with or who are most important (1–10 persons). Zone 2 (intimate) consists of close intimates (2–20). Zone 3 (extended) consists of those with whom you regularly interact but who are not as important to you (50–100). Zone 4 (nominal) consists of persons you know or interact with casually (around 500 persons). Zone 5 (extended) consists of people linked indirectly to you via persons in the other zones (around 1,000 persons).

The first two zones, called the intimate psychosocial network (twenty-five persons), form a relatively stable social system that mediates the relationships between the person and his social world (Pattison, Llamas, & Hurd, 1979). There are significant correlations between disturbances in this intimate social network and psychiatric disorders. It is important to note that social networks may be constructive and supportive, neutral, or destructive and pathogenic. Therefore a social network system should not be labeled a support system, because it may not operate as such.

The application of social network theory and analysis has resulted in new mental health interventions (Pattison, 1981). First are thematic social network intervention: the construction of crisis information centers, the activation of mutual assistance programs, and the organization of informal community networks. The intent of such clinical programs is to activate latent and indirect social links into an active and direct linkage. The resulting social network can then assist persons in crisis, respond to emergencies, and provide sustaining emotional and material support.

A second intervention strategy is screening-planning-linking. Here the focus is on an individual in crisis who lacks good network resources. The network convener screens inactive, latent, or indirect links, and convenes the personal network of the person to bring resources to his aid.

A third strategy is work with extended family, kin, and friend systems in which the social network is intact but dysfunctional. Here the network therapist, much as a family therapist, collates the network, identifies dysfunctional elements of the social system, and seeks to change the structure and function of the social network (Speck & Attneave, 1973).

A fourth strategy involves persons with pathological networks, such as drug and alcohol abusers, or inadequate networks such as chronic schizophrenics. Here the task of the network therapist is to recruit new members for the social network of the patient, constructing a new and more viable ongoing network.

The methods of social analysis can be applied to church and parish social systems (Pattison, 1977). The pastor can analyze the various social network themes that link parish members, as well as determine the social network resources available to an individual member. In turn, social network interventions can be employed to improve utilization of parish resources to meet the needs of the membership.

References

Gottlieb, B. (Ed.). *Social networks and social support in community mental health*. Beverly Hills, Calif.: Sage Publications, 1981.

Leinhardt, S. (Ed.). *Social networks: A developing paradigm*. New York: Academic Press, 1977.

Pattison, E. M. (Ed.). *Pastor and parish: A systems view*. Philadelphia: Fortress Press, 1977.

Pattison, E. M. (Ed.). *Clinical applications of social network theory*. New York: Human Sciences Press, 1981.

Pattison, E. M., Llamas, R., & Hurd, G. Social network mediation of anxiety. *Psychiatric Annals*, 1979, *9*, 56–67.

Speck, R. V., & Attneave, C. L. *Family networks*. New York: Pantheon, 1973.

59

Strategic Therapy
Vance L. Shepperson

$\mathbb{A}$ few major assumptions form the foundation for this type of therapy, which stems from the work of Erickson. First, it is a largely systemic therapy as it is practiced currently; that is, strategic practitioners think in terms of ongoing interactive sequences within a family system rather than individually rooted intrapsychic events. Another distinctive is that the practitioner rather than the client is assumed to be the primary source of change. A third hallmark is that strategic therapists think in terms of problem formation and problem resolution rather than in terms of helping the client to grow; consequently most strategic therapy is directive, brief therapy.

One of the most basic theoretical tenets of this approach is that clients come for help because they tend to mishandle everyday problems in living (Segal, 1981). When people ignore problems, take ineffective action on problems, or fail to realize that nothing can be done about a problem at the moment, they subsequently tend to try to solve their difficulties with "more of the same," or first-order change methods. The strategic therapist will often reframe the problems by applying second-order change tactics that redefine the meaning and nature of the difficulty.

A strategic style of intervention requires a facility for analogic or metaphoric thinking (see Rosen, 1982). For example, a strategic therapist would typically view a physical symptom as an indirect communicative tactic. Reframing a headache in analogic fashion might involve praising the patient for nobly sacrificing his own well-being in the service of bearing his family's pain for them. Alternately the therapist might weave a metaphor that matches the situation initially and then tag a more constructive, resourceful end onto the story (Madanes, 1981). One primary result of such an approach is the introduction of more choice into any one family system. The encrusted, repetitive sequence of interpersonal transactions is interrupted and a new range of creative problem-solving options is introduced.

It is assumed within this approach that very little is learned without the client doing something. Insight is viewed as nothing more than an intermittent and benign epiphenomenon of problem resolution. The primary mechanism for learning therefore becomes the directive rather than the interpretation.

The skillful use of directives is an art in itself (Haley, 1976). The first step is to motivate the individual, couple, or family to follow the therapist's directive. This basic first step, common to all therapies, involves establishing rapport and trust. The second step involves giving one's directives in a precise and clear fashion. Should the first strategy for effecting change not work, then it behooves the therapist to look at the problem from a different perspective and try another directive. Typically such a progression begins with straightforward, compliance-based directives that depend on the family doing what they are told to do. Should the family sabotage such directives with a variety of passive ploys (for which they typically eschew responsibility), then the therapist should move to defiance-based directives, which rely on paradox. Paradox in this context is best understood as instructing the family to continue in their plight or get worse. Many frameworks for understanding why paradox works are extant; we do know, however, that it is an effective technique that works.

A final distinguishing quality of the strategic school is the use of positive connotation or reframing (Stanton, 1981). The behaviors of clients are invariably accepted as they are without labeling them resistant. Further, clients are praised for their symptomatic behavior in that it is often labeled as self-sacrificial or protective of other family members. For example, because the father does not want others in the family to have to endure his angry feelings, he sacrifices his physical health and develops an ulcer; because the child does not want his mother or father to have to deal with their own difficulties, he generates problem behaviors at school. Most clients are used to being misunderstood and blamed; when instead they are accepted in the midst of their symptoms, most feel they have been really understood, perhaps for the first time. Further, because these positive ascriptions do have kernels of systemic truth tucked away within them, the technique is effective.

References

Haley, J. *Problem-solving therapy: New strategies for effective family therapy.* San Francisco: Jossey-Bass, 1976.

Madanes, C. *Strategic family therapy.* San Francisco: Jossey-Bass, 1981.

Rosen, S. *My voice will go with you: The teaching tales of Milton H. Erickson, M.D.* New York: Norton, 1982.

Segal, L. Brief therapy II. In R. Corsini (Ed.), *Handbook of innovative psychotherapies,* New York: Wiley, 1981.

Stanton, M. Strategic approaches to family therapy. In A. S. Gurman & D. P. Kniskern (Eds.), *Handbook of family therapy.* New York: Brunner/Mazel, 1981.

60

Structural Family Therapy
Brian L. Carlton

Structural family therapy is based on a body of theory and techniques dealing with the individual in his social context. Therapy based on this framework is directed toward changing the organization of the family. When the structure of the family group is transformed, the positions of members in that group are altered accordingly. As a result each individual's experiences change.

Structural family therapy is predicated on the fact that the individual is not an isolate. He or she is an acting and reacting member of social groups. To say that a person is influenced by his social context, which he also influences, may seem obvious. However, basing mental health techniques on this concept is a new approach.

The traditional techniques of mental health grew out of fascination with individual dynamics. This preoccupation dominated the field and led therapists to concentrate on exploring the intrapsychic. The resulting treatment techniques focused exclusively on the individual apart from his surroundings. An artificial boundary was drawn between the individual and his social context. The practice of intrapsychic psychotherapy maintained and reinforced the artificial boundary. Consequently, the individual came to be viewed as the site of pathology.

Structural family therapy was developed in the second half of the twentieth century by Salvador Minuchin and his co-workers. *Families of the Slums* (Minuchin, Montalvo, Guerney, Rosman, & Schumer, 1967) was the first attempt at a comprehensive exposition of structural family therapy. Minuchin and his colleagues were working with poverty-stricken underprivileged families grappling with day-to-day survival. There was a sense of urgency and necessity in approaching these families in a practical way that would alleviate stress. Therapies aimed toward understanding and insight rather than action seemed too far removed from the pressures of everyday problems of poor families. Minuchin and his co-workers developed a therapeutic approach that was founded on the immediacy of the present reality, was oriented toward solving problems, and, most importantly, viewed human problems within their social context. Other influences in structural family therapy are Haley's (1976) problem-solving approach and strategic techniques.

During the 1970s and 80s structural family therapists broadened their scope and began using their approach with middle-class psychosomatic families. Unlike most therapies, which had their roots in the middle class and were adapted to work with lower socioeconomic patients, structural family therapy was generated from work with the poor and subsequently expanded to other socioeconomic strata.

The theoretical underpinnings of structural family therapy rest on the belief that "the whole and the parts can be properly explained only in terms of the relations that exist between the parts" (Lane, 1970). Thus, focus is on the relationships that connect one part of the whole to another. Structuralism approaches all human phenomena with the intent of identifying the codes that regulate human relationships. Structure refers to the regulating codes manifested in the operational patterns through which people relate to one another in order to carry out functions. The repertoire of structure that the family develops to carry out its ongoing functions takes on a character that is as unique to each family as the personality structure is to the individual.

The structural dimensions of transactions most often identified in structural family therapy are boundary, alignment, and power. According to Minuchin, "The boundaries of a subsystem are the rules defining who participates and how" (1974, p. 53). These rules dictate who is in and who is out of an operation. The clarity of boundaries within a family is a useful parameter for the evaluation of family functioning. Families can be conceived of as falling somewhere along a continuum whose poles are the two extremes of diffuse (enmeshed) and rigid (disengaged) boundaries. Most healthy families fall within the middle range of clearly defined boundaries.

Aponte speaks of alignment as the "joining or opposition of one member of a system to another in carrying out an operation" (1976, p. 434). Alignment statements, for example, would indicate whether the father agrees or disagrees with his wife's disciplinary action toward the children.

Power refers to the relative influence of each family member on the outcome of an activity. Power is not an absolute attribute but is relative to the operation. An indicator of power might be who speaks first or who becomes the gatekeeper of communication flow in the session.

The scope of the family therapist and the techniques he uses to pursue his goals are determined by his theoretical framework. Structural family therapy is a therapy of action. The focus of this therapy is to modify the present, not to explore or interpret the past. The therapist actively directs his own behavior and communications with the family so as to influence selected aspects of the family's transactions within or outside of the session. The therapist's task is to develop relational contexts that will allow, stimulate, and provoke change in transactional patterns associated with the problem.

References

Aponte, H. J. Underorganization in the poor family. In P. J. Guerin (Ed.), *Family therapy: Theory and practice.* New York: Gardner, 1976.

Haley, J. *Problem-solving therapy.* San Francisco: Jossey-Bass, 1976.

Lane, M. *Introduction to structuralism.* New York: Basic Books, 1970.

Minuchin, S. *Families and family therapy.* Cambridge: Harvard University Press, 1974.

Minuchin, S., Montalvo, B., Guerney, B., Rosman, B., & Schumer, F. *Families of the slums.* New York: Basic Books, 1967.

61

Therapeutic Community
Glenn C. Taylor

A constant concern throughout history has been the development of effective and responsible ways of relating to members of our society who, for whatever reason, deviate from the norms. We have passed through many reforms as definitions of deviance and society's response to it have evolved. Therapeutic community stands as one example of a more humanitarian approach to mental illness that began in the late nineteenth century and gained momentum in the twentieth century.

Therapeutic community involves the self-conscious creation of a social organization within which the total resources of both patients and staff, as well as the total environment, will be used to their optimum potential to further treatment. The total organization is seen as a vital force in determining therapeutic outcome. Patients are involved in leadership and treatment. All relationships, whether patient-staff, patient-patient, or staff-staff, are seen as potentially therapeutic and examined to maximize this potential. The emotional climate and the physical environment are created to facilitate treatment.

Origins and Development

The therapeutic community approach evolved in the historical context of psychiatry's pursuit of more humanitarian treatment of those suffering from mental illness. The humanitarian approach looked on mental illness as sickness and the sufferers as persons in need of care, comfort, and cleanliness in their surroundings. Other important influences were interpersonal psychology and psychiatry, milieu therapy, group therapeutic techniques, social psychiatry, and administrative therapy (Almond, 1974).

During the 1940s much research and analysis brought into perspective the psychiatric hospital as a small society, the dynamics of which could either facilitate or inhibit treatment. It was recognized that the institution was a hybrid form of society that disregarded family needs; the benefits and needs of relationships between the opposite sex and various age groups were ignored. Instead it created subcultures in which the patient insulated himself from staff and treatment personnel, who in turn insulated themselves from the controlling bureaucracy. These decision makers were removed from the patient to such an extent as to be almost unaware of his needs.

Social and administrative therapies focused on the organizational, administrative, and sociocultural processes in terms of their role in treatment. Sullivan's emphasis on communication, the role of culture, the significance of the intensity and meaning of behavior, the role of the environment in determining the functional use of behavior, the definition of the role of the psychiatrist as a participant-observer, and the training of staff in interpersonal skills contributed to this new approach to mental illness (Sullivan, 1953, 1956).

Milieu therapy, with its focus on the physical environment and social structure, developed at the same time as the therapeutic community approach. It essentially involved paying attention to and using the environment of the patient toward therapeutic goals. This concept was eventually expanded to include the role of all persons relating to the patient as significant in the treatment process.

Prior to 1935 psychopathology was usually understood in terms of intrapsychic conflict, even though social adjustment was the criterion most often used for measuring improvement. A new interest in the social relationships of patients led to the concept of group treatment techniques. Thus, the treatment of individuals through the medium of the group developed and made a significant contribution to the therapeutic community approach.

The merging of psychiatric and sociological concepts of mental illness in social psychiatry led to a serious study of potentialities for treatment inherent within community relationships. This included staff-patient, patient-patient, and patient-administrator relationships. Interpersonal relations and environmental influences were considered important factors in etiology, diagnosis, and treatment (Greenblatt, York, & Brown, 1955; Freeman, 1965).

The term *administrative therapy* was used by some to describe an approach developed at this time that emphasized open doors, increased liberty and self-determination, a meaningful work program with appropriate incentives, and useful and healthy use of leisure time (Clark, 1964; Taylor, 1958). Those using this term distinguish between administrative therapy and therapeutic community. The lines of separation between the approaches are, however, sketchy.

From this brief historical sketch it can be seen how influential the various therapeutic developments of the day were in the evolution of the therapeutic community concept of treatment. This was a period of major advance in the treatment of mental illness, and therapeutic community was one dimension of that development.

Almond (1974) identifies the beginnings of therapeutic community in the work of Maxwell Jones at Belmont Hospital in England during the years 1947–1959. However, while Jones is definitely the individual most clearly identified with the development of therapeutic community, others were also involved in similar activities.

Bion and Rickman (Taylor, 1958) introduced and developed new principles of treatment at the Northfield Military Hospital Training Wing in 1943 to bring unruly soldiers under control. They used group methods and a reduction of the traditional authoritarian structure to create a feeling of belonging and a social environment. They felt this gave the men a sense of responsibility and enabled them to deal with their own problems and antisocial behavior. In 1946 Bion's methods were further developed in the second Northfield experiment. An open-door policy, more parole, improved nurse-patient relationships, gainful employment, and a general focus on interpersonal relationships was also being introduced in several other hospitals at the same time. As early as 1938 Bierer introduced therapeutic social clubs at Runwell Mental Hospital for inpatients.

Maxwell Jones served at the Effort Syndrome Unit, Mill Hill, from 1939 to 1945. Several principles developed in this unit were later refined and modified to form the therapeutic community model. The authoritarian hierarchy was broken to permit free communications among all staff and patients, nurses were actively involved in treatment, and patients were educated concerning their symptomatology. Additionally, sociodrama and role playing as therapeutic techniques were practiced, treatment was defined as all-pervasive in the patient's total experience, and problem solving through group discussion rather than appeal to authority was introduced. Many of these concepts were poorly developed and very much in an experimental stage.

From 1945 to 1947 Jones developed the Ex-Prisoner-of-War Unit, Dartford, Kent. Repatriated prisoners of war were the patients. The experimental nature of this unit allowed for the development of the principles introduced at Mill Hill, and an extensive work therapy program was an added feature. The use of psychodrama and group therapy was greatly developed. From 1947 to 1959 Jones was associated with the Neurosis Unit, Belmont Hospital. During these years the concept of therapeutic community matured and was articulated and refined through scholarly interaction. From 1959 to 1962 Jones served in several capacities in the United States, which served to make his work more widely known. He returned to Scotland in 1963, and there developed a therapeutic community at Melrose (Dingleton Hospital) that embodied the principles of therapeutic community.

Sullivan's early emphasis on the part played by the hospital environment and the role of nurses is a precursor to the use of the therapeutic community model in the United States and Canada. One of the best-known therapeutic community programs in the United States was the Yale–New Haven Community Hospital, which opened in January, 1960. Under the medical direction of Thomas Detre this unit, known as Tompkins I, developed clearly as a therapeutic community. The consultation work carried on by Jones in North America during the 1960s and 1970s also assisted in the adoption of the principles of therapeutic community in numerous other psychiatric hospitals.

Principles of Therapeutic Community

Since the concepts of therapeutic community developed over a period of time, a description of its principles must specify the period being described. Because the most careful studies of therapeutic community were conducted on its application by Jones at Dingleton Hospital from 1963 onward, and because this program was the basis of many of Jones's own observations (Jones, 1966, 1968b), it is the basis of the following discussion.

The total community as treatment agent

Jones felt that the major distinctive of therapeutic community is the way in which an institution's total resources are self-consciously pooled to facilitate treatment (Jones, 1959). Administrators, clinicians, support staff, and patients were all viewed as a part of the total treatment team. All would also be involved in community meetings where the question of their positive or negative influence on treatment was discussed. These groups were designed to enhance the sensitivity of staff to their role in treatment.

This approach led to a redefining of the roles of those normally defined as treatment staff (psychiatrists, psychologists, and social workers) so as to permit the inclusion of nurses, administrators, maintenance staff, and recreational staff in the treatment team. This was accomplished through the blurring of role distinctions and the inclusion of all relevant staff in patient assessment and treatment groups. One of the ways this blurring was accomplished was through the discouragement of dress distinction perpetuated through uniforms or typical attire for various professional groups.

Perhaps the best example of this principle is the treatment role established for nurses. Jones began involving nurses in discussion groups with patients and as participants in sociodrama. They soon were referred to as social therapists and were recognized as important culture carriers. Because of their intensive involvement with patients they were accepted as key contributors to diagnosis and treatment discussions.

The role of the patient evolved from essentially a passive role to one in which the patient was urged to assume all the responsibility he or she was capable of assuming for his or her own progress toward health and the improvement of fellow patients. Some emphasis on patients' learning to understand their problems began early. The patient was then expected to participate in discussion groups to help others to understand their problems. Patients were given opportunity and encouraged to provide meaningful feedback to fellow patients concerning their behavior and its effects. The patient's role was defined as that of a collaborator in treatment and later as that of a culture carrier in relation to the orientation of new patients.

It is obvious that to accomplish such a redefinition of role for nurses and patients a corresponding change of role for psychologists, social workers, and doctors was needed. The flattening of the traditional hierarchical structure and the facilitation of open communication was essential.

The creation of community

The concept of culture and the role it plays in therapy are crucial. Jones defined culture as "a cluster of socially determined attitudes and behavior patterns grouped and elaborated around structurally defined roles and relationships" (1952, p. 66). The culture was created with the intent of maximizing the resocialization of patients. In this context he spoke of doctors as social engineers. The staff and patients who had been in the institution for some time were described as culture carriers whose responsibility was to transmit the culture of the institution to new members. A treatment goal was to help the patient to adapt to the culture of the program and to learn to find new and satisfying roles in such a social context. The assumption was that he would then become more effective in adapting in the community after discharge. Psychopathology was expressed in relationships and could be dealt with through education, confrontation, and modeling by staff and patients.

An underlying principle was that of permissiveness. A pervasive attitude of permissiveness facilitated the patient's expression of symptomatology, which was dealt with through a supportive teaching of new behavior as the unacceptable behavior was confronted. The culture of the society was described in terms of permissiveness, understanding, helpfulness, mutual responsibility, inquiry, expression of feeling, democratic-equalitarian organization, and the facing of tensions, conflicts, or role confusion that arise (Rapoport, 1959). The redefinition of the patient in this culture gave him a strong sense of belonging and facilitated his identification with the culture and his motivation toward treatment.

The principle of open communication, which negated the traditional concept of lines of communication, was recognized early and developed to play an increasingly important role. The goal was to develop the freest communication possible between patients and staff. It was discovered that this eliminated much distortion that often occurred if communication was limited to formalized channels. Nonverbal communication was studied, and acting out was viewed as communication. The giving and receiving of feedback was encouraged. The question of confidentiality or privileged communication was dealt with by extending the circumference of confidentiality to include the total community, and the sharing of the most intimate material in the group became the norm (Jones, 1953).

Permissiveness coupled with open communication and the broader concept of confidentiality made it possible to deal with unacceptable deviations from the cultural norms in a group context. This reduced manipulation and the playing of one staff against another. In the context of an accepting group a person was encouraged and, if necessary, required to look at his behavior and its implications. Through group discussion the patient was helped to discuss his deviant behavior and to recognize its outcome for self and others (Jones, 1968a). This was spoken of as social learning.

All of this had implications for the role of leadership and the exercise of authority in the community. The hierarchical structure of the organization was flattened. Authority was dispersed through the community on a horizontal plane, with staff and patients assuming authority commensurate with their function. Authority was experienced as residing in the official leader only at times of crisis when it was necessary that he function decisively. Otherwise, Jones described his function as leadership from behind or as a catalyst. This concept of latent leadership permitted the development of leadership skills and functions among staff and patients.

Programs and techniques in theory

A summary of approaches used in therapeutic community philosophy included learning theory, psychodrama, work therapy, and a problem-solving orientation, in addition to the more traditional use of drug therapy, psychoanalytic techniques, and group therapy. These more specific approaches were used in the context of a community designed for treatment.

General learning theory and the Gestalt theory of learning were used to explain the social learning approach practiced. The focus was on understanding and unlearning habitual patterns of behavior found to be ineffectual and the learning of new, more adequate and satisfying ways of coping. Acknowledging and revising the emotional responses to behaviors was central, and for this reason there was a strong emphasis on the expression of feelings (Jones, 1968b).

Psychodrama was used to facilitate the expression and identification of feelings. Buried dynamics of behavior were explored through projective techniques. Work therapy was developed into a very useful approach with helpful outcomes in patient self-worth and constructive use of time. With the emphasis on treatment being the function of all staff, the personnel in the work therapy program took on real significance. Work therapy was also developed to contribute to a sense of community as well as training skills.

Decision making by consensus was one of the more radical focuses of therapeutic community. Any unilateral decision was seen as contradictory to its basic philosophy. A genuine attempt at reaching unanimity required providing rationale for decisions to patients and staff, which often involved sharing of information not traditionally available to either patients or frontline staff. However, the communication of respect and significance to members of the community proved to be of great benefit, especially to patients. The mutual education and learning that grew out of this approach was deemed to justify the large amount of time consumed in the process.

Out of this grew an approach to problem solving that became clearly defined. The approach was to solve community problems, which often involved a person's personal problems, by group discussion rather than through appeal to authority. Third party intervention was not accepted as a way of resolving interpersonal or personal issues. Turning the community problem into what is referred to as a living-learning situation, the process involved bringing together all involved parties in the presence of a group facilitator and the airing of all feelings, interpretations, expectations, and accusations. The facilitator sought to create a social learning experience for participants as they moved toward resolution and reconciliation. The timing of these encounters and the skill of the therapists were crucial. The confrontation was sought as close to the experience as possible unless the situation was such as to suggest delay would be more effective. These concepts were applied to staff as well as to patients.

Another process developed was the "postmortem meeting," which followed many activities and was intended to maximize the learning potential in each experience. The modeling provided by the more expert staff for other staff and patients in these activities was very helpful and educative.

Current Status

Since Jones's early work therapeutic communities have proliferated. Many applications of the concept, however, bear little resemblance to the original communities developed by Jones. Therapeutic community approaches have continued to be utilized in psychiatric hospitals and have also been adopted in a number of nonhospital drug treatment programs. Residential programs such as Synanon and Daytop Village are therapeutic community programs. Freudenberger (1972) has described an application of therapeutic community principles within a psychoanalytic private practice, and a number of other nonresidential applications have been described (e.g., Siroka & Siroka, 1971). While therapeutic community is certainly not a major contemporary treatment modality or approach, it has played an important role in shaping much current mental health philosophy.

References

Almond, R. *The healing community.* New York: Aronson, 1974.

Clark, D. H. *Administrative therapy.* Philadelphia: Lippincott, 1964.

Freeman, H. L. (Ed.). *Psychiatric hospital care.* London: Bailliere, Tindall, & Cassell, 1965.

Freudenberger, H. J. The therapeutic community in private practice. *Psychoanalytic Review,* 1972, *59,* 375–388.

Greenblatt, M., York, R. H., & Brown, E. L. *From custodial to therapeutic care in mental hospitals.* New York: Russell Sage Foundation, 1955.

Jones, M. *Social psychiatry.* London: Tavistock Publications, 1952.

Jones, M. *Therapeutic community.* New York: Basic Books, 1953.

Jones, M. Towards a clarification of the "therapeutic community" concept. *British Journal of Medical Psychology,* 1959, *32,* 200–205.

Jones, M. Therapeutic community practice. *American Journal of Psychiatry,* 1966, *122,* 1275–1279.

Jones, M. *Beyond therapeutic community.* New Haven: Yale University Press, 1968. (a)

Jones, M. *Social psychiatry in practice.* Hammondsworth: Penguin, 1968. (b)

Rapoport, R. N. *Community as doctor.* Springfield, Ill.: Thomas, 1960.

Siroka, R. W., & Siroka, E. K. Psychodrama and the therapeutic community. In L. Plank, G. B. Gottsegen, & M. G. Gottsegen (Eds.), *Confrontation.* New York: Macmillan, 1971.

Sullivan, H. S. *The interpersonal theory of psychiatry.* H. S. Perry & M. L. Gawel (Eds.). New York: Norton, 1953.

Sullivan, H. S. *Clinical studies in psychiatry.* H. S. Perry, M. L. Gawel, & M. Gibbon (Eds.). New York: Norton, 1956.

Taylor, F. K. A history of group and administrative therapy in Great Britain. *British Journal of Medical Psychology,* 1958, *31,* 153–173.

62

Triadic-based Family Therapy
Vance L. Shepperson

The focus on an interpersonal triangle within the family cuts across most of the traditional schools of family therapy; this is true regardless of whether the theoretical orientation is psychoanalytic, structural, strategic, problem-solving, experiential, or communicational. Historically family therapy grew from an initial focus on dyads (e.g., the mother-child dyad as exemplified in the schizophrenogenic mother notion of Fromm-Reichman, 1948). Since that time a major shift has taken place, and many individuals have focused on triads as opposed to individuals, dyads, or larger units of study. Ravich (1967) notes that there is a vast difference between a two-person and a three-person system.

Triadic-based family therapy is primarily identified with the work of Zuk (1969, 1971). Haley (1976, 1980) and Bowen (1966) have also made important contributions.

Theoretical Considerations

One of the best-known claims for the importance of triadic family therapy was made by Bowen: "The basic building block of any emotional system is the triangle. When emotional tension in a two person system exceeds a certain level it triangles in a third person, permitting the tension to shift around within the triangle. Any two in the original triangle can add a new member. An emotional system is composed of a series of interlocking triangles. It is a clinical fact that the original two person tension system will resolve itself automatically when contained within a three person system, one of whom remains emotionally detached" (1966, p. 368). Haley (1967) has elaborated on this theoretical foundation by describing three primary characteristics of the "perverse" triangle:

1. The members are not peers; one is in a different generation from the other two.
2. In the process of interaction one person forms a coalition with the single person from the other generation against the remaining third party. This coalition is not an alliance in which the two operate independently of the third; rather, it is a process of dual action against the third person.
3. The emotional coalition between the two persons is denied frequently, especially when the parties are queried regarding a specific act.

This pattern is seen most frequently in a clinical situation when a family appears with a symptomatic child connected to one overinvolved parent and one emotionally detached parent. This particular pattern of family interaction has been intrapersonalized and institutionalized by psychoanalytic theory as the oedipal conflict.

When the typical family is broken down into triads, a staggering complexity of units for study is generated; in the average American family of two parents, two children, and two sets of grandparents, this group of eight people generates 56 possible triangles. Any one person in the family is involved in 21 different triangles concurrently, each of which has the potential for an intergenerational coalition of a perverse nature. Within this network no two individuals are in the same position relative to the overall context. These triangles are intimately related. Adaptive behavior within one triangle may have maladaptive repercussions in another triangle. When all triangles are amicable, no problems appear; but when one individual is the nexus for two triangles that are in conflict, tension is generated within that individual. If the tension exceeds a certain critical level, it may manifest itself in symptomatic behavior. This behavior is seen in this theoretical framework as both a cry for help and protection from the anxiety generated by the triadic conflict.

Treatment Considerations

High levels of therapist activity within this primarily brief treatment modality are almost always required for effective treatment. The primary role of the triadic therapist is to serve as a flexible mediator, challenger, positive reframer of transactions, and shifting coalition partner within the extant family triangles (Haley, 1976; Zuk, 1971). The goal is to shift the balance of pathogenic relating among family members so that newer, more constructive family hierarchies (composed of interlocking series of triangles) become possible. It is assumed that once the structure of the family is rearranged, communication patterns will be forced to change and individual symptomatic behavior will improve (Haley, 1980). Change comes about when families begin behaving differently, whether or not insight into their own interaction process occurs.

It is inevitable that the family will involve the therapist in their covert triangulations. It is therefore critical that the therapist take cognizance of his or her coalition status at any one point in time. An excellent method for maintaining coalition neutrality has been proposed by Palazzoli-Selvini, Boscolo, Cecchin, and Prata (1980). In this method the therapist, in front of the whole family, systematically queries each family member in turn regarding specific aspects of the relationship between any other two family members ("Johnny, can you tell me what Mommie and Suzie fight the most about?"). This method serves to make implicit family triangulations explicit and to keep the net coalition valence of the therapist neutral at the end of such a circular interview.

This intervention style and way of thinking about families constitutes a growing edge within the field. It is highly likely that the focus on triads, combined with innovative therapeutic methods, will provide a cutting edge for continued growth and development within the mainstream of systems therapy.

References

Bowen, M. The use of family theory in clinical practice. *Comprehensive Psychiatry*, 1966, *7*, 345–374.

Fromm-Reichman, F. Notes on the development of treatment of schizophrenics by psychoanalytic psychotherapy. *Psychiatry*, 1948, *11*, 263–273.

Haley, J. Toward a theory of pathological systems. In G. Zuk & I. Boszormenyi-Nagy (Eds.), *Family therapy and disturbed families*. Palo Alto, Calif.: Science & Behavior Books, 1967.

Haley, J. *Problem solving therapy*. San Francisco: Jossey-Bass, 1976.

Haley, J. *Leaving home.* New York: McGraw-Hill, 1980.

Palazzoli-Selvini, M., Boscolo, L., Cecchin, G., & Prata, G. Hypothesizing, circularity, neutrality: Three guidelines for the conductor of the session. *Family Process,* 1980, *19,* 3–12.

Ravich, R. Psychotherapy for the whole family. *American Journal of Psychotherapy,* 1967, *21,* 132–134.

Zuk, G. H. Triadic-based family therapy. *International Journal of Psychiatry,* 1969, *8,* 539–548.

Zuk, G. H. *Family therapy.* New York: Behavior Publications, 1971.

Subject Index

ABAB design, 99–100
Academic psychology, 7
Adlerian psychotherapy, 93–96; central constructs in, 95; goals of, 9; process of, 94–96; theoretical roots of, 94
Administrative therapy, 352
Adult ego states, 276
Aggression, assertiveness versus, 104
Alignment, 349
Alternativists, 19–20
Analysis, levels of, 341. *See* Psychoanalysis
Analytical psychology. *See* Jungian analysis
Anchoring, 198–99
Anxiety: reduction of, 29; sources of, 150, 153, 155, 156
Anxiety management training, 141
Applied behavior analysis, 97–102; applications of, 100–1; current issues in, 102; effectiveness of, 101–2; future directions of, 102; origins of, 97–99; strategies for, 99–100, 117
Archetype, 184–85, 188
Assertiveness, 103–4
Assertiveness training, 103–17; biblical/

theological perspectives on, 106–7; effectiveness of, 68; objectives of, 104–6; origins of, 103; process of 104–5; theoretical foundations of, 103–4
Attendance rates, 67
Auxiliary egos, 315
Aversion therapy, 108–12; aversive counterconditioning procedures in, 109–10, 284; common features in, 108; effectiveness of, 111; ethical issues in, 110–11; punishment procedures in, 108–9
Avoidance training, 109
Awareness, 160

Behaviorism: applications of, 8; metaphysical versus methodological, 135; nature of, 7, 113
Behavior marital therapy, 283–86; biblical/theological perspective on, 286; effectiveness of, 285–86; goal of, 284; theoretical foundations of, 283–84; therapeutic process in, 284–85
Behavior modification, 8, 98–99
Behavior therapy, 113–20; approaches to, 116, 126, 190, 263–64; biblical/theological perspective on, 119–20;

344–46; structural, 347–49; systems, 294–97; triadic-based, 359–62

Feeling(s): in bioenergetic analysis, 128–29; change in, 5; in nouthetic counseling, 202; suppression of, 227–28. *See also* Emotion(s)

Focal conflict, 312

Forgiveness, as healing factor, 43

Free association, 227

Freedom, in existentialism, 150, 153, 154

Functional family therapy, 301–8; assessment criteria in, 306; Christian perspective on, 307–8; effectiveness of, 307; intervention goals of, 306–7; systems-behavioristic approach to, 305–6; therapist skills necessary for, 307

Functional professional, 88. *See also* Paraprofessional therapy

Fusion, emotional, 296

Games, transactional, 274, 278

General systems theory. *See* Systems theory

Gestalt prayer, 159

Gestalt therapy, 158, 158–63; biblical/theological evaluation of, 162; criticisms of, 161–62; effectiveness of, 161; goal of, 10, 158, 160–61; group approach to, 316; Jungian analysis versus, 189; theoretical roots of, 158–60; treatment approaches in, 159–61

Ghosts, in families, 339

Global studies, 65

God: as healing factor, 43–44; as parent figure, 43, 45; transference and, 41–42

Group-centered group therapy, 313–14

Group psychotherapy, 309–20; biblical/theological perspective on, 319–20; coining of term, 315; curative factors of, 317–19; effectiveness of, 318–19; origins of, 309–10; research data on, 317–19; transference in, 311

Group therapy(ies), approaches to: encounter group, 310, 316–17; existential, 312–13; Gestalt, 316; group dynamic, 311–12; here-and-now/process, 314–15; nondirective, 313–14; psychoanalytic, 310–11; psychodrama, 315; social network analysis, 341–43; strategic, 344–46; therapeutic community, 350–58

Growth model, 288

Guided imagery, 176–78

Guilt, 18; origins of, 180; resolution of, 149, 182; sources of, 150, 154; treatment conflict over, 63; true versus false, 215

Here-and-now/process, 314

Holy Spirit, healing by, 43–44

Homeostasis, 143–44

Humanistic therapy(ies), 158, 182, 387–89; assumptions of, 7, 53–54, 159

Human nature, views on, 38, 118–19, 148–49, 152–54

Hypnotherapy, 10, 164–70; authoritarian versus permissive, 164; Christian integrative potential of, 168–69; guided imagery therapy and, 176–78; indirect, 164–65; induction procedures in, 165–68; intervention procedure in, 167–68; metaphor use in, 166–69; principles of, 165; seeding tactic of, 169; trance-deepening procedure in, 165

Identity, individual, 128, 215

Imago Dei doctrine, 17–18; applications of, 122, 177, 202

Individual psychology, 94

Individuation, 302

Informed consent, 49, 110–11

Inner healing, 22, 171–79; critique of, 178–79; forms of, 171–73; guided imagery and, 176–78; hypnotherapy and, 176–77; by secular healers, 172–73; techniques for, 173–76

Insight, as therapeutic goal, 8, 126–27, 221, 227, 278

Insight therapy, 227

Integrity therapy, 180–83; biblical/theological perspective on, 182–83; comparative analysis of, 181; effectiveness of, 182; theoretical foundations of, 180–81; treatment approaches of, 181

Intensive therapy, 94, 156

Interdependence, 155

Interpersonal psychotherapy, 9

Interpretation, 95–96

Interrelation, 155

Intimacy, 278, 279, 342

Intrapsychic disease approach, 114

Isolation, 150, 153

Author Index